The Missionary Oblates
of Mary Immaculate
A Clerical Religious Congregation
With Brothers

The Missionary Oblates
of Mary Immaculate
A Clerical Religious Congregation
With Brothers

William H. Woestman, O.M.I.

Faculty of Canon Law
Saint Paul University
Ottawa – 1995

Canadian Cataloguing in Publication Data
    Woestman, William H., 1929-
        The Missionary Oblates of Mary Immaculate : a clerical religious
    congregation with brothers

    2nd. ed.
    Includes bibliographical references and index.
    ISBN 0-919261-37-X (bound) —

        1. Oblates of Mary Immaculate.   I. Saint Paul University
    (Ottawa, Ont.). Faculty of Canon Law. II. Title.

    BX3821.W64 1995   255'.76   C95-900428-9

Imprimi potest
Benoît Garceau, O.M.I., Provincial Superior
Montréal, March, 13, 1995

Nihil obstat
Michael O'Reilly, O.M.I., *censor deputatus*
Norbert M. Andradi, O.M.I. *censor deputatus*

Legal deposit, 3rd quarter 1995, National Library of Canada

Printed in Canada

Dedicated to

Charles-Joseph-Eugène de Mazenod

priest, missionary, founder, religious, bishop, saint,

zealous servant of the universal Church

Table of Contents

Table of Contents ix

Abbreviations xi

Introductions and Acknowledgements xiii

Illustration—Reproduction of Eugene de Mazenod's
Autograph of the 1826 Constitutions xix

Chapter I. Son of Provence, Priest, Missionary 1
   Family Background 1
   The French Revolution and Exile 2
   First Signs of a Vocation 3
   Eugene's Return from Exile 5
   Interior Crisis and Conversion 6
   Seminarian at Saint-sulpice 8
   Ordination 10
   First Years as a Priest in Aix 12
   Pastoral Renewal Through Missions 18
   De Mazenod's Decision To Found a Mission Society 21
   Summary 22

Chapter II. Foundation and Papal Approval 25
   Foundation of the Missionaries of Provence 25
   Introduction of Vows 27
   Successes and Crises 36
   Approval by Leo XII 42
   Summary 49

Chapter III. Historical and Juridical Development 51
   The 1826 Constitutions 52
   Development 1826-1861 58
   Revisions of the Constitutions 1843-1850 65
   Denial of Exemption 78
   Decade of Crises 84
   The 1917 Code of Canon Law and Revision 93
   Beginning a Thirty Year Process 97
   The 1966 Constitutions *Ad Experimentum* 98
   The 1972 and 1974 General Chapters 106
   The 1982 Constitutions and Rules 110
   The 1986 and 1992 General Chapters 118
   Summary 120

Chapter IV. Juridical Status of Pontifical Clerical Religious Congregations . . . 123
    The Evolution of the Juridical Status of Religious Congregations
        with Simple Vows 124
    Congregations with Simple Vows Recognized as Religious Institutes 129
    Trend Toward Uniformity in the Constitutions of Religious Institutes . . . 133
    Emphasis on the Particular Charism and Traditions of Each Institute 135
    Clerical Religious Institutes 140
    Summary 145
Chapter V. A Clerical Religious Congregation 147
    A Religious Congregation 147
    De Mazenod's Intent and Purpose as Founder 149
    "Mission" and "Missionary" 151
    De Mazenod's Use of the Word "Missionary" 155
    Evangelizare Pauperibus Misit Me, Pauperes Evangelizantur 161
    No Identity Crisis 173
    Similar Institutions 174
    Propositions of Union 175
    Tradition 177
    Proportion of Clerics 187
    Governed by Clerics 189
    Approval by the Holy See As a Clerical Institute 192
    Summary 198
Chapter VI. The Brothers 201
    Sons of the Congregation 201
    De Mazenod and the Brothers 205
    Instruction of Poor Children 207
    Extended Apostolic Role 209
    Oblates and Missionaries 214
    The Name "Brother" 217
    Oblation 220
    Religious Garb 222
    Formation 228
    Diaconate 230
    Change of Category 232
    Brothers as Superiors 234
    Summary 244
Epilogue 247
Sources and Select Bibliography 249
Appendix I–Marcello Zago,"The Priestly Character of the Congregation" . . . 269
Appendix II–John Paul II Addresses Religious Men 281
Appendix III–Indults Permitting a Brother to be Appointed Superior . . . 287
Index 289

Abbreviations

AG	*Ad genes divintus*, Vatican Council II, Decree on Church's Missionary Activity
AAG–OMI	*Acta Administrations Generalis O.M.I.*
AAS	*Acta Apostolicæ Sedis*
art.	article(s)
ASS	*Acta Sanctæ Sedis*
C., CC.	article(s) of the O.M.I. Constitutions
c., cc.	canon(s)
CIC¹	*Codex Iuris Canonici* – 1917
CIC	*Codex Iuris Canonici* – 1983
CICLSAL	Congregation for Institutes of Consecrated Life and Societies of Apostolic Life
DM	Rome, Postulation Archives, O.M.I., Documents de Mazenod
FB	Rome, Postulation Archives, O.M.I., Fonds Boisgelin
JM	Rome, Postulation Archives, O.M.I., Journals of de Mazenod
LG	*Lumen gentium*, Vatican II, Dogmatic Constitution on the Church
LM	Rome, Postulation Archives, O.M.I., Letters to and from de Mazenod
OR	*Osservatore Romano*
ORe	*Osservatore Romano*, English edition
PC	*Perfectæ caritatis*, Vatican II, Decree on the Renewal of Religious Life
R., RR.	article(s) of the O.M.I. Rules
SCRIS	Sacred Congregation of Religious and Secular Insitutes

Introduction and Acknowledgements

Toward the end of October 1981, Father Benito Gangioti, O.P., then the dean of the Faculty of Canon Law of the Pontifical University of St. Thomas Aquinas *in Urbe*, suggested to the students in the first year of the licentiate program that, if they intended to work toward the doctorate, they choose a subject that we could develop as a doctoral dissertation. If they would elect for their seminar such a topic and continue working on it throughout the licentiate cycle, it would be possible to finish a dissertation within the minimum of three years required for obtaining a doctorate in canon law.

Since I intended to specialize in canon law for religious, I began to search for an apt topic in that field. A few days later at breakfast, I asked Father Francis Morrisey, O.M.I., who was then dean of the Faculty of Canon Law at Saint Paul University, Ottawa, if he could give me an idea for a topic. He suggested that I might do something on the brothers in the Congregation.

This idea appealed to me, and I spoke about it with Father Michael O'Reilly, O.M.I., the Oblate procurator to the Holy See, and Father Fernand Jetté, O.M.I., superior general. Both encouraged me to pursue this line of thought. I soon realized that it would be impossible to adequately study the juridical aspects of the brothers without first considering the nature of the Missionary Oblates of Mary Immaculate as a religious congregation. The result of this line of investigation is this thesis—a study of the juridical nature of the Congregation and the status of the brothers in the Congregation.

Since a particular religious institute is not an abstract idea that can be studied *a priori*, it has to be considered in the concrete reality in which it had its origin through divine grace working in real people at a definite time and place in the Church to meet specific needs of a certain age.

Consequently, this thesis begins with a consideration of Eugene de Mazenod, the man called by God to found the Missionary Oblates of Mary Immaculate. His background and personal history are examined only insofar as they influenced him as founder and bear on the nature of the institute which he founded.

Because a religious institute is in fact constituted only by the hierarchical Church and given by it a juridical personality, it is necessary also to study the laws and practice of the Church relating to congregations with simple vows, their eventual recognition as religious institutes, and the law relating specifically to clerical institutes. This work pays special attention to the law as determining whether an institute is lay or clerical.

I had the advantage of researching and writing Chapter IV after the promulgation of the *Code of Canon Law* by Pope John Paul II on January 25,

1983. I would hesitate to say that I broke new ground here, but I was able to examine the evolution of the practice of the Church's approach to religious institutes by the Fathers of Vatican II and the subsequent emphasis placed upon the *patrimonium spirituale*, the spiritual patrimony, as a determining force in the internal life of each religious institute and in specifying its juridical nature.

I first look as the practice of the Holy See as seen in the *Normæ* of 1901, the 1917 Code, and the practice of the Sacred Congregations. With this background, it is possible to understand the radical change initiated by Vatican II with *Lumen gentium* and *Perfectæ caritatis* and its implementation in the post-conciliar era. The reports of the Commission for the reform of the Code reveal its determined perseverance to incorporate this new approach into the Code. It is clearly the policy of the Church to protect and promote the spiritual patrimony of each institute and to require that every institute's particular law enshrine its own spiritual patrimony.

I demonstrate that a special application of this principle is found in the canon legislating the determination of whether an institute is clerical or lay. To do this, I examine first the 1917 Code and then point out the improvement and refinement found in the 1983 Code. I show that this change is solidly based on the teaching of Vatican II in its insistence that the intentions of the founder and the approved traditions of each institute are the deciding factors in determining the nature of the institute.

The Congregation of the Missionary Oblates of Mary Immaculate is then examined in light of this legislation. Since Eugene de Mazenod founded the Oblates of Mary Immaculate, to preach missions—to evangelize the poor—I examine what he meant by preaching the Gospel to the poor, and what it has meant and means in the Congregation. I also found it necessary to give special attention to the meaning of and the use of the word *missionary*, by carefully analyzing his writings. The reason is that the sense of this word has evolved almost imperceptibly, but greatly, since the time of de Mazenod. In fact, a great evolution took place with Vatican II. For example, prior to 1966 the Oblate Constitutions used the word *missionary* to designate only the priest members of the Congregation as distinguished from the scholastics and the brothers.

This detailed study of the word *missionary* and its use is important for a proper understanding of the name of the Congregation and the nature of its ministry, which is seen to be essentially that of the ministerial or ordained priesthood. I examine all changes in the Oblate Constitutions through 1982 to show that the modifications did not alter the nature of the Congregation established by de Mazenod and approved by Leo XII. I demonstrate that the Congregation is essentially priestly or sacerdotal; its purpose is the exercise of the ministerial priesthood. Consequently, it is clerical in nature. This is its internal reality revealed in the constant tradition of the Congregation, and is not something imposed from without.

This thesis is the first study that considers directly the clerical status of the Congregation and the basis for it.

I prove that the reality of the Missionary Oblates of Mary Immaculate as a society dedicated to priestly ministry precedes its recognition as a clerical institute by the Church. In fact, it is its inmost reality that determines its recognition as a clerical institute.

Needless to say, the theological basis for the distinction between clerical and lay institutes is the essential difference between the common priesthood of the faithful and the ministerial priesthood of the ordained. Vatican II clearly expressed this traditional teaching in the Dogmatic Constitution on the Church *Lumen gentium* (no. 10).

Only after this analysis of the Congregation and its nature is it possible to study the role of the brothers in the Congregation. Previous detailed studies of the brothers were made before 1972 and the implementation of *Clericalia instituta*. An examination of the question of brothers as superiors is made in light of the nature of the Congregation and the vocation of the brothers. I then evaluate the decision of the Sacred Congregation of Religious and Secular Institutes as to how this was to be expressed in the Constitutions.

As we will see from the many sources cited and the bibliography, especially during the 1950s, many works and articles were published on the history of de Mazenod and the Congregation. Of special note are the works of the Oblates Duval, Cosentino, and Pielorz. Also, special mention must be given to the multitude of articles published in *Études Oblates*, now called *Vie Oblate Life*, founded by Father Maurice Gilbert, O.M.I.. Without these publications, my research would have been most difficult, if not almost possible. Since most of these writings are in French, they are unfortunately closed to a greater part of the Congregation. This explains in part my extensive use of quotations throughout this dissertation and their translation into English in the published version.

My research was greatly facilitated by the well-organized archives and the extensive canonical libraries of the Oblate General House. Most of the research material needed was readily available under my own roof. Those in charge of the various archives not only assisted me in finding the necessary material, but gave me the required keys, so that I could consult the documents at my own convenience.

To Father Fernand Jetté, superior general, I owe a special debt of gratitude for my obedience to the General House and the opportunity, time, and encouragement needed to accomplish the research and writing of this dissertation. I hope that the Congregation will be repaid by the benefits derived from this work. I must thank Father Francis George, O.M.I. vicar general, for luring me back to Rome and prompting me to return to school after thirty-one years of oblation and after having been ordained for twenty-five years.

I have spent many hours at the feet of Father O'Reilly, tapping his vast sources of knowledge acquired as procurator to the Holy See, consultor of the Sacred Congregations of Religious and Secular Institutes and of the Clergy, and professor of canon law for over forty years. His instant recall of where to find papal documents and the literature available saved me hours of work and opened many sources to me.

If I were to mention by name the other members of my community who helped me, by proofreading, listening to me, helping me clarify my ideas, and by their truly fraternal encouragement, this introduction would have an excessive length. Most of all, I must thank them for living with me and listening patiently to me talk about this work and its progress.

I must, however, mention by name Father Maurice Gilbert for not only proofreading most of the thesis but for his insights and help in finding various items of information or articles. I must point out that he was most helpful, even when positions presented in this paper differed from his own stance.

The Dominican professors at the Pontifical University of Saint Thomas *in Urbe* have given me a deep appreciation for the law of the Church. I hope that I have absorbed a portion, not only of their vast learning, but especially of their deep love and respect for the Church as revealed in its law, an essential part of its pastoral office. They have shared with us students a true love of the Church and a real understanding of its human face as manifested in its law—a law that protects, determines, and respects the rights of all for the *salus animarum*, the salvation of souls.

Father José Castaño, O.P., the director of this dissertation, during these three years has constantly manifested kindness and a gentle guiding hand in directing this mature-aged student. His moderating assistance was ever prudent and learned, while allowing me to develop this dissertation in my own way.

The final word of thanks must go to the Lord for my vocation as a Missionary Oblate of Mary Immaculate. Writing this thesis has brought me to a deeper appreciation of what He has done through the Congregation founded by Blessed Charles Joseph Eugene de Mazenod for the preaching of the Gospel to the poor.

October 9, 1984
Rome

William H. WOESTMAN, O.M.I.

Introduction and Acknowledgements
to the Second Edition

At the ordinary public consistory held on April 10, 1995, John Paul II approved the canonization of Charles Joseph Eugene de Mazenod, bishop of Marseille and founder of the Missionary Oblates of Mary Immaculate. At the same celebration it was announced that Eugene de Mazenod will be canonized on Sunday, December 3, 1995.

For many years I have wanted to revise and have printed in a more permanent form my doctoral dissertation in canon law. The de Mazenod year honoring our founder and his canonization has spurred me to complete this task as my contribution to the celebration.

Since the initial writing of this work more than ten years ago, Father Fernand Jetté, O.M.I., former superior general, and Father Marcello Zago, O.M.I., superior general, have in their writings reaffirmed the basic tenet of this thesis: that the ministerial priesthood is an essential element of the Missionary Oblates of Mary Immaculate—that the Congregation founded by de Mazenod necessarily includes the ministry of ordained priests in order to fulfill its goal of evangelizing the poor—and that consequently the Church has recognized the institute as a clerical religious congregation. I have attempted to incorporate their teaching in revising this book.

Shortly after the first publication of the dissertation in 1985, Fathers Józef Pielorz, O.M.I., and Aloysius Kedl, O.M.I., had the kindness to supply me with written observations, recommendations, and corrections for the improvement of this work. Father Michael O'Reilly, O.M.I. also pointed out several things for its amelioration. I wish to express my appreciation for their consideration and helpfulness. Their suggestions have been taken into account during the revision process.

A special word of thanks is due to Father Norbert Andradi, O.M.I., for spending many hours in checking the various references for accuracy and for making other valuable suggestions for improving the text. Father Michael O'Reilly, O.M.I., painstakingly reviewed the manuscript and from his immense treasure of canonical and historical knowledge proposed a number of changes to enrich the work.

I can never sufficiently express my gratitude to Father Jean Thorn, dean of the Faculty of Canon Law since 1984, for his encouraging my writing and making possible the publication of my works. Ms. Cherry Heard meticulously

xvii

retyped the original work, as well as proofread the revised manuscript, and made a number of suggestions for improvement of the style.

I wish to acknowledge the assistance of all these persons, and the encouragement of many others for the appreciation they expressed for the original work. Among these I include the late Father Jean Drouart, O.M.I., who many years ago as superior of the Roman scholasticate, prepared the groundwork for this study.

May this book be a tool for a better understanding of and love for the Congregation founded by Eugene de Mazenod for the evangelization of the poor. May his canonization impel his spiritual sons to strive more diligently "for their own sanctification and for the salvation of souls."[1]

Ottawa
Solemnity of Saints Peter and Paul
June 29, 1995   William H. Woestman, O.M.I.

---

[1] Preface.

Pars Prima

Constitutionum et Institutorum Societatis

Missionariorum Oblatorum

Sanctissimæ et Immaculatæ Virginis Mariæ

Gallo-Provinciæ nuncupatorum.

Caput Primum

De Fine Societatis.

Art. 1. Finis hujus parvæ Societatis Missionariorum Oblatorum Sanctissimæ et Immaculatæ Virginis Mariæ, Gallo-Provinciæ dictorum a Provincia in quâ habuere initium, est 1.° ut coadunati Sacerdotes Sæculares, et ut fratres habitantes in unam, præcipuam dent operam — pauperibus evangelizandis, virtutes et exempla Salvatoris nostri Jesu Christi assidua imitatione prosequendo.

This is a reproduction of the copy of the Constitutions approved by Leo XII on February 17, 1816. Eugene de Mazenod's autograph is preserved in the Postulator's Archives O.M.I., Rome.

Although all my limbs are numb, my dear Tempier, with the penal labor that I have just undergone, I thought I would write you at least a half a sheet . . . I calculated that it would about fifty hours of writing [to copy the only Latin manuscript of the Constitutions]; I barged through this job in three days and part of the nights; I must admit it was an enormous task; I can also say that I was in it from head to toe; with head, chest, arms, hands, legs, feet, and an unmentionable part of me being cruelly tired (DE MAZENOD, to Tempier, February 27, 1826, in *Letters*, vol. 7, no. 227, p. 43).

Chapter I
Son of Provence, Priest, Missionary

I n order to have a real grasp of a religious movement in the Church, it is necessary to have a thorough understanding of the men or women who began the particular project, development or institution. It is only in knowing the founders and the actual working of divine grace in their lives, that it is possible to comprehend God's intervention in the Church and in the world.

> In God's work . . . everything is composed mainly of initiatives from God. For this reason the development does not have a kind of automatic continuity, but is governed by the vocations that God gives to persons who are in a special way "men and women of God" . . .[1]

This same idea was clearly expressed and applied to religious institutes by Paul VI in his apostolic exhortation on the renewal of religious life, *Evangelica testificatio*:

> In reality, the charism of the religious life, far from being an impulse born "of flesh and blood" (*Jn* 1:13) or one derived from a mentality which "conforms itself to this world" (*Rom* 12:2) is the fruit of the Holy Spirit, who is always at work within the Church.[2]

However, the Holy Spirit does not work in a vacuum, but in the real world and in real people. For a comprehension of the Holy Spirit's operation in the founding of an institute of consecrated life, one must have a knowledge and understanding of the founder, his or her background, and historical environment. Only then is it possible to comprehend the work of the hand of the living God.

Family Background

The de Mazenod family was firmly rooted in the pre-Revolution history and traditions of Provence. They were strong supporters of the king, anti-Jansenist, and vigorous advocates of papal authority. The family was ennobled

---

[1] Y.-M.-J. CONGAR, O.P., *Vraie et fausse réforme dans l'Église*, Unam Sanctam, no. 20, Paris, Éditions du Cerf, 1950, p. 134.

Minor editorial modifications, e.g., capitalization, spelling, inclusive language, have been made in some of the quotations to conform to the adopted style for this work. Whenever the source of the English translation is not given, the translation was made by the author of this work.

[2] PAUL VI, apostolic exhortation, *Evangelica testificatio*, June 29, 1971, *AAS*, 63 (1971), pp. 503–504, no. 11; trans. in Austin FLANNERY, O.P., ed., *Vatican Council II, the Conciliar and Post Conciliar Documents*, Newport, NY, Costello Publishing Company, 1986, pp. 685–686.

in 1653. Eugene's father, Charles-Antoine de Mazenod, Seigneur de Saint-Laurent-du-Verdon, noble of the robe, was president of the Court of Accounts, Aids, and Finances of Provence, and later was president *à mortier* of the parliament of Provence. Both he and his father, who held similar positions, maintained a life-style befitting their social standing, but unrealistic in reference to their income, and were constantly in debt.

The thirty-three year old magistrate solved his financial embarrassment in the accepted way—by marrying eighteen year old Marie-Rose Joannis. Her father was professor of medicine at the royal faculty of Aix, and his daugther's dowry indicates that he was a wealthy man. Charles-Antoine brought the marriage prestige and social position; Marie-Rose brought the means to gild the family coat of arms.[3]

Charles-Antoine had two younger brothers, Canon Charles-Fortuné, vicar general of Aix and later bishop of Marseille, and Charles-Louis-Eugène. The latter was a naval captain at the time of the Revolution. Canon Charles-Auguste-André, Eugene's great-uncle, was vicar general of Marseille.

Charles-Joseph-Eugene de Mazenod was born in Aix-en-Provence on August 1, 1782 and baptized the following day in the parish church of St. Mary Magdalen, patroness of Provence. The first eight years of his life rooted Eugene in his native Provence. His parents were at the top of the social ladder in the provençal capital as he grew up in one of the stately mansions on the main boulevard. From his grandfather Joannis and his old nurse, he learned Provençal, the language of the ordinary people.

Eugene was enrolled as a boarding student at Collège Bourbon in Aix, the alma mater of his father and uncles. However, a radical change had been made in the quality of the school since the suppression of the Jesuits in 1767. First the Oratorians attempted to run the institution but had to give it up because of a lack of personnel. It was then confided to the Doctrinaires (Priests of Christian Doctrine), whose theological, political, social, and pedagogical principles were considerably different from those of the Jesuits.[4]

The French Revolution and Exile

Throughout 1790 the political situation in Aix became inflamed. In December because of the danger to his life President Charles-Antoine de Mazenod slipped quietly out of Aix and took up residence in Nice, which

---

[3] See Jean LEFLON, *Eugene de Mazenod*, trans. in F.D. FLANAGAN, 4 vols., New York, Fordham University Press, 1961–1970, vol. 1, pp. 3–33.

[4] See LEFLON, *De Mazenod*, vol. 1, pp. 63–68, 75–78.

belonged at that time to the kingdom of Sardinia, not to France. His flight was none too soon. The full force of the Revolution reached Aix a few days later. Several political figures were forcefully taken from the King's Jail by a mob and hanged from lamp posts within view of the *hôtel* de Mazenod.

Fearing for the life of his son, Charles-Antoine sent for him to join him in Nice. No doubt this decision was also based in part on the fact that the Doctrinaires on January 30, 1791 solemnly took the oath to uphold the Constitution of the Clergy as prescribed by the National Assembly on November 30, 1790. The oath had been condemned as schismatic by the French bishops.

Eugene arrived in Nice in April. Shortly afterward he was followed by his mother and other members of the family. In the fall of that year, they moved to Turin, where nine year old Eugene was enrolled as a boarder in the Royal College of Nobles. The school was under the direction of the Barnabites. He remained there as a student until the family moved to Venice in April 1794.

While in Venice the president became involved in a number of unsuccessful financial ventures. Meanwhile, the situation in France had become more peaceful, and his wife returned to Aix in 1795 in order to recover her dowry; the couple was never reunited. Eugene remained with his father and uncles, who had more important things to do than care for Eugene, who was left on his own.

First Signs of a Vocation

It was in Venice that divine providence exerted its influence in his life through the person of Bartolo Zinelli, a cultured and devout priest, the son of a rich merchant family.

> Don Bartolo welcomed me with great goodness; he had me look all through his library, and I went from there into the study where he worked at a great table with his brother, Don Pietro, who was still only a deacon. "All our books are at your disposition," said Don Bartolo to me. Then he added, "This is where my brother and I study; you see there the seat which was occupied by another of my brothers whom the good God has called to Himself. If it were agreeable to you to take his place, you have only to say the word, we would make it a pleasure to have you continue your classes, which no doubt you have not finished." . . . From then on, every day for nearly four years, I went after Mass to these volunteer teachers who made me work up until noon. After dinner, Don Bartolo, whose health needed great care, came to take me for an outing with him ending at some church where we stopped to pray. On returning, I sat down again to work, which lasted until evening. Several priests met together about that time to recite the office in common. We then went down into the salon where friends and family indulged in quiet recreation. Coffee was served and then they

withdrew, but not I, being in a way already a member of the family, hence
I remained for supper and to say the rosary and prayers according to the
pious custom of that country, then so good . . .

Shall I ever be able to thank God enough for having procured for me
such help precisely at the most difficult age of my life, the decisive period
for me when a man of God laid in my soul, prepared by his sure hand and
by the grace of the Holy Spirit whose instrument he was, the bases of
religion and piety on which the mercy of God has constructed the edifice
of my spiritual life?[5]

It was during this period that Canon Charles-Auguste-André, who died in
Venice in November 1795, asked Eugene if he wanted to be a priest.

"Why yes, uncle," I replied without hesitation. "What, child! You can
make such a resolve? Do you not know that you are the sole offspring of
our family which will die out with you?" Surprised at such a reflection
coming from the mouth of so venerable a man, I retorted quickly, "What
then, uncle? Would it not be a great honor for our family to finish with a
priest?" My uncle was amused and touched to hear a child of thirteen years
reply to him thus, he embraced and blessed me. This precocious vocation
could not possibly be realized until much later. It was necessary for me to
go through other trials. We were in full flight, and my exile would last still
many years.[6]

In November 1797, the de Mazenods left for Naples where they lived on
a pension from Queen Caroline. Toward the end of December the court
retreated to Palermo to escape the advancing Republican troops. The de
Mazenods followed on January 3, 1799 sailing with the Portuguese naval
squadron. In Palermo Eugene was embraced by the family of the Duke of
Cannizaro. In his memoirs de Mazenod states very simply:

Providence which has always watched over me since my tenderest
infancy opened the doors of a Sicilian family into which I was admitted from
the beginning as a child of the house.[7]

The death of the duchess, "a saint," "whom I rightly called my mother,"[8]
was a severe blow for Eugene. Much of his fervor vanished, and therein lay the

---

[5] DE MAZENOD, "Souvenirs de Famille," in *Missions O.M.I.*, 5 (1866), pp. 126–129; trans. in
Missions O.M.I., 79 (1952), pp. 643–645.

[6] DE MAZENOD, "Souvenirs," in *Missions O.M.I.* 5 (1866), p. 129; trans. in *Missions O.M.I.*, 79
(1952), p. 646.

[7] DE MAZENOD, "Souvenirs," in *Missions O.M.I.*, 5 (1866), p. 289; trans. in *Missions O.M.I.* 79
(1952), p. 682.

[8] DE MAZENOD, "Souvenirs," in *Missions O.M.I.*, 5 (1866), pp. 289–290; trans. in *Missions O.M.I.*
79 (1952), pp. 682–683.

preparation, if not the actual beginning, of the moral and spiritual crisis that he was to stress repeatedly in his intimate notes.[9]

Eugene's Return from Exile

Complying with his mother's urgent requests, Eugene returned to France on October 24, 1802 to end his eleven year exile and seven year separation from her. He experienced anything but the happy homecoming that he had expected. In order to establish a legal residence at Saint-Laurent, the family fief, so that he could avoid paying a large sum to escape military conscription, he was forced to live there a good part of the time. This, however, was not the greatest of his trials. The estrangement of his parents increased with time and separation. Matters were made worse by his mother's relatives, and Eugene was caught in the middle. To acquire the right to recover and administer the family possessions, she had obtained a civil divorce. This made her the sole owner of all the property. Thus, her husband was penniless and unable to return to France because of the debts he had inherited from his father. Eugene's parents were never reunited, even after his father's return to France in 1817.

Prior to Eugene's return to France, his mother began arrangements for a proper marriage for him with an heiress. Because of the young woman's untimely death from consumption, the plan fell through. Later Eugene, fed up with the whole situation, came up with the plan to return to Sicily and become a citizen of that country. He would then become an officer in the palatine guard, buy property, receive a title, and even become a court chamberlain.[10] This plan never got on foot because he was unable to get a passport to leave France.[11]

His mother and Roze-Joannis, a relative of his mother whom he called uncle, had other plans for a marriage, but it fell through because the dowry was too small.

> She was not from Aix, and of a family of *mezzi cavalieri* (semi-knights). You can imagine how interested I was in all this. Forty thousand francs, when I want at least 150,000.[12]

---

[9] LEFLON, *De Mazenod*, vol. 1, p. 225.

[10] DE MAZENOD, to his father, September 21, 1804, FB, I, no. 1.

[11] DE MAZENOD, to his father, November 1, 1805, FB, I, no. 1.

[12] DE MAZENOD, to his father, January 18, 1805, FB, I, no. 1.

It is evident that the idea of priesthood was far from his mind. The only vocation that he had in mind was to restore the aristocratic status that the Revolution had stolen from him and his family.[13]

Interior Crisis and Conversion

The earlier biographers make no mention of these things, nor of the interior crisis that Eugene was soon to suffer. It was this crisis that reawakened his priestly vocation. Through the consideration of a letter to his mother in 1809 to assure her that his decision to become a priest was not an impulsive one, we can trace the beginning of the crisis as far back as 1806.

> By next Christmas, the time at which I will probably be ordained subdeacon, it will be three years that I consider this matter.[14]

It was in 1806 that his lifelong friendship with Charles de Forbin-Janson began. De Forbin-Janson, also a provençal noble, entered Saint-Sulpice Seminary the year before de Mazenod, became a priest, missionary, co-founder of the Missionaries of France, bishop of Nancy, and founder of the Pontifical Association of the Holy Childhood. It was that same year that Eugene composed a refutation of Jansenism.[15] This was occasioned by the disputes with Uncle Roze-Joannis, a dyed-in-the-wool Jansenist. It was also the year that the mayor of Aix appointed him along with five other men as directors of the confraternity for the spiritual and material assistance of the inmates of the Aix prisons.[16]

It was on Good Friday 1807, that this crisis came to a head.

> Shall I ever forget those bitter tears which the sight of the Cross drew from my eyes one Good Friday? Ah! They welled up from the depths of my heart, and I was unable to check them. So abundant were they that I could not hide them from the people attending that impressive service. My soul was in mortal sin, and it was this that caused my sorrow. At that moment and also on a few other occasions I could tell the difference.[17] Never was my soul more relieved, and never did it feel happier. And it was simply because, during that shower of tears, in spite of my grief, or better, by reason of it, my thirsting soul reached up to its Final End, to God, its only good, whose lack it felt so keenly. Why say more? Could I ever express

---

[13] See LEFLON, *De Mazenod*, vol. 1, p. 260.

[14] DE MAZENOD, to his mother, April 4–7, 1809, FB, I, no. 7.

[15] DE MAZENOD, "Jansénisme," 1806, DM, II, no. 6a.

[16] See LEFLON, *De Mazenod*, vol. 1, pp. 281–282.

[17] Cf. Józef PIELORZ, O.M.I., *La vie spirituelle de Mgr de Mazenod (1782-1812), étude critique*, Ottawa, Éditions des Études Oblates, 1956, p. 130, note 11.

what I felt at that moment. The very thought of it fills my heart with sweet consolation.[18]

This text is cited not to prove a sudden conversion, but to indicate a step in the events and graces that would lead Eugene to a profound change in his life—a process that lasted over an extended period of time.[19]

It also gives an indication of an important element in his spirituality—Jesus as Savior. His earlier retreat notes express mostly a deep sense of his sinfulness. Later there is a greater emphasis on Jesus as Savior, then on identification with Jesus as Savior in sharing in the redemption of those who are to be evangelized.[20]

In 1815 in a letter to de Forbin-Janson, he explained in this way his decision to found a group of missionaries:

It is the second time in my life that I see myself moved to resolve something of utmost seriousness as if by a strong impulse from without (*par une forte secousse étrangère*). When I reflect on it, I am convinced that it so pleases God to put an end to my irresolution . . .[21]

That the Good Friday experience was the first time that he was moved by a *secousse étrangère* is a reasonable inference.[22]

In addition to speaking with his confessor, he consulted Father Magy, who had been a Jesuit until the suppression of the Society, and made a trip to Paris to see M. Duclaux at Saint-Sulpice. Magy wrote, ". . . your vocation is as radiant as high noon on the most beautiful day."[23]

De Mazenod had not revealed his plans to his mother, who still had in mind a fitting marriage for him. Writing from Saint-Julien, he sought to convince her.

---

[18] DE MAZENOD, "Retreat Notes 1814," DM, IV, no. 2.

[19] PIELORZ, *La vie spirituelle*, pp. 125–142; LEFLON, *De Mazenod*, vol. 1, pp. 267–281.

[20] See H. GRATTON, O.M.I., "La dévotion salvatorienne du Fondateur," in *Études Oblates* 1 (1942), pp. 158–171.

[21] DE MAZENOD, to de Forbin-Janson, October 23–24, 1815, Holy Childhood Archives, Rome, in *Oblate Writings*, vol. 6, no. 5, p. 8. These archives were in Paris until about 1984, when they were transferred to Rome along with the international office of the Holy Childhood.

[22] See PIELORZ, *La vie spirituelle*, pp. 152–155; Alexandre TACHÉ, O.M.I., *La vie spirituelle d'Eugène de Mazenod, aux origines de la Société (1812–1818)* (=*La vie spirtuelle*), Rome, Gregorian University, 1963, pp. 60–69; J. MORABITO, O.M.I., *Je serai prêtre*, Ottawa, Édition des Études Oblates, 1954, pp. 112–113; for the latter also *Études Oblates* 13 (1954), pp. 112–113.

[23] MAGY, to de Mazenod, cited by A. REY, O.M.I., *Historie de Monseigneur Charles-Joseph-Eugène de Mazenod*, 2 vols., Rome, Maison Générale, 1928, vol. 1, p. 82.

That is why I asked my uncle [Roze-Joannis], who understands the ways of God, to acquaint you with the designs of the Master whom we are all obliged to obey under pain of damnation, and to answer any objections you might bring up. In short, I wanted him to speak first so that, by explaining my reasons to you, he might obtain your approval of a plan which must surely have come from God since it has survived the trials demanded of any inspiration that appears to be out of the ordinary, and since it has the approval of all those who take God's place in my regard.

. . . What He asks of me is that I renounce the world where it is well nigh impossible to save one's soul, so widespread is apostasy there. He is asking me to devote myself in a special way to His service so that I might rekindle the fire of faith which has all but died out among the poor. In short, He is asking me to prepare for the day when I can do everything He demands of me for His glory and for the salvation of souls redeemed by His Precious Blood.[24]

Seminarian at Saint-Sulpice

On October 12, 1808 Eugene de Mazenod entered Saint-Sulpice, the only seminary in France that accepted nobles. His interior dispositions may be judged from the conference that he gave after receiving the tonsure in November of that year.

Not having imitated my Model in His innocence, will I be denied the grace to imitate Him in his dedication to the glory of His Father and the salvation of men? . . . Armed with the Sacred Sign, the symbol of Your victory over hell, and interiorly ablaze with the fire that You came to kindle upon the earth, I will pounce upon Your enemies as a roaring lion in order to recapture the prey that they have stolen from You.[25]

All the seminarians were members of the Sodality of the Blessed Virgin.[26] De Mazenod was also a member of a missionary association founded by de Forbin-Janson. This latter organization greatly influenced de Mazenod's future

---

[24] DE MAZENOD, to his mother, June 29, 1808, FB, I. no. 7.

[25] DE MAZENOD, conference given after tonsure, DM, V, no. 1.

[26] The Sodality of the Blessed Virgin Mary (Congrégation de la Sainte-Vierge, Congregazione Mariana) was founded at the Collegio Romano by the Jesuits and spread to many countries. After the Revolution Father Delpuits revived this institution that had once borne great fruit in Jesuit colleges. Its purpose was to train its members in the practice of piety and in the works of Christian charity. In recent years the sodalities have been known as Christian Life Communities. Cf. LEFLON, De Mazenod, vol. 1, p. 336; Enciclopedia Cattolica, s.v. "Congregazione Mariana," by E. VILLARET; The Catholic Encyclopedia, s.v. "Sodality," by J. HILGERS.

orientation toward the foreign missions.[27] Within the Sodality there was a special group known as the "Association of Piety" and designated by the letters "Aa." Later, de Mazenod was also a member of this group. Like the Sodality, it was Jesuit in origin.

At Saint-Sulpice, both the Sodality and Aa were under the leadership of the seminary staff. The Aa consisted of the elite of the students and had a double purpose—the improvement of the spiritual life of the members and their orientation toward the apostolate. It was a kind of a secret sodality. It seems that for a time its main goal was to help the new arrivals to adapt to seminary life and to assure the fervor of the seminary.[28] As the crisis between Napoleon and the Church became more acute, various Aa's throughout France formed a network to promote the welfare of the Church and defend it against the encroachment of the emperor.

Napoleon's success on the battlefield only served to whet his thirst for power. Seeing himself as the new Charlemagne, he sought complete domination of the Church. The situation had become worse with the occupation of Rome by French troops on February 2, 1808. This was followed by the expulsion of the cardinals, annexation of the Papal States, his excommunication, and the imprisonment of Pius VII in July of the same year. In 1809 there was his divorce from Josephine, and in 1810 his marriage to Marie-Louise. When thirteen cardinals refused to attend the marriage, Napoleon forbade them to dress according to their rank, and deprived them of their income and a place to live.[29] This was followed by the imperial council in 1811.

Under the leadership of M. Emery, the Sulpician superior general, Saint-Sulpice was a center of opposition to the emperor. De Mazenod was one of the group of trusted seminarians that participated in the organized resistance: he helped copy the bull of excommunication for dissemination throughout Brittany, as well as other correspondence of Pius VII for secret distribution; served as a secret messenger between the cardinals; also helped the *black* cardinals—so called because they could not wear the color of their rank—find places to live.

---

[27] See LEFLON, *De Mazenod*, vol. 1, p. 339.

[28] See LEFLON, *De Mazenod*, vol. 1, pp. 336–349.

[29] See J. LEFLON, *La crise révolutionnaire 1789–1846*, Fliche-Martin, no. 20, Paris, Bloud et Gay, 1949, p. 259; Fernand MOURNE, S.S., *A History of the Catholic Church*, trans. Newton THOMPSON, Saint Louis and London, B. Herder Book Co., 1955, vol. 7, p. 435; Karl BIHLMEYER and Hermann TÜCHLE, *Kirchengeschichte*, Padebron, Verlag Ferdinand Schönigh, 1956, vol. 3, p. 304.

> While only a deacon and then as a young priest, I had the privilege, despite the most active surveillance of a suspicious police force, of devoting myself to the daily contacts in the service of the Roman cardinals, who at the time had been brought to Paris and shortly afterward persecuted because of their loyalty to the Holy See. The good fortune of being useful to these exiles and of being increasingly inspired by their spirit compensated me for the danger to which I was exposed.[30]

It is not hard to understand that his own ultramontane position was strengthened by this experience.

After the death of M. Emery and the expulsion of the Sulpicians from the seminary by Napoleon, de Mazenod, who was still a deacon, was named by the Sulpicians as one of the directors to keep the seminary in operation.

Earlier his mother had vigorously opposed his preparation for the priesthood, but once he had completed his studies, she urged him to be ordained and to return home. In reply, he wrote her on October 14, 1811:

> Our directors have definitely been sent away from the seminary and must return to their own homes . . . Their departure makes it imperative that I remain here. My leaving at this time would cause the greatest drawbacks since my example might influence others to leave also. At the present moment, the government is keeping a close watch on everything that goes on here. Since I am one of the most prominent in the house, and in a certain sense, perhaps the most prominent, my departure would create a scandal that couldn't be ignored. What is more important, the welfare of the house, and consequently of the Church, demands that I stay.[31]

Ordination

He had postponed his ordination to the priesthood because he felt that he was not sufficiently prepared. He was also determined not to be ordained by Cardinal Maury, Napoleon's uncle, whom de Mazenod considered a tool of the emperor and on the edge of schism for accepting the nomination as archbishop of Paris without the approval of Pius VII. Now that he had been named a director of the seminary, his ordination could not be put off any longer.

Bishop de Demandolx of Amiens, an old friend of the family, came to his rescue and invited him to come to Amiens and be ordained by him. On December 21, 1811 he was ordained a priest. Following the custom of the

---

[30] DE MAZENOD, to Cardinal Gousset, July 21,1852, Registre Lettres Administratives, Évêché de Marseille; copy LM.

[31] DE MAZENOD, to his mother, October 14, 1811, FB, I, no. 7.

time, he remained on retreat until Christmas and then celebrated Mass for the
first time. His retreat notes preserve the many intentions that he had for the
three Masses on Christmas. Among the intentions for the midnight Mass are
found:

> The grace to repair my faults, that I may save souls by living wholly
> and solely in the service of God, that I may be filled with the spirit of Jesus
> Christ, that I may gain final perseverance and even martyrdom, or at least
> death in the service of those stricken by the plague or any other kind of
> death that will bring glory to God and save souls.[32]

It would be easy to attribute these intentions written during the fervor
of a retreat to a very pious imagination that was out of contact with the real
world. Death by martyrdom and from the plague in the historical context were
hardly farfetched dreams, but real possibilities. Many priests were killed during
the French Revolution. In March 1814, de Mazenod will almost die from typhus,
"prison sickness," contracted while ministering to the Austrian prisoners of war
in Aix.

Joseph Morabito concluded his consideration of de Mazenod's vocation
in *Je serai prêtre* by stating:

> From what we have said one conclusion naturally follows necessarily:
> this very original personality of the Founder, which opened the road over
> such difficulties and such struggles, is a truly *priestly personality* everything
> else for him is at the service of and in function of the priesthood. The
> Founder is *priest before all else. . .*
>
> "*I will be a priest.*" These words that he had spoken at Venice and
> which by being fleshed out during his youth embraced all the greatness of
> the redemptive priesthood of Jesus, and were finally brought to fulfilment
> at Saint-Sulpice the day of his ordination. These words explain the whole
> personality of the Founder. The other motifs are but rays from this center,
> as from the core of this rich personality. They are the rays of this vocation
> and this charity, which are above all else a priestly vocation and priestly
> charity. The love of souls, the love of the Church, the love of the poor are
> all the same love—the same priestly charity. This intense charity embraces
> the whole field of action of the sublime priesthood of Christ the
> Redeemer.[33]

Józef Pielorz in his dissertation on de Mazenod's spiritual life cited the
above quoted text of intentions for his first Mass and then commented:

---

[32] DE MAZENOD, "Intentions de mes messes," (1811), DM, IV, no. 1.

[33] MORABITO, *Je serai prêtre*, pp. 197–199; *Études Oblates,* 13 (1954), pp. 197–199.

The characteristic expressions that we have frequently met return here to prove that the apostolate, or more precisely apostolic-immolation correspond to a deep need of his soul—enthusiastic with love of Jesus and completely contrite for having sinned. For Eugene it is at this point that the love of Jesus and the esteem for the priesthood grow and unite. Action, natural propensity to get to the base of things, keen sense of sin, need of reparation and expiation, sense of gratitude for divine gifts, loving desire to follow Jesus to the Cross—*all this is joined in the formula: priest-apostle-victim.* This formula is neither berullian nor ignatian, but a synthesis of his life. It will be at the base of the new society that he will found in 1816.[34]

Bishop de Demandolx, feeling the weight of age and moved by the zeal of the newly ordained priest, asked him to remain in Amiens as his vicar general. He offered de Mazenod a free hand in establishing works and preaching. The latter pleaded his youth and inexperience, and the necessity of returning to Saint-Sulpice as director.[35]

When he returned to Paris in January, all the Sulpicians had been forced to leave the seminary. He assumed his role as director of the major seminary and was also confessor at the minor seminary. At the end of the school year he spent the summer vacation with the seminarians at the country villa. This gave him also time to continue his personal studies and to prepare for his return to Aix as soon as the new directors took charge in October.

First Years as a Priest in Aix

It would be less than three years before he would buy a house for the band of missionaries that he was to found. These three years in Aix are most important, not only because they were a time for his maturing as a priest and preparing the way for the foundation of his society, but also because his experiences during these years would be paramount in determining the nature of that society and the works that it would undertake.

Rather than accept a privileged appointment, as was to be expected at that time for one of his social position, he requested and received permission

---

[34] J. PIELORZ, O.M.I., "La vie spirituelle de Mgr de Mazenod, Fondateur de la Congrégation des Missionnaires Oblats de Marie Immaculée, première partie: 1782-1812, étude critique," S.T.D. dissertation, Gregorian University, 1954, pp. 402-403. The published version of this dissertation contains the same idea, but it is not expressed as succinctly (see PIELORZ, *La vie spirituelle*, pp. 255-257).

[35] See REY, *Histoire*, vol. 1, p. 133.

from the vicar capitular,[36] who was the bishop of Metz, to be free to choose his own ministry.

> There was not a hair of my head which would dream of obtaining for itself, because of my social position, pretensions that everyone at that epoch found reasonable. *I had rather lie at the threshold of the house of my God*—this was my motto . . . That is the true expression of the secret of my vocation. I answered the bishop of Metz that my only ambition was to consecrate myself to the service of the poor and the young.[37]

Commenting on this, Leflon adds, "It may be that, secretly, the vicars [captitular] breathed a great sigh of relief over this ready made solution, since this noble, who was such a dynamic individualist, would not have been easily regimented; better to keep him out of the ranks."[38]

The effects of the French Revolution were keenly felt in the shortage of priests.

> Since 1789 there were very few ordinations and persecution, deportation, and exile had decimated the clergy. Most of the priests were old and tired. In 1809 out of 31,870, 10,613, i.e., one-third, were over 60. There were only 933 priests less than 40 years old, i.e., about ten per diocese. As the years passed the voids opened up with the disappearance of the older men. From 31,870 in 1809, the total decreased from 25,057 in 1814 to 24,874 in 1815. Between 1809 and 1815 the number of active priests dropped by 6,996.[39]

One must not forget that all religious communities of men and women had been suppressed, and that their return to France was a slow process.

On the positive side the number of ordinations was increasing almost each year.

> The number of ordinations increased progressively and rose from 344 in 1807 to 618 in 1810, to 907 in 1812, to 1,504 in 1816. Nevertheless, in all of France under the Consulate and the Empire the total hardly exceeded

---

[36] Gaspard-Jean-André-Joseph Jauffret became bishop of Metz in 1806, and in 1811 Napoleon nominated him to be archbishop of Aix. Because of the conflict between Napoleon and Pius VII, the latter refused to appoint any of the emperor's candidates for vacant sees. Jauffret administered the archdiocese of Aix as vicar capitular, i.e., diocesan administrator according to today's terminology, from 1811 to 1814, when he resume the pastoral governance of the diocese of Metz (cf. *Larousse du XXe Siècle*, Paris, 1931, vol. 4, p. 160).

[37] DE MAZENOD, "Journal," March 31, 1839, JM.

[38] LEFLON, *De Mazenod*, vol. 1, p. 404.

[39] J. LEFLON, *La crise révolutionnaire*, p. 213.

6000, i.e., the number that a single year furnished prior to 1789. The balance was not re-established until under the Restoration.[40]

De Mazenod saw that the Church was not answering the needs of all the people. It was barely reaching out to those that remained faithful. It was not that the clergy lacked zeal, but their number was greatly reduced, and they were getting old. The pastoral situation had changed, and he saw that special methods were needed. De Mazenod became part of the pastoral renewal of the Church as he faced the situation first in Aix and then in Provence. [41]

Upon his return to Aix he took up residence in his mother's house with Maur, a Camaldolese lay brother, who was secularized when his monastery was closed by Napoleon in 1811. Maur was both his servant and companion, and would remain with him until September 15, 1815. At that time he entered the Trappist monastery of Port-du-Salut.[42]

Before beginning his ministry, de Mazenod made a retreat at the seminary of Aix, and drew up a schedule for his daily life. Commenting on his schedule one author wrote:

> The Founder seems to have had an idea of the concrete life of a priest that was much more contemplative than pastoral. In any case his daily schedule was still that of a good seminarian.[43]

De Mazenod sent a copy of his resolutions and schedule to M. Duclaux, his Sulpician spiritual director, who replied, "Don't change a comma without a necessity."[44] Commenting on this, Taché wrote:

> If Saint-Sulpice rightly insisted on prayer and study, it did not open sufficiently the way to the apostolic life . . . This encouragement from M. Duclaux only enclosed M. de Mazenod in this seminary schedule. While he approved the plans inspired by his zeal, this advise will not aid him to leave behind this schedule when the demands of the apostolate will require it.[45]

---

[40] Ibid. p. 214.

[41] LEFLON, De Mazenod, vol 1, pp. 403-404.

[42] See J-M. LAROSE, O.M.I., "Étude sur l'origine des frères convers chez les Oblats (1815–1861)," in Études Oblates 12 (1953), pp. 66–69; J. PIELORZ, O.M.I., "À propos du F. Maur," in Études Oblates 13 (1954), pp. 248–249; REY, Histoire, vol. 1, p. 126.

[43] Fernand JETTÉ, O.M.I., review of "Vie Spirituelle d'Eugène de Mazenod," in Études Oblates, 20 (1961), p. 88.

[44] DUCLAUX, to de Mazenod, February 23, 1813, cited by REY, Histoire, vol. 1, p. 152.

[45] Alexandre TACHÉ, O.M.I., "La vie spirituelle d'Eugène de Mazenod Fondateur des Mission-naires Oblats de Marie Immaculée aux origines de la société (1812–1818)," S.T.D. dissertation, Gregorian University, 1960, pp. 90–91.

After his retreat de Mazenod continued to visit the Aix seminary, and it became, in fact, a field of his ministry. He soon established an association of piety, an Aa, modelling it on the one at Saint-Sulpice. However, at Aix it was not a secret society.[46]

> Since the establishment of the association, everything has taken a complete change . . . One cannot help but see the punctuality, the recollection, the meticulousness in little things, the renewal of fervor, the more frequent reception of the sacraments . . . In sum, I can tell you that I never leave these little meetings without feeling myself permeated by the example of these angels, and filled with the desire for my own perfection.[47]

At the same time, he began to hold regular meetings with some of the priests of Aix. Duclaux wrote, "I am elated about what you told me about beginning to get together with several pious priests to hold together conferences and conversations on the duties of the priesthood."[48]

According to all of de Mazenod's biographers the people of his social class awaited with curiosity for the first sermon of one of their own. Much to the surprise of all, he began with a series of lenten conferences for the workers, servants, and beggars at 6:00 A.M. on Sundays in the church of Saint Mary Magdalen in Aix. Breaking with the general practice of preaching only in French as was the custom after the Revolution, he spoke in Provençal, the language of the ordinary people.[49] As if this were not enough, he addressed them in a way that was most extraordinary for a noble.

> Artisans! How does the world look upon you? In its eyes, you are a class of people who were meant to toil laboriously all your lives in an obscure occupation which deprives you of your independence and makes you dependent upon the whim of those from whom you must solicit your employment.
>
> Servants! What are you in the eyes of this world? A class of people enslaved by those who pay your wages, subject to contempt, injustice, and even ill treatment on the part of exacting masters who think that they have the right to treat you harshly simply because of the niggardly salary they pay you.
>
> And you farm hands and peasants! What are you in the eyes of the world? No matter how valuable your work may be, your worth is deter-

---

[46] See LEFLON, *De Mazenod*, vol. 1, pp. 407–408 and 482, note 35.

[47] DE MAZENOD, to de Forbin-Janson, May 12, 1813, Holy Childhood Archives, Rome.

[48] REY, *Histoire*, vol. 1, p. 152.

[49] In an effort to bring about greater national unity, French alone was to be used as a public language. Consequently, the public officials could have easily taken umbrage at his preaching in Provençal.

mined simply by the strength of your arms; and if those who hire you give attention to the sweat of your brow, distasteful as it is to them, it is only because they wish to see it enrich the earth.

And what shall we say of you paupers who are forced by the injustice of men and the harshness of fate to beg for you pitiful sustenance and to grovel before the rich while you plead for the bread you need for staying alive? The world looks upon you as the scum of humanity, intolerable to look at, and it turns away from you to avoid being moved with pity for your condition of life, since it has no desire to ease it . . .

Come then, and learn what you are in the eyes of God! All you poor of Jesus Christ, you afflicted, unfortunate, suffering, infirm, diseased, covered with ulcers, you who are crushed by misery, my brothers, my very dear brothers, my revered brothers, listen to me.

You are the children of God, the brothers of Jesus Christ, co-heirs of His eternal kingdom, the cherished portion of His inheritance . . .[50]

Already on the first Sunday the large church was full. Each week the crowd increased, and soon "the huge building could not contain the affluence of persons eager to hear a sermon in the language of the people which penetrated its way into their hearts with the charm of the mother tongue . . ."[51]

Already as a seminarian de Mazenod demonstrated that he had the natural ability to reach children through teaching catechism. He had been assigned to the poorest of the parish, the children of the tavern keepers.[52] This was a valuable preparation for his future ministry in forcing him to present what he had learned in a way that was understandable to his audience.

Yesterday, Quinquagesima Sunday,[53] I had to give them a lesson on the mysteries of the Trinity and the Incarnation . . . I find an advantage for myself in giving these classes. First of all I get a much clearer idea of the things that I have to treat. I chew them well in order to be able to present them to the children. I get used to speaking in public, for fifty children and twenty curious onlookers, including some from the house, are really a public . . .[54]

---

[50] DE MAZENOD, "Instructions en Provençal à la Magdeleine," DM, V, no 3. In the same file is also the Provençal ms. in de Mazenod's hand.

[51] [Jaques] JEANCARD, Oraison funèbre de Monseigneur Charles-Joseph-Eugène de Mazenod, évêque de Marseille; prononcée le 4 juillet 1861, dans l'Église Saint-Martin (cathédrale provisoire) à Marseille, Marseille, 1861, p. 12; also in Missions O.M.I. 17 (1879), p. 119.

[52] See PIELORZ, La vie spirituelle, pp. 277–280.

[53] I.e., the Sunday before Ash Wednesday.

[54] DE MAZENOD, to his mother, February 13–14, 1809, FB, I, no. 7.

It was not only the poor and the common people that were suffering from the shortage of priests, and a lack of religious instructions. The teenaged students of the middle and upper classes were in great need.

It is not difficult to perceive that the plan of the impious Buonaparte (sic) and his infamous government is to completely destroy the Catholic religion in the states that he had usurped . . . The success of his measures is frightening. Already the surface of France is covered with secondary schools, military schools, and other establishments where impiety is encouraged, bad morals are at least tolerated, and materialism is prompted and applauded.[55]

Napoleon had in 1809 forbidden all religious groups that might be suspected of giving support to the Roman resistance to his regime. For this reason he had suppressed the Sodality and other similar organizations.

This, however, did not stop de Mazenod. On Low Sunday 1813, he held the first meeting of what was to become the "Association de la Jeunesse chrétienne" (Association of Christian Youth). The first seven members were students of Collège Bourbon, which was now under the control of the university. They were sons of the first families of Aix. The group was founded "sous l'invocation de l'Immaculée Conception de la Très-Sainte Vierge" (under the title of the Immaculate Conception of the Most Holy Virgin).[56]

Since it was in fact a sodality, great pains were taken to avoid the suspicion of the imperial police. The meetings, which were a time of prayer, instruction, and wholesome recreation, were conducted under the guise of games. The statutes drawn up by de Mazenod were a rule of life for the members.

The Association of Christian Youth was certainly for M. de Mazenod the principal work of the first years of his priesthood. He dedicated to it his soul, his heart, his time, his worries, and a good part of his income.[57]

The association soon had twenty members, and in a few years there were three hundred in Aix, which was a relatively small city.[58] Three of them later joined the Missionaries of Provence.

---

[55] DE MAZENOD, "Journal des délibérations, lois et coutumes de l'Association de la Jeunesse chrétienne, établie à Aix, sous les auspices de la Très sainte Vierge," April 15, 1813, DM, VIII, no. 2a.

[56] DE MAZENOD, "Consécration et Protestation de la Jeunesse Chrétienne," DM, VIII, no. 3.

[57] TACHÉ, "La vie spirituelle," p. 115. CF. REY, Histoire, vol. 1, p. 136.

[58] See [Toussaint] RAMBERT, Vie de Monseigneur Charles-Joseph-Eugène de Mazenod, évêque de Marseille, 2 vols., Tours, Mame et fils, 1883, vol. 1, pp. 129–135.

Duclaux, his director, referred to de Mazenod's preaching a mission in which he mentioned the "extraordinary attendance at your talks."[59] No other information is available concerning this mission.

Already in the first part of 1813, de Mazenod began to work among the prisoners in Aix. In April he wrote de Forbin-Janson:

> Still on Sundays I go to the prisons to give these poor people a talk in French. Afterward I go to the confessional until six P.M. to hear all the prisoners who come. Before and after the talk we sing hymns. I finish by having evening prayer.[60]

His prison ministry came to the attention of the general public by the conversion of a notorious woman, who had been sentenced to death for the enormity of her crimes. According to an eye-witness "they blessed outloud the charitable apostle who had contributed so effectively to bring about this miracle of grace."[61]

The following year, 1814, was marked by the passage of Pius VII through Provence on his return to Rome. This gave de Mazenod the opportunity to demonstrate his devotion to the pope. A number of the cardinals benefited from the hospitality of his mother as they passed through Aix.

The retreat of the imperial armies forced the transfer of many prisoners of war to southern France; some two thousand Austrians were sent to the old barracks in Aix. When the doctors and the chaplain fell victims to typhus, de Mazenod volunteered to take the latter's place. It was only a matter of days until he too fell ill from the dreaded disease and almost died. He attributed his recovery to the prayers of the members of the youth association.[62]

Pastoral Renewal through Missions

With the abdication of Napoleon there was a revival of a method of spiritual renewal that had a long and glorious history in France—parish missions. It is sufficient to merely mention the preaching of St. Bernard in the twelfth century, the Franciscans and Dominicans in the thirteenth, St. Vincent Ferrer in the fifteenth, St. Francis de Sales in the sixteenth, St. John Francis Regis and St. Vincent de Paul in the seventeenth.[63]

---

[59] DUCLAUX, to de Mazenod, September 10, 1813, cited by REY, *Histoire*, vol. 1, p. 157.

[60] DE MAZENOD to de Forbin-Janson, April 9, 1813, Holy Childhood Archives, Rome.

[61] MARTIN, "Mémoires," cited by REY, *Histoire*, vol. 1, no. 158.

[62] See REY, *Histoire*, vol. 1, pp. 164–166.

[63] E. SEVRIN, *Les missions religieuses en France sous la Restauration (1815–1830)*, vol. 1, Paris, Procure des Prêtres de la Miséricorde, 1948; vol. 2. Paris, Libraire Philosophique Vain, 1959; vol.

This tried and proven system of extraordinary preaching that was much in vogue prior to the Revolution was used again from 1803. For a while the missions were approved and even subsidized by the emperor. The success in bringing back the people to religious practices was truly astonishing. By the Decree of Schoenbrün (September 26, 1809) all missions were forbidden by Napoleon. In spite of this, there were still a few missions preached after the decree.[64]

De Mazenod's talented and zealous friend de Forbin-Janson wanted to do something great for the Church. He had been preaching with great success, but was drawn by the challenge of his old desire of going to China as a missionary. Travelling to Rome, de Forbin-Janson presented his project to Pius VII. The pope replied:

> Without a doubt your project is good, but it is more important to help the people that surround us; *especially our brothers in the faith.* In France, especially there is a need of missions for the people and retreats for clergy.[65]

Not one to lose any time, de Forbin-Janson started immediately. He joined Jean-Baptiste Rauzan in founding the Missionaries of France, and urged de Mazenod to join them. Already in 1814 he presented a petition for royal approval of his plan, "Mémoire au Roi sur un établissement de mission pour la France."[66]

De Mazenod, by nature, was not one to make quick decisions in important matters. This can be seen in his reply:

> The king has granted you 150 thousand francs for your first establishment. When will you start it, and do you count on moving in there soon? You are quite numerous, since you count on two houses. I keenly desire to know your Constitutions, not that I think I will probably come to join you. I still do not know what God wants of me but am so resolved to do His will as soon as it is known to me, I would leave tomorrow for the moon, if I had to. I keep nothing secret from you. So, I will tell you without ado that I am hesitating between two plans: either to go off and bury myself in some well regulated community of an order that I have always loved; or do in my diocese exactly what you have done successfully at Paris. My illness has played havoc with me. I was feeling more inclined to the first plan because, to tell the truth, I was quite sick of living solely for others. It has come to pass that I have not had time to go to confession for three whole weeks.

1, pp. 4–11.

[64] Sevrin, *Les missions,* vol. 1, pp. 12–21.

[65] de Mazenod, "Mémoires," cited by Rey, *Histoire,* vol. 1, p. 169.

[66] Sevrin, *Les missions,* vol. 1, pp. 25–33, 52–61.

You can see for yourself how tied down I am. The second plan, however, seems to me more useful, given the dreadful plight to which the people have been reduced.[67]

The fact that he was leaning in the latter direction is indicated later in the same letter by his reflections on how to obtain a house, and on the rules that he was already formulating in his mind:

But what must be remembered is that our regions are without any help, that their people offer hopeful signs of being converted and must not therefore be abandoned. Yet abandon them we would if we joined you because we alone, and not you, can help them. We have to speak in their own tongue in order to be understood by them. We have to preach in Provençal.[68]

In December he made an eight day retreat at the Aix seminary and used as the basis of his meditations "Retraite selon l'esprit de la méthode de Saint Ignace pour les ecclésiastiques" by François Nepveu, S.J. The meditations on the Kingdom of Jesus Christ, the standards, and apostolic service met his spiritual needs and affirmed him in his apostolic orientation, although it did not bring him to a definitive answer as to the form of his ministry.[69]

In February 1815 Napoleon secretly left Elba and arrived at Cannes on March the first. From there, he marched in triumph to Paris. It did not take de Mazenod long to act. He wrote to Duke d'Angoulême, the commander of the king's army, volunteering his services, "Not being able to serve my king with the sword, I must serve him by all the means that my ministry gives me."[70] As far as is known, he did not receive a response.

Napoleon's triumph ended with his second abdication on June 22. Aix was liberated on June 25, and Louis XVIII returned to Paris on July 8. With the king's return a new era of the Church in France began—that of the popular missions.

In his two volume study, "Les missions religieuses en France sous la Restauration," Sevrin states that between 1815 and 1830 about forty-five dioceses in France had societies formed for the preaching of missions. The precise form that these societies took varied from diocese to diocese. Some were very informal groups, while others were religious communities or formally

---

[67] DE MAZENOD, to de Forbin-Janson, October 28, 1814, Holy Childhood Archives, Rome, in *Oblate Writings* vol. 6, no. 2, pp. 2–3, all except the first three sentences.

[68] Ibid., pp. 3–4.

[69] See JETTÉ, "La vie spirituelle," p. 89; TACHÉ, "La vie spirituelle," pp. 55–56.

[70] DE MAZENOD, to his father, March 26, 1815, FB, I, no. 1.

established societies of diocesan priests. This missionary movement extended throughout France.[71]

De Mazenod's Decision to Found a Mission Society

On October 23-24, 1815 de Mazenod wrote de Forbin-Janson that he had made the decision to found a band of missionaries. By using the date of this letter as a reference point, one may conclude that it was in late August or early September that he made up his mind.

Now I ask you and I ask myself how I, hitherto unable to make up my mind in this matter suddenly find myself setting wheels in motion, renouncing my comfort and risking my fortune by launching an enterprise of which I know the worth, but for which I only had a liking negated by other and diametrically opposed views! This is a riddle to me, and it is the second time in my life that I see myself moved to resolve something of the utmost seriousness as if by a strong impulse from without. When I reflect on it, I am convinced that it so pleases God to put an end to my irresolution. And in such a way that I am engaged to the hilt! I assure you that in such circumstances I am quite another man. You would no longer tell me to get the lead out of my ass,[72] if you were to see how I fly around. I am well nigh up to your standard in acting with so much authority . . . It is nearly two months now that I fight on at my own expense, sometimes openly, sometimes discreetly . . .[73]

On October 2 de Mazenod bought the choir of the church of the Carmelites in Aix and a portion of the adjoining convent to house his mission

---

[71] See Sevrin, *Les missions*, vol. 1, pp. 48–50.

[72] Flanagan translated "Tu ne m'appellerais plus 'cul-de-plomb,' " as "You won't be able to call me a lazy bum any more" (Leflon, *De Mazenod*, vol. 2, p. 32). John Witherspoon Mole translated it as "You would no longer call me a stick-in-the-mud" (*Oblate Writings*, vol. 6, p. 8). Are these bowdlerizations to avoid offending the very delicate? It seems that neither translation renders the full meaning or the verbal impact of the expression "cul-de-plomb." For that reason the author of this dissertation uses in his rendition the current American-English slang expression to better convey both the meaning and force of the French expression.

Something similar is found in the practice of many early writers on de Mazenod. Frequently in his letters to Oblates he used the familiar form of you, *tu*. This offended their sensitivities, since it was forbidden to *tutoyer* in the Congregation. De Mazenod was excused by these writers because he was the founder, but in order to remove the "bad example," the published writings and quotations were modified by using *vous* in place of *tu*. Cf. "Registre des Délibérations des Chapitres Généraux de la Société des Missionnaires dits de Provence," 1837, pp. 53, 64; cited by J. Pielorz, o.m.i., *Les Chapitres Généraux au temps du Fondateur*, 2 vol., Ottawa, Éditions des Études Oblates, 1968, vol. 1, pp. 138 and 168.

[73] De Mazenod, to de Forbin-Janson, October 23-24, 1815, Holy Childhood Archives, Rome, in *Oblate Writings* vol. 6, no. 5, pp. 8–9.

society. In addition to this he contacted a number of priests and invited them to join them. On October 9 he wrote l'abbé Henri Tempier:

> My dear friend, read this letter at the foot of your crucifix with a mind to heed only God and what is demanded in the interests of his glory and of the salvation of souls from a priest like yourself. Stifle the voice of cupidity, love of comfort and convenience; dwell deeply on the plight of our country people, their situation, the apostasy that daily spreads wider with dreadfully ravaging effects . . .

> Since the head of the Church is persuaded that, given the wretched state in which France finds herself, only missions can bring people back to the Faith which they have practically abandoned, good priests (ecclésiastiques)[74] from different dioceses are banding together in response to the views of the supreme Pastor. We likewise feel that it is utterly necessary to employ the same remedy in our regions and, full of confidence in the goodness of Providence, have laid down the foundations of an establishment which will steadily furnish our countryside with fervent missionaires.

> . . . You will have *four companions* If presently we are not more numerous, it means we wish to choose men who have the will and the courage to walk in the footsteps of apostles.[75]

Summary

Returning to Aix after his eleven year exile in Italy, Eugene de Mazenod found the religious situation in his native Provence desperate because of the aftermath of the French Revolution. While struggling to reunite his family, and solve its financial problems, he began to experience a religious conversion. During the Good Friday liturgy at the unveiling of the cross, he was overwhelmed by his own sinfulness and divine grace. Marked by this experience of Jesus as Savior and feeling the call to the priesthood, he entered Saint-Sulpice Seminary.

After ordination, he returned to his native Aix. With the permission of the diocesan authorities, he devoted himself to his own ministry—preaching to the poor and ordinary people, an organization for students, direction of the seminarians, spiritual care of the prisoners. He almost died because of his ministry to the typhus-ridden Austrian prisoners of war.

---

[74] In *Oblate Writings*, vol. 6, no. 4, p. 6 the word *ecclésiastiques* is translated as "good men of the Church." This is hardly a precise translation. In fact *ecclésiastiques* in this context means *priests*.

[75] DE MAZENOD, to Tempier, October 9, 1815, cited by REY, *Histoire*, vol. 1, p. 181; *Oblate Writings*, vol. 6, no. 4, pp. 6–7.

Realizing that the parishes were not meeting the spiritual needs of the most of the people and following the advice of Pius VII to de Forbin-Janson, de Mazenod in 1815 decided to found a house of diocesan missionaries.

Religion is truly in a deplorable state in the rural areas, where the inhabitants seem to have rejected the faith of the fathers. A group of priests, who have been deeply moved by this situation, have probed the depth of this wound and have decided to dedicate themselves completely to the work of the missions in order to try and bring back the people to religious principles . . .

They are optimist enough to expect to get sufficient men to join them, that some will be able to spend time in prayer, study, and meditation on the holy truths, while others spread throughout the country to announce the Word of God and restore the practice of the gospel precepts.[76]

---

[76] "Prospectus pour les Missions," DM, IX, no. 1; *Écrits du Fondateur*, vol. 4, p. 274. This ms. is in an unknown handwriting, although the title is in de Mazenod's. The date assigned by Pielorz is from October 1815 to January 25, 1816, i.e., between de Mazenod's decision to found and the actual foundation of the Missionaries of Provence. However, DUVAL in "Écrits" opts for January 29, 1816 as the earliest possible date (*Écrits* vol. 4, pp. 273-274). See J. PIELORZ, O.M.I., "Nouvelles Recherches sur la Fondation de notre Congrégation," *Missions O.M.I.* 83 (1956), pp. 244-245.

This document is a letter sent to prospective benefactors to sollicit their financial support. Undoubtedly it is the first example of Oblate fund raising by direct mail. After explaining the need of the people to be evangelized and the work and life of the missionaries it concludes:

"Daily prayers for the benefactors will be recited by the Church of the Missions in Aix; during the missions the people will be asked to do the likewise.

"*Subscription form.* 'I promise to pay each year for (_____) years, as long as my means permit me to do so, the sum of _____ to contribute to the expense of the establishment of the house of the Missions of Provence, founded in Aix in the old convent of the Carmelites.'

P[raised be] J[esus] C[hrist]."

CHAPTER II
Foundation and Papal Approbation

Foundation of the Missionaries of Provence

Some twenty-five years after the foundation of the Missionary Oblates of Mary Immaculate Eugene de Mazenod summed up his intentions at that time:

> It was in 1815 that I lay the footings of our little society. I proposed as the principal end the preaching of the Gospel to the poor, the prisoners, and the young. I had to have companions who could enter into this idea with which the Lord had inspired me. We had to consecrate ourselves to the apostolic ministry; it was necessary to have mortified men who wanted to walk in the footsteps of the apostles by the practice of the evangelical counsels. I could not conceive how it would be possible to do the good that I was undertaking on any other condition.[1]

Tempier was the first to take up residence in the former Carmelite convent. On the feast of the Conversion of St. Paul, January 25, 1816, de Mazenod and another priest—probably Icard moved in with him. It was on that feast that they began common life.[2] Their other three companions moved in shortly afterward. It was also on January 25 that de Mazenod addressed a formal petition to the vicars capitular general of Aix requesting approval for their community, ministry, and way of life. All six of them signed this petition which stated the purposes of their community in this way:

> The undersigned priests have been deeply moved by the deplorable situation of the small towns and villages of Provence which have almost completely lost their faith . . .
>
> Being convinced that Missions are the only means available to move these strayed people from their senseless ways . . .
>
> The end of this society is not only to work for the salvation of one's neighbor by the ministry, it has also principally the purpose of giving its members the means of practising the religious virtues. They have such a great attraction for these virtues that most of them would consecrate themselves to observe them their whole life in some religious order, if they

---

[1] DE MAZENOD, "Mémoires," cited by [Toussaint] RAMBERT, O.M.I., *Vie de Monseigneur Charles-Joseph-Eugène de Mazenod*, 2 vols., Tours, Mame et fils, 1883, vol. 1, p. 164.

[2] See Józef PIELORZ, O.M.I., "Nouvelles recherches sur la Fondation de notre Congrégation," in *Études Oblates*, 84 (1957), pp. 130–136.

did not have the hope of finding in the community of missionaries about the same advantages that they would find in the religious state to which they would like to dedicate themselves . . . Their life will be then divided between prayer . . . study . . . preaching and the direction of youth.

On entering the society the missionaries must have the intention of persevering for their whole life.[3]

Although the petition speaks of the practice of religious virtues, and the desire of most of the members for religious life, there is no mention of religious vows. In a draft of the petition de Mazenod had written, "The missionaries are free; they do not make vows."[4] This change in the final text indicates, it would seem, an evolution in de Mazenod's thought.[5] This is seen very clearly when it is compared with his letter to Tempier the previous October.

For the rest, we will not be bound by vows. But I hope that it will be the same with us as with the disciples of St. Philip Neri who, free as we shall remain, would die before thinking of leaving a congregation for which they have the same affection as for their mother.[6]

Their first mission at Grans—from February 11 to March 17, 1816—was so successful that it had to be extended in order to have the time needed to hear the confessions of the men.[7] It was during this mission, according to Rey, that de Mazenod realized the necessity of permanent commitment.

The mission at Grans gave him the opportunity to experience the good will and the dispositions of his confreres, and at the same time to realize the great difficulty of apostolic ministry, if the minds and hearts are not united by bonds—if not by insoluble bonds.[8]

---

[3] DE MAZENOD, "Supplique," DM, IX, no. 1, in A. REY, O.M I., *Histoire de Monseigneur Charles-Joseph-Eugène de Mazenod*, Rome, Maison Générale, 1928, vol. 1, pp. 190–191; Józef PIELORZ, O.M.I., "Nouvelles recherches sur la fondation de notre Congrégation," in *Missions O.M.I.*, 84 (1957), p. 141.

[4] DE MAZENOD, draft of "Supplique," DM, IX, no. 1, J. PIRLORZ, O.M.I., "Nouvelles recherches," in *Missions O.M.I.*, 84 (1957), p. 141. This article prints the draft and the final petition in parallel columns for easy comparison.

[5] Ibid., p. 146.

[6] DE MAZENOD, to Tempier, October 9, 1815, in RAMBERT, *Vie*, vol. 1, p. 166; *Oblate Writings*, vol. 6, no. 4, p. 7.

[7] See DE MAZENOD, to Tempier, March, 1, 1816, in RAMBERT, *Vie*, vol. 1, pp. 181–182; *Oblate Writings* vol. 6, no. 11, p. 19.

[8] REY, *Histoire* , vol. 1, p. 195.

Could the necessity to expel from the group Icard, "a miserable priest who had to be sent away after the first mission,"[9] have been the reason why de Mazenod reached this conclusion?

The name *Missionaries of Provence* was adopted from the beginning. No explanation for this was needed—they were to preach missions in Provence in Provençal. It also distinguished them from the *Missionnaires de France* founded by Jean-Baptiste Rauzan and de Forbin-Janson.

De Mazenod before long obtained possession of the former Carmelite church attached to the convent and after the necessary repairs it was opened to the public on Palm Sunday, April 7. From the beginning it was called the church *de la Mission*, and was dedicated to St. Vincent de Paul, founder of the Congregation of the Mission, for whom de Mazenod had a special devotion.[10] Because of the zeal and talent of the missionaries, much to the chagrin of the clergy of Aix, the beautiful church was soon a very popular place of worship. The pastors resented their parishioners forsaking them for the missionaries and considered this opposed to their parochial rights.

Introduction of Vows

In his memoirs, de Mazenod explained the difficulties that he encountered in introducing vows.

It was always my firm idea that our little family must consecrate itself to God and the service of the Church by vows of religion. The difficulty was to bring my first companions to appreciate this teaching, that is a bit hard for beginners, especially during a period which has lost the vestiges of this tradition. We were at the end of a revolution that had dispersed, I will say almost destroyed, all the religious orders. Nevertheless I broached this idea with the first of them, Father Tempier, whom I had chosen as my director, and he had chosen me as his. He was pleased with the proposition which corresponded to his own thoughts, and we agreed, M. Tempier and I, to follow through with this plan . . . In a word, Father Tempier and I judged that we should not delay any longer. On Holy Thursday [April 11, 1816] beneath the canopy of the beautiful repository which we had raised over the main altar of the church of the mission, during the night of that holy day, we made our vows with undescribable joy.[11]

---

[9] RAMBERT, *Vie* , vol. 1, p. 164.

[10] See J.-P. GUIGOU, O.M.I., Decree permitting the publication of indulgences, January 25, 1818, in *Recueil de cantiques et de prières à l'usage des Missions de Provence,* Avignon, Aubanel, 1819, pp. 5–6; *Missions O.M.I.,* 79 (1952), p. 122; *Écrits du Fondateur,* vol. 3, p. 122.

[11] DE MAZENOD, *Memoires,* in RAMBERT, *Vie,* vol. 1, p. 187.

In his study, "Introduction des vœux dans notre Congrégation,"[12] Cosentino shows that on Holy Thursday 1816 de Mazenod and Tempier made vows of obedience to each other. They were already bound by celibacy by their ordination to the subdiaconate, and the vow of poverty was soon to follow.

From October 1816 to November 1817, seven young students joined them and began their novitiate. Writing from Paris to Tempier, the novice master, de Mazenod insisted on the regularity of these young men. They were attending classes at the major seminary of Aix, and he was concerned about the example they should give the seminarians.

> I quite insist that all give a good example at the seminary . . . They ought not to forget that we are a Congregation of regular clerics (*clercs réguliers*), that we ought in consequence to be more fervent than simple seminarians, that we are called to replace in the Church the piety and all the virtues of the religious Orders . . .[13]

Although they were a group of secular priests living and working together without a rule and vows, de Mazenod already considered the Missionaries of Provence to be a congregation of religious priests (*clercs réguliers*).

De Mazenod began by founding a house that would work only in the diocese of Aix. He had written to de Forbin-Janson in 1815 that the vicars capitular of Aix had opposed his plans until they understood that he did not plan to take the much needed priests out of the diocese.

> Well did I see, my dear friend, that what decidedly cooled the ardor of our grand vicars for mission work was the fear of seeing themselves deprived of people truly needed for the diocese. All obstacles fell before the decision I took. The proposal that the missionaries I would band together would not go outside the diocese calmed them so well that they became avowed protectors of our enterprise.[14]

This too was soon to change. In August 1818 the bishop of Digne offered to the Missionaries of Provence the Shrine of Notre-Dame-du-Laus. De Mazenod called together the six other priests and the three theology students, who were in minor orders, to discuss the offer and the consequences of accepting it. It would be necessary to have real constitutions, tighten the bonds (*des liens plus étroits*), and a hierarchy to coordinate everything in order to maintain the same

---

[12] G. COSENTINO, O.M.I., "L'introduction des vœux dans notre Congrégation," in *Études Oblates*, 13 (1954), p. 297.

[13] DE MAZENOD, to Tempier, November 4, 1817, in REY, *Histoire*, vol. 1, pp. 222–223; *Oblate Writings*, vol. 6, no. 29, p. 45.

[14] DE MAZENOD, to de Forbin-Janson, October 23, 1815, Holy Childhood Archives, Rome, in *Oblate Writings*, vol, 6, no. 5, p. 8. See REY, *Histoire*, vol. 1, p. 228.

will and spirit.[15] All were of one mind and asked de Mazenod to start drafting constitutions immediately. He left for Saint-Laurent-du-Verdon for a much needed rest. During this time he worked on the constitutions. J. Pielorz rejects with well reasoned arguments the traditional view that de Mazenod completed his task while there.[16] He points out that de Mazenod went to Saint-Laurent precisely because he was rundown and needed a rest; during this time he recovered his health, made all the spiritual exercises with the two young Oblates who accompanied him; preached in the parish church on Sundays, etc. He simply did not have time to do all this and recover his health within the time frame.[17] He must have begun writing the Constitutions before going to Saint-Laurent.

The first part of the Constitutions listed the ends of the society as three: preaching the word of God, taking the place of the religious suppressed by the Revolution, and the reform of the clergy. Next were listed the apostolic works to be performed: missions, extraordinary preaching, direction of youth, work among prisoners, care of the dying, recitation of divine office in common, and the religious services in the churches of the society.[18]

Having completed his task de Mazenod returned to Aix in time for the annual retreat. According to the reconstruction of the sequence of events by J. Pielorz, de Mazenod read the Constitutions to the assembled priests on the morning of October 24. All went well up to his text on vows. Umtil then there had been a few objections on minor points, and he willingly incorporated the suggestions. The proposed text included perpetual vows of obedience and celibacy, and a perpetual vow and oath of perseverance in the institute. There were immediate objections from four of the six other priests that they had not thought of vows. Evidently they had not understood what de Mazenod had meant by *"liens plus étroits."*

---

[15] DE MAZENOD, "Mémoires," in RAMBERT, *Vie*, vol. 1, p. 282.

[16] According to the traditional opinion, this was possible through his intense labor and by relying heavily on the Constitutions of the Redemptorists written by the recently beatified Alphonsus Liguori. In fact, he frequently translated paragraphs word for word. See J. LEFLON, *Eugene de Mazenod*, 4 vols., New York, Fordham University Press, 1966), vol. 2, 160; G. COSENTINO, O.M.I., *Histoire de nos Règles*, 6 vols., Ottawa, Édition des Études Oblates, 1955. The first volume studies in detail the various sources used by de Mazenod. The treatment of the influence of the Constitutions of Alphonsus Liguori takes almost sixty pages (71–130).

[17] See Józef PIELORZ, "Le séjour du Fondateur à St-Laurent et la rédaction de nos Règles (août–octobre 1818)," in *Missions O.M.I.*, 84 (1957), pp. 297–322.

[18] "Constitutions et Règles de la Société des Missionaries de Provence," (first French ms., 1818), DM, XI, no. 1, in *Missions O.M.I.*, 78 (1951), pp. 11–97; *Écrits du Fondateur*, vol. 1, pp. 11–97.

It was a critical moment, and there was a danger of a complete rupture. In order to convince them that vows were not something so dreadful (*si effrayant*) to the other members of the society, during the afternoon de Mazenod called together the three students in minor orders to the meeting, read to them the part on vows, and asked their opinion. All three were in favor. De Mazenod then convoked the community in general chapter, and gave the students deliberative vote. This was the only session at which they assisted. The assembly recognized itself as constituted as a society and meeting as a general chapter in light of the Constitutions they had just accepted, and vows were approved by vote of six to four—with four of the priests casting a negative vote. De Mazenod was unanimously recognized as superior general, and the other officers were elected.[19]

The annual retreat began the following morning. Before the end of the retreat two of the priests who had voted negatively changed their position. At the close of the retreat on November 1, 1818 eight members of the Missionaries of Provence, five priests and three students for the priesthood made perpetual vows. Of the two not making perpetual vows, one made vows for one year, and the other remained for the time being in the institute without vows.

One may judge the spirit of peace that had returned to the community by the fact that de Mazenod was unanimously elected superior general for life, and the two priests not making perpetual vows were elected first and second assistants general.

The first article contains a resumé of the Constitutions. It reads:

> The end of the Missionaries of Provence is first of all to form a group of secular priests who live together and strive to imitate the virtues and example of our Savior Jesus Christ principally by preaching the Word of God to the poor.[20]

However, there was still one thing missing in this article that de Mazenod considered essential, religious vows. This would come in time.

During his monthly day of retreat the previous May, he had written:

> A quick glance at the saints of our time, such as Blessed Leonard of Port Maurice and Blessed Alphonsus Liguori, seemed to encourage and strengthen me. The means that must be taken to succeed far from frightening me, confirmed me in this confidence, since they were easy. The view of religious perfection, the observance of the evangelical counsels revealed

---

[19] Józef PIELORZ, O.M.I., *Les chapitres Généraux au temps du Fondateur*, 2 vols., Ottawa, Éditions des Études Oblates, 1968, vol. 1, pp. 6-9.

[20] "Constitutions 1818," in *Missions O.M.I.*, 78 (1951), p. 13; *Écrits*, vol. 1, p. 13.

themselves to my spirit disengaged from the difficulties that I had experienced up to the present moment.

I asked myself why I should not add the vow of poverty to the vows of chastity and obedience which I have already made? Having passed in review the different obligations that evangelical poverty would impose on me, I see that there are none before which I would retreat.[21]

The time was not yet ripe for the vow of poverty when the Constitutions were composed. This is alluded to in the first chapter of the second part "Des obligations particulières des missionnaires" entitled "De l'esprit de pauvreté, et des vœux—de chasteté et de persévérance."

Voluntary poverty has always been regarded by the founders of religious orders as the foundation and the support of spiritual perfection, as the impregnable bulwark of religious life, and as the virtue which enables us the more easily to acquire the other virtues and to devote ourselves to good works . . . Since it is our aim to walk in the footsteps of the first Christians and according to the spirit of the holiest religious orders, the foregoing reasons would be more than sufficient to persuade us to embrace this essential point of the perfect and religious life . . .

The present situation impedes us for the moment from this ideal. Thus, we leave to future general chapters to perfect this point of our Rule, whenever they judge before God that it is the opportune moment to do so.[22]

To understand the difficulty of introducing the vow of poverty, one must recall the events of the French Revolution, the ensuing suppression of all religious houses in France, and also the forced secularization of countless religious institutions in much of Europe in the wake of the revolutionary armies.

Moreover, during that epoch there was no example of the practice of the vow of poverty, for the hindrances of the laws bequeathed by the Revolution prevented the strict observance of this vow. It seemed that it was impossible for the vow to exist with the inherent right of every French citizen to dispose of his own property up until his death. In addition, it must be acknowledged, that apart from one, none of Father de Mazenod's associates had ever thought of consecrating themselves to God by religious vows.[23]

Since the Missionaries of Provence were not a formally approved institute with public vows, the priests could be called back by their bishops to their

---

[21] DE MAZENOD, "Journal," in RAMBERT, Vie, vol. 1, pp. 272–273.

[22] "Constitutions 1818," in Missions O.M.I., 78 (1951), pp. 44–45; Écrits, vol. 1, pp. 44–45.

[23] RAMBERT, Vie, vol. 1, pp. 333–334.

dioceses. In fact in 1823 the bishop of Fréjus would declare the vows of two priests null and call them back to his diocese.[24]

These problems were soon overcome. Cosentino affirms that de Mazenod was the first to make a vow of poverty, but he gives no documentation to support the statement. The novices sent him a collective letter in October 1820 requesting his approval to add the vow of poverty at their profession.[25] Tempier, the novice master, made a vow of poverty the following November 21 with the condition "if ratified" by de Mazenod.[26]

At the second general chapter, on October 21, 1821, the vow of poverty was introduced in the institute. Rey says:

> . . . the first was a decree, issued by a unanimous vote, imposing the obligation on all the Missionaries of Provence to add to the three vows of chastity, obedience, and perseverance the vow of poverty . . .[27]

A different version was presented by Jeancard in 1826 when he wrote the acts of the 1821 general chapter:

> The Most Reverend Father General gave various explanations relative to the practice of poverty; he declared that it was the spirit of our Rules that it was to be lived as if it were under the most austere rules. Thereupon the proposal was made that the profession of the vow of poverty be prescribed by the Rule. After this was said, our Most Reverend Father General, using the authority that he had as founder, forthwith decided and inserted into the Rules that the vow of poverty will be obligatory in order to be received into our Society.[28]

A third version of what happened is presented by Suzanne in his draft of the chapter minutes. He said very simply, ". . . it was resolved first that the vow of poverty will be obligatory in order to be received into the society."[29]

---

[24] See REY, *Histoire*, vol. 1, pp. 316–317; G. COSENTINO, O.M.I., "Existence juridique de notre Congrégation pendant ses dix premières années (1816–1826)," in *Études Oblates*, 12 (1953), p. 15.

[25] See Th. ORTOLON, O.M.I., *Les Oblats de Marie Immaculée durant le premier siècle de leur existence*, 2 vol., Paris, Librairie Saint-Paul, 1914, vol. 1, p. 129.

[26] See REY, *Histoire*, vol. 1, p. 259.

[27] Ibid., p. 279.

[28] "Registre des Délibérations des Chapitres Généraux de la Société des Missionnaires dite de Provence," 1821, p. 17, in General Archives O.M.I.; *Missions O.M.I.*, 79 (1952), p. 49; *Écrits*, vol. 3, p. 49; PIRLORZ, *Les Chapitres*, vol. 1, p. 27.

[29] Draft of minutes, in General Archives O.M.I., in *Missions O.M.I.*, 79 (1952), p. 48; *Écrits*, vol. 3, p. 48.

Suzanne, who wrote his draft in 1826, was present at the 1821 chapter. Jeancard was not yet professed and consequently not present at the chapter.[30] Perhaps the explanation attributed to Cardinal Villeneuve of what really happened is as good an interpretation as any. It is that the motion was accepted unanimously by acclamation, and that de Mazenod sanctioned it by placing it in the Constitutions.[31]

In any case the 1821 chapter was peaceful, and the vow of poverty was accepted without any turmoil. At the end of the annual retreat following the chapter all made a vow of poverty with the exception of Dupuy. It was with de Mazenod's authorization that he never made a vow of poverty—even after papal approval of the Congregation.[32]

In a culture that is much more conscious of the forms of address than ours, another item was considered at the 1821 chapter.

> On the motion of a member that none should no longer be called by the word *monsieur*, it was unanimously decided that one is to be called *père*, with the designation *most reverend* for the superior general, and that of *reverend* for the other members of the Society.[33]

Until this time they were called *monsieur l'abbé,* as was the custom for the members of institutes without public vows, such as the Vincentians and Missionnaires de France, as well as the secular clergy. By deciding that henceforth they would be called *père,* they were stating that they considered themselves members of the religious clergy.

In accordance with the abovementioned decision the professed students for the priesthood were also addressed as *père*.[34] This was changed at the 1826 general chapter when it was decided that they should be addressed as *frère*.[35]

---

[30] See PIRLORZ, *Les Chapitres*, vol. 1, pp. 11. Jacques Jeancard (1799–1875), who had previously been a novice, again entered the on December 21, 1821; made his oblation on May 30, 1822 (ibid. p. 46); and was dispensed from his vows on July 23, 1834 (ibid., p. 115). For many years he was archdeacon of the cathedral chapter and vicar general of Marseilles as well as de Mazenod's secretary, who consecrated him as his auxiliary bishop on October 28, 1858.

[31] See PIRLORZ, *Les Chapitres*, vol. 1, p. 23, note 15.

[32] See PIRLORZ, *Les Chapitres*, vol. 1, p. 24.

[33] "Registre," 1821, pp. 17 and 30, in *Missions O.M.I.*, 79 (1952), pp. 50–51; *Écrits*, vol. 3, pp. 50–51; PIRLORZ, *Les Chapitres*, vol. 1, p. 27.

[34] PIRLORZ, *Les Chapitres*, vol. 1, p. 34.

[35] Registre," 1826, p. 24, in *Écrits*, vol. 4, p. 232; PIRLORZ, *Les Chapitres*, vol. 1, p. 72.

The first article of the 1818 Constitutions called the society the "Institut des Missionnaires dits de Provence."[36] This name was in common usage for a number of years even after papal approval and the official adoption of the name of Missionary Oblates of Mary Immaculate. For example, the acts of the general chapters were written from 1826 until 1856 in the official book with the title "Registre des délibérations des Chapitres généraux de la Société des Missionnaires dits de Provence."[37] In chapter five of this dissertation will be found an analysis of the use and the meaning of the word "missionary" in the Constitutions and by de Mazenod and his contemporaries.[38] It will be seen that in the Constitutions a missionary in the strict use of the word applied only to the priests, who were members of the institute, and was applied to the brothers only when it referred to all the members of the society.[39] Such usage, as will be seen, was the exception.

Ordinarily the priests added to their signature either "prêtre missionnaire" or an abbreviation for it such as *p.m.* or *ptre mre* or *p.mis.* This was done from the time of their entry into the novitiate by the priests. Other similar abbreviations were used by the candidates for the priesthood. Examples of this are *sous-diacre miss., t[onsu]ré m., acoly[te] miss., eccl[ésiastique] miss., n[ovi]ce m[issionnai]re.* By this practice they were affirming their double vocation—as priests (candidates for the priesthood) and missionaries.[40]

Until 1818 all the candidates were known as novices. This applied both to the students in theology and those who today are called juniors or minor seminarians or pre-novices.[41] In the Constitutions the word used for religious profession or the making of vows was *oblation.* This is a direct translation of *oblazione,* the word used by Alphonsus Liguori.[42] After the chapter in conformity with the Constitutions, the professed students for the priesthood were called *oblats* (oblates) or *simples oblats* (simple oblates).[43] Could the reason for the latter be that they were not yet missionaries, since they were not yet priests, but were oblates by their profession?

---

[36] See "Constitutions 1818," I partie, c. I, §1, art. 1.

[37] "Registre," title page.

[38] Infra pp. 151–161.

[39] Infra pp. 155–158.

[40] "Registre des formules d'admissions au Noviciat: 1815–1850," in General Archives O.M.I., in *Missions O.M.I.,* 79 (1952), pp. 7–34; *Écrits,* vol. 3, pp. 7–34.

[41] See PIRLORZ, *Les Chapitres,* vol. 1, p. 10.

[42] COSENTINO, *Histoire,* vol. 1, p. 124.

[43] See PIRLORZ, *Les Chapitres,* vol. 1, p. 34.

The first brother joined the community in 1820 and began his novitiate on May 30, 1822. There was another brother novice in 1823 and a third in 1825. In the written request for entry into the novitiate the words "en qualité de frère convers" (as a lay brother) were added to the standard formula.[44] None of the three finished the novitiate or made his oblation. If they had, in light of the 1821 decision concerning the titles, would they have been called *père*? It would seem not, since *frère* is not only a title of address, but also the word for a particular vocation, and the role of the brothers was not that of a spiritual father. The decision of 1826 chapter concerning the use of *père* referred only to the *simples oblats*, and no mention was made of the brothers in that context.

> A member of the chapter asked if the title of father, which according to the words of our previous chapters, should be given to the members of the Society, should be extended to the simple oblates who are not yet priests. The question was resolved negatively. As a result of this, it was decided that the oblates should be given the title of brother.[45]

A careful reading of minutes of the 1826 chapter indicates that the decision of the 1821 chapter had been understood as applying the professed students (*simples oblats*), and this was changed. There is no indication that it was ever understood as applying to the brothers (*frères convers*).

A profound change had taken place in de Mazenod's interior life during the early period of the foundation of the Missionaries of Provence. This change would affect not just de Mazenod but his Congregation. During the first months of the foundation he was utterly torn in all directions by his many responsibilities and his personal program of prayer and penance. His health was suffering, and he began to vomit blood. Upon the recommendation of de Mazenod's physician, Tempier ordered him to the country for a period of rest in July 1816. He took the opportunity to make a retreat, and it was during this retreat that he was given the light to realize that God's will for him was not the life of a monk. For him, holiness was to be found in the active ministry.

> After two years of apostolic work, the retreat notes registered only impatience and confusion for having not been able to give the desired care for his spiritual life and a strong inclination to achieve in solitude "his" ideal of perfection. The notes of 1816 reflect an interior climate that was more serene, more confident, more patient. He understands better now how true holiness consists in a perfect union with God's will. What God wants now is that he consecrate himself to the apostolate. It is in the active life that he

---

[44] "Registre du Noviciat," passim, in *Missions O.M.I.*, 79 (1952), pp. 7–34, passim; *Écrits*, vol. 3, pp. 7–34, passim.

[45] "Registre," 1826, p. 24, in *Écrits*, vol. 4, p. 220; PIRLORZ, *Les Chapitres*. vol. 1, p. 72.

must sanctify himself.[46]

De Mazenod handed on to his sons the enlightenment which he had received in prayer. The resolution of the seeming dilemma that faces every apostolic worker striving for personal holiness while engaged in very active ministry is outlined in the Constitutions.

> Whether out on the missions or at home, their chief study will always be to make progress in the way of priestly and religious perfection. They will cultivate the virtues of humility, poverty, self-denial, interior mortification, purity of intention, and faith. In a word, they will seek to become other Jesus Christs spreading abroad everywhere the fragrance of his amiable virtues.[47]

Successes and Crises

The success stories of the missions sound so fantastic to modern ears, that they are hard to believe. The crowds filled the churches, and the people on the outside tried to break down the doors to enter. The team of missionaries heard confession day and night to the point of exhaustion, etc. No doubt this was due not only to the zeal of the missionaries and the working of divine grace, but in part to the intensity with which the people of Provence lived. This same intensity is seen in the quarrels among the clergy and the crises experienced by the Missionaries of Provence.

While devoting himself to this ministry and the foundation of the Congregation, de Mazenod did not neglect the needs of his family. Already in 1814 he had begun steps to have Canon Fortuné de Mazenod, his uncle, made a bishop. There was a sustained effort to obtain pensions from the government for his father and other uncle, the former naval officer. He was successful in obtaining for the latter the promotion to the rank of retired rear admiral and the corresponding pension. Success escaped him in regard to his father.

---

[46] Alexandre TACHÉ, O.M.I., "La vie spirituelle d'Eugène de Mazenod, Fondateur des Missionnaires Oblats de Marie Immaculée, aux origines de la Société (1812–1818)," S.T.D. dissertation, Pontifical Gregorian University, 1960, p. 279.

[47] "Constitutions 1818," II partie, c. I, Des autres principales observances, in *Missions O.M.I.,* 78 (1951), pp. 55; *Écrits.* vol. 1, p. 55.

In the Latin translation, the phrase "il tâcheront de devenir d'autres Jésus-Christ" became "instar Christi Domini" (*Constitutiones 1826*, pars II, c. III, #1, art. III). This was rendered in English as "in imitation of Jesus Christ" (*Constitutiones 1928*, art. 290). With each translation the meaning was watered down or weakened. This weakening of de Mazenod's words was changed with the publication of *Constitutions 1982* which has in its quoting of *Constitutions 1818*; "they will strive to become other Christs" (p. 40).

While in Paris in 1817, de Mazenod personally undertook the cause of Canon Fortuné. Cardinal Talleyrand, the *grand aumônier*, was in charge of episcopal appointments, and his brother was Baron de Talleyrand, Louis XVI's last ambassador to the king of Naples. He was still there during the de Mazenods' stay in Naples, and a friend of Fortuné. The cardinal readily accepted Eugene's proposal that his uncle be made a bishop, and the semi-official announcement of Fortuné's appointment to the restored see of Marseille was made in September of that year. Because of this the three brothers left Palermo in December and returned to France after an exile of twenty-seven years.[48]

The president and the retired rear admiral took up residence in Marseille. Canon Fortuné moved into the house of the Mission in Aix.

The family support was not onesided. Fortuné, now sixty-eight years old, generously devoted himself to the ministry of the church of the Mission, hearing confessions daily by the hour. The president translated the life of Blessed Alphonsus Liguori from Italian into French in order to further his son's promotion of the teaching of and devotion to the founder of the Redemptorists. With an annual allowance of 1000 francs, de Mazenod's mother helped support Eugene and the Missionaries of Provence. Roze-Joannis, his Jansenist uncle, encouraged him and gave him 300 francs.

De Mazenod's background, convictions, and personality hardly endeared him to the local clergy. He was a noble, royalist, anti-Jansenist, and ultramontane. His preaching in Provençal gained him no popularity with his own social class. The very success of his youth organization was resented by the pastors and considered an infringement on their rights. His introduction of the moral theology of Alphonsus Liguori was considered laxist.[49] His vocal defence of papal authority won him no friends among the Gallicans.

The crucial point that repeatedly reared its head and threatened the very existence of the Missionaries of Provence was the absence of a firm juridical basis for the society. Could the bishops call the priests back to their dioceses? Could the members desiring to leave the society seek a dispensation of their vows from their bishops in spite of the vow of perseverance and the prescriptions of the Constitutions reserving the dispensation to the pope and the superior general?

---

[48] See Jean LEFLON, *Eugene de Mazenod*, trans. F.D. FLANAGAN, 4 vols., New York, Fordham University Press, 1961–1970, vol. 2, p. 84.

[49] See LEFLON, *De Mazenod*, vol. 2, pp. 129–130.

In January 1816 the vicar capitular of Aix had given only preliminary approval to the Missionaries of Provence:

> . . . [we] have authorized Messieurs de Mazenod, Maunier, Deblieu, Tempier, and Mie to form a community in the house that is called that of the Carmelites in Aix . . . we, however, reserve the right to grant a more ample and more formal approval with the changes in the regulations that experience may show to be useful, if that is necessary.[50]

Following the adoption of the Constitutions in 1818, de Mazenod again sought approval from Canon Guigou, vicar capitular general of Aix. The reply was a confirmation of the approval of 1816:

> . . . wishing to consolidate, insofar as it depends on us, an institution that is so beneficial to religion, and which many dioceses seem recently to have taken as a model by establishing similar societies, we have authorized, as we authorize by the present, insofar as it depends on us, the aforementioned institution for the exercise of the abovenamed works and for the dedication to said duties and to live observing the regulation that was provisionally approved by us on January 29, 1816 . . .[51]

It is to be noted that neither of these decrees approved the Constitutions. In the case of the 1816 decree, the Constitutions had not been written, and in the case that of the 1818 decree, de Mazenod had not submitted the Constitutions for approval. The vow of poverty was not introduced until 1821. Prior to that the Constitutions of the Missionaries of Provence could not have been approved as those of a *religious* institute.

To assure the legal status of his society, de Mazenod sought already in 1816 through Guigou authorization from the French government. The political situation prevented the approval at that time. Because of disputes with the Aix pastors, the situation became urgent, and de Mazenod made a special trip to Paris in July of the following year to obtain the desired recognition. There was no possibility of getting a bill through the Chamber of Deputies. De Mazenod's enemies knew why he had gone to Paris, and to return to Aix without approval would place his institute in real jeopardy.[52] Unwittingly one of the priests, who by an anonymous letter hoped to harm him, gave the minister of worship the means to come to de Mazenod's aid.

> You can let it be known throughout the city, my dear friend, for the consolation of worthy people and to the despair of the wicked, that we are recognized by the government and authorized to continue *the functions* that

---

[50] Decree of approbation, Aix, January 29, 1816, DM VIII, no. 1b; *Écrits*, vol. 4, pp. 273–274.

[51] Confirmation of decree of approbation, Aix, November 13, 1818, DM VIII ia; *Écrits*, vol. 4, pp. 276–278.

[52] See LEFLON, *De Mazenod*, vol. 2, p. 62.

we have so *happily begun*. These are the very terms of the letter which the minister has just addressed to *M. de Mazenod, superior of the Missions of Aix*. You will note that M. de Mazenod had never assumed this title in speaking or in writing to the minister. Apparently it is to belie the author of the anonymous letter which denounced me to the minister while designating me, such is the regard he has for my person, as *a certain Sieur de Mazenod, priest of this diocese, calling himself a missionary.*[53]

This was hardly official recognition from the government. So, de Mazenod embarked on an alternative plan of having Fortuné become a bishop so that he could be the protector of the Missionaries of Provence.

> The motive that inspired Eugene de Mazenod [to seek the elevation of his uncle to the episcopacy], when a young layman, was the duty of reuniting his family by obtaining for its members a post in keeping with the profession or the vocation of each of them. But when he became a priest, the reasons that prevailed in him were mainly the desire to give the Church a worthy bishop, able to collaborate with Pius VII in his views of France, and the necessity of providing for his Congregation in jeopardy a protection that the government refused.[54]

As mentioned above success seemed immediate with Fortuné's semi-official nomination to the see of Marseille in September 1817.[55] However, because of the disagreement between the Holy See and the French government over the Concordat, Fortuné's appointment did not become official until January 1823.

The success of this plan to guarantee the protection of the society almost destroyed it. Fortuné was by this time seventy-three years old, and he would accept the appointment only if de Mazenod would agree to be his vicar general. De Mazenod had no choice but to accept. On the insistence of the minister of worship, Fortuné accompanied by de Mazenod left for Paris on February 9, 1823. Because of a delay in the arrival of the bull from Rome, he was not consecrated bishop until July sixth, and went on to Marseille on the tenth. Tempier also accepted to be a vicar general along with de Mazenod. Both of them were also named canons of the cathedral with de Mazenod as provost and Tempier as archdeacon, and they moved to Marseille to assist Fortuné in the administration of the diocese.

---

[53] DE MAZENOD, to Tempier, August 5, 1817, in *Oblate Writings*, vol. 6, no. 19, pp. 29–30.

[54] A. MITRI, O.M.I., *Blessed Eugene de Mazenod, His Life and Work, His Beatification Cause*, Rome, Postulation O.M.I., 1979, pp. 35–36.

[55] Supra pp. 36–37.

This caused the greatest crisis in the history of the institute. At that time they numbered only thirteen priests. De Mazenod and Tempier were accused of compromising the very existence of the society, of sacrificing it to the interests of one diocese, and of giving in to personal ambition.[56]

But that was not all. Deblieu and Maunier, two of the original members and at that moment first and second assistants general, were recalled to their diocese by the bishop of Fréjus. The episcopal council of Fréjus had unanimously declared:

> . . . your so-called vows are null: firstly, by the lack of authority on the part of your superior, who without the authorization of the Holy See, cannot impose any obligation on those who join in his good work; secondly, because the vow of stability in the association of the mission rend illusory the obedience that you promised to your bishop at your priestly ordination, and a vow can never be made that is prejudicial to a third party.
>
> The council also decided that, even if your vow were valid, your superior could not reserve to the pope the right to release you from it, thus prejudicing the rights of the bishop.[57]

The newly appointed archbishop of Aix supported this position and threatened to recall all the priests of his diocese. Two other priests were ready to leave, one to become a Trappist and the other for his diocese. De Mazenod returned to Aix for the annual retreat and was able to calm the community.

In spite of all arguments to the contrary the Missionaries of Provence were not a canonically established institute, their Constitutions had not been approved by a competent authority, and their vows were merely private vows. The only solution was to obtain approval from the Holy See.[58]

Nevertheless, de Mazenod seemed in no great rush to get papal approbation. Jeancard in his recollections of the early days of the Congregation gave the reasons for de Mazenod's hesitation:

> Although it may have been desirable to obtain the approval of the Sovereign Pontiff, it was also most important that this approval be direct and efficacious in such a manner as to establish the Congregation in the fullness of prerogatives of a religious institute. But how could one hope to take rank among the religious societies? We were so few, so small, so obscure. Did not modesty demand that we content ourselves to do good in the hinterlands of the provinces where we were born, and where circumstances

---

[56] See REY, *Histoire*, vol. 1, p. 315.

[57] REY, *Histoire*, vol. 1, p. 316.

[58] See COSENTINO, *Histoire*, vol. 2, pp. 72–78; id., "Existence juridique de notre Congrégation pendant ses dix premières années (1816–1826)," in *Études Oblates* 12 (1953), pp. 3–24.

had relegated us, rather than show ourselves in daylight by seeking to climb the mountain? . . . It was his humility itself that he had to fight. He said to himself, I heard him murmur it several times, that he was not of the stature to have himself recognized by the Church as a founder of a religious order; that it would be presumptuous for him to go and claim this title from the Sovereign Pontiff, or at least an act that would imply this title; . . . On the other side, he felt that if he did not succeed in the steps taken with the Holy See, this publicly known failure would cast disfavor on his Congregation and if, in place of direct approbation, he received only words of praise and encouragement, which seemed probable, the question of the raising of the Congregation to the rank of religious societies recognized and constituted by the Church would be prejudiced in such a manner that being not only a postponement, it would be of such a nature as to harm the future hopes by postponing indefinitely its realization.[59]

The 1824 general chapter was a peaceful event. By that time internal calm seems to have been restored to the society. All of the eleven priests, who had made their oblation, were members of the chapter.[60]

> Before proceeding to any other consideration, he [de Mazenod] wanted to know the opinion of the chapter as whether it was opportune for the good of the society for him to continue to serve as vicar general of the bishop of Marseille. The chapter took a secret vote, and the result of the ballot was unanimously affirmative.[61]

During the chapter, one of the members introduced a proposal that the article of the Constitutions forbidding the direction of institutions which would lead the society away from its end be changed, but the chapter rejected the proposition. The question then arose whether or not the article in question also referred to seminaries. They unanimously agreed that the running of seminaries would not be contrary to the letter or the spirit of the Constitutions and asked de Mazenod, the founder, to modify the Constitutions to state that the running of *maisons ecclésiastiques* would not be forbidden.[62]

> . . . the superior general, taking into consideration the unanimous vote of the general chapter and recognizing that this change would not in fact be contrary to the spirit of the institute, consented to express it in our Rules.[63]

---

[59] [Jacques] JEANCARD, *Mélanges Historiques sur la Congrégation des Oblats de Marie Immaculée*, Tours, Mame, 1872, pp. 226–228.

[60] See PIRLORZ, *Histoire*, vol. 1, p. 34.

[61] "Registre," 1824, p. 1, in *Missions O.M.I* 79 (1952), pp. 54–55; *Écrits*, vol. 3, pp. 54–55.

[62] See "Registre," 1824, 4, in *Missions O.M.I.*, 79 (1952), pp. 57–59; *Écrits*, vol. 3, pp. 57–59.

[63] "Registre," 1824, pp. 3–4, in *Missions O.M.I.*, 79 (1952), pp. 58–59; *Écrits*, vol. 3, pp. 58–59.

In the 1818 Constitutions, it had been expressly forbidden to direct semi-naries.[64] Thus, there had been an evolution in what works could be undertaken while respecting the end of the Congregation.

In 1825 de Mazenod obtained letters of praise from seven diocesan bishops, including the archbishop of Aix and the bishop of Fréjus, who had claimed that the vows of the priests were contrary to the rights of diocesan bishops.[65]

Six of seven referred to the Congregation as the Oblates of Saint Charles. No extant sources give further information on the when or how the name was changed. The name Missionaries of Provence had become a misnomer now that the society was reaching beyond Provence. St. Charles Borromeo was the patron of the de Mazenod family.[66]

Approval by Leo XII

Armed with the seven letters of recommendation, de Mazenod set off for Rome on October 30, 1825.

> He was pushed, not only by the wishes of all the members of the Congregation, but especially by Father Albini. Between the two of them there were many conversations. I don't know all the details, but they were decisive in determining the founder. I heard him say many times: "Father Albini ended by saying: Go, Father, go. While uttering this, "he pushed me on with both hands on my shoulders."[67]

On his way to Rome, de Mazenod went through Turin to visit the court in an effort to arrange for a foundation in Nice, which was then a part of the kingdom of Sardinia. Although he was unsuccessful, while there he met Pio Bruno Lanteri, the founder of the Oblates of the Virgin Mary. On November 16 he wrote Tempier:

---

[64] See "Constitutions 1818," I partie, c. II, #1, art. 16, in *Missions O.M.I.*, 78 (1951), p. 22; *Écrits*, vol. 1, p. 22.

The decision taken in 1824 did not resolve the question of running seminaries. Fortuné was pressing de Mazenod at the time to undertake the direction of the seminary at Marseille. De Mazenod finally resolved the question by requesting and obtaining a response from Leo XII. The running of seminaries was not included in the Constitutions until 1850. Cf. infra p. 67.

[65] See *Missions O.M.I.*, 79 (1952), pp. 410–420; *Écrits*, vol. 4, pp. 10–20.

[66] See LEFLON, *De Mazenod*, vol. 2, p. 251; R. MOOSBRUGGER, O.M.I., *The Spirituality of Blessed Eugene de Mazenod (1818–1837)*, S.T.D. diss., Pontifical Gregorian University, Rome, Catholic Book Agency, 1981, p. 45.

[67] JEANCARD, *Mélanges*, pp. 229–230.

> I did not have time to finish my letter at Turin because the great theologian Lanteri, having arrived, asked me for the favor of granting all the free time that I would have before my departure. There was altogether so much to gain from his conversation that I had no trouble in granting him a favor from which I ought to derive more benefit than he . . . I cannot tell you in writing what was the subject of the ten or twelve hours of these conferences; the subject was worth the trouble.[68]

Other evidence leaves no doubt that the two founders had discussed the merger of their societies. It did not take place because of the opposition of Lanteri's associates. A lasting memorial of the meeting of these two men of God may well be the name of de Mazenod's Congregation. Just a few weeks later on December 8 in the French draft of his petition to Leo XII, de Mazenod wrote: "Your Holiness is requested to please . . . give them the name of Oblates of the most holy and immaculate Virgin Mary in place of Oblates of St. Charles . . ."[69] There is no indication that he had consulted his members about this change of name. It is probable that it was made to facilitate the union of the two societies. However, it should be recalled that the youth organization founded by de Mazenod in Aix was "under the title of the Immaculate Conception of the Most Holy Virgin."[70]

De Mazenod arrived in Rome on November 26 and took up residence with the Vincentians at St. Sylvester's near the Quirinal. Immediately he began to make the rounds calling on the various cardinals and officials of the curia. Although he was told that the pope would see him, it seemed that he would never get called for an audience. So, on December 20 he presented himself without a formal invitation, knowing that he might have to wait for hours in the antechamber.[71] First were the audiences of the curial officials.

> Who will they call next? The general of the Dominicans [Joachim Briz], whose stomach noised its hunger, would have wagered that it would be he; not at all, it was I. I arrived at the door with the dignity you know me to have, but I left it there to pick up again on coming out . . .
>
> When I had finished speaking, he [Leo XII] took up the discourse and spoke for quite a long time himself about the same subject . . . "The great

---

[68] DE MAZENOD, to Tempier, November 16, 1825, in *Oblate Writings*, vol. 6, no. 207, pp. 196–197.

[69] Draft of petition to Leo XII, Vatican Archives, S.C.VV. e RR., Fondo Vescovi, 1846 Marsiglia, Vatican City; copy DM XXII, no. 2a, in *Missions O.M.I.*, 79 (1952), p. 461; *Écrits*, vol. 4, p. 61.

See J. THIEL, O.M.I., "Relations du Fondateur avec le P. Lanteri," in *Études Oblates*, 5 (1946), pp. 129–142; LEFLON, *De Mazenod*, vol. 2, pp. 256–260.

[70] Supra p. 17.

[71] See LEFLON, *De Mazenod*, vol. 2, p. 262.

number of these requests, which are coming to us especially from France, has made the Congregation [of Bishops and Regulars] adopt a particular mode of approbation, which consists of praising, of encouraging, without formally approving." I was not afraid to manifest to the Holy Father that this mode would not satisfy me, and I dared to hope they would do something more for us. . . .

As you will understand, I kept nothing from the Holy Father. When I told him what we were doing: "Quite right," he said, nodding his head, "the dispensation is reserved to the superior general and to the sovereign pontiff." He approved again with a nod of his head and did as much when I gave the motive of this reservation: "That is so," I said, "in the rule of Saint Vincent de Paul." The Pope added, "And in that of Blessed Ligouri." . . . "Does your Holiness approve that the members, etc., continue to live according to the Rules previously approved by such and such bishops?"— Reply in the affirmative. "Does your Holiness approve that the dispensation of this and that (I named each thing by its proper name) be reserved to the superior general and to the sovereign Pontiff, and that the members of the society can only ask the dispensation from them?"—Reply in the affirmative. "Does your Holiness approve that he who has been superior general be such and does your Holiness deign to recognize him in the capacity?"—Reply in the affirmative. "Does your Holiness approve that the society take the name of Oblates of the Most Holy and Immaculate Virgin Mary instead of that of Oblates of Saint Charles which it had previously taken?"—The Pope said neither yes nor no; I think I understood that he said it should be put in the report . . . This change has seemed necessary to me in order not to be confused with an infinite number of communities which have the same name . . .[72]

The following day the Archpriest Pietro Adinolfi, under-secretary of the Congregation of Bishops and Regulars, discussed the matter with Leo XII. The next morning, December 22, de Mazenod called on Adinolfi for a report on what had transpired.

He [Adinolfi] first read to me the succinct report that he made to the Holy Father which, it must be said, basically contained my memoir and the essential points which ought to stand out but, as he had given me to understand the day before yesterday, he concluded in favor of the *laudanda* after the text had been examined to see if there was anything to change. But, give praise to the goodness of God and unite yourselves, all of you, to me to thank Him! Such was not the mind of the Holy Father: "No," said the Pontiff, "This society pleases me; I know the good it does, etc., etc." And he

---

[72] DE MAZENOD, to Tempier, December 22, 1825, in *Oblate Writings*, vol. 6, no. 213, pp. 217–220.

entered into multiple details which surprised the archpriest to the utter-
most. "I wish to favor it. Choose a cardinal, one of the mildest of the
Congregation, to be the *ponens* of this cause; go to him on my behalf and
tell him my intention is not merely that these Rules be praised but that they
be approved."[73]

In his official petition to Leo XII de Mazenod expressed very succinctly the
various ministries to be exercised by the Congregation. The running of
seminaries was included.

> The missionaries dedicate themselves principally to the missions, the
> main end of their institute, always preferring the most neglected towns,
> where they preach in the common language, i.e., in *patois*, the dialect of the
> people, for in those out of the way towns French is not well understood.
> Help is given to the clergy for the reform of morals through retreats and
> good clerical education in seminaries. They care for youth by forming
> Christian societies in order to withdraw them from the corruption of the
> world. Lastly, all of them devote themselves to the service of the poor
> prisoners. They instruct them, administer the sacraments, and accompany
> them to the scaffold when they are condemned to death.[74]

Upon de Mazenod's request a commission of three cardinals was named
to study the Constitution in order to speed up the process. Otherwise all eight
cardinals of the Congregation would have had to study them. On January 2, he
wrote to Cardinal Carlo Pedicini, the *ponens* of the cause:

> It seems to me that I understood the last time that I had the honor
> to be in contact with your Eminence, that you thought that we have asked
> for specific approval of our congregation only for France. It would be a very
> harmful error to the good that the congregation proposes to do with God's
> help. For this reason I feel obliged by means of this letter to assure you that
> one of the principal reasons why we are brought to seek the approval of the
> Holy See is precisely the great desire that we have to spread the fruit of our
> ministry to which are dedicated the members of our society in any part of
> the Catholic world we may be called by the common father of all the
> faithful, or by the respective bishops of different dioceses.

He then mentioned the desire to work in Nice, the dioceses of Savoy, and
Sardinia.

> Some members of the congregation could willingly preach among the
> infidels, and when the members are more numerous, it could be that the
> superiors will send them to America, either to come to the aid of the poor

---

[73] DE MAZENOD, to Tempier, December 22, 1825, in *Oblate Writings*, vol. 6, no. 213, pp. 222–223.

[74] Petition to Leo XII, Vatican Archives, S.C. VV. e RR., Fondo Vescovi, 1846 Marsiglia, Vatican City, in *Missions O.M.I.*, 79 (1952), pp. 477–478; *Écrits*, vol. 4, pp. 77–78.

Catholics lacking every spiritual good, or to make new conquests for the faith.[75]

Three of the bishops who had given letters of recommendation to de Mazenod had second thoughts and wrote again to the Holy See. The bishop of Gap on December 8 addressed a letter to Cardinal Castiglioni, the future Pius VIII. It was probably on the same day that the archbishop of Aix and the bishops of Digne and Gap sent a common letter to Leo XII. Both letters are in the handwriting of the secretary of the bishop of Gap. The basic argument is the same in both.

> Before his departure [for Rome], he requested our signature for his statutes. We were not well informed and did not pay enough attention to several things that are harmful to our rights.
>
> An oath of stability in the congregation and obedience to the superior is required. Neither the missionary is free to back out nor can his own bishop release him from the oath. Hence, it is evident that such an oath is given preference to the oath that was made to the bishop on the very day of ordination. This completely destroys the whole canonical order.
>
> Your Holiness will also notice that the aforementioned statutes are internally contradictory by supposing that the congregation is both subject to the local ordinaries and exempt. This latter is against the present civil laws of France, according to which no religious society may be outside the jurisdiction of the ordinary. Wherefore, we urgently request your Holiness that care be taken to remove from the aforesaid statutes everything that is opposed to the rights of the local ordinaries.[76]

On December 29 de Mazenod knew that something was amiss when he met Adinolfi, who told him that things were *"un peu gâtées"* (a bit spoiled).[77] There was no time for a discussion, and de Mazenod was left in suspense. His concern became even greater on January 2. Cardinal Castiglione, major peniten-

---

[75] DE MAZENOD, to Pedicini, July 2, 1826, Vatican Archives, S.C. VV. e RR., Fondo Vescovi, 1846 Marsiglia, Vatican City, in *Missions O.M.I.*, 79 (1952), pp. 483–484; *Écrits*, vol. 4, pp. 83–84.

[76] BAUSSET-ROQUEFORT et al., to Leo XII, December 8, 1825, Vatican Archives, S.C. VV. e RR., Fondo Vescovi, 1846 Marsiglia, Vatican City, in *Missions O.M.I.*, 79 (1952), pp. 430–432; *Écrits*, vol. 4, pp. 30–32.

It would be a mistake to be too hard in one's judgment of these bishops. They were still suffering from a severe shortage of ablebodied priests. Jeancard also points out that the bishop of Gap was involved in an ongoing battle over the teachings of Lamennais. "He sustained this controversy with indefatigable ardor by means of continuous publications. For it seemed to him, and not without reason, that M. de Lamennais and a large number of his partisans tended to diminish and almost negate the authority of the bishops by zealously boasting of the authority of the Holy See with an insulting arrogance" (JEANCARD, *Mélanges*, p. 249).

[77] DE MAZENOD, to Tempier, December 29, 1825, in *Oblate Writings*, vol. 6, no. 214, p. 226.

tiary, invited him for a visit and during their conversation gave the impression that he was opposed to the pope's attitude of quick approval of the institute.[78] By January 4 he had learned what had happened.

> I do not know yet who this man is. May God judge him, who has just dealt such a terrible blow to God's work. It is my opinion that it can only be the bishop of Gap. This is the recognition that he gives for all the good that we have done in his diocese . . .
>
> What a betrayal on the part of this bishop. And he is a bishop only because I did not accept his see! . . . This unworthy and hollow complaint has done nothing less than weaken all the recommendations, made them, as it were, worthless. What harm this man has done us! . . .
>
> But for the present everything is to be feared if things take their ordinary course because of the wild panic the opposition of one French bishop causes. They imagine it puts all the Gauls on the move.[79]

The following day he again saw Adinolfi, who told him the whole story of the common letter "which did not have common sense and which was completely anticanonical."[80] De Mazenod went then to see Cardinal Pedicini, who personally answered all the objections as de Mazenod read the letter aloud at the cardinal's request. De Mazenod's comment was, ". . . this is a pitiable affair. I blush for the honor of our episcopate."[81]

By the time the letters arrived in Rome Leo XII had already made up his mind to approve de Mazenod's institute. In fact the letters had an effect just the opposite to the one intended by the three bishops. The appeal to the laws of France and the authority of the bishops raised specters of Gallicanism.

> I don't need to tell you that he [Leo XII] did not stop for one minute because of these complaints which he learned about. They did not give him a good estimation of the one who had the sorry thought to do it, for they attack his sovereign jurisdiction. He pointed this out, and from it would follow that no pope could ever have approved in the Church the religious orders of regular congregations. All of which are exempt . . .[82]

The commission of cardinals approved the Constitutions with a few minor amendments on February 15. Two days later Leo XII gave his formal approval.

---

[78] See DE MAZENOD, to Tempier, January 1–3, 1816, in *Oblate Writings*, vol. 7, no. 215, p. 2.

[79] DE MAZENOD, to Tempier, January 4–5, 1826, in *Oblate Writings*, vol. 7, no. 216, pp. 6–7.

[80] DE MAZENOD, to Tempier, January 5, 1826, in *Oblate Writings*, vol. 7, no. 216, p. 8.

[81] DE MAZENOD, to Tempier, January 5, 1826, in *Oblate Writings*, vol. 7, no. 216, p. 9.

[82] DE MAZENOD, to Tempier, February 18, 1826, in *Oblate Writings*. vol. 7, no. 226, p. 39. In this letter he mentioned that Leo XII specified a number of things that were to be placed in the brief of approval, including "particularly the previous approval of the bishops, which is especially pleasing . . ."

> My dear friend, my dear brothers, yesterday evening, February 17, 1826, the Sovereign Pontiff Leo XII confirmed the decision of the Congregation of cardinals and specifically approved the Institute, Rules, and Constitutions of the Missionary Oblates of the most holy and immaculate Virgin Mary, and accompanied this solemn act of his pontifical authority with most flattering words for those who have the blessing of forming part of the Society, of which the head of the Church expects so much good.[83]

While waiting for the papal brief of approval de Mazenod had time to reflect on what had happened. He was overwhelmed by the thought that his little society was along with the great orders and congregations counted among those communities approved by the pope. All his requests had been granted. Only one was an innovation, the name of the institute. On March the ninth, he added *"Oblat de Marie"* to his name.[84]

> Would that we really could understand who we are! I hope that the Lord will give us the grace for that with the help and the protection of our holy Mother, the Immaculate. We must have a special devotion for her in the Congregation. Does it not seem to you to be a sign of predestination to carry the name of Oblates of Mary, that is consecrated to God under the auspices of Mary. The Congregation carries her name as a family name which is in common with the most holy and immaculate Mother of God.[85]

De Mazenod's first audience with Leo XII was on December 20, 1825. Three months and one day later, March 21, 1826, the apostolic letter *Si tempus unquam* was signed approving the Missionary Oblates of Mary Immaculate:

> If there was ever a time when this Apostolic See endeavored to encourage and support by every means at its command the zeal of those priests, who, burning with the fire of holy love, preach the Gospel throughout the whole world, and labor to implant in the minds of men the precepts and duties of the Christian religion, and to instruct the people to be subject to lawful authority, We think of no more fitting occasion to this than at the present . . .
>
> This Society has as its aim the following objects: its members, who are bound by simple but perpetual vows of poverty, chastity, obedience, and perseverance in the Institute itself . . . devote themselves principally to the work of preaching missions to the poor classes in the common tongue, especially in places destitute of the aid of religion; they give assistance to the clergy by providing them with suitable training in seminaries, and by being continually ready to assist parish priests and other pastors in the work of reforming the morals of the people through preaching and other

---

[83] De Mazenod, to Tempier, February 18, 1826, in *Oblate Writings*, vol. 7, no. 226, p. 39.

[84] De Mazenod, to Tempier, March 9, 1826, in *Oblate Writings*. vol. 7, no. 229, p. 57.

[85] De Mazenod, to Tempier, March 20, 1826, in *Oblate Writings*, vol. 7, no. 231, p. 63.

spiritual exercises; they generously bestow devoted care on the young, and they strive to withdraw this chosen portion of the Christian people from the seductions of the world by forming them into pious associations; lastly, they preach the divine word and administer the sacraments to those in prison, and accompany to the scaffold those condemned to death. When, indeed, the great benefits flowing from this Society were perceived by all, its priests soon came to be spread far and wide . . .

. . . We hereby with a ready and willing mind, establish it, to be known by the name of the Congregation of the Missionary Oblates of the Most Holy Virgin Mary, conceived without sin . . .

This approbation and commendation are given all the more willingly to such a salutary enterprise, because the members of this Congregation in their exterior ministry of preaching the word of God and of administering the sacraments make an open profession of reverence, submission, and obedience to all bishops in communion with the Roman See who wish to employ their aid and services in their respective dioceses, and we feel convinced that they will continue to act in this manner.

. . . Finally, since the exercise of supreme authority in this Congregation serves as its special strength and support, and since also from its very beginning, and in conformity with its Rules, this same Charles Joseph Eugene de Mazenod has been entrusted with it, We, in view of his personal merits, by the bestowal of Our own approval, maintain him as its superior general. These things We decree and sanction, and it is Our will that this Letter be now and in the future firm, valid, and efficacious . . .[86]

Summary

On January 25, 1816, the feast of the Conversion of Saint Paul, l'abbé Eugene de Mazenod and five other secular priests petitioned the vicars general capitular of Aix to approve a diocesan mission society to be established in that city in the old Carmelite convent. The purpose of the group was to preach missions to the common people in Provençal especially in the country areas of Provence. Following de Mazenod's example, they also dedicated themselves to others who were not being adequately reached by the parish clergy: youth, dying, prisoners, and those condemned to death.

The first mission made de Mazenod realize the need of firm bonds of unity for the members to assure effectiveness and solidarity in their ministry. Feeling personally called to replace by their dedication, as well as by their

---

[86] Leo XII, apostolic letter, *Si tempus unquam*, March 21, 1826, MD XII, no. 2b, in *Bullarii romani continuatio*, Prati, Aldina, 1854, vol. 16, pp. 413b–415a; *Constitutiones 1826*, pp 173–180; *Constitutiones 1853*, pp. 183–188; *Constitutiones 1894*, pp. 189–194; *Constitutiones 1910*, pp. 164–168; *Constitutiones 1928*, pp. 188–193; *Écrits*, vol. 4, pp. 167–173.

ministry, the religious communities suppressed by the French Revolution, he and Tempier made vows of mutual obedience on Holy Thursday, 1816.

The spectacular success of the missions was followed by new members, and the opportunity to open another house. This necessitated the writing of Constitutions in 1818 to guarantee unity between the two houses. Along with the Constitutions adopted in October of that year, perpetual vows of celibacy, obedience, and perseverance were embraced. The vow of poverty was added in 1821. The society of diocesan missionaries had become a *religious* community of priests dedicated to preaching missions.

Since the bishops were severely handicapped by a shortage of active priests, there was a constant danger of the individual bishops declaring the vows null as contrary to the ordination promise of obedience, and recalling their priests. Consequently the very existence of the society was in constant peril. Even Fortuné's becoming bishop of Marseille in order to have an episcopal protector was not sufficient to remove this danger. In fact, it provoked an internal crisis by de Mazenod's and Tempier's becoming vicars general of Marseille, and being named provost and archdeacon of the cathedral chapter.

Upon the urging of the members, de Mazenod arrived in Rome at the end of November 1825. He was discouraged when he learned that according to the practice of Congregation of Bishops and Regulars that all he could hope for was a decree of praise and encouragement. However, much to the surprise of the curial officials, Leo XII made it known that he wanted to approve the institute and granted all de Mazenod's requests, including the new name of Missionary Oblates of Mary Immaculate, on February 17, 1826.

> The Oblates of the Holy and Immaculate Virgin Mary are a body, a society, otherwise called a Congregation in the Church, I have already told you that, just like the Lazarists [i.e., Vincentians], the Passionists, the Ligourists [i.e., Redemptorists], etc. . . .[87]

---

[87] DE MAZENOD, to Tempier, March 9, 1826, in *Oblate Writings*, vol. 7, no. 229, p. 53.

Chapter III
Historical and Juridical Development

S ince the time of Saints Basil and Benedict the rule has played a major role in the lives of religious and their institutes. Perhaps it would be better to say that the rule has played many roles in religious life. The rule is much more than a set of laws for internal government. It contains the basic inspiration of the founder as founder and is the written instrument for transmitting the spirit and intentions for the ends and nature of the society that he or she founded. It is above all the norm for the spiritual formation of the members.

In addition to the ancient rules of Saints Augustine, Basil, Benedict, and Francis the Church has accepted and approved since the XVI century the basic documents of other religious founders. In contrast to the ancient rules that are immutable general documents that are further determined by changeable constitutions, the latter are more specific documents that are modified according to changing circumstances. These are also commonly called constitutions. They play the same role for an institute and its members as the ancient rules. These constitutions are approved by the Holy See or a diocesan bishop as the particular law for a religious institute and serve as the norm both for internal government, apostolic work, and the community and spiritual life of the members.

The 1983 Code of Canon Law summarizes this traditional practice by stating that the fundamental code of each religious institute should contain both the institute's spiritual patrimony which consists of the intentions of the founder, of all that the competent ecclesiastical authority has approved concerning the nature, purpose, spirit, and character of the institute, and its sound traditions, as well as the basic norms of government, discipline, admission, and formation, and also the proper object of the bonds of the members.[1]

It was such a document that de Mazenod had presented to the Holy See for approval in 1826. Although the complete title was "Constitutiones et Regulæ et Instituta Societatis Missionariorum Oblatorum Sanctissimæ et Immaculatæ Virginis Mariæ Gallo-Provinciæ nuncupatorum,"[2] de Mazenod usually spoke

---

[1] See c. 587, §1.

[2] The title page reads: *Constitutiones et Regulæ Congregationis Missionariorum Oblatorum Sanctissimæ et Immaculatæ Virginis Mariæ, A Sanctissimo in Christo Patre et Domino, Domino Nostro Leone*

simply of the "Règle" or the "Règles" (the Rule or Rules). In conformity with the current practice the word *Constitutions* is used in this work.

Through a brief examination of the Constitutions, development in the ministry, and subsequent changes in the Constitutions it will be possible to understand the nature of the Missionary Oblates of Mary Immaculate—who they are, and what they are called by vocation and by approval of the Holy See to be.

The 1826 Constitutions

The formal approval of the Missionary Oblates of Mary Immaculate as a congregation and its Constitutions by Leo XII transferred these from the category of regulations of a private association or society to that of particular law of an officially approved institute in the Church. De Mazenod was very conscious of this as can be seen from the notes that he wrote after his retreat in 1831:

> In the course of my meditations, the thought came to me that we shall never be able to thank the good God sufficiently for having given us these Rules—for God is indeed and beyond all dispute their author. He who wrote them does not recognize in them anything that came from himself, so he can judge them impartially as if he had never seen them before. But why should I speak of judging them, when the Head of the Church has already spoken!
>
> We, with the plenitude of Our Apostolic Authority, approve and confirm its Constitutions . . . *We further command that these Constitutions be faithfully observed* by all the members of the Congregation, whatever be the position they hold in it. This approbation and commendation are given all the more willingly to such a salutary enterprise, etc.

Papa XII, Una Cum Instituto in Forma Specifica Approbatæ, Galliopoli, 1827. De Mazenod brought to Rome the one and only final copy of the text of the Constitutions for approval. This had to be left with the Sacred Congregation of Bishops and Regulars, and de Mazenod himself copied the entire text in order to have a copy. This copy is in the Postulation Archives O.M.I. (DM XI, no. 6). See DE MAZENOD to Tempier, February 27, 1826, in *Oblate Writings*, vol. 7, no. 227, p. 43. The original text cannot be found in the Vatican Archives.

In this work the various editions of the Constitutions will be designated by the year of the printed edition with the exception of the Constitutions approved by Leo XII in 1826, which are called *Constitutiones 1826*. This text was reprinted in *Écrits*, vol. 2, pp. 20–154; *Missions O.M.I.*, 78 (1951), pp. 340–474.

See A. DUMAS, O.M.I., "Galliopolis?" *Études Oblates*, 6 (1947), pp. 209–210 for an explanation of Galliopolis.

These are the words of Pope Leo XII in his apostolic letter of approbation. Judgment, therefore, has been given by infallible authority . . .[3]

This text reveals not only de Mazenod's attitude toward the authority of the pope, but also gives us an insight as to how he viewed his role as author of the Constitutions. With papal approval they were no longer his work, but the work of the Church. The Constitutions were now a sacred rule of life. They made known to the members of his institute the divine plan for their ministry and their own salvation.

> . . . What a consoling thought this is—in obeying our Rule, we obey the Church! And as our Rule covers our entire conduct and also the spirit which ought to animate our conduct, it follows that all our actions have in them something of the wonderful merit of obedience to the Church. Furthermore, as the Church commands nothing but what is good, nothing that does not lead to eternal salvation, in obeying our Rule, we advance steadily along the road to heaven. This conclusion cannot be challenged . . .

> And this sublime vocation, shall we ever have an adequate conception of it? To arrive at this, one must comprehend how excellent is the name of our Institute. It is, undoubtedly, the most perfect that one can set before himself in this world, for the end of our Institute is that which the Son of God set before himself when He came on earth, namely—the glory of his heavenly Father and the salvation of souls, "The Son of Man has come to search out and save what is lost." He was sent particularly to the poor—"He sent me to preach the Gospel to the poor," and we are established precisely to work for the conversion of souls, and particularly to preach the Gospel to the poor . . .[4]

With papal approval changes will be made in the Constitutions both during de Mazenod's lifetime and after his death. Through the course of this chapter it will be shown that all changes were made in accordance with the end of the institute, the preaching of the Gospel to the poor. It will be seen that the essentials have always remained intact, and that all modifications have been but adaptation to meet changing times, circumstances, and understanding of what the Church asks of the Congregation.

De Mazenod, conscious of his particular role as founder, alone during his lifetime would determine what the Constitutions mean. As will be seen, when

---

[3] DE MAZENOD, "Nos Saintes Règles," October 8, 1831, in *Circulaires Administratives des supérieurs Généraux aux membres de la Congrégation des Missionaires Oblats de M.I.* [=*Circulaires*], no. 14, vol. 1, pp. 121–122; English trans. in *Missions O.M.I.*, 77 (1950), pp. 362–363.

[4] Ibid., pp. 112–113. Cf. DE MAZENOD to Tempier, February 18, 1826, *Letters,* vol. 7, no. 226, p. 40.

there was a question during a general chapter concerning the interpretation of the Constitutions, his word was final:

> . . . which is ridiculous, absurd, out of line during the lifetime of the founder to claim to understand differently than the the the spirit and the direction of the Society.[5]

The 1826 Constitutions are also of a major historical and spiritual importance because all the subsequent revisions until 1966 were but adaptations of and additions to the 1826 text. Even with its dated language and theology it is more than an interesting and venerable relic. It reveals not only de Mazenod as founder, but it is the text that inspired and formed all Oblates for almost 150 years. It is the primary document of the spiritual heritage or patrimony of the Missionary Oblates of Mary Immaculate.[6] All subsequent Constitutions must embrace the same values and mission. Otherwise they would alter the nature of the Congregation founded by de Mazenod.

The 1826 Constitutions will be surveyed in order to highlight the essential elements. Then subsequent modifications of the text and the completely new texts—the 1966 Constitutions *ad experimentum* and the 1982 Constitutions—will be examined for their conformity in essentials to the 1826 Constitutions.

The 1826 Constitutions consist of the Preface and three parts. The first part treats the end of the Congregation and its works, the second part the vows, religious exercises, observances, illness, death, burial, and suffrages for the deceased members, and the third part government, various offices, admission, oblation, brothers, and dismissal.

The Preface vividly presents the sad condition of the Church and the clergy in the aftermath of the French Revolution. The moral situation of many persons is worse than it was for the gentile nations before the Redemption. What did Jesus do? He chose a group of apostles, formed them, filled them with his Spirit, and sent them out to convert the world. A group of priests have decided to follow the example of Jesus and the Apostles, to join forces to work more securely for the salvation of souls and their own sanctification:

---

[5] DE MAZENOD, to Tempier, June 24, 1851, LM.

Later on de Mazenod would accept the decision of the majority during a general chapter (see Józef PIELORZ, "Le rôle du Fondateur dans les six premiers Chapitres généraux," in *Études Oblates*, 24 (1965), p. 367.

[6] The committee for the revision of the Constitutions in preparation for the 1980 general chapter recognized this, and in the printed text they placed parallel to the major passages of the new text passages from de Mazenod's Constitutions. The chapter accepted this mode of presentation as a means of keeping before the eyes of present and future Oblates de Mazenod's own words.

Wherefore, while pledging themselves to all the works of zeal which priestly charity can inspire—above all, to the work of the missions, which is the main reason for their union—these priests, joined together in a society, resolve to obey the following Constitutions and Rules; by living them they hope to obtain all the benefits they need for their sanctification and for the salvation of their souls.[7]

With the stage thus set, the Constitutions in the first part state in three chapters how this is to be done. The first chapter "De fine Societatis" begins with the key article that contains de Mazenod's basic inspiration and intention as founder.

Art. 1. The end of this humble Society of Missionary Oblates of the Most Holy and Immaculate Virgin Mary, called the Missionaries of Provence from the place of its origin, is that secular priests, living together as brothers in community, diligently striving to imitate the virtues and example of our Savior Jesus Christ, may devote themselves principally to the preaching of the Gospel to the poor.[8]

Everything else follows from this—a group of priests living together as brothers, imitating the virtues and example of Jesus for the evangelization of the poor.

The second article speaks of the ministry of preaching missions, retreats, catechetics, etc. to the spiritually neglected people in the country and the villages. Articles three and four enumerate the virtues to be practised and the apostolic works to be done to replace the religious institutes destroyed by the Revolution. The sixth article as well as the seventh mention specifically repairing the damage caused by the defection of priests, and calling priests back to the height of their vocation by prayer, example, counsel, and welcoming them into the houses of the society.

Chapter two with ninety-three articles is devoted to the missions, "præcipuus Instituti scopus" (prinicipal end of the Institute).[9] Nothing is to distract the missionaries from this "præcipuum vocationis nostræ finem"

---

[7] *Constitutiones 1826*, Preface.

[8] *Constitutiones 1826*, pars I, c. I, art. I.

The expression *sacerdotes sæculares* (secular priests) reflects their juridical status at the time. As will be seen in the next chapter members of congregations with simple vows were not considered to be religious. De Mazenod based this article on the Constitutions of Alphonsus Liguori (see G. COSENTINO, O.M.I., *Histoire de nos Règles [=Histoire]*, Ottawa, Éditions des Études Oblates, 1955, vol. 1, pp. 77–78).

The words *Religionis votis obligati* (bound by vows of religions) were added in the 1850 revision of the Constitutions (*Constitutiones 1853*, pars I, c. I., art. I).

[9] *Constitutiones 1826*, pars I, c. II, art. I.

(principal end of our vocation). [10] Consequently they are forbidden to partake in processions and public ceremonies, to be the directors of religious women, to preach their retreats (except on the occasion of a mission or pious exercises in the vicinity), to be in charge of parishes, and to preach lenten sermons.

The third chapter deals with other priestly ministry: preaching, hearing confessions, direction of youth, pastoral care of prisoners and those condemned to death, assisting the dying, and the recitation of divine office in common, and the public exercises in the churches of the society. In the first chapter it was stated that the common recitation of divine office is considered as one of the works that is undertaken in order to replace the religious institutes destroyed by the Revolution. [11]

The government of the Congregation was completely in the hands of the priests. The superior general appoints in the local superiors, "inter presbyteros Instituti spectabilissimos" (from among the most outstanding priests of the Institute). [12] The assistants general, the superior general's admonitor, and the procurator (treasurer) general must be priests. [13] The same is true of the members of the general chapter. [14] However, if there are not enough priests who have made their oblation for three years to hold the chapter, except in the case of a chapter called to elect a new superior general, the superior general may call "nonnullos alios oblatos" (some other oblates) to the chapter. [15] These latter have only consultative vote, unless the superior general judges it opportune to grant them a deliberative vote. The understanding at the time of the word *oblati* as used here can be seen from the use in the 1853 Constitutions in reference to the *oblati* being present at the local chapter, and the interpretation given to that regulation.

> VI. The other oblates are called to the local chapter, but since they have only a consultative vote, they will vote first in order that their desires may be known, and then the others will cast their votes. [16]

---

[10] Ibid., pars I, c. II, art. XXII.

[11] Ibid., pars I, c. I, art. IV.

[12] Ibid., pars III, c. I, §VII, art. IV.

[13] Ibid., part III, c. I, §I, art. LIV.

[14] Ibid., pars III, c. I, §I, art. IV.

[15] Ibid., pars III, c. I, §XI. See infra pp. 189–190, the discussion at the 1904 chapter because the brothers had been given consultative vote at a vicarial chapter.

[16] *Constitutiones 1853*, pars III, c. I, §IX, art. VI.

In 1867 Joseph Fabre, superior general, issued a circular letter with instructions for conducting the local and provincial chapters in preparation for the next general chapter.

> Art. 11 The local superior, all the professed priests, and the scholastic oblates of the house, if there are some, will go to the community meeting room . . .
>
> Art. 12 . . . in the houses where there are some scholastic oblates, the superior will ask them to vote, which vote is only consultative . . .
>
> Art. 13 Once the consultative vote has taken place, in the presence of the oblate brothers the election will take place for the delegate of the house to the provincial chapter.[17]

The use of the word *oblate* was in conformity with the practice mentioned in the previous chapter of speaking of the scholastics as "oblats" or "simples oblats."[18] In a word only the scholastics, and not the brothers, had a consultative vote.

The article containing requisites for a person to be elected superior general does not explicitly state that he must be a priest.

> III. No one can be elected superior general unless he has lived an edifying life in the Society for at least ten years, is thirty years old, is experienced in the ministry of the Missions, and has served as local superior or assistant.[19]

There cannot be any doubt that the superior general had to be a priest since it was required that the local superior be a priest, as was seen above.[20] There is also the provision that to be elected superior general, one had to be "in Missionum ministerio exercitatus" (experienced in the ministry of the missions). This excluded the brothers from eligibility.

The understanding of the members of the congregation at that time may be seen from the acts of the 1831 chapter. The question being treated was the presence of the brothers at the *coulpe*, i.e., the chapter of faults against the Constitutions. Should they be present during the accusation of the others? It was the unanimous decision of the general chapter that all the brothers,

---

[17] *Circulaires*, April 21, 1867, no. 18, vol. 1, p. 171.

[18] Supra p. 34.

It would seem that the word *scholastic* came into use prior to 1850. The 1853 Constitutions, which were revised during the 1850 general chapter, have "oblati scholastici" (pars II, c. II, §IV, art. XI). *Personnel 1854* also uses the word "scolastique" (pp. 2 and 7).

[19] *Constitutiones 1826*, pars III, c. I, §2, art. III.

[20] Supra p. 56.

novices and professed, should absent themselves before the accusation of the other members of the community. The reason given for the decision was:

> The chapter based itself on the fact that our Congregation is a society of priests, and not of brothers as are, for example, the Franciscans . . .[21]

Development 1826–1861

At the time of the 1826 chapter the institute consisted of 15 priests, seven professed students for the priesthood, and probably eight novices. De Mazenod and Tempier were vicars general of Marseille and members of the cathedral chapter. This left thirteen priests to staff the four houses of the society, conduct the missions, and form the professed students and novices. How were they to do all the works that were set before them? Was de Mazenod a dreamer? If so, he was a dreamer with both feet on the ground, a sound administrator, and his dreams were blessed by divine providence.

In 1827 de Mazenod accepted the administration of the major seminary of Marseille after his uncle had been unsuccessful in getting another society to assume the responsibility. The question of accepting seminaries had been discussed at the 1824 chapter.

> . . . The chapter wanted to examine at this time whether seminaries were to be considered one of the works that would turn us away from the end of our Institute. The chapter having found that they would be contrary to the letter rather than the spirit of our Constitutions unanimously requested the superior general, the founder of the Society, to express in our Rules that in case of need it would not be forbidden to take charge of houses for ecclesiastics. Taking into account the unanimous desire of the general chapter the superior general agreed that this change would not be contrary to the spirit of the Institute, and to place it in the Rules.[22]

As was seen in the previous chapter de Mazenod had in his petition for approval to Leo XII included seminaries as a work of the Congregation, and this was specifically mentioned in the brief of approval, although it had not been added to the Constitutions: " . . . they give assistance to the clergy by providing them with suitable training in seminaries . . ."[23]

---

[21] "Registre des Délibérations des Chapitres Généraux de la Société des Missionnaires dits de Province" [="Registre"], 1831, p. 38, in Józef PIELORZ, Les Chapitres généraux au temps du Fondateur [Les Chapitres], 2 vols., Ottawa, Études Oblates, 1968, vol. 1, p. 107.

[22] "Registre," 1824, p. 3; in Missions O.M.I., 79 (1952), p. 58; Écrits, 3, 58.

[23] ". . . clero in seminariis versantur, amica præbeant subsidia . . ." (Leo XII, apostolic letter, Si tempus unquam, March 21, 1826, in MD XII 2b; Bullarii romani continuatio, Prati, Aldina, 1854, vol. 16, pp. 413b–415a; Constitutiones 1826, pp. 173–180; Constitutiones 1853, pp. 183–188; Constitutiones

Tempier was named rector of the Marseille seminary and held the post for some twenty-seven years until 1854. Four other members were appointed professors. The major seminary of Ajaccio was accepted in 1835, and the seminaries of Fréjus (1851), Romans (1853–1857), and Quimper (1856–1857) were to follow.

At the time of the 1831 general chapter the number of members had increased to twenty-two priests, ten scholastics, and two brothers. The chapter voted unanimously for sending men to the foreign missions. A proposal to accept teaching youth was rejected as contrary to the letter and the spirit of the institute. However, an exception could be made for such works overseas, since there such institutions could be considered as a means to arrive at the prical end of the institute rather than a goal according to a declaration made by de Mazenod.[24]

In 1832 de Mazenod was appointed by the Holy See apostolic visitor of the missions of Tunisia and Tripolitania, and consecrated bishop of Icosia *in partibus*." His residence was to be in Marseille. Since there was a movement on the part of the government to suppress the see of Marseille upon the death of Fortuné de Mazenod, this was devised as a means to assure the continuity of the diocese. After his reconciliation with the government over his episcopal ordination without royal approval, and the resignation of Fortuné in 1837 de Mazenod succeeded his uncle as diocesan bishop. He was fifty-five at the time.[25]

Would it be stretching the truth to say that Corsica was the Oblate's first *foreign mission*? The minutes of the 1837 general chapter give the background for the foundation earlier that year of two houses in Corsica:

> . . . which has as its goal the renewal of a clergy that is the scandal of Europe, and a people that is its dismay. He had always resisted the thought and the ideas of certain members to spread out to distant places to preach the Gospel to the barbarians. But here are these barbarians, for whom we must obtain with the torch of an enlightened religion what civilization could not. We know how our fathers have looked on this mission, and how the students placed under their direction and the people

---

1894, pp. 189–194; *Constitutiones 1910*, pp. 164–168; *Constitutiones 1928*, pp. 188–193; *Écrits*, vol. 4, pp. 167–173).

[24] "Registre," 1831, p. 37; in PIELORZ, *Les Chapitres*, vol. 1, pp. 104–106.

[25] See LEFLON, *De Mazenod*, vol. 2, pp. 429–516; R. BOUDENS, O.M.I., *Mgr Ch.-J.-E. de Mazenod, Évêque de Marseille (1837–1861), et la Politique*, Lyon, Éditions du Chalet, 1951, pp. 49–98.

spread throughout this half wild island respond to their unselfish work. Certainly this is for the glory of God and the salvation of their souls.[26]

In 1826 de Mazenod entrusted to his missionaries at Calvaire in Marseille the responsibility for the large group of Italian immigrants in the city. Dominic Albini, later known as the apostle of Corsica, for many years was the mainstay of the "Œuvres des Italiens."[27] Thirty years later in 1856 a similar "Œuvres des Allemands" was established for German speaking immigrants to the city.[28] Just as de Mazenod had spent himself in caring for the Austrian prisoners of war in Aix,[29] he assigned his sons to the spiritual needs of these people who were far from their native lands and gave them priests who knew their language to care for them spiritually.

In 1841 de Mazenod was presented with two opportunities for the foreign missions. Bishop Bourget made an offer that he could not turn down.

> . . . The Bishop of Montreal proposes to call our Congregation into his vast diocese to evangelize its inhabitants and perforce even to venture amongst the savage tribes which are in trading relations with his people.[30]

De Mazenod first consulted the men living in Marseille, and then wrote all the superiors asking them to consult their communities. The response was unanimous in favor of the foundation, and four priests and two brothers were assigned to the mission and arrived in Montreal on December 2, 1841. De Mazenod gave Honorat, the superior of the group, a formal letter of assignment in Latin:

> . . . For the rest, brothers, take comfort in the Lord and in the might of His power. Put on the armor of God, hold yourselves erect, loins girded with truth, wearing the breastplate of justice and your feet shod in readiness to evangelize; so that the Lord may help you to announce the Word mightily, to withdraw from sin the sons of the Church and lead them to holiness; and that He may open your mouth with assurance to make known the mystery of the Gospel to those ignorant of it, and go astray.[31]

---

[26] "Registre," 1837, p. 45; in PIELORZ, Les Chapitres, vol. 1, p. 123.

[27] See "Registre," 1850, p. 85; in PIELORZ, Les Chapitres, vol. 1, p. 267; and vol. 2, pp. 3, and 111. Charles-Felix, king of Sardenia (Piedmont) in 1827 named de Mazenod a knight of the Religious and Military Order of Saints Maurice and Lazarus in recognition for his pastoral zeal for the Italian immigrants in Marseille. For the same motive in 1836 Charles Albert raised him to the rank of commander, and in 1856 Victor Emmanuel II raised his rank to that of first class commander. See DM VII 2.

[28] PIELORZ, Les Chapitres, vol. 2, p. 111.

[29] Supra p. 18.

[30] DE MAZENOD, to Mille, July 17, 1841, Lettres, vol. 1, no. 1, no. 2., p. 2.

[31] DE MAZENOD, to Honorat, September 29, 1841, in Archives Deschâtelets, Ottawa; copy LM;

While urging the observance of the Constitutions, he gave Honorat the authority to dispense and modify whatever he considered opportune while maintaing the spirit of the institute. He also gave him the authority to accept candidates and have them do their novitiate in the house to be founded. However, he reserved to himself with his council the authority to admit to profession.[32]

Montreal was but the toehold in North America. One foundation after another followed—Bytown (Ottawa) in 1844, Red River in 1845,[33] Oregon, Alberta, and Saskatchewan in 1847, Ceylon (Sri Lanka) in 1847, Brownsville and Galveston, Texas in 1849, Natal in 1852, Quebec and Plattsburg, New York in 1853, and Mexico in 1858.

In May 1841 de Mazenod had sent newly ordained William Daly to England and Ireland to investigate the possibility of a foundation.

> The purpose of this trip is to examine on the spot how a foundation of missionaries of our Congregation could be made in order to work for the conversion of the English heretics, and even if there is a need and we have enough people to go to the colonies, or the newly conquered places in America or any other part of the world.[34]

After several unsuccessful attempts to open a house in Ireland, in 1843 the first house of the *foreign mission* was founded at Penzance and was soon followed by other houses.

In 1847 de Mazenod accepted the invitation to send his missionaries to Ceylon.

> . . . What a field has opened for us! One million-five-hundred-thousand gentiles to convert in this most beautiful country of the world. Five-hundred-thousand Christians to instruct. This whole immense population disposed by its goodness and its character, and by a certain attraction for religion to listen with docility to the voice of God's messengers.[35]

In February 1848 de Mazenod's dreams of working in Algeria were seemingly fulfilled. However, eighteen months later the mission was given up because of a disagreement with the bishop over the nature of the work that the missionaries were to do.

---

translation in *Lettres*, vol. 1, no. 8, pp. 12–15.

[32] Ibid.

[33] The region of Red River was sold by the Hudson's Bay Company to the Dominion of Canada and became the province of Manitoba in 1870.

[34] DE MAZENOD, "Journal," July 16, 1841; cited by A. REY, O.M.I., *Historie de Monseigneur Charles-Joseph-Eugène de Mazenod* [=Histoire], 2 vols., Rome, Maison Générale, 1928, vol. 2, p. 106.

[35] DE MAZENOD, to Vincens, August 12, 1847, LM.

> We have recognized that the ministry that our missionaries went to Algeria to do, is not what they are required to do. The bishop does not see things in conformity with our spirit. He had agreed to give them at Blidah the kind of place that essentially community men need. He went back on this decision and reduced our fathers to being simple pastors of little villages, where there is not much to do . . . In conclusion, our fathers are not in their proper place in Algeria, and since another opportunity is opening for us . . . Thus, it is the case to prefer a mission that is offered us by the office of the head of the Church, and which is, in addition to that, eminently conform to the spirit of our Institute and the end of our Congregation.[36]

The Congregation de Propaganda Fide had offered de Mazenod a new vicariate apostolic, Natal in southern Africa. He hastened to accept it. Because of the experience of working with non-oblate bishops in Oregon and Ceylon, as well as Algeria, who did not understand his missionaries and the spirit of the Congregation, de Mazenod requested that the vicar apostolic be one of his own men.[37] Upon de Mazenod's recommendation Jean-François Allard, the novice master in Canada, was appointed vicar apostolic and consecrated bishop "in partibus," i.e., a titular bishop according to our terminology. After a four month journey he and the other missionaries arrived in Durban in March 1852.

De Mazenod wrote to Propaganda repeatedly concerning the problems that his men were having with the bishops in Ceylon and Oregon. In reference to Jaffna he said:

> Your Eminence believes that matters will proceed in a better way in the future. So may it be! I had understood that there was very little to be done in those countries, and even that to the detriment of my poor sons. That is the reason why I had agreed for them to go somewhere else to exercise their zeal. So many requests are made! However, the Sacred Congregation wants us to remain there, and we will remain. I will write in this same sense to the superior of that mission who is very discouraged, but ready to persevere in his sacrifice.
>
> Discord such as this does not exist where a Congregation is in charge of a vicariate. When that element is missing it is impossible to rely on the stability which is so necessary for the accomplishment of good that demands considerable time.[38]

---

[36] DE MAZENOD, *Journal*, March 28, 1850, JM.

[37] DE MAZENOD, to Barnabò, secretary of Propaganda Fide, March 30, 1850, ACTA, vol. 212 (1849–1850), ff. 511–512, Propaganda Archives; trans. in *Oblate Writings*, vol. 5, p. 40.

[38] DE MAZENOD, to Fransoni, prefect of Propaganda Fide, April 8, 1853, Scrit. rif. nei Congressi, America Centrale, vol. 16 (1852–1854), ff. 563–564, Propaganda Archives; trans. in *Oblate Writings*, vol. 5, pp. 67–68.

He continued by requesting that Stephan Semeria, the superior of the Oblates in Ceylon, be made bishop and coadjutor vicar apostolic of Jaffna. This was done in 1856. Upon the death of the vicar apostolic the following year he succeeded him, and in 1861 the vicariate was confided to the Oblates by Propaganda.

During this period there was a corresponding development within France. The missions continued to be the major ministry. At the 1843 general chapter it was reported that at least 65 missions and retreats had been given during the previous year.[39] The Constitutions specified that a mission should be at least three weeks long, and be given by a minimum of two missionaries.[40] During de Mazenod's life the Oblates preached in France about 3000 parish missions and retreats to religious, triduums, and lenten and advent series.[41] In 1861 there were in France seven mission houses. In addition to this the Oblates staffed six shrines dedicated to Mary—Notre-Dame de Lumière (1837), Notre-Dame de Bon Secours (1846), Notre-Dame de la Garde (1850), Notre-Dame de Talence (1853), Notre-Dame de Sion (1853), and Notre-Dame de Cléry (1854). In addition to the work of evangelization and hearing confessions, and promoting devotion to the Blessed Virgin, the priests stationed at three of these shrines also conducted missions.[42]

At the time of the 1843 general chapter there were 68 professed oblates— 44 priests (including two bishops, de Mazenod and Guibert of Viviers), 13 scholastics, and 11 brothers. The great expansion in works was possible because of the phenomenal increase in the number of candidates. In the years 1847 and 1848, one hundred and fifteen entered the novitiate.[43] At the time of de Mazenod's death in 1861, there were 414 Oblates—6 bishops, 267 priests, 53 scholastics, and 88 brothers.[44]

---

[39] See "Registre," 1843, p. 73; in PIELORZ, Les Chapitres, vol. 1, p. 191.

[40] See Constitutiones 1826, pars I, c. II, art. 6 and 16.

[41] See PIELORZ, Les Chapitres, vol. 2, p. 116.

[42] See Donat LEVASSEUR, O.M.I., A History of the Missionary Oblates of Mary Immaculate, 2 vol., Rome, General House, 1985–1989, vol. 1, pp. 110–111.

[43] See ibid., vol. 1, pp. 115–116.

[44] PIELORZ, Les Chapitres, vol. 2, p. 140.

Until the acceptance of the foreign missions there had been little growth in the Congregation. Why did the Missionary Oblates of Mary Immaculate not only survive—unlike many contemporary religious and missionary institutes founded in France at about the same time—but become one of the Church's major congregations of men?

The present author sees the answer in de Mazenod's dedication of being at the service of the Church in preaching the Gospel to the most neglected souls, and his pragmatic adaptability to

In 1850 the legislative assembly increased the funds for naval chaplains, and the government was disposed to have religious priests as chaplains. De Mazenod was asked to furnish priests for the ships sailing from Toulon. He declined the offer, not because he considered the ministry opposed to the end of the Congregation, but because of the extreme youth of the priests available.

> Just as you, I see the advantages that such a mission could bring to the Congregation, but our family is too young. We would delude ourselves to think that we could fulfil it with honor. Our young priests do not have enough experience, and are not strengthened in virtue to be exposed to the dangers to be feared from being completely alone on a ship with depraved youth . . . We are not in a condition to do it either from the number or the quality of men needed.[45]

It should be pointed out that he did not hesitate to call military chaplaincy a *mission*. Should one be surprised at this? If these men lacked priests to serve them, they were "les âmes abondonnées" (the neglected souls) to be evangelized.[46]

---

change with the times according to the needs that were most pressing. This led him to sending his priests and brothers to the foreign missions.

It was only then that the real expansion of the Congregation began. The foreign mission spirit was at a high point, and France was *the* mission sending country in the nineteenth century. The Oblates were blessed at that moment with many missionary vocations. Historically, a high percentage of the men who joined the Congregation in France and also in the rest of Europe—and to a certain extent in North America—did so in order to go to the foreign missions. The various expulsions from France in turn led to foundations in Belgium, Netherlands, Germany, Italy and Spain.

De Mazenod's decision from the very beginning of the foreign missions that novitiates should be opened to receive new local members for his Congregation should not be discounted. Wherever the Congregation went, it sank deep roots by local recruitment to its ranks.

To a great extent, de Mazenod's sons have maintained his pastoral and missionary pragmatism and have adapted their ministry and pastoral methods according to the needs of the people with whom they worked.

This position differs from that expressed by F. Ciardi: "L'originalità va piuttosto cercata nel particolare stile di vita impresso alla propria comunità, che la differenzia dagli altri gruppi missionari contemporanei. In questo sta la causa più profonda che spiega la sua sopravvivenza e la sua estensione, quando la stragrande maggioranza delle creazioni coeve ha vita breve et circoscritta" (F. CIARDI, O.M.I., *I Fondatori Uomini Dello Spirito*, Rome, Città Nuova, 1982, p. 254). The same author elsewhere wrote, "Gli O[blati], fin dal loro sorgere, mostrarono tuttavia elementi caratteristici—quali l'apertura universale e lo spiccato senso della comunità e della ricerca della perfezione religiosa—che determinarono la loro permanenza e il loro sviluppo, rispetto alle altre società" (id., "Oblati di Maria Immacolata," in *Dizionario degli Istituti di Perfezione*, Rome, Edizioni Paoline, 1980, vol. 6, p. 625).

[45] DE MAZENOD, to Tempier, June 27, 1850, LM.

[46] Cf. William H. WOESTMAN, O.M.I., "De Mazenod and Military Chaplaincy," in *Vie Oblate Life*,

In spite of the absolute prohibition of the Constitutions to minister to communities of religious women, except in special cases, from the beginning of the Congregation de Mazenod authorized a number of priests to found such communities and to be the ecclesiastical superiors of women's communities.[47] A member of the 1850 general chapter proposed that there be strict conformity to the Constitutions. This was the occasion of "longs et vifs débats." Finally it was left up to de Mazenod to settle the question:

> . . . The Most Reverend Superior General said that nothing had been done in this matter without prior authorization. The chapter unanimously agreed that this work should peacefully continue the course it has taken.[48]

Less than five months before his death de Mazenod, having consulted the Congregation, approved a spiritual association between "la Congrégation des Pères Oblats de Marie Immaculée et l'Association de la Sainte-Famille" of Bordeaux. By this agreement the superior general of the Oblates assumed a special responsibility in the government of the Holy Family Congregation. He was represented by a delegate for the affairs of this Congregation.[49]

Revisions of the Constitutions 1843-1850

Since the Constitutions were written for a small congregation in southern France, no provision was made for provinces and foreign missions. In his opening address to the 1843 general chapter de Mazenod spoke of the necessity to bring the Constitutions into harmony with the expansion of the Congregation. In spite of this the only change made concerned the frequency of general chapters. This was changed from every three to every six years. On March 20, 1846 Gregory XVI issued the brief *Quam multa sit messis* approving the modifications.[50]

---

47 (1988), pp. 41-43.

[47] See J. PIETSCH, O.M.I., "Notre Fondateur et les communautés religieuses de Marseille," *Études oblates*, 6 (1947), pp. 157–182; 7 (1948), pp. 211–228, 263–286.

[48] "Registre," 1850, p. 102; PIELORZ, *Les Chapitres*, vol. 1, p. 290.

[49] See *Circulaires*, November 16, 1860, vol. 1, p. 17; March 15, 1861, vol. 1, p. 35. See Congregation of Bishops and Regulars, response, April 11, 1862, in P. GASPARRI, *Fontes*, vol. 4, no. 1983, pp. 967–168.

The Constitutions for the Holy Family from 1903 until 1958 contained a chapter on the relations between the two Congregation. By mutual agreement after Vatican II the Oblate superior general did not appoint a delegate, pro-director, to the Holy Family. There is still a fraternal relationship between the two congregations on the level of the general administrations although the formal relationship of the 1861 agreement had *de facto* ceased to exist.

[50] Gregory XVI, apostolic letter, *Quum multa sit messis*, March 20, 1846, in *Constitutiones 1853*, pp. 189–192; *Constitutiones 1894*, pp. 195–198; *Constitutiones 1910*, pp. 169–171.

When there was no intermediate governmental structure between the local superior and the superior general, as a stopgap measure de Mazenod delegated very broad powers to the superiors of missions and to visitors.

> . . . If I were in Marseille I would get all these faculties written specifically as I have for all the heads of distant missions. Since you will not have any official documents I shall make this present letter serve and it will be short.
>
> I give you for your mission territory of Natal and for the Seychelles Islands if we take charge of them, all my powers as superior general with the exception of the final admission of subjects, whom you will be able to admit to the Oblate community without the Congregation being bound to them in any way before I give my approval. In case, which God forbid, you were obliged for the gravest reasons to expel someone without being able to consult me first, you could nevertheless not release him from his vows.
>
> These are the only restrictions I am placing on the wide powers I am giving you. You are thus more than a provincial, since I am confidently making you an *alter ego* as it were.[51]

On March 19, 1850 de Mazenod issued a circular letter announcing that the next general chapter would take place the following August. At the same time he made a number of determinations concerning governmental structures, who would be the capitulants *ex officio*, and the election process for the delegates. This was necessary because of the rapid expansion since the last chapter, and the impossibility of all those attending, who would have been entitled to do so according to the Constitutions. As a part of this communication he announced the establishment of permanent visitors for the more distant missions—Oregon, Red River, and Ceylon.

> IX. Since the great expansion of the Congregation demands that the authority of the superior general be represented everywhere, and that recourse to him become easier, we institute *permanent visitors*, who in the places assigned to them for a set time enjoy all the ordinary rights of a visitor and even more ample authority if the superior general judges it opportune.[52]

The houses, residences, and territory placed under the authority of a permanent visitor were called a vicariate.[53]

The 1850 general chapter made extensive modifications in the governmental structure in the Constitutions to bring them in conformity with the expanded Congregation, and other changes that had taken place since 1826.

---

[51] DE MAZENOD, to Allard, October 24, 1851, in *Oblate Writings*, vol. 4, pp. 192–193.

[52] *Circulaires*, March 19, 1850, vol. 1, p. 4.

[53] See ibid., p. 5.

The first article of the Constitutions was modified to express clearly that it was a congregation of priests with vows by the addition of the words "Religionis votis obligati" (bound by vows of religion).[54] Although along with the other institutes with simple vows the Oblates were not officially considered to be religious but seculars, this important element of their life was now explicitly stated in the first article of the Constitutions.

A long chapter with forty-eight articles on seminaries was introduced immediately after the chapter on missions. This indicates the importance given this ministry. It was entitled "De Institutione Clericorum in Seminariis." The first article of this chapter clearly states the stress placed on the running of major seminaries.

> Art. (I). After the missions, the most important work of our Congregation is undoubtedly the direction of seminaries, in which clerics receive their own special training . . . In vain would the missionaires labor for the conversion of sinners, if the parochial clergy were not men filled with the Holy Spirit, earnestly following in the footsteps of the Divine Shepherd, and feeding with watchful and constant care the sheep that have returned to Him.

However, the major change was the division of the entire Congregation into provinces and vicariates of mission.[55] A province was subject to common law and consisted of at least three houses and had to have sufficient ordinary revenue to support its members and their missionary activity. A vicariate of missions could have fewer houses and permanent residences with a smaller number of religious, and in addition to general statutes was governed by decrees given by the superior general with the consent of his council to fit the particular situation.[56] Both provincials and vicars of missions had to be at least thirty years of age, seven years in the Congregation, and have served as a local superior.[57] Provincials were named for a term of three years. Vicars were appointed for a term determined by the superior general with the consent of his council. However, ordinarily the time was not to be greater than six years.[58]

Even though the Congregation was divided into provinces and vicariates, the authority of the superior general remained very great. It could seem that

---

[54] *Constitutiones 1853*, pars I, c. I, art. I. These words were added to modify *sacerdotes sæculares*. Thus it read: "ut coadunati sacerdotes sæculares, Religionis votis obligati" (secular priests bound by vows of religion)."

[55] See *Constitutiones 1853*, pars III, c. I, §VII, art. I.

[56] See ibid., pars III, c. I, §VII, art. II.

[57] See ibid., pars III, c. I, §VII, art. V.

[58] See ibid., pars III, c. I, §VII, art. VII.

in a certain sense that the provincials and vicars of missions were almost visitors or delegates of the superior general rather than full superiors in their own right. Did de Mazenod understand these articles in that way?

> IX. The superior general is invested with absolute authority for interior and domestic government over all persons subject to him, over the provinces and houses of the whole Congregation.[59]

> Art. I Since it would be very difficult for the superior general personally to care for everything that pertains to the various houses, their superiors, subjects, and items of business, the whole Congregation is divided into provinces and vicariates. Provincials and vicars of missions are responsible for their immediate government.[60]

Thus, the Congregation was divided into provinces and vicariates because of necessity, and there was a real concern to maintain unity. Hence the crucial role of the superior general, "who is to be considered in the Institute as the soul of the whole Society."[61]

Local superiors and directors of residences were required to write to the superior general at least once each year and report to him, "how everything is going in his community concerning the things and persons committed to their care."[62] The following article of the Constitutions encourages all individuals to write personally to the superior general and open their hearts to him, to seek light and direction. The superior general had the authority to transfer the professed members and the novices from one province or vicariate to another province or vicariate "which authority he will use as often as he judges it will serve the welfare of the Society or an individual . . ."[63]

In spite of the extraordinary development of the Congregation during the previous nine years because of the foreign missions there was no explicit mention of them in the revised Constitutions. Of course, the treatment of the vicariates of missions and vicars of missions is an implicit treatment of the foreign missions.

The lacuna was filled by an appendix to the Constitutions entitled "Appendix de Exteris Missionibus Instructio Illustrissimi ac Reverendissimi D.D. Caroli-Joseph-Eugenii de Mazenod . . ."[64]

---

59 Ibid., pars III, c. I, §II, art. IX.

60 Ibid., pars III, c. I, §VII, art. I.

61 Ibid., pars III, c. II, §I, art. V.

62 Ibid., pars III, c. I, §VII, art. XXIII.

63 Ibid., pars III, c. I, §VII, art. XXV.

64 Ibid., pp. 167–182; *Constitutiones 1894*, pp. 211–226; *Constitutiones 1910*, pp. 201–214.

In treating the government of the foreign missions the instruction states:

As far as government is concerned there are two types of foreign missions. Some belong to the Congregation in such a way that the whole territory is placed under the jurisdiction of one of our members, who has the title of vicar apostolic or bishop; in others, the members of our Society are called by the ordinary of the place or the vicar apostolic, to preach the Gospel under the jurisdiction of that ordinary or vicar, who has that region assigned to him. In the first case, most often the bishop is both the ecclesiastical and regular superior of our missionaries. He shares the common life with them, directs their external ministry, and also everything that pertains to the interior administration of our houses. In a word he enjoys the faculties which our Constitutions grant a vicar of missions.[65]

In this way de Mazenod solved the problem that his missionaries had encountered in Algeria, Oregon, and Jaffna. As a general rule, in the foreign missions assigned to the Congregation the local ordinary would be also the religious superior. At the time of de Mazenod's death there were six Oblate bishops, and three of them were vicars of mission—Allard of Natal, Taché of Red River, and Semeria of Jaffna. A fourth, Guigues of Ottawa, was provincial of the province of Canada.[66]

In spite of the prescription of the Constitutions that a vicar of missions should not ordinarily serve for more than six years, the norm of the "Instruc-

---

Cf. Claude CHAMPAGNE, O.M.I., "Instruction de Monseigneur de Mazenod relative aux missions étrangères," in *Kerygma*, 9 (1975), pp. 164–177.

[65] *Constitutiones 1853*, p. 170; *Constitutiones 1894*, p. 214; *Constitutiones 1910*, pp. 203–204.

[66] See A. BOUCHER, O.M.I., *Provinciaux et Vicaires des Missions dans la Congrégation des Missionnaires Oblats de Marie-Immaculée 1841-1948*, Ottawa, Éditions des Études Oblates, 1949, pp. 44, 53, 97, and 107.

Lower Canada (Quebec) and Upper Canada (Ontario) were united from 1841 until 1867 when Ontario and Quebec as separate provinces formed a confederation with the provinces of New Brunswick and Nova Scotia to become the Dominion of Canada.

There seems to be an anachronism in *Atlas O.M.I. 1990* published by the general administration when it speaks of the erection of the province of "Canada-Est" in 1851. This denomination corresponds neither to the political reality of the time nor to the name given to the province by de Mazenod. This same error has been repeated frequently, e.g., *Personnel O.M.I.*, 1967, p. 124. All the earlier editions of *Personnel O.M.I.* from 1880 to 1956 (e.g., 1880, p. 21; 1882, p. 25; 1895, p. 35; 1921, p. 36; 1947, p. 38; 1956, p. 68) have "Province du Canada." No doubt the usage of the name "Canada Est" began because subsequently there were many other oblate provinces within Canada, whose boundaries with time extended far beyond those when the province was erected in 1851. In the decree dividing the province, Leo Deschâtelets, superior general, spoke of "Provincia hucusque de 'Canada' nuncupata . . . supradicta Provincia de Canada . . . " (January 7, 1957). He also on the same date signed a letter "Aux Religieux Oblats de Marie immaculée de la Province du Canada (Est)" (in Archives Deschâtelets, LCB, 2002, .M81R, 1 and 2).

tio," that in the territories confided to the Congregation the vicar apostolic would be also vicar of missions in fact, prevailed. For example three succeeding vicars apostolic were the vicars of missions of Natal in South Africa for almost eighty-four years, from 1851 to 1936.[67]

The vicars of missions, as well as the provincials, were *ex officio* members of the general chapters.[68] Because of their long tenure in office as vicars of

---

[67] See ibid., p. 197.

The Servant of God Ovide Charlebois is an outstanding example of a vicar apostolic who was simultaneously religious superior as vicar of missions. When the vicariate apostolic of Keewatin was founded in 1910, it was the largest in the world, extending all the way to the North Pole. In this immense territory there were only thirteen thousand people.

Because of other commitments the superior general refused to accept the responsibility of supplying the vicariate with missionaries. After Propaganda named Charlebois vicar apostolic and he was ordained bishop, the superior general the following year appointed him vicar of missions ("Procès verbaux des Conseils Généraux O.M.I." May 14, 1911, vol. 8, p. 113). However, the Congregation still made no commitment of personnel. On December 11, 1911 Charlebois was given permission to open a novitiate (ibid., p. 144). When the master of novices became ill in 1915, Charlebois was also novice master for a time (ibid., p. 245). In 1917 he began a scholasticate at Beauval which existed until 1935. He recruited candidates as well as accepting scholastics whose health prevented them from completing their studies elsewhere. In 1932 he had eight brother novices and eight scholastics (*Rapports sur les Provinces et Vicariats 1932*, 1932). At one time Beauval had as many as fifteen scholastics (see G. CARRIÈRE, O.M.I., *Le Père du Keewatin*, Montréal, Rayonnement, 1962).

The vicars apostolic of Bay James, Labrador, and Prince Rupert, who were bishops, were at one time the vice-provincials of the vicarial districts of provinces in Canada. As vice-provincials they were the vicars of the provincials who were priests (see *Personnel O.M.I. 1954*, pp. 158, 161, and 177).

In 1981 René Toussaint, former bishop of Idiofa, was appointed provincial treasurer of the vice-province of Zaïre.

[68] See *Constitutiones 1853*, pars III, c. I., §VII, art. V.

Exercising his right as superior general to appoint a number of capitulants, in 1867 Fabre, de Mazenod's successor, called to the chapter Archbishop Guibert, Bishop Guigues, and Bishop Grandin.

The question of bishops being members of the general chapter was raised, and Corne, the procurator to the Holy See, after making inquiries in Rome responded, "Religious who have become bishops enjoy neither active nor passive voice in orders with solemn vows: such is, I believe, the practice. The reason is easy to understand: the bishops are not held to the observance of their rules and their vows save *quoad substantiam*: how could they be the *form for religious*? Do not ask for an official response on this matter from the Sacred Congregation. The answer could give you difficulty and cause your established practice to become illegal. Concerning the rest of the question, for the vicars apostolic, Propaganda advises you to give them authority as provincial over the religious of their vicariate—Propaganda does it *in the name of the Holy See*, that ratifies everything. For the practice you have of calling bishops, even regular diocesan bishops, to the general chapter, you can continue to do so until an explicit contrary decision renders it illegal. Do not provoke a decision" ("Procès verbaux des Conseils Généraux," August 8, 1870, vol. 2, p. 389). On July 7, 1871 the decision was made, "to maintain our practice, which is to call some of our Oblate bishops to our

missions, many bishops were members of many consecutive general chapters, and consequently for almost one hundred years there were many bishops, and often the same ones, who were capitulants.

The bishops and priests in the vicariates as well as those in the provinces had the right to elect one delegate to the general chapters. Since many of the vicariates, although vast in territory, had very few members, these had proportionately a much greater role in the chapters.[69]

---

general chapters" (ibid., p. 404). To the 1879 chapter Fabre invited Balain, bishop of Nice, and Guibert, cardinal and archbishop of Paris. The latter attended only one afternoon.

The photographs of the members of the various general chapters clearly show the number of bishops (and frequently the same ones) present during the latter part of the nineteenth century and the first part of this century. This group of almost perpetual capitulars exercised, it would seem, a large influence within the chapters.

Perhaps the most outstanding example of a bishop being a member of general chapters is Gabriel Breynat. He was vicar apostolic and vicar of missions of Mackenzie from 1901 to 1943. As vicar of missions he was *ex officio* member of seven consecutive general chapters (1904, 1906, 1908, 1920, 1926, 1932, 1938). In 1936 he was appointed bishop assistant and palatine count to the pontifical throne, and titular archbishop in 1939. He died in 1954. In addition to several books on his missionary experiences, he is the author of a short theological work, *Saint Joseph, Père Vierge de Jésus*, 2 ed., Montréal, Fides, 1944). His ability as a theologian has frequently been the source of humor within the Congregation. His reputation of power and even intrigue still exists.

Archbishop Dontenwill, as superior general, had invited Bishop Brault of Jaffna to the 1920 general chapter. To remove a doubt concerning the validity of his convocation because of canon 629 of the newly promulgated Code of Canon Law, the capitulants petitioned the Holy Father just before the chapter elections to give Brault active vote. At the bottom of the petition the pope wrote, "Petitam facultatem, quantenus opus sit concedimus die 21 octobris 1920 Benedictus PP XV" (III-s, Procurator's Archives, O.M.I.). It would seem that for subsequent chapters until 1974 there was no such doubt. Indults were requested in 1974, 1979, and 1992 (Francis G. MORRISEY, O.M.I., "The Juridical Situation of Oblate Bishops in the Congregation," in *Vie Oblate Life*, 54 (1995), pp. 65–81).

In 1953 there were two bishops, who were were vicars of missions, but only one attended the chapter. In 1959 there was only one bishop, a vicar of missions, and he did not come to the chapter (see "Registre," 1953 and 1959).

The 1972 chapter decided that bishops have active voice in elections, but not passive voice (*Administrative Structures*, 1972, p. 17, no. 6). The 1974 chapter stated that bishops have both active and passive voice (*Acts of the General Chapter 1974*, p. 33, footnote). According to *Constitutions 1982*: "All Oblates in perpetual vows enjoy active and passive voice, saving exceptions foreseen in canon law and in the Constitutions and Rules" (C. 86.)

Two bishops were members of the 1992 general chapter. Gilles Cazabon, vicar general at the time of his appointment as bishop of Timmins, received an indult to participate in the chapter (Prot. No. 25250/92, June 30, 1992, in *AAG O.M.I.*, 15 [1992], p. 4). Vincent Cadieux, elected delegate for St. Joseph Province and subsequently appointed bishop of Moosonee, was given an indult granting him active and passive voice in the Congregation (Prot. No. 2525/92, in *AAG O.M.I.*, 15 [1992], p. 3).

[69] The provincial and vicarial chapters met only prior to a general chapter in order to elect

The prohibition to minister to religious women was modified by the clause "nisi de Superioris generalis licentia" (unless they have the superior general's permission).[70] The similar prohibition to have parishes and preach lenten series was also relaxed.

> XXIV. For the same reason it is not permitted to take charge of parishes, except for grave reasons, and then only rarely, with the consent of the superior general. Nor is it permitted to preach a course of lenten sermons without the provincial's mandate.[71]

The changes in the Constitutions were approved by the Sacred Congregation of Bishops and Regulars, and Pius IX gave his approval with the apostolic letter, *Quum nullo umquam tempore*, on March 28, 1851.[72]

At the 1843 general chapter there had been a proposal to exempt the scholastics from the recitation of office because many of them had poor health, and the need of more time for study. The proposal was rejected by a vote of nineteen to three. Prior to the vote, de Mazenod had been requested to explain the obligation for scholastics to recite the office in common.

> In recalling his concerns at the time of the foundation of the Society, our superior general and founder said that one of his principal thoughts had been to replace in God's Church the ancient religious institutions. He had been in particular painfully hurt by the suppression of the divine office, and consequently he had decided to impose on our members, priests and simple oblates, the same obligation carried by the members of the other religious orders.[73]

---

a delegate for the general chapter. The chapter could not do any other business or discuss any question unless the superior general requested in writing the opinion of the members of the chapter. The members were the provincial or vicar of missions, the members of the council, provincial (vicarial) treasurer, local superiors, and one delegate from each house with four members (*Constitutiones 1853*, pars III, c. I, §IX, De conventu Provinciæ et Vicariatus). This was not changed until the 1966 Constitutions *ad experimentum*.

See *Personnel O.M.I. 1950*. The Whitehorse vicariate of missions had 28 members, Pilcomayo had 30, and Laos had 23, while the province of Canada had 898 members. Each of these units had the right to have one delegate at the 1953 general chapter in addition to the provincial or vicar of missions.

[70] See *Constitutiones 1853*, pars I, c. II, §I, art. XXIII.

[71] Ibid., pars I, c. II, §I, art. XXIV. De Mazenod accepted the parishes at Notre-Dame de Talence in 1852, at Notre-Dame de Cléry in 1854, in Autun in 1858, at Notre-Dame de l'Osier in 1834, in Ottawa in 1844, and St. Sauveur, Québec in 1854.

[72] Pius IX, apostolic letter, *Quum nullo unquam tempore*, March 28, 1851, DM 4, in *Constitutiones 1853*, pp. 193–197; *Constitutiones 1894*, pp. 199–202; *Constitutiones 1910*, pp. 172–175.

[73] "Registre," 1843; p. 74, in PIELORZ, *Les Chapitres*, vol. 1, p. 193–195.

During the 1856 chapter the question concerning the scholastics and the office came up again. The health of the students was poor according to many because of the excessive number of spiritual exercises and so much time given to study. At the time of the chapter there were twenty-nine scholastics. Eight scholastics had died since the previous chapter, including three in the previous three months.[74] The recommendation was that only those in holy orders recite office in common, and that they would be joined by several of the others taking their turn. De Mazenod found this difficult to accept as contrary to the letter and spirit of the Constitutions, but said that the chapter should discuss it seriously. One of the members came up with the suggestion that the scholastics recite the office of the lay brothers. This consisted of a number of Credos, Our Fathers, Hail Marys, and Glory Bes replacing the psalms of the office.

> All the fathers of the chapter rallied around this view, and it seemed to our most reverend superior general to have less drawbacks.[75]

With de Mazenod's death on May 21, 1861 a new era began. The tenth general chapter met in Paris on December 5–8 of the same year. Tempier, de Mazenod's first companion and vicar general of the Congregation, asked the capitulants not to consider him for the post of general because of his age and health. Archbishop Guibert of Tours rose and spoke in the name of the bishops present at the chapter. They felt that it would be inopportune to elect a bishop, because Rome might not approve and because of problems that this could cause within the Congregation. Courtès responded in giving the advantages of having a bishop as superior general and said the chapter should not renounce its right to elect a bishop. This proposition was adopted by the chapter.

That afternoon they elected on the first ballot thirty-seven year old Joseph Fabre, who was at the time simultaneously rector of the Marseille major seminary, vicar general of the diocese, assistant general, and treasurer general of the Oblates. The vote was nineteen to one, with obviously only Fabre voting for another person.[76]

---

[74] See PIELORZ, *Les Chapitres*, vol. 2, pp. 15–16. All but one of them died in France, and he died in England. Between 1856 and the next general chapter four scholastics died, all in France. There were at the time of the 1861 chapter 53 scholastics. Cf. ibid., vol. 2, pp. 131 and 141.

Until the 1950s, tuberculosis, a frequent cause of death, was not uncommon.

[75] "Registre," 1856, p. 146; PIELORZ, *Les Chapitres*, vol. 2, p. 54.

[76] The Constitutions stated, "Nemo eligi poterit (Superior generalis) nisi saltem . . . et in missionum ministerio exercitatus . . ." (No one can be elected [superior general] unless he had worked in the ministry of the missions) (*Constitutiones 1853*, pars III, c. I, §II, art. III). It would seem that Fabre lacked this qualification. His ministry had always been in education and formation. After

Fabre remained in office until his death almost thirty-one years later in 1892. This was a time of continual growth both in Europe and in the missions in spite of the persecution of religious in France. The positive side of the expulsion from France was the establishment of the Congregation in Italy, Spain, Netherlands, Belgium, and Germany. The Congregation accepted new territory in Canada and the vicariate apostolic of Colombo, Ceylon. The greatest growth was in personnel, which tripled during the period. At the time of the 1893 general chapter there 10 bishops, 648 priests, 201 scholastics, 352 brothers, 91 scholastic novices, and 37 brother novices.[77]

The Congregation's dedication to the foreign missions can be seen in the report to the 1873 general chapter. In the previous six years the superior general assigned 46 new priests to the houses in France and Great Britain, and sent 64 priests to Canada and the other foreign missions.[78]

In the previous decades the Congregation had spread to the four corners of the world. It was spread thin. Many of the missionaries were obliged to live for long periods of time at a great distance from their brothers, and community life was difficult. There was a need for organization and consolidation. Fabre's background and temperament had prepared him for this. His sense of loyalty demanded that he and the Congregation walk faithfully in de Mazenod's footsteps, and for him the Constitutions were the clear map for doing this. Five days after his election he wrote:

> Let us be united in heart and soul, and we will be strong for doing good. Let us be united by the memory of a Father who will always be loved. I had the blessing of knowing his heart that was so good, so great . . . I will do everything to walk in the footsteps of him, whom we will always mourn. His noble and dedicated soul lives among us in the blessed Rules that he left us as a pledge of his love . . . I have promised faithful and fervent keeping of them; I have solemnly promised to demand of everyone a timely observance of them. I ask the Lord not to permit that this sacred deposit be lost in our hands, that not even the least minute part of this precious

---

de Mazenod's death seventy-three year old Tempier made "le voyage de Rome" (cf. "Fabre, J.", in *Notices necrologiques O.M.I.*, vol 2, p. 103). This trip was mentioned in the context of his acting as vicar general and preparing for the general chapter. Was the trip made to seek a dispensation from this requirement?

The chapter may have judged that it had the right to dispense from this article of the Constitutions: "Capitulo dumtaxet generali competit jus dispensationes generales et perpetuas concedendi, quo jure utetur solummodo ob causas gravissimas" (pars III, c. I, §I, art. XLII).

[77] *Notices necrologiques*, vol. 7, p. 538.

[78] See *Circulaires*, vol. 1, p. 284.

gift be squandered. Our joy and strength will be in the complete obedience to all their prescriptions.[79]

Unfortunately Fabre's temperament and lack of missionary experience gave him a narrow approach to the apparent dilemma that faces every active religious—how to meet simultaneously the demands of the ministry and the necessity of solitude and prayer for growth in the spiritual life. While de Mazenod continually insisted on the observance of the Constitutions, he did not hesitate to adapt and dispense when the missionaries were faced with real problems. De Mazenod had met this same problem in his own life, as was seen in first two chapters. He had learned to adjust in a very pragmatic way the principles that he had laid down in the Constitutions when he or his missionaries encountered the demands of the ministry and religious observance that seemingly were in conflict. He had stated clearly in the first article of the Constitutions that the principal work of the Congregation was the imitation of the example and virtues of Jesus Christ by the preaching of the Gospel to the poor.

Fabre saw that faithfulness to de Mazenod demanded the exact observance of the Constitutions especially in those elements that pertain to the *regular* or *religious* life of the Oblates. For him the *regular* aspect prevailed over the *missionary*. It would seem that he separated the religious and missionary facets of oblate life rather than consider them as parts of a unified whole.[80]

> We are priests, we are religious; these two qualities impose obligations which we must never be mistaken about, and which we must never forget. Work for the sanctification of others by exterior ministry is a very beautiful mission, but it is only a part of our holy vocation . . . Do not lose sight that to obtain this goal [our own sanctification] our holy Rules prescribe that we *spend a considerable part of the year* within our houses in

---

[79] *Circulaires*, December 10, 1861, no. 10, vol. 1, p. 2.

[80] Fabre has been described as "the enthusiast (*der Eiferer*) for the holy Rule . . . Father General Fabre was thoroughly aware that the main task of the successor of a founder is to preserve intact the holy inheritance that the founder bequeathed to his community and to pass it on undamaged . . . and to do all this through the conscientious observance of the holy Rule.

"For this reason Fabre was the great enthusiast for the holy Rule. Thus, the holy Rule was the main idea of his administration, the first and last word in his acts of visitation, his circular letters, his conferences. From the moment of taking office his life was an unrelenting battle against every relaxation of discipline, every neglect of common or individual exercises, every unfaithfulness to the Rule, a tireless struggle to stop the sources from which every fault flows, every effort to keep aware among the Oblates loyalty to the holy Rule" (P. SCHARSCH, O.M.I., *Geschichte der Kongregation der Oblaten der Unbefleckten Jungfrau Maria*, St. Karl, 1953, vol. II², pp. 10–11).

order to work on our sanctification and to become by the practice of all the religious virtues worthy instruments of God's grace.[81]

These words were written some three months after his election in a circular to commemorate the thirty-sixth anniversary of the approval of the Constitutions. In November 1863, a little less than two years later he sent another circular.

> Above all it is the life of faith that makes us appreciate our ministry, and makes it possible for us to become saints according to the Heart of Jesus Christ. But in order that we may live ever more such a life, let us make it a duty to spend *half the year* in the community loving solitude and recollection . . .[82]

The importance that Fabre placed on these circulars can be seen from the prescription that both of them were to be read each year during the annual retreat along with two circulars written by de Mazenod.[83]

Fabre's interpretation of the Constitutions is foreign not only to de Mazenod's practice, but to his intentions. While reading the following quote from the 1818 Constitutions one should recall the personal struggle that de Mazenod experienced to reconcile the active ministry with personal holiness. It was only during his retreat of 1816, as was seen in the previous chapter,[84] that he came to realize that God's will for him was to be found in his apostolic activity, and it was there that he would have to find holiness.

---

[81] *Circulaires,* March 21, 1862, no. 11, vol. 1, p. 3 [79], emphasis added.

[82] *Circulaires,* March 21, 1863, no. 13, vol. 1, p. 15 [97], emphasis added.

An interesting point to investigate would be to see if Fabre was influenced by the Redemptorists in his interpretation of a half a year. Louis Hernot, O.M.I., who was for many years a missionary in Laos, told me that the American Redemptorists in the Vicariate Apostolic of Oudon, Thailand in the 1960s would spend fifteen days in community, and fifteen days in the villages. Is this a standard practice in the Redemptorist missions?

[83] See ibid., p. 23. See E. LAMIRANDE, "Les 'deux parts' dans la vie de l'homme apostolique d'après Mgr de Mazenod," in *Études Oblates,* 25 (1966), pp. 177-204.

These two circular letters were still being read publicly each year in some parts of the Congregation in the 1940s. It seems that there has never been a formal abrogation of the prescription that they be read publicly each year. Needless to say they have almost passed into oblivion.

In this same circular Fabre insisted on the observance of the 1856 chapter directive requiring each member of the Congregation to personally write to the superior general each year a letter of spiritual direction. The concluding sentences of the same paragraph give an indication of his concept of primacy of obedience: "Therefore, let us be in everything and everywhere the faithful disciples of obedience. We are religious in name, we are not religious in fact every time that we avoid the first duty of religion: *I vow perpetual obedience*" (ibid., p. 11).

[84] Supra pp. 35-36.

It has already been said that the missionaries ought, as far as human nature allows, to imitate in everything the example of Jesus Christ our Lord, the chief founder of our Society, and that of the apostles, our first fathers.

Following in their footsteps, the missionaries will give one portion of their life to prayer, recollection, and contemplation, while living together in the seclusion of God's house.

The other portion of their life they will zealously devote to the works of the ministry, to missions, preaching, the hearing of confessions, catechizing, directing the young, visiting the sick and prisoners, giving retreats, and other works of this kind.

Whether out on the missions or at home, their chief study will always be to make progress in the way of priestly and religious perfection. They will cultivate the virtues of humility, poverty, self-denial, interior mortification, purity of intention, and faith. In a word, they will seek to become other Jesus Christs spreading abroad everywhere the fragrance of his amiable virtues.[85]

These words were divided into a preamble and three articles and became part of the approved Constitutions, and remained so until 1966. A careful reading reveals that the missionaries both at home and while out on the active ministry were to strive for priestly and religious holiness. Nothing is said about a considerable part of the year at home in the religious house. It is a question of a part of their lives and not a part of the year. This is not the same thing. Much of the pastoral work mentioned in the third paragraph was done, as de Mazenod himself had done as a young priest, while at home.[86]

If Fabre had examined the Constitutions more closely he would have found that de Mazenod expected the missionaries to spend the greater part of the year away from their communities, "the greater portion of the year, namely

---

[85] "Constitutions 1818," Deuxième partie, c. I, Des autres principales observances, in *Missions O.M.I.*, 78 (1951), pp. 54–55; *Écrits*, vol. 1, pp. 54–55. In *Constitutiones 1826*, this passage became pars II, c. III, §1; in *Constitutiones 1928* it is art. 287–290.

[86] An example of the suffering that this narrow interpretation of the Constitution caused can be seen in the mission of Brownsville, Texas, a small border town in the Wild West along the Rio Grande River. The superior Gaudet never learned Spanish, and knew very little English. Without these languages he could do no external priestly ministry. He was an "exemplary religious" but not a missionary. He was ill at ease with the Americans, felt antipathy toward the Mexicans, and kept all contact with outsiders to a minimum. This was sad enough but he imposed his way of doing things under the guise of the necessities of religious life on the missionary priests (see B. DOYON, O.M.I., *The Cavalry of Christ on the Rio Grande*, Milwaukee, Bruce, 1956, pp. 79 and 183–184). As superior he kept most of the nine priests at home most of the time in this small town to maintain regular community life. At the same time the poor Mexican people were spiritually neglected, and had no other priests to minister to them. Fabre knew the situation, and Gaudet was superior for sixteen years (cf. MUREL, to Fabre, February 26, 1865 and January 7, 1867, General Archives O.M.I.).

that devoted to missions and the spiritual exercises that follow them is spent in the world."[87] In the same paragraph he said that it is only for shorter periods that they are home, "in the brief intervals of this perilous ministry." It should be recalled that these words were written long before the acceptance of the foreign missions, while their ministry was confined to southern France.

Special note should be taken of two ideas that go together in de Mazenod's thought—the danger of the ministry and the necessity for humility. Why was the ministry so dangerous? The success of the missions was so great that the missionaries could easily attribute it to themselves, and not to the grace of Jesus. Consequently the need for great humility. All the virtues that are specified in the fourth paragraph of the quote refer to various aspects of humility to counteract the danger of pride. Certainly this was not the main spiritual danger to the missionaries in the foreign missions where physical hardship, discouragement, and often meagre success were their daily lot.

> V. By this mode of life they will become well versed in humility, a virtue that they will not cease to implore from God, since it is so necessary for the perilous ministry in which they are engaged. Rich, indeed, are the fruits of this ministry, yet it is to be feared that such marvellous achievements, due as they are to grace alone and whose glory consequently belongs only to God, might prove a dangerous snare for imperfect missionaries, who have not sufficiently cultivated this fundamental and absolutely necessary virtue of humility.[88]

Denial of Exemption

As part of his organization of the Congregation, Fabre went to Rome and on December 22, 1862 presented to Pius IX a report on the state of the Congregation. He also decided that it was time to have a procurator to the Holy See resident in Rome. The necessary rescript for this was granted on February 23, 1863, and in March Fabre named Ambrose Tamburini to fill this office. One of his first acts in Rome was to present to the Sacred Congregation of Bishops and Regulars a petition from Fabre for the faculty to dispense from the defect of age for ordination to the priesthood.

> The same Joseph Fabre humbly requests your Holiness that the faculty, which the Most Reverend Frederick Gabriel Mary Francis de Marguerye, bishop of Autun, already has of promoting to the priesthood some of the

---

[87] *Constitutiones 1853*, pars II, c. II, §I, N.B. 3°.

[88] Ibid., pars II, c. III, §I, art. V. The same idea is expressed in the section on preaching and on the dangers to the preacher "in this perilous ministry, which so many vain and proud priests have exercised to their own misfortune and without benefit to the souls of others. We shall not attain it, however, unless we renounce our own personal glory . . ." (pars I, c. IV, §IV, art. V).

students of his seminary before they have reached the canonical age, be graciously extended to the aforementioned Oblates of Mary Immaculate, so that each year ten deacons of their Congregation may be promoted to the priesthood, as long as they are at least twenty-two years and six months of age.[89]

Unwittingly Tamburini opened Pandora's box as far as the Oblates were concerned. The pro-secretary of the Sacred Congregation of Bishops and Regulars, Stanislao Svegliati, acting on the premise that the Oblates were not exempt, wrote the following memorandum:

From the Secretariat of Bishops and Regulars, June 20, 1863. The undersigned maintains that the dispensations from age for the Oblates of Autun, who are to be ordained priests, should direct themselves to the bishop of Autun. Stanislaus Svegliati, pro-secretary.[90]

The memorandum was presented to Pius IX and the response was, "From the audience of July 3, 1863. Refer the matter to the bishop."[91] Since the personnel of the Secretariat of Briefs had a doubt concerning the exemption of the Oblates,[92] an inquiry was made:

From the audience of July 3, 1863. Refer the matter to the bishop. The substitute of the Secretariat of Briefs doubting whether the said Congregation is or is not exempt from the jurisdiction of the bishops has returned the request for the relative rescript.[93]

When the indult for the dispensations was denied, Tamburini went to Propaganda and obtained it there. He wrote Fabre to inform him of what had happened, and the minutes of the general council meeting of July 15, 1863 laconically read:

On the occasion of ordinations a number of dispensations from age were required; they were granted at Propaganda, but previously the procurator of the Congregation addressed the secretariat of Bishops and Regulars. There they questioned the exemption which the Congregation enjoys. This matter must be treated with prudence. Exemption with certain

---

[89] TAMBRUINI to Pius IX (no date), CICLSAL Archives, M. 29. This document and all others cited from CICLSAL Archives M. 29 are found in COSENTINO, *Histoire*, vols. 4 and 5 in the original language in the notes at the end of the volumes and in French in the text. There are photocopies in the General Archives O.M.I.

[90] M. 29, CICLSAL Archives. The scholastics were students at the scholasticate in Autum.

[91] M. 29, CICLSAL Archives.

[92] Ibid. He wrote on the memorandum, "N.B. Check to see if the commission should be made to the bishop or the superior of the institute since it has a rescript of communication of privileges of the Redemptorists and all the regular orders."

[93] Ibid.

restrictions seems to us to be certain, but it will be necessary to prepare a work on this subject.[94]

Svegliati studied the case and formulated twenty-one questions that he presented to the pope on August 14. There were two key questions—exemption and the approval of the Constitutions *in forma specifica*. This latter question will be considered later.

> 9. Finally, on the occasion of a request sent to obtain the dispensation from age for several *ordinandi*, the doubt arose as to whether the Oblates are exempt from the jurisdiction of the ordinaries? Since there are no institutes with simple vows which enjoy exemption, it seems that the Oblates do not have it, and it is not contained in the apostolic brief of approval of that Institute.[95]

As was to be expected when the question was so presented, the response of the pope was a simple "negative." Although he gave an affirmative answer to question 21, which was whether a decree was to be issued, this was not done, and consequently Fabre was not informed that the Holy Father had spoken.

The Oblates until this time had no doubt that they were exempt. In April 1826 de Mazenod had petitioned Leo XII for complete communication of privileges, including exemption, with the Redemptorists:

> to grant to this little Congregation, which a short while ago Your Holiness established by approving *in forma specifica* the institute, the constitutions and rules with your brief of March [21], of this year, all the privileges, exemptions, indults and other spiritual graces granted by your predecessors as supreme pontiffs to the Congregation of the Most Holy Redeemer, its superiors, members, churches, and houses whether generally or specifically; and not only those granted to the aforementioned Congregation of the Most Holy Redeemer, but in addition those granted to it by

---

[94] "Procès verbaux," July 15, 1863, vol. 2, p. 70. Would the whole question of exemption have been raised at all if Tamburini had sought the indult from Propaganda in the first place, and dealt with Propaganda as de Mazenod seems to have been doing rather than with the Congregation of Bishops and Regulars? Would a more experienced procurator have known how to avoid the whole issue being considered?

[95] "Ex audientia die 14 Augusti 1863," M. 29, in CICLSAL Archives. Svegliati seems to have based his case on a series of articles "Traité des Congrégations seculières" in *Analecta Juris Pontificii*, 3 (1861), pp. 52–103, and 147–217. The anonymous author stated, "From what has been said, it seems that it has been established that in the case of non-regular congregations of ecclesiastics the ordinary jurisdiction of the bishops is complete, except for questions concerning the rule, the observance of the constitutions, and also internal finances . . ." (p. 149). The author did not realize that this statement was not accurate, since the Passionists and the Redemptorists, both clerical congregations with simple vows, were exempt. Cf. infra p. 82.

communication with other congregations and religious orders; whether through graces, privileges, exemptions, indults already granted, or through those which will be granted in the future . . .[96]

On April 28 the secretary of the Sacred Congregation of Bishops and Regulars presented the petition to Leo XII. The hand written note of the audience records the concession of the petition.

From the audience of His Holiness, April 28, 1826.

His Holiness orders that the customary rescript of participation be granted in the most ample form (*forma amplissima*).

J[oannes] arch[bishop] of Ancyra, secretary.[97]

De Mazenod was informed of the result of the audience on April 30, and he wrote in his journal, "It is true that until the very last moment the Holy Father has poured out in my favor a full measure."[98] Since he had left Marseille for Rome on the previous October 30, he had been away for six months and did not want to delay his return. It had taken more than a month to receive the brief of approbation of the Congregation. Because he thought that a brief was not necessary, it is easy to understand why he did not want to remain in Rome to receive one confirming the communication of all the privileges with the Redemptorists. On his way back to Marseille he wanted to go to Chambéry to meet Joseph-Marie Favre, a well-known missionary, in order to explore the possibility of a merger with his group of missionaries.[99]

From that moment de Mazenod and all the Oblates took for granted that they were exempt. De Mazenod and Fabre granted dimissorial letters for ordination, granted the necessary dispensations for ordinations *extra tempora*, and the faculty to hear the confessions of Oblates. They also thought that the faculty to hear confessions from a diocese was not sufficient for an Oblate to receive absolution, since they thought that they were, as exempt, outside the bishop's jurisdiction. The general chapters established reserved sins. The Oblate candidates for sacred orders were ordained with the title *mensæ communis*. The Oblates did not consider themselves subject to the jurisdiction of the local

---

[96] DE MAZENOD, to Leo XII, April 28, 1826, in Vatican Archives, S.C. VV. e RR., Fondo Vescovi, 1846 Marsiglia, Vatican City; in *Écrits*, vol. 4, pp. 189–190.

[97] Ibid.; in *Écrits*, vol. 4, pp. 193–194. In the report after the audience in which the secretary mentioned all the various categories of favors requested save exemptions (ibid.). Was this just an oversight on his part?

[98] *Missions O.M.I.*, 10 (1872), p. 472. See DE MAZENOD, to Tempier, May 26, 1826, *Lettres* 7, no. 238, p. 91.

[99] DE MAZENOD, to Honorat, May 28, 1826; to Tempier, May 29, May 30, June 10, 1826, *Lettres* 7, nos. 244–248, pp. 102–114.

pastors for the reception of Easter Communion, viaticum, extreme unction and burial.[100]

The question of non-exemption was first raised in June 1863, and dragged on until January 1866 before the Oblates were given a final answer. An internal memorandum of the Sacred Congregation in September 1865 complained, "The request of the Oblates concerning the alleged exemption from the bishops is back for the third time. In July 1863 a full report of the whole affair was made to the Holy Father . . . His Holiness gave instructions to answer *negative* . . ."[101] As far as the Sacred Congregation was concerned the whole question was solved, but they had not gotten around to informing the Oblates that such was the case. They had been told that their response was to come at the same time as that of the Redemptorists, who were given a reply in September 1864 denying they were regulars, but confirming their exemption.[102] Finally on January 5, 1866, Cardinal Quaglia, the prefect, wrote Fabre. The general council minutes record Fabre's reaction to the letter and decree:

> . . . Our Most Reverend Father General with great emotion communicated a decree of the Sacred Congregation of Bishops and Regulars. The Congregation decided that our society does not possess the privilege of exemption because the conferral is not explicitly mentioned in the brief of

---

[100] See *Circulaires*, June 29, 1866, no. 17, vol. 1, p. 156.

[101] CICLSAL Archives, M. 29, September 11, 1865. In the same document it is stated: "Since the mentioned dispositions have not been communicated to the Oblates, as could be done with a nice decree, these gentlemen have come back to insist."

[102] See "Procès verbaux," May 25, 1864, vol. 2, p. 107,. On November 19, 1864 Tamburini sent a copy and a French translation of the petition of the superior general of the Redemptorists, the *votum* (April 16, 1864) of Girolamo Priori, a Carmelite consultor, and the *relatio* (September 1864) of Cardinal Quaglia, the ponens ("Communication de Privilèges avec Redemptoristes," XXII, in Procurator's Archives O.M.I.). In his letter of November 19, 1864, Tamburini said that the Redemptorists may never know of the consultor's report, but that the archivist of the Sacred Congregation had loaned it to him (ibid.). He then remarked that it is easy to see the great influence in the business of the Church exerted by the consultors of the Sacred Congregation, who are to a great extent members of the ancient orders. In reading the "Annuaire Pontifical" he did not find one consultor that belonged to a modern congregation. In all fairness it must be pointed out that in 1864 the congregations with simple vows were, by today's reckoning, few and small in number of members. Cf. P. GASPARRI, *Fontes*, vol. 4, no. 1993 for the text of the response given to the Redemptorists subsequent to Quaglia's *relatio* mentioned above.

This whole question must be seen as part of the Sacred Congregation's effort to put in order the institutes with simple vows. Cf. A. BIZZARDI, *Collectanæ in usum Secretariæ Sacræ Congregationis Episcoporum et Regularium*, Rome, 1885, passim. As will be seen in the next chapter, this process culminated with the publication of the *Normæ* of 1901.

approbation . . . This is a great trial, and there is nothing else to do but to turn to God.[103]

Quaglia's letter stated: "Since the members of the said pious Congregation are not exempt from the jurisdiction of the ordinaries, which you know well from the decree . . ."[104] The letter does not contain any reason for non-exemption. The reason given in the decree itself is that the members have only simple vows:

> 6° Since the members of the pious Congregation make simple vows, the jurisdiction of the ordinaries remains as far as they are concerned always and at all times in conformity with the Sacred Canons and Apostolic Constitutions.[105]

Both the Passionists and the Redemptorists have simple vows and are exempt. It is not hard to see here the influence of the articles in *Analecta Juris Pontificii,* which were mentioned in Quaglia's *relatio.* However, another reason is given in the internal documents of the Sacred Congregation:

> The privilege of exemption is prejudicial to the ordinary jurisdiction of the bishops, and consequently one cannot admit that the Holy See intends to grant it except when clear expressions are used . . .[106]

Shortly afterward Fabre went to Rome and was graciously received by everyone in the curia and especially by Pius IX.[107] He was advised to request all the faculties that were needed, and all his petitions were granted. Although the Oblates were not exempt, the superiors were given all the authority that they needed to govern the Congregation without continual recourse to the

---

[103] *Procès verbaux,* January 29, 1866, vol. 2, p. 188.

[104] QUAGLIA, to Fabre, January 5, 1866, XXIII, 4, Procurator's Archives O.M.I. This letter includes an absolution from all ecclesiastical penalties that may have been incurred by the use of the presumed privileges.

[105] SACRED CONGREGATION OF BISHOPS AND REGULARS, decree, January 5, 1866, in II, 1, Procurator's Archives O.M.I. Seventeen of the twenty decisions of August 14, 1863 were imposed by this decree. A number of them refer to irregularities of not requesting required indults, v.g., to erect provinces, to take charge of parishes, etc., but some of them are rather petty, v.g., the denial of the privilege to celebrate Mass two hours before dawn or after noon when travelling, for confessors not to wear both surplice and stole, to omit the divine office during the missions when the ministry requires it. In reference to the latter point Fabre in his letter to the Oblates pointed out that sound theological principles exist concerning the cessation to the obligation of praying the office (June 29, 1866, no. 17, *Circulaires,* vol. 1, p. 158).

De Mazenod had received from Leo XII indults for the office and hours of celebration of Mass (see memo, April 15, 1826, XXIII, 1ª, Procurator's Archives O.M.I. and note that the pope had given de Mazenod the authority to make an official record of these indults).

[106] *Votum,* 1864, M. 29, in CICLSAL Archives.

[107] *Circulaires,* June 29, 1866, no. 17, vol. 1, p. 153.

local bishops, or the pastors for the sacraments. There was little de facto change in dealing with the diocesan authorities. On June 29, 1866 Fabre addressed the Congregation and explained what had happened and the main points in the decree. His own interior sentiments are reflected in the following words:

> We must look upon the act which emanated from the Holy See on January 5, 1866 as the coronation of the edifice constructed by our venerated Founder . . . Let us thank the Lord for this precious grace . . .[108]

The various indults were regularly renewed by the Holy See until they were no longer necessary with the publication of the pontifical rescript *Cum admotæ* on November 6, 1964.[109]

The decree of 1866 stated explicitly that the members in simple vows and not in holy orders were bound to recite the divine office in virtue of the Constitutions, and not by a precept of the Church.[110]

The 1867 general chapter added two new chapters to the Constitutions: the one concerned the direction of parishes and the other the office of procurator to the Holy See.[111] However, a new edition of the Constitutions was not published until 1894.

Decade of Crises

The Missionary Oblates of Mary Immaculate began the twentieth century full of optimism and enthusiasm. Although they were a young religious community, they had been blessed with singular success. Within France they had an abundance of vocations. The same was true in eastern Canada and in the recently (1895) founded German province that had about thirty novices each year. In the United States there would soon be two scholasticates. In France they were in charge of eight shrines, including the Basilica of the Sacred Heart on Montmartre in Paris. It had been confided to them by their own Cardinal Archbishop Guibert of Paris. Soon they would be asked to take charge of the construction of a similar shrine in honor of the Sacred Heart in Brussels. The Holy See had confided to the Congregation more mission territory than it

---

[108] Ibid., p. 164. Fabre concluded the circular letter by asking each house to contribute to the Peter's pence collection in appreciation and filial devotion to the Holy Father, and for all of them to encourage the faithful to do likewise (ibid., pp. 165–166).

[109] PAUL VI, pontifical rescript, *Cum admotæ*, November 6, 1964, in *AAS*, 59 (1967), pp. 374–378; trans in *CLD*, vol. 6, pp. 147–152.

[110] Decree, no. 9, January 5, 1866, II, 1, Procurator's Archives O.M.I.; cf. *Circulaires*, vol. 1, p. 158.

[111] See COSENTINO, *Histoire*, vol. 4, pp. 25–32.

had to any other religious community. In Canada the success was phenomenal. In addition to many other ministries theirs was the growing university in Ottawa, the capital, and in the west their mission territory was bounded on the west by the Pacific and in the north by the Arctic Ocean, and by the United States to the south. Little did anyone dream that they would soon be faced with three crises caused by the masonic anti-clerical government in France, a financial debacle, and, if these were not enough, a threat from the Sacred Congregation of Bishops and Regulars to conform their Constitutions to the 1901 Normæ.[112]

On July 1, 1901 a law was passed obliging all religious communities in France to be either authorized (under what many judged to be humiliating conditions) by the government or to be dissolved. After much soul searching Cassian Augier, de Mazenod's third successor as superior general, with the approval of his council requested authorization, but the request was rejected without serious consideration.

In 1903 the novices, scholastics, brothers, and priests responsible for them were sent to Ireland, Belgium, Italy, and Spain. The superiors resisted to the very end, but all the houses were taken over by armed force, to use their expression, manu militari. The doors were literally broken open, and the authorities entered by force of arms. The doors were sealed, and the priests were fined. A number of the priests volunteered for the foreign missions, and the rest were not permitted to live in community. In 1904 all the houses of the Midi province were in Italy and Spain, and those of the Nord province in Jersey, Belgium, and Luxembourg. This situation remained until World War I.[113]

Expulsion by the government was nothing new for the Congregation in France. The first expulsion was in 1830, and this was followed by that of November 1880. At that time they were expelled from sixteen of their houses. The seventeenth general chapter at Liège in August 1904 seems to have taken the recent event in stride. The provincial treasurers of Midi and Nord, however, reported that their provinces were operating with deficits without means to cover them.[114] Pierre Longeon, the recently appointed treasurer general, gave a very positive report. There was a very favorable rate of interest on the debt for the construction of the public chapel at the general house on rue de St.

---

[112] See Sacred Congregation for Bishops and Regulars, Normæ secundum quas S. Cong. Episcoporum et Regularium procedere solet in approbandis novis institutis votorum simplicium, Rome, Typis S.C. de Propaganda Fide, 1901.

[113] See Circulaires, May 3, 1903, no. 76, vol. 3, p. 11; Missions O.M.I., 41 (1903), pp. 68–125, 280–302, and 348–354; 42 (1904), pp. 188–192; Personnel O.M.I. 1904, pp. 22–29.

[114] "Registre," 1904, pp. 6–7.

Pétersbourg (which had been seized by the government), and it should be repaid shortly. He hoped to raise the income to support the scholastics and to buy back the expropriated houses of the mission in Aix and the Calvaire, the first house in Marseille.[115]

Vocations were abundant; there were six scholasticates—Liège (Belgium), Rome, Ottawa, Hünfeld (Germany), Belmont (Ireland), and San Antonio, Texas. A seventh scholasticate would open the following year in Tewksbury, Massachusetts. There were 264 scholastics, 76 scholastic novices, and 46 brother novices. The chapter minutes state that there were 1915 members, including novices.[116]

The treasurer general, however, neglected to mention in his report that he had invested money on deposit with him in stocks of Gold Run, a mining venture in the Yukon, Canada, and that the superior of the scholasticate in Rome was investing money in an electric power mill in Avezzano. As far as the Congregation was concerned both were disasters. All the liquid assets would soon be gone, and the Congregation would be responsible for the money on deposit with it.[117] The treasurer general and the superior of the Roman scholasticate were dismissed from the Congregation, and the superior general

---

[115] See "Registre," 1904, p. 4. The minutes of the chapter reflect much concern about the finances, and perhaps even more about financial management, the observance of regulations, and sound record keeping by treasurers at all levels—general, provincial, local. However, a proposal to have an assistant treasurer general was rejected, although it was said that it would be advantageous to have someone in the administration or outside it who would know the accounts of the treasurer general, and that the usefulness of such had been shown by experience (see ibid., p. 29).

Auguste Lavillardière spontaneously asked for the floor to explain in full the financial situation of the construction of the house in Lyon. He wanted to put to rest the legend in the Congregation that had circulated for the previous seven or eight years that this house had put the province of Midi in financial danger. At the end of his presentation he was given a long applause, and the superior general thanked him in the name of the whole Congregation (see ibid., pp. 6–7). Later another capitulant complained that the minutes did not state that Lavillardière had donated 345,000 francs for the house (ibid., p. 7). Two years later Lavillardière was elected superior general.

There was also concern about some member of the Congregation who was involved in some business deal, and the reporter of the finance committee gave "very minute details . . . about a very delicate affair, but fortunately neither the honor or the finances of the Congregation had been compromised" (ibid., p. 43). With the discretion of the time no names were mentioned.

[116] See "Registre," p. 5. The Personnel O.M.I., 1904 gives 1678 professed plus 122 novices for a total of 1800. It seems that the difference of 115 is to be explained from the fact that the priests living dispersed in France are not listed because of the political situation. This is confirmed by comparing the statistics with those in Personnel O.M.I., 1899.

[117] The general administration had a deficit of 2,280,542 francs (see "Registre," 1906, p. 103). This history of the financial difficulties is yet to be written. Abundant documentation is to be found in the General Archives.

resigned. At the request of the assistants general the Sacred Congregation of Bishops and Regulars deprived him of active and passive voice.[118]

At the chapter of 1867 the decision was made that the scholasticates would be directly subject to the superior general and not under the jurisdiction of the provincials. At subsequent chapters the question was again considered but it was not until 1906 that it was decided to place all the scholasticates, except the one in Rome, just as other houses, under the jurisdiction of the provincials. The provincials were for the change, but it was opposed by the scholasticate superiors, who feared interference, and the vicars of missions, who feared that they would not receive as many priests as formerly.

---

[118] See "Registre," 1906, p. 78. It may have been that the assistants feared that Augier would be reelected. The report to the chapter was given by Eugene Baffie, who had been elected vicar general by the other assistants. The tradition in the Congregation is that he made matters worse because of personal differences with Augier, including very divergent positions on French politics. It would seem that Augier was politically too progressive for Baffie and others. Baffie may also have feared a strong intervention by the Holy See and the appointment of an apostolic visitor.

Bishop William Miller, vicar apostolic and vicar of missions of Transvaal, during the 1906 chapter stated that as assistant general in 1904 he knew nothing of what was going on, that at that chapter he had spontaneously declined to be part of the new general administration. He requested that his statement be placed in the archives "for his honor as bishop."

Lavillardière, the newly elected superior general, then addressed the chapter, " '. . . It is necessary that our Holy Rules be vindicated . . . I request that the chapter attribute to the former superior general, who resigned, a *formal rebuke* (blâme). All who judge the former superior general guilty and worthy of rebuke, stand!' Solemnly the whole assembly got to its feet. What a moment!" In order to temper justice with mercy, he then told the chapter that Augier was doing expiation in silence, penance, and prayer. They agreed to send Augier an expression of compassion. The minutes continue, ". . . It seemed that after this act of justice the Congregation, according to the words of Most Reverend Father General, had washed its tarnished honor, and that the halo was returned to the post and the dignity of the head of the family" (ibid., pp. 81–82). It was decided to write the cardinal prefect of the Sacred Congregation of this statement of culpability, and that the Holy Father should be informed.

As far as could be ascertained the Holy See allowed the Oblates to handle the whole question as an internal problem without interference. During the whole time the Oblates were treated by the Holy See with great understanding and support.

Archbishop Dontenwill, who was elected superior general after Lavillardière's death in 1908, petitioned the Sacred Congregation to restore passive voice to Augier. This was done with the restriction that he could not be elected superior general, treasurer general, or procurator to the Holy See without the permission of the Holy See.

Augier spent his last years in Naples, and at the time of his death in 1927 had a reputation of sanctity. It seems that his fault was in trusting too much to the treasurer general, and in not bringing the financial problems to the attention of his council and the 1904 general chapter. It was a case of negligence, and the 1906 chapter recognized this (see "Registre," 1906, p. 82). The Oblate family tradition treats Augier very differently than his contemporaries did. The same can also be said for Baffie.

Until that time, the greatest expense of the general administration was the support of the scholasticates. In 1904 out of the 1915 members of the Congregation, 415 (priests, scholastics, and brothers) were assigned to the scholasticates, and were immediately subject to the superior general.[119] The provincials had to support the novices and the juniors. Each province and vicariate was taxed to support the scholasticates. Under the new system adopted in 1906 the practice of a tax on each priest to be paid to the general treasurer was maintained, and the superior general had to send a regular allowance to each scholasticate for the support of the students.[120]

To avoid the dangers entailed in making the scholasticates directly subject to the provincials, the Constitutions were to be changed to provide that the appointment of the staff members of scholasticates had to be approved by the superior general, and the practice of all first obediences being given by the superior general was maintained. A priest finishing his studies did not belong to a province or vicariate of missions until he was given such an assignment by the superior general.

The 1906 general chapter proposed a number of other changes in the Constitutions. Several resulted from the religious political situation in France— the elimination of the prescription requiring the superior general to live in France and his taking an oath to comply with this obligation, the right of the four senior local superiors of the province of the residence of the deceased superior general to be members of the chapter called to elect his successor.

The internal financial crisis was the occasion of several other modifications:

1—In the article referring to the superior general and his authority, the word *suprema* was substituted for *absoluta*;

2—A complete list of cases requiring the deliberative vote of the general council was drawn up;

3—The provision requiring the treasurer general to give a financial report to the general council every six months was changed to every month.[121]

---

[119] See *Personnel O.M.I.*, 1904, p. 109.

[120] The importance given to these decisions can be seen from the amount of space devoted to them in the superior general's report to the Congregation on the chapter (*Circulaires*, vol. 3, pp. 181–188, April 21, 1907). These decisions are incorporated in the present Constitutions and have been the constant practice in the Congregation. In addition it has always been the right of the superior general to transfer an Oblate from one province or vicariate to another, even after the first obedience. The *Constitutions 1982* state: "It pertains to the Superior General to give the first obedience and to transfer a member from one Province to another" (art. 117).

[121] See "Registre," 1906, pp. 143–147.

The number of Masses to be celebrated by the priests for the deceased members of the Congregation was also revised. This was necessary because the greatly increased membership in the Congregation had placed too heavy a burden of celebrating the great number of Masses previously prescribed.[122]

The Holy See was petitioned to approve all these changes plus some others proposed by the chapter. Tommaso Esser, a Dominican consultor of the Sacred Congregation of Bishops and Regulars, submitted a *votum* after a study of the whole Oblate file since the 1860s.[123] His recommendations were accepted by the commission of the Sacred Congregation.

> All the consultors agreed with the *votum* of Father Esser to reform the Constitutions and not only to approve the corrections proposed by the last general chapter, all the more so since the modifications contained in the decree of the Sacred Congregation in 1866 and 1869 until now have not been inserted in the Constitutions. In addition to that the Most Reverend Consultors find the words of the title of the Constitutions, which say that they were approved *in forma specifica* to be false, since the necessary formality for such an approbation is lacking.
>
> Rome, December 24, 1907.   D. Pietro Bastien, o.s.b., sect.[124]

The communication of this decision came as a great shock to the general council. How could they avoid a radical modification of the Constitutions that would give them a code of law almost completely different from the one they had received from de Mazenod and approved by Leo XII? As will be seen in the next chapter complete conformity to the *Normæ* would have entailed the elimination of the Preface and all the spiritual and scriptural texts, and would have left a cold manual of law with no heart.[125] This was the real danger, although the *Normæ* by their very title were to be followed for "novis institutis votorum simplicium" (for new insitutes with simple vows),[126] and not for institutes already approved.

The Constitutions so dear to de Mazenod and his sons would have been confined to the archives, and would no longer be a part of the life of the Congregation. Such was the practice of the Sacred Congregation of Bishops and Regulars at that time. The superior general and his council instructed the procurator general:

---

[122] See "Registre," 1904, pp. 83–84; "Registre," pp. 143–147.

[123] Tomasso ESSER, O.P., *votum*, May 20, 1907, M. 29, CICLSAL Archives.

[124] M. 29, CICLSAL Archives.

[125] Infra pp. 133–135.

[126] Supra p. 85, note 112.

. . . to obtain, as an exception, that the question not be considered by the commission of religious institutes, of which Father Esser was the consultor, and where his influence is very great. In addition this commission has the tendency to want to conform all the constitutions that fall into its hands with the *Normæ*, which it wrote.[127]

Joseph Lemius, the procurator to the Holy See, wrote to the commission, and explained that everything in the decrees of 1866 and 1869 had been communicated to the whole Congregation and put into practice, although they had not been inserted into the Constitutions. The same was true of the general decrees for all religious. He assured the president of the commission that all these things would be placed in the Constitutions. On behalf of the vicar general and the assistants he requested approval of the changes proposed by the 1906 chapter.[128]

When these changes were not approved, the Oblates requested the acceptance of the modifications concerning the residence of the superior general, the oath not to move the general house outside France, and the suppression of the privilege of the four senior superiors of the province in which the deceased superior general lived to attend the chapter to elect his successor. This was granted, and the obligation was imposed, "of reviewing the entire Constitutions of the Institute in the next general chapter and bringing them into conformity with the *Normæ* in so far as possible . . ."[129] It could be said that the battle was won. The changes would be made by the Oblates in general chapter, and not by someone in the Sacred Congregation, and conformity to the *Normæ* would have to be only *in so far as possible*.[130]

---

[127] "Procès verbaux," January 3, 1908, vol. 7, p. 287. Because of his poor health Lavillardière had appointed Baffie vicar general to govern the Congregation (*Circulaires*, September 23, 1907, no. 97, vol. 3, pp. 215–217). He died on January 28, 1908. In accordance with the Constitutions he had left a sealed letter dated November 30, 1907 naming Frédéric Favier, who was not a member of the general council, as vicar general in case of his death (see *Circulaires*, February 6, 1908, no. 101, vol. 3, pp. 224–225). The following September Archbishop Dontenwill of Vancouver was elected superior general.

[128] See "Procès verbaux," January 3, 1908, vol. 7, pp. 288–290, for copy of letter from Lemius to Vincenzo La Puma, of the Sacred Congregation of Bishops and Regulars.

[129] S.C. Bishops and Regulars, decree, January 24, 1908, Constitutions et Règles 1908 (3), Cong. Gen., in General Archives O.M.I.

[130] Joseph Lemius (1860–1923) is credited by the Oblates with saving their Constitutions. He was consultor of many congregations of the curia, and is the author of a portion of the encyclical *Pascendi*. His personal files on Modernism and the drafts for the encyclical are filed under his name in General Archives O.M.I. Cf. two letters found in *Bulletin de Littérature Ecclesiastique*, (Toulouse) 9 (1946), pp. 242–243.

At his first audience after his election as superior general with Pius X, Dontenwill expressed to the pope his fears and misgivings about his new charge. Pius X replied: "Have confidence in God,

Esser had objected,[131] and was sustained in his objection by the other consultors,[132] to the title page of the Constitutions, which read:

A LEONE PAPA XII
UNA CUM INSTITUTO
IN FORMA SPECIFICA APPROBATÆ
A GREGORIO XVI CONFIRMATÆ
ET JUXTA PII IX APOSTOLICAS LITTERAS EDITÆ.[133]

In his *votum* he referred to the notes of Svegliati and the audience of August 14, 1863, which stated:

> 20. The Oblates are persuaded that the Constitutions of the Institute were approved by the Holy See *in forma specifica*, as is printed on the title page; and afterward (p. 96) grant the general chapter the authority to give general and perpetual dispensations, and to the superior general (p. 104) the faculty to give general dispensations for a time, and then in particular cases.—The truth is that the Constitutions were not inserted in the brief of Leo XII, and cannot be said to be confirmed *in forma specifica*, even though the same brief states *We command them to be carefully observed*. This could be revised by declaring that the general could give permissions (licenze) in particular cases for a reasonable cause.   Approved.[134]

As was stated above the Oblates were not informed of that audience and of the decision given until January 1866. Although the decree issued at that time in number 17 restricted the authority to dispense, and to change the Constitutions without express approval, no mention was made that the Holy See did not consider the Constitutions to be approved *in forma specifica*. Pius IX had been asked to make a decision on the case without the Oblates being told that there was a problem, and they were not informed of the decision until 1908, almost forty-five years later. To say the least, communications were a bit slow. It seems that no protest concerning the decision was made at that late date. The main concern then was to keep the commission for religious

---

and keep in mind that you have at your side a firm support in the person of Father Lemius. He is a man of great knowledge, extensive experience, and can take anything" (*Circulaires*, October 28, 1923, no. 131, vol. 4, pp. 12–13).

Lemius had two brothers who were also Oblate priests. Jean-Baptiste (1851–1938) was an outstanding preacher, superior of the Basilica of the Sacred Heart, Montmartre in Paris and provincial of Nord; and François (1848–1933) was the saint of the family.

[131] Tommaso ESSER, O.P., *votum*, May 20, 1907, M. 29 CICLSAL Archives.

[132] Minutes of meeting of December 24, 1907, M. 29 CICLSAL Archives.

[133] *Constitutiones 1894.*

[134] "Ex audientia die 14 Augusti 1863," M. 29, CICLSAL Archives.

Cf. Francisco Javier URRUTIA, S.J., "Quando habeatur approbatio «*in forma specifica*»," in *Periodica*, 80 (1991), pp. 3–17.

institutes from itself revising the Constitutions. In any case by then, the question had become more historical than actual, because of the changes that had already been made and were to be made in the Constitutions.[135]

After Lavillardière's death at the end of January 1908, the general administration began immediately to prepare for a general chapter and the modification of the Constitutions. The 1908 general chapter worked seriously to implement the orders of the Sacred Congregation, and afterwards a post-capitular commission completed the work, which was presented to the Holy See for approval.

The revised Constitutions stated very clearly that since the members had only simple vows, "the jurisdiction of the ordinaries remains in conformity to the sacred canons and apostolic constitutions."[136] In addition to the changes required by the Sacred Congregation, sections were added on the scholasticates and the foreign missions.[137] Much of the material on the foreign missions was taken almost verbatim from the 1853 *Instructio*.[138]

The 1904 decision to place the scholasticates directly under the provincials was incorporated into the Constitutions (art. 787). At the same time the scholasticates were committed to the care and the vigilance of the superior general (art. 788), and the scholasticate superiors were bound to give an account of each scholastic every month to the provincial or vicar of missions and every three months to the superior general (art. 793). The superior general was to give the first obedience at the completion of the studies (art. 794).

---

[135] It seems that Svegliati had based his argument uniquely on the fact that the Constitutions were not included in Leo XII's Brief. For a contrary opinion see Paul-Henri LAFONTAINE, O.M.I., "Nature de l'approbation de nos Règles," in *Études Oblates*, 6 (1947), pp. 91–116. Cosentino accepts without hesitation the position of Svegliati and Esser (*Histoire*, vol. 2, pp. 125–151).

[136] *Constitutiones 1910*, art. 9. In compliance with the *Normæ* the paragraphs are given for the first time consecutive arabic numbers. Without doubt this was a great improvement.

[137] Cf. COSENTINO, *Histoire*, vol. 5, pp. 21–47. Both the 1906 and the 1908 general chapters worked on the chapter on scholsticates.

[138] Cf. "Statutum auctoritate Summi Pontificis a Sacra Congregatione de Propaganda Fide ad septennium approbatum pro missionibus Congregationi Oblatorum B.M.V. Immaculatæ concreditis," June 1, 1912 (printed separately, not in Missions, O.M.I.); "Statutum auctoritate Summi Pontificis a S. Congregatione de Propaganda Fide definitive approbatum pro missionibus Missionariorum Oblatorum B. Mariæ Virginis Immaculatæ concessis," January 30, 1934, in *Missions O.M.I.*, 82 (1955) pp. 434–486, with French and English translations.

Cf. Xaverius PAVENTI, "De statutis pro missionibus," in *Commentarium pro religiosis*, 26 (1947), pp.289–297; particular conventions for some of the mission territories confided to the Oblates are on p. 293.

Although the foreign missions had been very much a part of the life of the Congregation since 1841, they had never been treated explicitly in the Constitutions. Various general chapters had spoken of this, and the 1894 chapter had written: "By law, the superiors can send to the foreign missions a member who has not requested to go, and he is required to obey."[139] Even the 1908 general chapter did not add a section on the foreign missions to the Constitutions. It was the post-capitular commission that took on its own to do something about this lacuna.

> 39. Missions to the heathen and non-Catholics are included among the pious ministries of our Society. Consequently, the vow and the virtue of obedience also extend to these missions and all the good works to be carried out therein.[140]

The 1920 general chapter expressed its appreciation for the addition of this section to the Constitutions: ". . . our missionaries can say to themselves that there is no shadow on this truth, which is as old as their missions, namely they are completely in the life of the Congregation."[141]

The Sacred Congregation of Religious issued a decree on December 21, 1909 approving the revised Constitutions.[142] This approbation was confirmed by Pius X with the brief *Decessorum nostrorum vestigiis*.[143]

The 1917 Code of Canon Law and Revision

With the promulgation of the Code of Canon Law in 1917, all religious institutes had to conform their particular law to the universal law of the Church. Because of the immensity of the task, it was impossible for the 1920 general chapter to undertake a complete revision of the Constitutions. A special commission was appointed to prepare the work for the 1926 chapter, which was to work almost exclusively on the revision of the Constitutions. Dontenwill wrote to the Congregation to explain not only what had been done,

---

[139] *Circulaires*, March 26, 1894, no. 57, vol. 2, pp. 185. The 1887 general chapter, after discussing whether or not the vow of obedience included the foreign missions declared: "Since our vow of obedience is absolute, the superior general can assign the individual members of the Congregation and send them anywhere" ("Registre," 1887, p. 299).

[140] *Constitutiones 1910*.

[141] *Circulaires*, April 13, 1921, no. 128, vol. 3, pp. 369–370.

[142] See Constitutions et Règles 1908 (3), Con. Gen., General Archives O.M.I.

[143] PIUS X, apostolic letter, *Decessorum nostrorum vestigiis*, September 7, 1910; original in Constitutions et Règles 1908 (3), Con. Gen., General Archives, O.M.I.; copies in *AAS*, 2 (1910), pp. 901–903; *Constitutiones 1910*, pp. v–viii.

but how it was done. Faithfulness to de Mazenod was paramount in the minds of the capitulants.[144]

Two things should be pointed out in the first chapter of the revised Constitutions. In the first article the phrase "*secular* priests, living together as brothers in community, bound by the vows of religion"[145] became "priests, living together as brothers in community, bound by the vows of religion."[146] This reflected the Code which recognized the members of congregations with simple vows as religious, and they were no longer called seculars.[147] The other change was the moving of the first article on the brothers from the place it had occupied since the 1820s to the first chapter. It would seem that the capitulants attached no special importance for the position of the brothers in the Congregation in this change. In his letter to the Congregation, Dontenwill said very simply that this was done to be in conformity with other constitutions recently approved by the Holy See.[148]

Scholastics were no longer given a consultative vote at local chapters to choose the delegate to a provincial or vicarial chapter to elect a delegate to the general chapter. Nor is any mention of them being present at the meeting of the chapter as had been the case.[149]

In his circular letter presenting the revised Constitutions to the Congregation Dontenwill wrote:

> Finally the 1920 chapter had decided during its twentieth session to take advantage of the obligatory revisions of the holy Rule to ask the Holy See to approve an article expressly permitting the acceptance of educational institutions (*Circulaires*, vol. 3, pp. 380–381). The present article 133 was written to implement that decree. Henceforth, there can be no doubt: we can accept schools of every level, whether they be of secondary or higher education. It is true, however, that education is but a secondary end of our Institute.[150]

---

[144] *Circulaires*, July 16, 1928, no. 140, vol. 4, p. 113.

[145] *Constitutiones 1910*, art. 1.

[146] *Constitutiones 1928*, art. 1.

[147] See *CIC¹*, c. 488, 1°, 7°.

[148] *Circulaires*, July 16, 1928, no. 140, vol. 4, pp. 116–117. In the notes in the General Archives O.M.I. of the file of the preparatory work for the revision it is mentioned that the first chapter should contain both categories of Oblates. The documentary evidence gives no special importance to this change.

[149] See *Constitutiones 1928*, art. 565.

[150] *Circulaires*, July 16, 1928, no. 140, vol. 4, pp. 118–119.

This paragraph alludes to the long controversy in the Congregation concerning whether or not the operation of secondary schools and universities was within the purpose of the institute. Acting on a motion of Louis Soullier, the 1867 general chapter unanimously approved having secondary schools.[151] The 1898 chapter further declared that such schools "are not opposed to the ends of the Institute, on the contrary they are completely conformed to them."[152] Still opposition to schools continued. In addition to the financial crisis that was the main issue of the 1906 chapter, this question again came to the center of the stage.

The unspoken bone of contention was the growing University of Ottawa. It had been founded by the Oblates in 1848 upon the request of Eugene Guigues, an Oblate and the first bishop of the diocese. By a contract between de Mazenod and Guigues the institution was given permanently to the Congregation in 1856.[153] In 1906 the main opponent was Baffie, and he was supported by Lemius. The principal proponent was Dontenwill, bishop of New Westminster and vicar of missions of British Columbia. The result was a victory for Baffie with the amendment of the previously mentioned chapter to read,

---

[151] "Registre," vol. 2, pp. 78–80. Louis Soullier (1826–1897) was assistant general from 1867 until he was elected third superior general in 1893. He died less than five years later. Because of Fabre's poor health, Soullier spent a great part of his time as assistant general visiting the foreign missions.

[152] *Acta Capitulorum Generalium Congregations O.M.I. 1899*, no. 2.

[153] See Donat LEVASSEUR, *History*, vol. 1, pp. 137–138.

"The College of Bytown" was founded on September 26, 1848, by Bishop Joseph-Eugène Guigues, O.M.I., who in 1856 entrusted the College to the Missionary Oblates of Mary Immaculate. In 1861 the College of Bytown was renamed "College of Ottawa" and in August 1866 was granted university status by the Government of the United Canada. With the apostolic letter *Cum apostolica sedes* Leo XIII granted on February 5, 1889 the university its pontifical charter.

In the years following World War II, the University progressed rapidly and by 1965 had established nine faculties and four schools. On July 1 of that year, through an act of the Ontario Provincial Legislature, the institution heretofore designated as the University of Ottawa became Saint Paul University, nonetheless keeping its civil and canonical charters. At the same time the Ontario provincial government formed a new institution to be known as the University of Ottawa to which Saint Paul University conceded the majority of its holdings. The two universities became a federated complex and according to mutual agreement were to share existing schools and faculties.

Under the terms of the present contract, Saint Paul University agrees to extend its teaching only to the faculties of theology and canon law and related institutes. In addition to conferring its own degrees, Saint Paul University reserves the right to present its candidates to the senate of the University of Ottawa for joint conferment (Saint Paul University–University of Ottawa) of its certificates, diplomas, and civil degrees.

"on the contrary, they are completely conformed to them, *within the limits defined in the Instruction of our Founder on the Foreign Missions.*"[154]

With the passage of time England, Ireland, and parts of North America were no longer considered to be foreign missions. However, the chapter decision was not put into practice. Baffie, still assistant general, died a few months prior to the 1920 chapter. This was the first general chapter to meet after Dontenwill's election as superior general. The new article added to the 1928 Constitutions states merely that such schools must be for the *good of souls*.[155]

Although the 1928 Constitutions maintained the recitation of divine office in common as a work of the Congregation, a new article recognized the custom existing since the beginning of the institute of permitting the superior to dispense the whole community from the choral recitation. In fact, a greater part of the priests could not say office in common because they lived in very small communities or alone in the foreign missions, or because of their active ministry. In practice, pastoral ministry had always taken precedence over the common recitation of office.[156] For communities where it was impossible to recite office in common, the provincial with his council was to determine to what extent the prescriptions of the Constitutions were to be observed.[157]

---

[154] *Circulaires* April 21, 1907, no. 92, vol. 3, pp. 167–181, (emphasis added). The importance attributed to this question can be seen from the treatment, both in length and in detail, given by the superior general in his report on the chapter to the Congregation.

[155] *Constitutiones 1928*, "Whenever the good of souls may seem to require it, and this may more easily happen in missionary countries, the Provincial and his Council, acting with the approval of the Superior General and his Council, may build or take charge of minor seminaries or colleges. And in such institutions the members of our society will earnestly endeavor to give the young an education that is not only Christian, but literary and scientific as well" (art. 133).

[156] See the report from a special committee in the German province, "Concerning 'the canonical hours in choir' *there is a great discrepancy between theory and practice*, which creates not a slight difficulty for the novice masters who must explain the Constitutions. Those who know best the state of the whole Congregation assert that two-thirds of the priests simply cannot observe this law. To these must be added the priests and the scholastics in houses of studies, including the juniorates, who in our province, e.g., are a third of the priests, and more than half of those in the whole province bound to choir.—In addition those who work in preaching missions are more than half of the year away from their house. Having returned home they are tired, and it would be hard for them to say the whole office every day while resting and preparing for new missions. ... Wherefore, all the members of our committee, save one, agree that it is to be strongly advised to reduce the obligation to choir *in order that the practice can be what the Constitutions prescribe*" (Constitutions et Règles 1926 (8), Cong. Gen. Allemagne (a) (b) 22, General Archives O.M.I.).

[157] See *Constitutiones 1928*, art. 147.

The Sacred Congregation of Religious issued a decree approving the revised Constitutions on July 2, 1927.[158] Dontenwill requested an apostolic letter, and the brief *Mirabili plane modo* was issued on May 21, 1928 approving the Constitutions *in forma specifica*.[159]

Beginning a Thirty Year Process

In 1907 Tomasso Esser, consultor of the Sacred Congregation of Bishops and Regulars, after reviewing the proposed changes in the Oblate Constitutions complained: "So, today we find ourselves facing the sixth revision, and really it will not be the last."[160] Was he a prophet, or was he especially perceptive in sensing that the Oblates seem to take a particular delight—in spite of protests to the contrary—in reworking their Constitutions? Little did the members of the 1953 general chapter realize that they were starting a thirty year process of writing and rewriting their Constitutions when they

> requested Most Reverend Father General and his council to constitute a committee which, after having consulted the provinces and mission vicariates, is to prepare the new edition [of the Constitutions]. The work is to be completed at least six months before the assembling of the next chapter.[161]

The 1959 general chapter began on September 1, and after six weeks of work on the revision of the Constitutions reached the decision on October 15

---

[158] General Archives O.M.I.

[159] Pius XI, apostolic letter, *Mirabili plane modo*, May 21, 1928, original in General Archives O.M.I.; *AAS*, 20 (1928), pp. 341–344; *Constitutiones 1928*, pp. 7–12, 183–185. In addition to including the Constitutions in the text of the brief, the apostolic letter states: "We, of Our own volition, certain knowledge and mature deliberation, and in the plenitude of Our Apostolic Authority, by the text of the present Letter . . . give our fullest approbation to the Missionary Oblates . . ." Dontenwill explained to the Congregation his surprise at the favor granted by Pius XI (*Circulaires*, vol. 4, p. 138, July 16, 1928).

The 1947 general chapter increased the number of assistants general from four to six (see *Circulaires*, November 1, 1947, no. 181, vol. 5, pp. 179–181; Eng. ed., pp. 50–52), and instituted the position of a special secretary for studies to assist the superior general (ibid., p. 191; Eng. ed., pp. 61–62).

[160] M. 29, CICLSAL Archives.

[161] *Circulaires*, December 8, 1953, no. 203, vol. 6, p. 111. During the 1930s for the first time some of the circulars of the superior general were published in languages other than French. With the election of Leo Deschâtelets (1899–1974), superior general (1947–1972), the circulars were published in both French and English. De Mazenod's decision to send his missionaries to the British Empire and the United States had had its effect on the languages used in his Congregation.

Dontenwill died in 1932, and was succeeded by Theodore Labouré (1883–1944), who died during World War II. Because of the war the general chapter to elect his successor did not meet until 1947. During his term there was no special juridical development. There was continued growth in personnel that was temporarily interrupted by the war.

to conclude immediately its work on the Constitutions and confide the completion of the task to a post-capitular commission. There was also agreement that the impending ecumenical council could make any work done at that time outdated.

The commission was given complete freedom in its method of work. When a new text was complete, it was to be sent to the provincials and vicars of missions for study in whatever way they judged best. After the latters' suggestions were received and the proposed text revised, it was to be sent to the provincials and vicars of missions in preparation for the next general chapter and eventual approval. In spite of the frustration of not having completed the task they had set for themselves, the members of the chapter felt that they had accomplished much by working together.[162]

The post-capitular commission was duly appointed and did its task as prescribed. The result was known as the *Textus Revisus*.[163] After the frustrating experience of 1959 of working hard for six weeks and not completing the revision of the Constitutions, many of the capitulants were determined that they would during the 1966 general chapter finish the work of revising the Constitutions. They felt that it was not good for the Congregation to continue without an agreed upon and accepted text.

The 1966 Constitutions *Ad Experimentum*

The chapter opened on January 25, 1966, the one hundred-fiftieth anniversary of the foundation of the institute. The *Textus Revisus* was presented by the president of the commission. It consisted of two complementary codes— Constitutions and capitulars rules. The text had been previously sent to the entire Congregation through its publication in *Missions des Oblats de Marie Immaculée*.[164] Although a few last minute changes had been made to bring the text into conformity with the Vatican II documents, the whole Congregation had had the opportunity to study the text. It was basically an updated version of de Mazenod's text.

On January 25 the following motion was made:

---

[162] *Circulaires*, November 22, 1959, no. 210, vol. 6, pp. 1–19. N.B. the page numbers are those of this circular, no. 210, and not those of the volume which are lacking for this particular letter.

[163] The complete title was *Textus Constitutionum Congregationis Missionariorum Oblatorum Sanctissimæ et Immaculatæ Virginis Mariæ a Commissione Post-Capitulari de Mandato Capituli Generalis Anno 1959 Celebrati a Rev.mo Patre Generali Instituta Revisus et Emendatus Capituli Generalis Proxime Venturi Approbationi Subiiciendus.*

[164] *Missions O.M.I.*, 92 (1965), pp. 335–534. A later version—revised to conform to the Vatican II documents—was presented to the capitulants for their work during the chapter.

That the *Textus Revisus*, presented by Father Fortin in the name of the post-capitular commission for the revision of the Rule be accepted as basis for the work of this chapter.[165]

To this motion the following two amendments were made and accepted by the chapter:

It being understood that the chapter does not in any fashion limit itself to the *textus revisus* either as far as content or as far as form.[166]

And on condition that each commission may use all the reports, commentaries, and proposals that have been sent concerning the textus revisus.[167]

In an address given later year Paul-Emile Pelletier, the author of the two amendments to the original motion, presented the situation as he saw it:

One remembers the last 25 January, when our General Chapter for renovation and adaptation opened, the last documents of the Council had been promulgated less than a month before.

On the other side, we were living in a sort of state of emergency. The 1959 Chapter had not succeeded in carrying out the revision decided in 1953. It was imperative that results be achieved.

"For twelve years," asserted our Father General, "the Congregation had been considering a revision of its Rules. This period of apparent incertitude, hesitation, suspense must end; it is prejudicial to the Institute and to the maintenance of its spirit." (Cir. 222, p. 8)

By scrutinizing the signs of the time, by the light of God's plan for mankind, the Church has felt the need to reflect on itself, to redefine itself, then to renew itself to begin the dialogue of salvation with the world of today.

In turn, the General Chapter had to undertake the same steps to answer the expectations of the Church, of the entire Congregation and of the world.

. . . the turn has taken the right direction.[168]

---

[165] "Registre," 1966, p. 70.

[166] "Registre," 1966, pp. 70–71.

[167] Ibid. The vote on the amended motion was: 97 affirmative, 3 negative.

The general administration did not take a stand supporting the *Textus revisus*. Without a doubt this weakened the support for the text. Was there a division among the members of the general council?

[168] Paul-Émile, PELLETIER, O.M.I., "The Church in the World of Today and our New Constitutions," in *Études Oblates*, 26 (1967), pp. 254–255. The enthusiasm portrayed in this article is representative of the naively optimistic attitude of many persons during and immediately after Vatican II.

By and large the most vocal French speaking Oblates—with notable exceptions—were for the rejection of the *textus revisus*; the opposite was the situation among most English speaking Oblates.

The capitulants were divided into committees and diligently began their task. After some two weeks the first reports of the committees were distributed and came to the floor. February 18 was a memorable day in the chapter. It was then that the question was raised as to the meaning of the motion accepted and adopted to guide the members in preparing the texts for the Constitutions. It seems that it was only then that some of the capitulants, including the one who had introduced the original motion, realized what had happened.

Although there was considerable opposition to the amendments, they had been adopted, and the amended motion was approved by the overwhelming majority of the chapter. This amended motion had for all practical purposes not approved the *Textus Revisus*, but had rejected it.[169] As the evolution of the chapter would soon show, the amended motion had in fact done what Tomasso Esser and the commission of religious institutes of the Sacred Congregation of Bishops and Regulars had failed to do in 1907—it had sent de Mazenod's Constitutions to the archives. With the exception of the Preface, there would be a completely new text as far as form and style were concerned. The language familiar to generations of Oblates since their novitiate had been discarded.

The turn of events would not have been a surprise to anyone who had read the documents sent to Rome, and were available to the capitulants. St. Joseph's Province, by far the largest in the Congregation, had made a thorough study of the *Textus Revisus*, and all the members of the province had been involved in the process. A 113 page summary of their work was published, and in the general conclusion is found:

> We are led to the following conclusion by the aggregate of depositions received: even if it is a step forward, and a big step in the right direction, the *Textus Revisus* of the Constitutions does not respond to the expectations of the members of the province. The matter is there in substance, but it lacks unity of inspiration, internal dynamism, and conciseness. There is a constant feeling of tension between the old and the new, which creates an impression of disparity and artificiality.

> Is it opportune to discuss this text at the next general chapter? The members of the committee do not think so; the *Textus Revisus* is not sufficiently perfected . . .

> The present committee would hope for a new text of Constitutions which would fully be in the orientation of the Council. It desires that the

---

Most of them were prepared to accept the *Textus Revisus* with appropriate amendments by the chapter.

[169] "Registre," 1966, pp. 132–133.

fundamental realities of Oblate life be clearly asserted, but also that they be in a style and a spirit that truly respond to the expectations of today's world.[170]

After the chapter, Deschâtelets wrote the Congregation to introduce the Constitutions:

> Everyone was agreed in conserving intact the present Preface of our Constitutions and Rules, drawn up by the Founder himself, and indicating in substance the spirit of the Institute and its basic principles, which still retain their relevance in face of the needs of the Church and of the contemporary world.[171]
>
> This Preface, inherited from Bishop de Mazenod, is a kind of birth certificate for the Institute, which it defines in the Church.
>
> In fiery terms, it portrays the Oblate, first and foremost as an apostolic man meant to alleviate, according to his modest means the distress of the Church, beloved Spouse of Christ, Savior of the world.
>
> . . . The formula is strikingly broad: *pledging themselves to all the works of zeal which priestly charity can inspire—above all the work of the missions . . . These men he sent forth . . . to conquer the world, which was to bow to his holy rule.*
>
> . . . The Constitutions and Rules simply add detailed precisions to the basic points outline in the Preface.[172]

There was not a list of the various works of the Congregation, but an insistence on its missionary character to preach the Gospel to the poor. The divine office was considered under liturgical life and as community prayer, and there is no mention of it being a work of the Congregation.[173] Although the common recitation of office was recommended, it was not prescribed.

The modifications in government that should be noted are: the superior general was to be elected for a twelve year term and not for life, and could be reelected once for a six year term (C. 132); the assistants general could be reelected for a second term only (C. 141); several changes in general chapter membership, including greater representation for larger provinces, elimination of the superior general's right to call four capitulants with deliberative vote, but granting him the right to call an unlimited number with consultative vote only (CC. 124–125); elimination of local and provincial chapters for choosing delegates to the general chapter, and substituting direct voting for delegates

---

[170] *Études de la Province Saint-Joseph sur le projet de revision des Constitutions et des Regulæ Capitulares paru dans les "Missions", Nos 317 et 317bis,* Montréal, Maison Provinciale, 1965, pp. 92–93. How many of the English speaking members of the genaral chapter had read this document?

[171] *Circulaires,* March 25, 1966, no. 226, vol. 7, p. 346.

[172] *Circulaires,* April 12, 1966, no. 227, vol. 7, pp. 354–355.

[173] See *Constitutiones 1966,* CC.. 50–51, pp, 18–19, and R. 109, p. 85.

(C. 126); granting the brothers in perpetual vows the right to vote (C. 126); requiring the consultation of members before the appointment of superiors and provincials (CC. 174 and 202); elimination of the term *vicariate of missions*, and the official introduction of the term *vice-province* (C. 166).

Other changes in government were: the establishment of a number of permanent secretariates, general conferences of specialists, various regional conferences, including regional conferences of provincials (CC. 158–160, 193–199); the establishment of an extraordinary general council that was to meet annually (CC. 154–157), extraordinary provincial councils and provincial congresses (CC. 187–192); the participation of the local community in discussing ministry, common life, and temporal affairs (CC. 210); and a whole change in the style of canonical visitations (CC. 161–165 and 173). Decentralization can be seen in the greater authority of provincials to make decisions without recourse to the superior general for confirmation or approval.

In his circular letter, Deschâtelets outlined the spirit that guided the drafting of the Constitutions:

> It constantly looked for the Founder's mind which in substance, remains amazingly apposite and in striking harmony with the directives of the IInd Vatican Council.
>
> The mind of the Founder, as enriched by the living tradition of the Institute, was the Chapter's main concern, updating it as to language, and pastoral orientation and liberating it from elements now superseded which had their *raison d'être* in the theology and circumstances of their time, but which now demand adaptation and renovation . . .
>
> This schema (End and Works of the Congregation) seeks to visualize the Congregation as an answer to the urgent call of God and of the Church and to describe its characteristic as a clerical Institute. Even though some of its members are not priests, all have the same religious and missionary obligations as cooperators with Christ, the Savior in the work of evangelization, and dedicate themselves primarily to the poor and the abandoned.[174]

These ideas were expressed especially in the first article of the Constitutions, which by tradition and practice usually contains the essential elements of a religious institute.

> 1—Our Lord Jesus Christ in the fullness of time called his disciples to follow Him and to share in His mission both by word and by work.
>
> In the Church the same Lord continually calls men to follow him. The Congregation of Missionary Oblates of the Most Holy and Immaculate Virgin Mary seeks in its own way to respond to this call. For this reason, priests in union with brothers, bound by religious vows and living together as

---

[174] *Circulaires*, April 12, 1966, no. 227, vol. 7, pp. 356–357.

brothers, closely cooperating with one another in Christ the Savior, devote themselves principally to the preaching the Gospel to the poor.[175]

After a post-capitular commission had completed its work of perfecting the Latin text, the Holy See was requested to give its approbation to use the text *ad experimentum*. The petition explained the process used, and the presentation of the *Textus Revisus* to the whole Congregation, and the incorporation of the latest changes because of *Perfectæ caritatis*.[176] The principal changes in the Constitutions approved by the chapter were outlined in the petition, but no mention was made of the fact that the final text bore little resemblance in form and language to the previous Constitutions or the *Textus Revisus*. The letter indicated that there was no essential change made in the Congregation, "Structura tamen Congregationis funditus immutata remanet."[177]

Cardinal Antoniuitti, prefect of the Sacred Congregation of Religious, gave the superior general permission to introduce the new Constitutions on a trial basis, "experimenti gratia in praxim."[178] Deschâtelets in his letter to the Congregation pointed out that, although there was not an approval of the text by the Holy See, permission had been granted to use it until the next chapter.[179]

While maintaining the essentials of the Oblate heritage, the new text incorporated not only the ideas of the Council, but it did so in language very similar to that of the Vatican II documents, often using the same words. De Mazenod's ideas and inspirations were present, but in a very different lan-

---

[175] *Constitutiones 1966*, art. 1. An informal consultation was made at the Sacred Congregation concerning the revision of the Constitutions, and the question was raised in reference to the mentioning of the brothers in the first article, and the clerical nature of the Congregation. The answer was given that this was not a problem, since it was clear from the part on government that the Congregation was clerical.

[176] Vatican II, decree on the renewal of religious life, *Perfecæ caritatis*, October 25, 1965.

[177] O'REILLY, to Holy Father, July 9, 1966, copy of original in Procurator's Archives O.M.I.; published in *Circulaires*, September 8, 1966, no. 233, vol. 7, pp. 426–428.

[178] ANTONIUTTI, prefect of SCRIS, to Deschâtelets, July 29, 1966, in Procurator's Archives O.M.I.; published in *Circulaires*, September 8, 1966, no. 233, vol. 7, p. 429.

[179] *Circulaires*, September 8, 1966, no. 233, vol. 7, p. 430.
The superior general requested and received special approval for some specific changes in the Constitutions, for which specific approval was required.
In response to a petition concerning some difficulties in applying the 1966 Constitutions *ad experimentum*, Antoniutti in his answer added that the response of July 29, 1966 was not an approval of the Constitutions, but permission to use them. In the same letter he granted the superior general with his council the faculty "ad instar dispositionis in the *motu proprio Ecclesiæ Sanctæ*, sub n. 7 partis secundæ" for solving difficulties (ANTONIUTTI, to Deschâtelets, February 27, 1967, in Procurator's Archives O.M.I.).

guage, and in a mode resembling the public face of the Church, and not the familiar expressions that many of his sons treasured. Some felt much the same as if they had been given a page of a papal encyclical on prayer in the place of the Our Father.

It would seem that there were two very different concepts of what the Constitutions should be. The chapter wrote a more abstract theological document. Those unhappy with it preferred a familiar book that touched the heart rather than primarily the intellect. The 1966 Constitutions *ad experimentum* are clearly a product of Vatican II. They came as a real shock to a number of Oblates, who were expecting a text based on the *Textus Revisus*, which seemingly had broad support in the Congregation. Fortin, the chairman of the commission that prepared the *Textus Revisus*, had reported that twenty-six provinces were favorable to the text, five or six opposed, and the others favorable *iuxta modum*.[180]

A concerted effort was made to gain acceptance of the 1966 Constitutions within the Congregation. Could one say that the troubled times, as much as the text, stood in the way of their whole hearted acceptance? The upheaval following the Council had shaken loose many roots, and a radical alteration in the Constitutions came in its wake.

Prior to the 1972 general chapter a survey was made among the members of the Congregation. Three thousand eight hundred and forty-three Oblates answered, i.e., 54.9% of the Congregation responded.[181] To the question, "Have you familiarized yourself with the text of the Constitutions and Rules *ad experimentum*?" The answers were:[182]

by a reflective reading and study of the text	29.60%
by a simple informative reading of the text	57.10%
I have not read the text	10.25%
no clear answer	.65%
no answer	2.40%

---

[180] See "Registre," 1966, p. 72. This was reported to the Congregation in the special newsletter for the chapter (*Bulletin de Nouvelles*, no. 1, p. 4).

Cf. J.-B. GUTHANS, O.M.I., "Quelques réflexions sur les 'Constitutions et Règles nouvelles,'" in *Études Oblates*, 28 (1969), pp. 201–218. He points out that not one of the 215 articles in the Constitutions kept de Mazenod's words (p. 203), and that the Congregation had not been consulted on the text adopted. He stated that this was contrary to the *motu proprio Ecclesiæ Sanctæ*, of August 6, 1966, which demanded a two or three year consultation before revision (pp. 204–205). The chapter finished its work on March 23, 1966. There had been a consultation on the *Textus Revisus*, but not on the text adopted.

[181] *Sociological Survey for the 1972 Chapter*, p. 35.

[182] Ibid., pp. 89–90.

Nearly one-third had read and carefully meditated upon the new text. Over one-half had been content with a simple informative reading, and one out of ten had not even read the text. What about the 45% of the Congregation that did not answer the questionnaire?

A further question revealed that approximately one out of four Oblates would accept the text as it was, and that half of the Oblates would accept it with modifications. Twenty percent said that they would prefer a completely new draft or a return to the 1928 text.[183]

This data indicates that there was far from universal acceptance. At the same time a number of persons, who expressed misgivings about the 1966 Constitutions, lived under a cloud. Although the text was only *ad experimentum*, it was not to be criticized. Because the general chapter had spoken, it was not permitted to have a different opinion.[184] Thus, the 1966 Constitutions were a divisive and not an unitive element in the life of the Congregation.

---

[183] See ibid., pp. 89–90.

A number of individuals who welcomed the 1966 Constitutions *ad experimentum* wrote and published studies and papers to show the values of the text to meet the needs of the Congregation and its mission in the modern world. Cf. G. DE BRETAGNE, O.M.I., "Impressions d'ensemble d'un professeur de Pastorale sur nos nouvelles Constitutions," in *Études Oblates*, 26 (1967), pp. 310–342; Maurice GILBERT, O.M.I., *Oblate Life, Some Reflections on the New Constitutions*, Ottawa, 1967, originally published as "Réflexions sur la vie oblate à la lumière des nouvelles Constitutions," in *Études Oblates*, 25 (1966), p. 273–353; P.-E. PELLETIER, O.M.I., "The Church in the World of Today and our New Constitutions," in *Études Oblates*, 26 (1967), pp. 254–272; *The Congregation Renewed*, Rome, The General House, 1968; F. TRUSSO, O.M.I., *Corso di Exercizi Spirituali sulla nuova Regola*, Marigliano, Piccola Opera della Redenzione, 1977.

On the other hand some Oblates, who were displeased with the 1966 Constitutions, composed and published a revised text, which they proposed for consideration, in which they incorporated into the traditional text from de Mazenod the principles of Vatican II. They entitled it *Constitutiones et Regulæ Congregationis Missionariorum Oblatorum Sanctissimæ et Immaculatæ Virginis Mariæ. Textus renovatus et accomdatus iuxta sacrosancti Concilii Vaticani Secundi prasecripta* (Rome, 1971). The collaborators working principally at Notre-Dame de Lumières included some of the more illustrious Oblates. Insofar as I can ascertain among the collaborators were: Agostino Argentieri, Ive Guéguen, Joseph Reslé, Amand Reuter, Edmund Servel. Few gave this text serious consideration—it was the work of old men out of touch with the modern world and Vatican II!

[184] This was told to me by Jean Drouart, O.M.I., superior of the international scholasticate (1947–1953), first assistant general (1953–1966), and subsequently itinerant spiritual animator of the Congregation until his death in 1989; and Amand Reuter, O.M.I., distinguished canonist, *peritus* for the theological commission of Vatican II, consultor of several Roman Congregation, and member of General House community until shortly before his death in 1992.

The 1972 and 1974 General Chapters

With the convocation of the XXVIII General Chapter Deschâtelets announced to the Congregation that during the chapter he would resign as superior general.[185] The chapter opened on April 11, 1972. With 140 capitulants it was the largest chapter in the history of the Congregation. In addition to the 120, who were present either as ex officio members or as duly elected delegates, the superior general in conformity with the 1966 Constitutions *ad experimentum* had invited twenty additional capitulants with consultative voice. These were to represent groups supposedly not otherwise represented—delegations, the young, and the brothers.

There was tension in the air from the very beginning of the chapter. Many factors were responsible—suspicion and mistrust because of the 1966 experience, the large number of capitulants making it difficult to operate, the discontent of many of the invited members. The Chapter granted the right to deliberative vote to the invited brothers, but denied it to the other invited capitulants. Although the latter came to the chapter knowing that according to the Constitutions they did not have the right to vote, some them were most piqued that they did not have an active voice. In addition to all these factors the Church and the Congregation were still in the post-council period of unrest and nervousness.[186]

In January 1967, right after the previous chapter, the Congregation was at its peak in membership after 150 years of existence. There were at that time 7540 Oblates—31 bishops, 5267 priests, 975 scholastics, and 1267 brothers. By January 1972 the total number of Oblates had decreased by 530 to 7010—36 bishops, 5250 priests, 581 scholastics, and 1143 brothers. The recent phenomenon of massive departures was accelerating.[187]

The 1972 chapter wrote two major documents "Missionary Outlook" and "Administrative Structures," and did the ground work for a third "Community," that was to be written by the members of the general council.[188]

---

[185] See *Circulaires*, November 19, 1970, no. 247, vol. 8, p. 298.

[186] The present author was a member of the 1972 and 1974 general chapters as delegate of the Central United States province, and of the 1980 general chapter as provincial of the same province.

[187] See *Circulaires*, April 11, 1972, no. 247, vol. 8, p. 384. N.B. A mathematical error has been corrected. The same error is found also in "Registre," 1972, p. 219.

[188] *Missionary Outlook*, Rome, Missionary Oblates of Mary Immaculate, 1972; *Administrative Structures*, Rome, Missionary Oblates of Mary Immaculate, 1972; *Community*, Rome, Missionary Oblates of Mary Immaculate, 1972.

In "Missionary Outlook" the members of the chapter reaffirmed their sharing the same faith and mission of de Mazenod, and established principles to guide the mission of the Congregation in a new age. The document concluded by stating:

> We see ourselves as apostles in the spirit of de Mazenod and in the fullest biblical sense of the word: men called to be witnesses of the living Lord to the very ends of the earth (*Acts* 1:8, 21–22); men who have first experienced in our own lives the loving kindness of God made visible in the person of Jesus (see *Titus* 2:11–13); men who are driven on by this love to risk our lives for the sake of his Gospel (see *2 Cor* 5:14 and *Acts* 15:26); men who live apostolic poverty so as to free ourselves from all that might obstruct us from our mission (see *Mt* 10:9–10); men who celebrate our common hope in the Kingdom by breaking the bread of the Lord together in joy and simplicity of heart (*Acts* 2:44–47); men gathered together with Mary, as were the first Apostles (*Acts* 1:14).[189]

The first part of "Administrative Structures" consists of a number of principles that should guide both the delineation of the governmental structures of the Congregation and the exercise of government. The second part consists of a number of decrees that modify the 1966 Constitutions *ad experimentum*. The general chapter had the authority to do this by virtue of *Ecclesiæ Sanctæ*: "This general chapter has the right to alter, temporarily, certain prescriptions of the constitutions . . . by way of experiment, provided that the purpose, nature, and character of the institute are safeguarded."[190]

There were a number of changes in the determination of membership in the general chapter (nos. 1, 2, 4).[191] Perhaps the biggest change was that only those provincials with at least one hundred members in their respectove province were ex officio members (no. 1). Active voice in the election for chapter delegates was given to all Oblates in perpetual vows. The same was true of passive voice as chapter delegates, "with the exception of bishops and ecclesiastical superiors (prefects apostolic, and administrators apostolic)" (no. 6). If less than six brothers were elected as delegates, the superior general could invite as many as six brothers to bring the total to six (no. 3).[192] The

---

[189] *Missionary Outlook*, pp. 27–28.

[190] PAUL VI, apostolic letter, *Ecclesiæ Sanctæ II*, August 6, 1966, in *AAS*, 58 (1966), p. 776, no. 6; trans. *CLD*, vol. 6, p. 285–286.

[191] N.B. the numbers refer to the paragraphs of *Administrative Structures*, 1972.

[192] Although it is not explicitly stated that the word *brothers* here did not include the scholastics, but only the brothers who were not candidates for the priesthood, this was evident from the context, and was so understood by all. It did include brothers who were permanent deacons.

superior general could invite as many as four other Oblates as capitulars (no. 3). All capitulars were given deliberative vote in all acts of the chapter (no. 3). Article 127 of the Constitutions was changed to allow the chapter to set its own order of business, inclusive of the time when elections were to be held (no. 7).

The superior general was to be elected for a six year term, and could be reelected for a second term, but not for a third consecutive term (no. 10). The post of permanent vicar general was established (no. 11), and the form of the general council was modified to be composed of the vicar general, two assistants general, and six general councillors for the six regions of the Congregation (no. 13). The treasurer general was no longer to be elected by the general chapter, but by the general council for a six year term (no. 20). The extraordinary general council and the general conferences of specialists, creatures of the 1966 chapter, were suppressed (nos. 25–26).

In preparation for the appointment of a provincial, all the members of the province were to be consulted, and the man to be appointed was to be asked if he would accept the office (no. 29). Provinces were given the authority to modify some details of their governmental structures, and to elect the provincial and provincial consultors with the approval of two-thirds of those in perpetual vows, and the consent of the general council in plenary session (no. 32).

It was also decided that the term *brothers* was to be applied to all Oblates who completed their novitiate, and were not ordained priests. Brothers preparing for the priesthood were called *scholastics* (no. 36). Brothers in perpetual vows became eligible for the offices of local assistant, provincial consultor, and member of the general council (no. 38). In addition a non-scholastic brother could be named local superior with the required indult from the Holy See (no. 38).[193] Approval was given to request the Holy See for permission to introduce the permanent diaconate into the Congregation.[194]

The chapter also decided that it was not yet opportune to present the Constitutions to the Holy See for definitive approval and decreed "the prolongation of the experimental period of the Constitutions and Rules, as

---

[193] For the authority for these changes see *Ecclesiæ Sanctæ II*, no. 27, and SACRED CONGREGATION OF RELIGIOUS AND SECULAR INSTITUTES, decree, *Clericalia instituta*, November 27, 1969, in *AAS*, 61 (1969), pp. 739–740; trans. in *CLD*, vol. 7, pp. 468–469. This decree determined which offices lay members could hold in clerical religious institutes.

[194] See PAUL VI, motu proprio, *Sacrum diaconatus ordinem*, June 18, 1967, in *AAS*, 59 (1967), p. 703, no. 32: "Diaconatum permanentem constituere apud religiosos ius proprium Sanctæ Sedis est, ad quam unice pertinet Capitulorum Generalium hac de re vota expendere atque probare" (trans. in *CLD*, vol. 6, pp. 563–584). The indult was granted by SCRIS on December 14, 1972, in *Acta Adminstrationis Generalis O.M.I.* [=AAG-OMI], 1 (1972), p. 7.

adopted in 1966 and amended in the 1972 Chapter, until the next General Chapter."[195]

On May 2, 1972 the chapter celebrated the twenty-fifth anniversary of Deschâtelets' election as superior general. He resigned on May 5 with the effective date of May 8, and the resignation was accepted by the chapter. The following day Richard Hanley was elected superior general.[196] In conformity with the change in the Constitutions, Fernand Jetté was elected to the newly created post of permanent vicar general.[197] Hanley submitted his resignation as superior general, and it was accepted by the Sacred Congregation of Religious and Secular Institutes on June 21, 1974.[198] The XXIX General Chapter convened on November 12 of that year, and Jetté was elected superior general on November 26, and reelected in 1980 for a second term.[199]

The 1974 chapter made several changes in the membership of future general chapters. The superior general was to invite a brother from each region, even if a brother had been elected from that region as delegate (no. 3).[200] All Oblates in perpetual vows, including bishops, etc., were granted both active and passive voice in the elections for delegates to the general chapter (no. 6).

The 1974 general chapter requested by the Holy See for permission to postpone until the next chapter the submission of a definitive text for the Constitutions. This permission was granted on November 29, 1974.[201]

The chapter decreed that a post-capitular commission was to be created to revise the Constitutions and to involve the whole Congregation in the process. Instructors were given that the "draft text will take the 1966 text as its starting point and basis; it will also use the previous texts, especially those of the Founder, as important reference and source material; it will also reflect the Chapter Documents of 1972."[202]

---

[195] *Administrative Structures*, 1972, p. 41.

[196] Richard Hanley (1931–) at the time of his election was provincial of the Western U.S. Province.

[197] Fernand Jetté (1921–) was vicar provincial of St. Joseph's Province.

[198] See Richard HANLEY, letter all Oblates, June 21, 1974, circular no. 257, *AAG-OMI*, 2 (1973), pp. 34–35; Fernand JETTÉ, vicar general, to provincials, June 22, 1974, circular no. 258, ibid., pp. 38–39; id., to all Oblates, June 22, 1974, circular no. 259, ibid. pp. 42–43.

[199] Francis E. George (1937–), provincial of the Central United States Province, was elected vicar general in both 1974 and 1980. In 1990 he became bishop of Yakima, Washington, U.S.A.

[200] See *Acts of the General Chapter 1974*, II, Administrative Structures.

[201] See ibid., pp. 57–58.

[202] Ibid., p. 60.

On October 19, 1975 Paul VI proclaimed Charles Joseph Eugene de Mazenod blessed. This was not only the occasion of joy and celebration, but even more importantly one of profound renewal in the Congregation founded by him.

The 1982 Constitutions and Rules

The first members of the post-capitular commission for the revision of the Constitutions and Rules were appointed in 1974, and others were added in 1978.[203] Work began in 1975 with the sending of a questionnaire to all Oblates. About 1500 responded either as individuals or as groups. All the replies were analyzed and classified. Following the mandate of the 1974 chapter, the commission based its revision on the text of the 1966 Constitutions *ad experimentum*. In 1977 and 1978 draft texts were completed and sent to the whole Congregation for comment and reaction.

The chairman and the secretary of the commission[204] made a presentation at the inter-capitular meeting of provincials with the general administration in April 1978. The reactions of the provincials were mixed—from those of complete approval to those of praise for the work of the commission but with disappointment that the text was not inspirational.[205] A number of persons expressed the idea that the commission had followed too closely the 1966 text, and that the proposed text would experience opposition at the upcoming general chapter. As a result of this observation the commission interpreted the mandate to base their work on the 1966 text with greater flexibility.[206]

---

[203] See *Constitutions and Rules of the Congregation of the Missionary Oblates of Mary Immaculate, Proposed Text Prepared by the Revision Commission for the General Chapter of 1980*, Rome, 1979. A summary of the history of the text and the method of working is found on pages i–vii.

　　The Congregation owes a special debt of gratitude to Paul Sion, former professor of literature and superior of the minor seminary in Paksane, Laos. After the fall of Laos to the communists with the departure of all the foreign missionaries, he became general archivist at the General House. He served as executive secretary of the commission from its establishment and devoted himself without stint through the preparation of the text for the chapter, during the chapter, final revisions after the chapter, nursing the text through the Sacred Congregation, and the printing of the approved text. Having accomplished this work for the Congregation, he died on March 19, 1983 at the age of 56.

[204] Alexandre Taché and Paul Sion, respectively.

[205] See "Rencontre des Provinciaux 1978, Minutes II," pp. 74–80, General Archives O.M.I.

[206] See A. TACHÉ, O.M.I., "1980 Constitutions and Rules Project, Principles Underlying the Drafting of the Revised Text," in *Documentation O.M.I.*, 97/80, September 1, 1980, 2. Taché in this article presents the criteria used by the commission in its work, and explains the basis for various decisions made concerning the text.

Commenting on the reactions presented at the meeting, the general council wrote:

> *Unanimously,* all the regions asked that the revision of the Constitutions and Rules be carried out so as to produce a text that inspires and points out the basic Oblate values and that can be approved without too much difficulty and too much time lost at the next General Chapter. To achieve this, we need continued participation at the grass roots, the diverse reactions of Oblates and constructive dialogue with the various tendencies in the Congregation.[207]

Taking into consideration all the suggestions submitted, by 1979 the commission was able to complete a proposed text for the consideration of all the members of the Congregation in French, English, German, Spanish, Italian, and Polish. Jetté wrote all Oblates on August 16, 1979 and requested them to study the text and to let the precapitular commission know before June 1, 1980 whether or not they were generally satisfied with the text, and to submit specific recommendations for changes of sections or articles. By June 20, 1980 all the responses were compiled in French and English in order to make them available for the capitulants.

The XXX general chapter convened on October 27 and adjourned on December 6, 1980. During that time each article of the Constitutions and Rules was scrutinized carefully, not once, but many times. Many were rewritten and amended. A separate vote was taken by the whole chapter on the final form of each article, and then a final vote on the Constitutions as a whole, and on the Rules as a whole. On December 3 the capitulants addressed all their Oblate brothers with these words:

> It is with a deep feeling of peace, joy and thanksgiving that we send you today our greetings in the Lord. Father General has just solemnly announced the results of the final vote on the full text of the Constitutions and Rules—unanimous approval of the Constitutions and only one dissenting vote on the Rules. It is an intensely moving moment. There is an awareness of a gift, a special grace from the Lord. It is like the long awaited answer to the prayers of the whole Congregation. The melody of the "Magnificat" fills the hall and we thank Mary, Eugene de Mazenod, and all the Oblates who have gone before us and are now with him.[208]

Toward the end of January 1981 the completed text of the Constitutions was presented to the Sacred Congregation of Religious and Secular Institutes for approval. The Rules, although approval from the Holy See was not required or sought, were also presented in order that their complementarity to and

---

[207] *AAG-OMI,* 4 (1975), pp. 156–157.

[208] *Information O.M.I.,* 171/80, December 1980, p. 1.

specification of the Constitutions could be readily seen by those assigned to review the latter.

A number of observations were made by the two consultors who examined the texts. Some of these definitely improved the text. In a number of instances, however, it would seem that there was an insistence that articles of the Rules be transferred to the Constitutions, when it would seem that *Ecclesiæ Sanctæ* left such a decision to the particular religious institute.

The position taken by the general administration was to attempt to maintain the text as approved by the general chapter, except in those cases where there was an evident improvement of the text, or that a change requested was clearly demanded by universal law. Evidently there was a difference in the interpretation of "normas iuridicas necessarias ad Instituti indolem."[209]

It was required that the first article of the Constitutions state that the Congregation was a *clerical institute of pontifical right*.[210] In all the previously approved texts of the Constitutions, including the 1928 text, which was approved *in forma specifica*, such a statement was not required. It was felt by the general administration that this addition was unnecessary as the clerical nature of the Congregation from its beginning was clear from de Mazenod's Preface which forms part of the Constitutions,[211] and that such an addition placed a juridical element in an article that was spiritual and theological.[212]

---

[209] *Ecclesiæ Sanctæ II*, no. 12.

[210] SCRIS, "Observations du 'Congresso,'" n. M. 29–1/80, March 25, 1982, in Procurator's Archives O.M.I., "Art., §2 Write: 'The Congregation, *clerical of pontifical right* . . . ,' the rest the same.

[211] Infra pp. 163–164.

[212] The statement: "The fact that the Congregation is classed as clerical is a canonical imposition that we were obliged to insert into the new Constitutions and Rules by the Sacred Congregation of Religious and Secular Institutes in 1982" (René MOTTE, O.M.I. and Alfred HUBENIG, O.M.I., "Saint Eugene de Mazenod," Ms. [1994], p. 29), is misleading to say the least. The general administration did not question that the Congregation is clerical, but merely the opportuneness of saying so in the first article of the Constitutions. Motte was an assistant general in 1982.

F. Jetté, superior general at the time, later wrote: "Pope Paul VI added a reason of theological order [to the one of the juridical order] in his speech to the Jesuits on December 3, 1974: 'You are *priests*: that is an essential mark of the Company . . . The priesthood is necessary to the Order that [your Founder] established with its principal aim of sanctifying people through the word and the sacraments. The priestly character is indeed required by the consecration of your energies to the apostolic life, 'pleno sensu,' we repeat. . . the Congregation's canonical nature [is that of] a religious clerical society that brings together priests and brothers who live together, bind themselves by the same vows and dedicate themselves mainly evangelizing the poor" (*O.M.I., The Apostolic Man, A Commentary on the 1982 Oblate Constitutions and Rules*, Rome, General House, 1992, p. 44).

1. The call of Jesus Christ, heard within the Church through people's need for salvation, draws us together as Missionary Oblates of Mary Immaculate. Christ thus invites us to follow him and to share in his mission through word and work.

We are a clerical Congregation of pontifical right. We come together in apostolic communities of priests and Brothers, united to God by vows of religion. Cooperating with the Savior and imitating his example, we commit ourselves principally to evangelizing the poor.[213]

The Sacred Congregation also requested that the Constitutions establish special requirements for a person to be eligible for the office of superior, and that the superiors be priests.[214] This requirement had not been placed in the Constitutions by the chapter, since universal law already required that superiors be clerics: "Non-clerics cannot exercise the office of superior or vicar, whether it be general, or provincial, or local."[215] This was in conformity with the policy adopted in drafting the Constitutions and Rules of not repeating universal law which applied to the Congregation.

82. An Oblate appointed or elected Superior, vicar or replacement of a Superior, must have finished his first formation, taken perpetual vows and been ordained a priest.

Beyond these conditions, an Oblate appointed or elected Superior of a Province or a Delegation must have actually finished three years in perpetual vows; to be elected Superior General, he must have finished five years in perpetual vows.[216]

The consultors questioned the advisability of requiring a two-thirds majority of the votes for the election of the superior general (C. 114). The revision committee had proposed that such a majority be required for the first three ballots, but that on subsequent ballots an absolute majority, i.e., more than half of the votes, suffice and explained the recommendation in this way, "The proposed norm comes nearer to that which prevails in many other

---

[213] *Constitutions et Règles de la Congrégation des Missionnaires Oblats de Marie Immaculée*, Rome, 1982. The 1980 general chapter wrote the Constitutions and Rules in both French and English, with the agreement that only the French text was to be submitted to the Holy See for approval. Consequently, the French text is the *official text*.

[214] SCRIS, "Observations du 'Congresso,' " "Art. 73—Incorporate *R. 101*. The clause 'the norms of the law being observed' is insufficient; write 'been ordained a priest.' After 'local superior' add: 'or local vicar.' "

Both consultors of SCRIS in their vota had recommended this change, and the procurator general in his comments presented to SCRIS pointed out that to require that superiors be priests went beyond the prescription of SCRIS in *Clericalia Instituta* and the *schema* for the reform of the code. Both documents spoke of *clerics* and not of *priests* (M. O'REILLY, July 27, 1981).

[215] *Clericalia Instituta*, no. 4.

[216] *Constitutions 1982*.

Religious Institutes."[217] In spite of this recommendation the chapter amended the text to require a two-thirds majority on all ballots. This particular article was unanimously approved (111—*placet*; 0—*non placet*).[218] Following the policy of seeking to maintain the text as accepted by the chapter, the general administration explained that in the past a two-thirds majority had not been a problem. The Sacred Congregation did not insist on a change.

In 1969 the superior general and his council, having fulfilled the norms of the instruction *Renovationis causam*, decreed its implementation throughout the Congregation.[219] The 1972 general chapter decreed the same.[220] The 1980 text of the Constitutions and Rules incorporated the option of permitting promises to the Congregation instead of temporary vows as permitted by *Renovationis causam* and granted promises the same juridical effect as vows. In light of the 1980 draft of the text for the renovation of the Code of Canon Law,[221] the Sacred Congregation was asked if this should be changed. Since the Sacred Congregation hesitated to give an answer, the general administration, following its policy of maintaining insofar as possible the text approved by the general chapter, did not modify the text. Consequently, C. 60 and RR. 46–49 in the approved printed text were not in conformity with canon 654 of the code promulgated on January 25, 1983 and had to be modified to conform to

---

[217] A. TACHÉ, "1980 Constitutions," in *Documentation O.M.I.*, 97/80, September 1980, p. 8.

The Constitutions prior to 1928 did not require a majority of two-thirds for the election of the superior general. After the revision of the Constitutions by the 1926 general chapter, which maintained the provision of the election of the superior general for life, the Congregation of Religious wanted this modified to correspond more fully to CIC^1, c. 505, which preferred terms for all superiors. When the superior general and his council insisted upon the maintenance of the election of the superior general for life, the Congregation of Religious imposed the requirement of a two-thirds majority (see *Circulaires*, August 24, 1927, vol. 4, no. 139, pp. 102–103).

[218] "Registre," 1980, p. 227. N.B. article of the proposed text is article 114 in *Constitutions 1982*.

[219] See SCRIS, instruction, *Renovationis causam*, January 6, 1969, in *AAS*, 61 (1969), pp. 103–120, nos. 34–36; trans. *CLD*, vol. 7, pp. 489–508; see also *Circulaires*, vol. 8, pp. 261–286, August 15, 1969.

[220] *Acts of the General Chapter 1974*, Appendix, "Text on Formation of the 1972 Chapter," p. 71, no. 2.

[221] PONT. COMMISSIO CIC CODICI RECOGNOSCENDO, *Schema Codicis Iuris Canonici* (Patribus Commissionis reservatum), Vatican City, Libreria editrice vaticana, 1980, c. 580. For the background of this canon: ". . . a number of Cardinals sent the proposition of a professor concerning the substitution of vows by other sacred bonds during temporary profession. R. This suggestion cannot be accepted by the Commission because the Supreme Pontiff gave his own position as negative to this question, as was communicated to us by a letter of the Secretariat of State, No. 41.829 on August 12, 1980" (*Communicationes*, 15 [1983], p. 58).

the Code.[222] The apppropriate changes were made by the 1986 general chapter.[223]

Although from a juridical perspective the appearance and format of the book of Constitutions and Rules are of no importance, psychologically they can be very significant. The same is true of the literary style. Just as in the business world an inviting package does much to sell the contents.

All the editions in the various languages are attractive compact books with a visually pleasing format. The Rules follow the various articles of the Constitutions that they complement, and are indented and printed in a slightly smaller typeface. The passages from de Mazenod are printed on the left hand pages opposite the articles of the Constitutions to which they correspond.

Great effort was made to make the text itself equally attractive. The style is not heavy and abstract, as in the 1966 Constitutions *ad experimentum*, but direct and personal. In the first two parts there is frequent use of first person plural pronouns in order to make the text more concrete and to show that it forms part of the lives of real men, the Oblates. Of course, this varies from language to language according to the usage of the particular language. The English and German editions make much greater use of the first person than do the French, Italian, and Spanish versions.[224] Perhaps the best way to illustrate the literary style is to give an example.

> 12. Our mission requires that, in a radical way, we follow Jesus who was chaste and poor and who redeemed mankind by his obedience. That is why, through a gift of the Father, we choose the way of the evangelical counsels.
>
> Community is the life-giving reality fashioned by the vows which bind us in love to the Lord and to his people. Thus we become a living cell in the Church in which we strive to bring the grace of our Baptism to its fullness.

The 1982 text with a total of 279 articles in the Constitutions and Rules is notably shorter than the previous editions. The 1966 text had 522 articles, and the 1928 text 798. Of course, the non-repetition of universal law does much to explain the shorter text.

---

[222] See SCRIS, decree, *Iuris Canonici Codice*, February 2, 1984; SCRIS, decree, *Præscriptis canonum*, February 2, 1984, in *AAS*, 76 (1984), pp. 498–500; trans. *CLD*, vol. 11, pp. 91–92.

[223] "Changes to the Constitutions and Rules as approved by the General Chapter of 1986, pp. 3 and 5.

[224] There are also Polish, Japanese, Dutch, and Swedish editions. However, the author is not in a position to evaluate them. There is an unpublished translation in Czech.

While the 1966 text was distinguished by the use of Vatican II documents, the 1982 text incorporates Holy Scripture. The revised text as presented to the chapter by the commission had 126 scripture references compared to the nine references and twenty allusions in the original French text of de Mazenod, but the 1966 text had three explicit scriptural quotations and eleven other approximate ones.

> In spite of its many references, the new text is not a mosaic of scriptural quotes . . . It should be stressed that the Oblate Constitutions, even the most inspirational, do not issue from an hermeneutic exercise; they are born of a spiritual and apostolic experience that was lived by the founding group, then enriched by a century and a half's efforts, gropings and conversions.[225]

In his analysis of the responses to the questionnaire concerning the revision of the Constitutions, the executive secretary wrote, "As to the wording, many would like to find again as much as possible his (de Mazenod's) words, his vigorous formulas which give to the basic text of the Constitutions 'a family character,' 'a more profound presence of the Founder.' "[226] The 1976 *Congress on the Founder's Charism Today* made the same request, ". . . include in the text not only the Founder's thought but his words as well."[227]

This, it would seem, was easier said than done. How could the unity of style be kept? Modernization of de Mazenod's style? This would not be faithful to the reactions to the questionnaire or the recommendation of the Congress on the Charism. The solution was the quotation of de Mazenod's pertinent articles on the facing page, without integrating them into the text.[228]

De Mazenod's Preface is for Oblates the key document proclaiming the mission of the Congregation. It is seen as enshrining the family heritage, or, to use the expression of Vatican II, its "patrimony."[229] The vote of the 1980

---

[225] M. BOBICHON, O.M.I., "Holy Scripture in the Revised Text of the Constitutions and Rules," in *Documentation O.M.I.*, 95/80, June 1, 1980, pp. 1-7. There is little or no change in the use of Scripture between the text proposed to the chapter, and the finally approved text.

[226] Quoted by J. DROUART, O.M.I., "The Place Given the the Founder's Thought and Texts in Drafting the Constitutions and Rules," in *Documentation O.M.I.*, 94/80, May 1, 1980, p. 2.

[227] "Acta of the Congress, the Charism of the Founder Today, Rome, 26 April—14 May 1976," in *Vie Oblate Life*, 36 (1977), p. 293; also in *Documentation O.M.I.*, 70/76, October 1, 1976, p. 7.

[228] See DROUART, "The Place Given," in *Documentation O.M.I.*, 94/80, p. 2.

E. DE MAZENOD, *Choix de Textes relatifs aux constitutions et Règles O.M.I.*, Rome, 1983; trans. by Bastiampillai RAYAPPU, O.M.I. *Selected Texts related to the O.M.I. Constitutions and Rules*, Rome, 1984. This is a companion volume to the Constitutions and Rules consisting of excerpts from de Mazenod's writings, especially his letters, as a guide to illuminate them.

[229] *PC*, no. 2b. Cf. *CIC*, c. 578.

general chapter to maintain the Preface as part of the Constitutions was unanimous.[230] On the recommendation of the revision commission a forward was added in order to introduce de Mazenod's words and situate them in their historical, spiritual, and pastoral context, and thus give them all the prominence that they still have for his sons.[231]

The 1966 Constitutions *ad experimentum* were divided into four parts: the end of the Congregation, the apostolic man, formation, and government. The revised text followed the same division, but modified the titles somewhat to better express the content: mission, community, formation, and organization.

In order to underscore the unity between mission and religious life in the Congregation, the first two were combined to form one part entitled "The Oblate Charism."[232] The first chapter is "Mission," and in it are gathered the constitutive elements of the Congregation—the call of Jesus Christ the Savior to join Him in his mission, and this call is to men who are united by religious vows in apostolic communities to evangelize the poor. Various ministries are not named or described. This was done expressly in order to avoid lengthiness and oversights. The second chapter is divided into three sections: "The Evangelical Counsels;" "Living in Faith," the prayer and liturgical life of the community and individual members; and "The Apostolic Community," fraternal sharing and support.

The second part considers "Formation" in its various stages as a progressive and never-completed process of apostolic men in which each individual, as well as the community and superiors, share responsibility.

"Organization," the third part of the Constitutions, emphasizes the spirit of unity and collaboration that must inspire the government of the institute. The organizational structures, with some changes in the membership of the general chapter, are the same as in the 1966 Constitutions as modified in 1972 and 1974.[233]

---

[230] See "Registre," 1980, p. 203.

[231] See TACHÉ, "1980 Constitutions," in *Documentation O.M.I.* 97/80, September 1, 1980, p. 3.

[232] See "Registre," 1980, pp. 205, 211, 226–227, 229.

[233] It would seem that the Oblates have a particular propensity to spend much time and energy on the question of membership in the general chapter. The basis of this is the difficulty to establish membership that assures in so far as possible the presence of the leaders of all provinces and semiautonomous units, while maintaining the right of all Oblates in perpetual vows to vote for a delegate that will represent them with an equitable relationship to the number of persons represented by the delegates, and at the same time to keep the number of capitulants from being much over one hundred.

The 1986 and 1992 General Chapters

On September 13, 1986, the XXXI general chapter elected Marcello Zago as superior general.[234] It elected Gilles Cazebon vicar general on September 24.[235] The chapter voted for the modification of four articles of the Constitutions to bring them in conformity with the 1983 Code of Canon Law,[236] which were subsequently approved by the Holy See.[237]

Because the Code abolished the option of temporary commitment after novitiate through promises rather than vows,[238] the principal change was in C. 60, and RR. 46–49, and 82. It also established that a perpetually professed oblate may with the permission of the superior general divest himself of his present and future possessions.[239]

The chapter also revised R. 3 to read:

> Brothers participate in the missionary work of building up the Church everywhere, especially in those areas where the Word is being first proclaimed. Missioned by the Church, their technical, professional or pastoral service, as well as the witness of their life, constitute their ministry of evangelization.[240]

The XXXII general chapter on September 15, 1992 reelected Marcello Zago as superior general, and on the following day elected Daniel Corijn vicar general.[241] The chapter ratified the changes in the Rules introduced by the previous chapter and added Rule 28A:

> Several religious and secular institutes have links to the Congregation because of their origin or because of their spirituality. Each province shall

---

[234] At the time of his election Zago (1932–) was secretary of the Secretariat for Non-Christians (which became in 1988 the Pontifical Council for Inter-religious Dialogue). Prior to this he had been a missionary in Laos, professor of missiology, assistant general, and superior of the Italian scholasticate.

[235] Cazabon (1933–) had been provincial of St. Joseph Province and afterward rector of St. Paul University Seminary in Ottawa.

[236] See *AAG-OMI*, 10 (1987), p. 23.

[237] See V. FAGIOLO, secretary of SCRIS, to Zago, August 29, 1987, in *AAG-OMI*, 10 (1987), p. 18; "Changes to the Constitutions and Rules as approved by the General Chapter of 1986."

[238] See cc. 653, §2 and 654–658. Cf. SCRIS, decree, February 2, 1984, in *AAS*, 76 (19840, p. 500; *CLD*, vol. 11, pp. 91–92; *Communicationes*, 16 (1984), p. 26; *The Pope Speaks*, 29, (1984), pp. 140–141.

[239] This modified C. 23. The chapter added R. 17a, which allowed the superior general to delegate this authority to other major superiors, with the consent of their respective councils.

[240] *AAG-OMI*, 10 (1987), p. 24.

[241] Daniel Corijn (1943–), a native of Belgium, had been vicar provincial of the delegation of West Transval.

seek to strengthen those spiritual bonds, and, if possible, to establish concrete forms of apostolic cooperation, with all due respect for the autonomy of these institutes.[242]

The XXXII general chapter in 1992 proved itself true to the longstanding Oblate tradition of taking particular delight in revising the Constitutions as was pointed out in 1907 by Tomasso Esser, O.P., consultor of the Sacred Congregation of Bishops and Regulars: "So, today we find ourselves facing the sixth revision, and really it will not be the last."[243] It seems that he was either a prophet, or at least especially perceptive in sensing that the Oblates take a particular delight, in spite of protests to the contrary, in reworking their Constitutions?

A number of proposals had been made to the pre-chapter commission relating to the governing structures. The chapter made a number of decisions related to structures. One of these is most extraordinary in that it delegated to the "Inter-Chapter Assembly of 1995 the right to determine representation at the 1998 General Chapter."[244] Since some Oblates questioned the authority the chapter to make such a decision, the superior general requested "ad cautelam et pro hac vice tantum, an indult authorizing this Assembly to implement the mandate of the 1992 General Chapter concerning the composition of the next chapter and to determine more precisely the number and distribution of elected delegates to the *next* chapter."[245] The petition explained that it was

---

[242] *AAG-OMI*, 15 (1992), p. 72.

Marcello Zago invited to a special meeting—April 22-27, 1991—the superiors general of all the religious congregations and secular institutes either founded by Oblates of Mary Immaculate or with a special link with the Congregation. Representatives of twenty–six institutes (five male and twenty-one female) were present. In addition to these there are twenty other institutes (seven male and thirteen female) not represented at the congress (*Information O.M.I.*, June 1991, pp. 1–2).

Cf. JOHN PAUL II, address to communities found by Oblates of Mary Immaculate, April 26, 1991, in *L'Osservatore romano*, English edition, May 6, 1991, p. 2.

[243] M. 29, CICLSAL Archives.

[244] *AAG-OMI*, 15 (1992), p. 76. This decision is indeed most extraordinary in light of c. 135, §2: "Legislative power is to be exercised in the manner prescribed by law; that which in the Church a legislator lower than the supreme authority has, cannot be delegated, unless the law explicitly provides otherwise. . ."

[245] Marcello ZAGO and Daniel CORIJN, to E. Martinez Somalo, prefect of CICSAL, July 16, 1994.

The petition contains as one the reasons for the chapter's decision: "the 1994 Chapter did not wish to enter into practical details of numbers and distribution, given the rapid changes that are taking place in many parts of the world." One may speculate that from the experience of previous chapters, the members of the chapter did not want to take an immense amount of time and energy to reach a consensus on this very delicate question. Did the chapter take the almost effortless path of delegating a difficult decision?

not a question of modifying the Constitutions, but of the Rules. The indult was granted "iuxta preces, servatis ceteris servantis."[246]

The chapter also decided:

> . . . Rule 135 which calls for the superior general with his council in plenary session to appoint major officials, will be understood to mean that the major officials need not necessarily be persons distinct from those who hold elected office on the general council.[247]

Since neither the Constitutions nor the Rules require that major officials be distinct from the members of the general council, it was not necessary for the chapter to even consider such a question.

It was especially in mandating the superior general in council to establish a post-chapter committee on structures that the chapter proved the Oblate propensity to revise Constitutions and Rules. The chapter determine in great detail the committee's composition, tasks, functioning in four phases, and time line.[248]

Summary

This chapter has traced the main lines of the historical development and juridical evolution of the Missionary Oblates of Mary Immaculate. At the time of the pontifical approval by Leo XII in 1826, the Congregation had four houses in southern France and counted as members fifteen priests and seven professed clerical students. At the end of 1982 there were 4478 priests and bishops, 827 brothers, and 384 scholastics for a total of 5689 professed members spread throughout the world.[249]

The situation of both the Church and secular society of post-revolutionary France was far different in almost every respect from that of the latter part of the twentieth century. Most of these changes are reflected in the religious family founded by de Mazenod. In spite of all this change, has the Congregation evolved in a way that is consistent with de Mazenod's basic inspirations and intentions?

The answer is "yes," if the 1982 Constitutions and Rules are faithful to the spirit and aims of de Mazenod, as well as the Congregation's sound traditions constituting the spiritual patrimony of the Missionary Oblates of Mary Immacu-

---

[246] CICSAL, indult, Prot. no. 29365/94, July 26, 1994.

[247] *AAG-OMI*, 15 (1992), p. 76.

[248] *AAG-OMI*, 15 (1992), pp. 77–80.

[249] "Comparative Statistics 1980–1982," *Information O.M.I.*, 195/83, February 1983, p. 1.

late.[250] If the response is "no," there has been a radical change in the Congregation. In fact, it would be an essentially different institute, and this would not only be contrary to canon law which forbids such a change, but also opposed to the acquired rights of the individual members of the Congregation.

A pertinent response is that the 1982 Constitutions were unanimously approved by the XXX general chapter, and the Rules were approved with only one dissenting vote. Is it possible that after five years of intensive study and prayer the superior general, the members of the general council, the majority of the provincials, and the elected delegates representing all the members of the Congregation acted contrary to the spiritual patrimony that they all profess to treasure?

The whole Congregation had beforehand the revised text presented to the chapter, and shortly after the chapter the text voted upon was sent to all members of the Congregation. The general chapter studied thoroughly the text and made a number of amendments before approving the text. Since then the text has been approved by the Holy See with non-essential modifications, and has been distributed to all the members. It has been peacefully, and even joyfully accepted by the rank and file of the Congregation.[251] Is this not an adequate reply to remove any possible doubt?[252]

In 1980 the general council requested an international group of five Oblates to make a historical-theological study of the text prepared for the chapter. The purpose of the study was to judge the continuity and non-continuity in the 1928, 1966, and the proposed text in relation to the fundamental values proposed by de Mazenod and lived throughout the history of the

---

[250] See PC, no. 2, b; and Ecclesiæ Sanctæ II, no. 12, a.

[251] There have been some objections to two changes insisted upon by the Holy See, the addition to the first article concerning the clerical nature of the Congregation, and the explicit mention in article 82 and R. 90 that superiors must be priests, unless an indult is granted. See Documentation O.M.I., 126/84, May 1984, p. 11. Since these changes are only explicit statements of what was already implicitly in the texts approved by the Chapter, these objections may be an indication of the opportuneness of the Holy See's insistence and of this thesis.

[252] After reading a draft of this thesis Jean Drouart, who accepted loyally the 1966 Constitutions ad experimentum as a devoted son of the Congregation because of obedience, but experienced the pain of the rejection of de Mazenod's text in 1966, said that the suffering was more than compensated for by the 1982 Constitutions. In the same context he insisted on the great value to the Congregation of de Mazenod's letters.

Drouart (1911–1989), superior of the International Scholasticate of Rome (1947–1953), and first assistant general (1953–1966), from 1966 until his death in 1989 spent most of his time—with the mandate of four successive superiors general—as an itinerant retreat master and lecturer on de Mazenod and the Congregation throughout the world.

institute. Since the texts approved by the chapter and the Holy See are essentially the same as those presented by the revision committee, the judgment of the study group provides a relevant evaluation of the faithfulness of the 1982 Constitutions to the Oblate traditions.

In the three editions the characteristics of the Congregation are preserved. They contain the fundamental values proposed by the Founder and kept intact in Oblate tradition: the following of Jesus Christ, service of the Church, zeal for the salvation of the world by evangelization (especially of the most neglected), consecration in apostolic religious life lived in communities of faith and charity with the hope that under the patronage of Mary Immaculate, Mother of Mercy, the Lord will grant the Oblates the means to respond to the calls of the Church and the contemporary world.[253]

The 1986 and 1992 general chapters also remained faithful to the Oblate tradition and delight in revising the Constitutions and Rules—although it often entails a difficult and often painful process. They also practically guaranteed that the next general chapter in 1998 will preserve intact this tradition.

A study of the various general chapters from the Congregation's foundation reveals a profound change, which no doubt reflects a change of mentality from the nineteenth century to the latter half of the twentieth century. Prior to the 1960s general chapters consecrated their energy producing *capitular acts*, i.e., minute prescriptions or regulations governing daily life to improve the quality of the religious and missionary life of the members of the Congregation. Since that time, the chapters have shown little interest in making a multitude of decrees or regulations—if you discount the question of representation at future general chapters—and have consecrated their time and energy in composing documents or statements to the Congregation with the goal of sharing the chapter experience with their brother Oblates for a revitalization of the Congregation.[254]

---

[253] "Constitutions et Règles O.M.I. 1928–1966–1980, Étude Comparative, July 2–12, 1980," p. 54, General Archives O.M.I.

[254] It would be interesting to know whether these documents, statements, and letters have really had the intended effect and have in fact touched the lives of many Oblates. Are these documents and statements much like well crafted homilies or sermons that benfit more the preacher than the congregation? In a word, is the present mode of acting really more successful than the earlier manner?

Chapter IV
Juridical Status of Pontifical Clerical Religious Congregations

The teaching and the practice of the Church in recognizing, encouraging, approving, and moderating institutes of consecrated life was succinctly summarized by the Fathers of Vatican II in the dogmatic constitution *Lumen gentium*.

Since it is the duty of the ecclesiastical hierarchy to feed the people of God and lead them to the richest of pastures (*Ez* 34:14), it is the task of the same hierarchy wisely to regulate by law the practice of the evangelical counsels by which perfect charity towards God and one's neighbor is encouraged in a special way. Moreover, in docile submission to the inspiration of the Holy Spirit, the hierarchy accepts rules put forward by outstanding men and women and, once these have been further revised, give them official approval. It also provides vigilant and protective authority to see that institutes that have been set up here and there for the building up of the body of Christ develop and flourish in accordance with the spirit of their founders.

To meet the needs of the whole of the Lord's flock more effectively, any institute of perfection and its individual members can, for the general good of the Church, be exempted by the supreme pontiff from the jurisdiction of local ordinaries and subjected to him alone; this is possible by reason of his primacy over the universal Church. Similarly they can be left or committed to their own patriarchal authorities. The members themselves, in carrying out their duty towards the Church which arises from their particular form of life, have a duty of reverence and obedience, in accordance with the canon laws, towards the bishops, because of their authority in the particular churches and because of the need for unity and harmony in apostolic work.[1]

Down through the centuries the Church has been blessed with countless religious communities of men and women. Each was founded to meet the needs of the people at a particular time. It suffices to call to mind the hermits, monastic orders, canons regular, mendicant orders, clerics regular, and religious congregations with simple vows to realize the evolution in the forms of

---

[1] VATICAN COUNCIL II, dogmatic constitution on the Church, *Lumen gentium* [=*LG*], November 21, 1964, in *AAS*, 57 (1965), pp. 5-71, no. 45; English trans. Norman P. TANNER, S.J., ed., *Decrees of the Ecumenical Councils*, Georgetown, Georgetown University Press, 1990, vol. 1, p. *886.

religious communities and their ministries that have taken place to respond to the needs of different periods in the life of the Church. There has been a similar evolution in theology, canonical legislation, and practice to meet the changing times and modes of consecrated life. Examples of this can be seen in the various explanations and norms concerning the choral recitation of divine office, the obligation of cloister for religious women, and the nature of religious commitment.[2]

The Evolution of the Juridical Status
of Religious Congregations with Simple Vows

The theology and juridical practice of simple vows and, consequently of religious congregations with simple vows, were developed slowly. A schematic outline of this evolution, insofar as it concerns male religious communities, will situate the approval and subsequent development of the Missionary Oblates of Mary Immaculate in the proper theological and juridical context.

After the declaration of Boniface VIII (1294–1303),[3] a person could enter the religious state only by making solemn vows in a religious institute approved by the Holy See. Dispensations from solemn vows were not granted. Although the faithful could make simple vows to observe the evangelical counsels, this was not considered to be a religious profession, and they did not thereby become religious and did not participate in the privileges and obligations of religious. In approving the Jesuits with simple vows for the spiritual and temporal coadjutors and the scholastics in 1550, Julius III gave the first pontifical approval of simple vows in a religious order:

> After completing the tests and time required by the Constitutions the spiritual and temporal coadjutors and scholastics were to be allowed, for their greater devotion and merit, to pronounce their vows, not as solemn vows, but as vows by which they were bound for whatever time the superior general of the aforementioned Society should see fit . . .[4]

---

[2] See G. COSENTINO, O.M.I., *Histoire de nos Règles*, Ottawa, Éditions des Études Oblates, 1955, vol. 1, pp. 53–71; R. HOSTIE, *Vie et mort des ordres religieux*, Paris, Desclée de Brouwer, 1972; G. LESAGE, O.M.I., *L'Accession des Congrégations à l'État religieux canonique*, Ottawa, Les Éditions de l'Université d'Ottawa, 1952; *Dictionnaire de droit canonique*, s.v. "Congrégation religieuse," by J. CREUSEN, S.J.; id., "De iuridica status religiosi evolutione brevis synopsis historica," in *Periodica*, 31 (1942), pp. 143–155, 216–241; A. LARRAONA, C.F.M., "Commentarium in partem secundam libri Codicis, quæ est: de religiosis," in *Commentarium pro religiosis*, 1 (1920), pp. 16–21, 45–50, 133–140, 171–177, 209–217.

[3] See Cap. un., in VI°, lib. III, t. 15, Friedburg vol. 1, col. 1053.

[4] JULIUS III, constitution, *Exposcit debitum*, July 21, 1550, in *Bullarium Romanum Tauriense*, vol.

This accepting of simple vows in the name of the Church was a new element upon which would be constructed the juridical foundation for congregations with simple vows.[5]

In his solicitude to implement the decrees of the Council of Trent and to remove the scandal to the faithful by the non-observance of the decrees of Trent concerning cloister for religious women and of male religious returning to secular life, Pius V issued two constitutions using the juridical means at his disposal—solemn vows. In *Circa pastoralis* he required all nuns to make solemn vows and to observe papal cloister.[6] Tertiaries with solemn vows were also required to observe papal cloister, and those without solemn vows were to be persuaded to make them and to observe papal cloister. If they refused to do so, and later caused scandal they were to be severely punished. They were also forbidden to receive any new members and were thus condemned to extinction. It would seem that *Circa pastoralis* did not apply to pious women not attached to any order.[7]

Shortly afterward for the same reasons Pius V issued another bull for male religious. In *Lubricum vitæ genus*[8] he imposed the obligation of making solemn vows on all men living in common under voluntary obedience, and wearing a habit different from that of the secular clergy. It did not forbid male institutes in which the members dressed like the secular priests.

Because of the controversy caused by the simple vows approved for the Jesuits and the nature and effect of these vows, Gregory XIII attempted to resolve the question with the bull *Quanto fructuosius*[9] in 1583 by declaring that the vows of the spiritual and temporal coadjutors and the scholastics made

---

6, pp. 425–426. See E. GAMBARI, "De votis simplicibus religionis in Societate Jesu eorumque momento in evolutione juris religiosorum," in *Ephemerides iuris canonici*, 3 (1947), pp. 87–122.

[5] The necessary theological elements, common life, rule, simple vows, were present already in the Dominican and Franciscan Tertiaries in the latter half of the XIII century. See I. CREUSEN,.S.J., "De iuridica status religiosi evolutione," in *Periodica*, 31 (1942), p. 222.

[6] PIUS V, constitution, *Circa pastoralis*, May 29, 1566, in *Bullarium Romanum Tauriense* vol. 7, pp. 447–450; Petrus Card. GASPARRI, *Fontes*, vol. 1, no. 112. See N. ONSTENK, "De Constitutione S. Pii V 'Circa Pastoralis' super clausura monialium et tertiariorum," in *Periodica*, 39 (1950), pp. 213–230, 317–363; 40 (1951), pp. 210–255.

[7] See N. ONSTENK, "De Constitutione," in *Periodica*, 40 (1951), p. 253. *Circa Pastoralis* often was so applied in fact.

[8] PIUS V, constitution, *Lubricum vitæ genus*, November 17, 1568, in *Bullarium Romanum Tauriense* vol. 7, pp. 725–726.

[9] GREGORY XIII, constitution, *Quanto fructuosius*, February 1, 1583, *Magnum Bullarium Romanum*, vol. 4,4, pp. 23–25; *Fontes*, vol. 1, no. 150.

them religious. Rather than end the discussion, it was said that the pope had spoken as a private doctor and had erred.

The following year in order to settle the question once and for all Gregory XIII issued the bull *Ascendente Domino*.[10] In it he first presented the position of those who refused to accept that the simple vows of the Jesuits were truly religious vows, "non considerantes voti solemnitatem sola Ecclesiæ constitutione inventam esse," and condemned that opinion. He then affirmed that the Jesuit simple vows were religious vows in an institute approved by the Holy See:

> §20. Desiring to give the firm support of this See to the said Society, by this Constitution with complete knowledge and the fullness of our authority we determine and establish that these vows, although they are simple, by the decision of this See, by our declaration and confirmation are truly and substantially religious vows, and have been accepted in the aforesaid Society, and so are accepted by Us. They can be dispensed only by Us and this See, nor can these vows cease in any other way save by legitimate dismissal from the Society.[11]

This ended the controversy. Simple vows were a special privilege of the Jesuits, and remained so for many years. Nevertheless the foundation had been laid for further juridical development.

From the beginning of the seventeenth century new institutions would be pulled in two directions—on the one side to avoid solemn vows with their irrevocability, and on the other to profess solemn vows for their theological and juridical prestige as well as to avoid the inherent instability of simple vows. Saint Vincent de Paul responded to the objections to simple vows by applying to them the thomistic theory of holocaust which the theologians up to that time had applied only to solemn vows, and by the introduction of the vow of perseverance and the reservation of simple vows to the pope.

Benedict XIII approved the constitutions of the Brothers of the Christian Schools by the bull *In Apostolicæ dignitatis solio* in 1725. This is the first papal approval of a congregation with simple vows, that has maintained simple vows:

> *Eighth*. We confirm, approve and grant by our inviolable Apostolic authority, that the brothers be accepted into the said Institute at the age of sixteen, make vows for only a three year period, and renew their vows each

---

[10] Gregory XIII, constitution, *Ascendente Domino*, May 25, 1584, in *Magnum Bullarium Romanum*, vol. 4,4, pp. 55–56; *Fontes*, vol. 1, no. 153.

[11] Ibid.

year until they are twenty-five years old, at which time they may be admitted to perpetual vows.

Ninth. That the brothers' vows are chastity, poverty, obedience, and perseverance in the said Institute, and also of teaching the poor gratis: with the provision that the governing Roman Pontiff can dispense the brothers from the simple vows.[12]

In addition to approving the simple vows and reserving their dispensation to the pope, the bull also restricted the right of transferring to a more strict religious institute:

In addition to this we decide that forever in the future no brother of the aforementioned Institute may without the express consent of the Superior General of the same Institute, even under the pretext of joining a more strict religious institute, leave the aforementioned Institute . . .[13]

In 1746 with the brief *Ad pastoralis dignitatis fastigium*[14] Benedict XIV approved the Passionists, a congregation of clerics with simple vows. Three years later the same pope approved the Redemptorists with the brief *Ad Pastoralis Dignitatis,*

Indeed our beloved sons, Alphonsus de Liguori of Naples and other priests of the Kingdom of Naples, informed us that some time ago, that is in 1732, they came together in order to live according to the Gospel and to provide for their own salvation and that of others. For this purpose they took simple vows of poverty, common life, chastity, and obedience. Thus, they established the Society or Congregation of secular Priests of Workers of the holy Gospel under the name of Most Holy Savior . . .

Wishing to favor the petitioners by our Apostolic Authority with these present confirm, and approve the aforementioned Institute of the Congregation of Priests of the Most Holy Redeemer, and their above inserted Constitutions or Rules, or Statutes, and add the inviolable strength of Apostolic authority . . .[15]

During the eighteenth century nine congregations of men received full approval. They were called secular congregations and not regular congregations, although they were like the formally approved religious institutes in all

---

[12] BENEDICT XIII, constitution, *In Apostolicæ dignitatis solio,* January 26, 1725, *Recueil des bulles, brefs, et rescripts accordés par le Saint-Siège à l'Institut des Frères des Écoles Chrétiennes,* Rome, l'Institut Pie IX, 1907, pp. 1–14.

[13] Ibid., p. 13.

[14] BENEDICT XIV, apostolic letter, *Ad pastoralis dignitatis fastigium,* April 18, 1746, in *Acta Congregationis SS. Crucis et Passione D.N.J.C.,* vol. 12, pp. 161–162.

[15] BENEDICT XIV, apostolic letter, *Ad pastoralis dignitatis,* February 25, 1749, in *Constitutiones et Regulæ Congregationis Sacerdotum sub titulo Sanctissimi Redemptoris,* Rome, Cuggiani, 1895.

except simple vows and were exempt only if the privilege was granted to them. By the end of the pontificate of Benedict XIV religious communities with simple vows had full juridical recognition, although of particular law, from the Holy See. Their simple vows were public vows considered as made in favor of a third part and reserved to the Holy See.[16]

The French Revolution and its aftermath set the stage for further development of communities with simple vows. Following the complete destruction of religious communities in France, and the secularization of numerous others in the path of the revolutionary armies, the Church was faced with challenges in a very different world. Civil laws in many countries no longer recognized the juridical effects of solemn vows. The needs of the people were met by newly formed communities to replace those destroyed and to face the new sociological and religious situations. Between 1800 and 1864 ninety-eight congregations of men and women were approved or given a decree of praise by the Holy See. This was but a fraction of the new institutes. By 1870 France alone had 530 separate mother houses, although some for them had common origins.[17]

At this time the congregations with simple vows possessed all the theological requirements necessary for the religious state by divine law, although not all the juridical requirements were present. By common law they possessed none of the rights or privileges of the orders with solemn vows. On the other hand they did possess by common law the characteristics of a state distinct from that of seculars, e.g., public vows reserved to the Holy See, the privilege of forum, etc. In addition, the institutes approved by the Holy See had a certain independence from the bishops, especially in regard to internal government. Some of the congregations, e.g., the Passionists and Redemptorists, by special privilege were exempt.[18]

During this time the Holy See still did not consider congregations with simple vows to be religious institutes. The term *religious* was reserved for the orders with solemn vows. This can be seen in a response of the Congregation of Bishops and Regulars to the superior general of the Redemptorists:

> But the following *ex officio* observations are opposed. It is indeed true that the solemnity of vows is not essential to the religious state by divine

---

[16] See LARRAONA, "Commentarium," in *Commentarium pro Religiosis*, 1 (1920), p. 49; LESAGE, *Accession*, pp. 150, 167.

[17] See LESAGE, *Accession*, p. 180; HOSTIE, *Vie et Mort*, pp. 336–337.

[18] See A. BIZZARRI, *Collectanæ in usum secretariæ Sacræ Congregationis Episcoporum et Regularium*, Rome, Typographia polyglotta, 1885, pp. 433 and 746.

law, but it is nevertheless required by ecclesiastical law. Wherefore a person is not truly a religious according to church discipline, who made only simple vows, unless by a special and expressed indult of the Holy See there is a derogation of the church law.[19]
Further on the Redemptorists, although their name is omitted in the published rescript, are spoken of as "la Congregazione de'Preti Secolari," the Congregation of Secular Priests. The priests in such an institute are juridically members of the secular clergy.

Congregations with Simple Vows Recognized as Religious Institutes

During the pontificate of Leo XIII the word *religious* was first applied by the Holy See to congregations with simple vows. In the decree *Ecclesia Catholica* they are spoken of as "congregationes religiosæ,"[20] in *Conditæ a Christo* is found "religiosæ familiæ," "religiosarum domus," and "habitum religiosum,"[21] and in the *Normæ* the expression "Instituta virorum religiosorum."[22] However, the terms *religio* and *regulares* are avoided. In *Conditæ a Christo* the authority of the local ordinaries over diocesan and papal congregations with simple vows is spelled out. The *Normæ* contain detailed requirements for the constitutions of institutes with simple vows and the requirements for their acceptance and approval. From this time religious congregations with simple vows have a place in the general law of the Church.

It was with the promulgation of the *Codex Iuris Canonici* by Benedict XIV in 1917 that congregations with simple vows received an official and permanent place in the legislation of the Church and were definitely accepted as religious institutes.

> Can. 487 — The religious state, that is, a permanent mode of community life by which the faithful undertake to observe, not only the precepts

---

[19] Congregation of Bishops and Regulars, response, *Congregationis Presbyterorum Sæcularium*, Sept. 16, 1864, *Fontes*, vol. 4, no. 1993. A 1864 handwritten copy of this response is found in the Procurator's Archives O.M.I. file XXII. The archivist of the Sacred Congregation at the time had loaned the original to the Oblate procurator general. See supra chapter 3, p. 82, note 102.

[20] Congregation of Bishops and Regulars, decree, *Ecclesia Catholica*, August 11, 1889, in *ASS*, 23 (1890–1891), pp. 634–636.

[21] Leo XIII, apostolic constitution, *Conditæ a Christo*, December 8, 1900, in *ASS*, 33 (1901), pp. 341–347; *Fontes*, vol. 3, no. 644

[22] Congregation of Bishops and Regulars, *Normæ secundum quas S. Cong. Episcoporum et Regularium procedere solet in approbandis novis institutis votorum simplicium*, Rome, Typis S.C. de Propaganda Fide, 1901.

common to all, but also the evangelical counsels by the vows of obedience, chastity, and poverty, must be held in honor by all.

Can. 488 — In the following canons the terms used are:

1° An *institute* (*religio*) is a society approved by legitimate ecclesiastical authority, the members of which in accordance with its laws, make public vows, either perpetual or temporary, provided they intend to renew the latter after their expiration, and through these means tend to evangelical perfection.

2° . . . An *exempt institute*, that has solemn or simple vows, is withdrawn from the jurisdiction of the local ordinary. A *religious congregation*, or simply a *congregation*, means an institute whose members profess simple vows, temporary or perpetual . . .

7° *Religious* designates all who have made vows in any religious institutes; *religious with simple vows* designates those who made vows in a religious congregation; . . .

Religious institutes with simple vows were not granted exemption by the Code; nevertheless they might be exempt by special concession from the pope. However, all pontifical institutes were granted autonomy from the local Ordinary for internal government and discipline except insofar as he was expressly granted jurisdiction by law (c. 618). Hence, although the word was not used, all pontifical institutes were partially exempt. Though the major superiors of pontifical non-exempt clerical institutes were not ordinaries in the strict sense, as were their exempt counterparts (c. 198, §1), they were the equivalent of ordinaries of their subjects in a number of cases.[23]

During Vatican II in response to the request of the superiors general of clerical religious institutes, Paul VI through the Secretariate of State with the pontifical rescript *Cum admotæ* granted on November 6, 1964 a number of faculties to the superiors general for their institutes.[24] The faculties are for all pontifical clerical religious institutes without distinction between orders and congregations, or between exempt and non-exempt institutes. Of special interest for the development in juridical practice in regard to non-exempt congregations with simple vows is:

13. To perform acts of jurisdiction for government and internal discipline after the manner (*ad instar*) of major superiors of regulars, always without prejudice to dependence on local ordinaries according to the norm of canon law: namely, when there is question of religious institutes which do not enjoy this kind of faculty from law (*CIC*, c. 501, §1; c. 198, §1).

---

[23] See A. Larraona, "Quæstio canonica," in *Commentarium pro Religiosis*, 4 (1923), pp. 113–119.

[24] See Paul VI, pontifical rescript, *Cum admotæ*, November 6, 1964, in *AAS*, 59 (1967), pp. 374–378; trans in *CLD*, vol. 6, pp. 147–152.

With the consent of their council they can subdelegate this faculty to other major superiors of the same religious institute.[25]

Although this favor did not confer on these superiors the office of ordinary, it did grant them the power of exercising jurisdiction for the internal government and discipline of their institutes with the authority *ad instar* of regular major superiors. In other words it made them quasi-ordinaries of their subjects.[26]

There was further development in this same line during the pontificate of Paul VI. In 1971 the Sacred Congregation for the Doctrine of Faith issued new norms for the laicization of priests. The letter is addressed to "Omnibus locorum Ordinariis et Moderatoribus Generalibus Religionum clericalium." Without distinction all clerical major superiors are called *ordinaries*:

... the ordinaries concerned, that is, diocesan ordinaries for secular priests, major superiors for religious . . .

. . . the proper ordinary, either diocesan, or religious . . .

The ordinaries concerned, among whom is the major religious superior . . . [27]

The following year Paul VI issued the motu proprio *Ministeria quædam* revising the minor orders and suppressing the subdeaconate for the Latin Church. In it all major superiors of clerical institutes are called ordinaries:

IX. The ministries are conferred by the ordinary (bishop and, in clerical institutes of perfection, the major superior) . . .[28]

This practice was confirmed and became law by the *Codex Iuris Canonici* promulgated by John Paul II on January 25, 1983. This further reduced the distinction between orders and congregations, and exempt and non-exempt religious.

Can. 134 –§1. In law the term ordinary means, apart from the roman pontiff, diocesan bishops . . . likewise, for their own members, it means the major superiors of clerical religious institutes of pontifical right and of clerical

---

[25] Ibid.

[26] See I.B. FUERTES, "Commentarium in rescriptum pontificium 'Cum admotæ,' Facultas n. 13," in *Commentarium pro Religiosis*, 45 (1966), pp. 52–69.

[27] CONGREGATION FOR THE DOCTRINE OF THE FAITH, *Normæ ad apparandas in curiis diocesanis et religiosis causas reductionis ad statum laicalem cum dispensatione ab obligationibus cum sacra Ordinatione conexis*, and circular letter, January 13, 1971, in *AAS*, 63 (1971), pp. 303–312; trans. in *CLD*, vol. 7, pp. 110–121.

[28] PAUL VI, motu proprio, *Ministeria quædam*, August 15, 1972, in *AAS*, 64 (1972), pp. 529–534; trans. in *CLD*, vol. 7, pp. 690–695.

societies of apostolic life of pontifical right, who have at least ordinary executive power.

Henceforth the major superiors of pontifical clerical institutes are the ordinaries of their members.[29]

The superiors and chapters of all pontifical clerical religious institutes likewise have ex officio the authority of ecclesiastical government, and not just the domestic authority as heads of religious families.

> Can. 596 — §2. In clerical religious institutes of pontifical right, they [superiors and chapters] have in addition the ecclesiastical power of governance, for both the external and the internal forum.[30]

In *Cum admotæ* this authority was granted only to the superiors general with the power to subdelegate it to the other major superiors of their institute. No mention was made of granting or delegating this authority to chapters.

Although the 1983 Code maintains the distinction between solemn and simple vows (c. 1192, §2), this distinction is not mentioned explicitly in the canons referring to religious. It is found implicitly in c. 668, §4 and §5 when religious poverty is treated. The disparity between solemn and simple vows is lessened by the effect of all religious vows of celibacy.

> Can. 1088 –Those who are bound by a public perpetual vow of chastity in a religious institute invalidly attempt marriage.

This impediment is reserved to the Holy See in the case of pontifical institutes (c. 1078, §2, 1°), and no distinction is made between solemn and simple vows of celibate chastity.[31]

It is the treatment of exemption that shows most clearly the narrowing of the juridical disparity among religious institutes. Only one canon (c. 591)

---

[29] *Communicationes*, 6 (1974), p. 58: ". . . the major superiors of non-exempt religious institutes also are considered to be ordinaries."

[30] See PONTIFICAL COMMISSION FOR THE REVISION OF THE CODE, *Schema Canonum de Institutis vitæ consecretæ per professionem conciliorum evangelicorum*, Rome, Typis Polyglottis Vaticanis, 1977); the corresponding canon had also the following text: "Canon 25, §3. In Institutis exemptis ad normam c. 17, Moderatores pleniorem obtinent potestatis ecclesiasticæ participationem . . ." This was not included in either the 1980 *schema* or in the 1983 Code. Thus, the Code does not affirm that the exempt major superiors have a *pleniorem participationem* than the non-exempt superiors.

[31] See *Communicationes*, 9 (1977), p. 58. In the *Prænotanda* to the 1977 *schema* on religious the commission wrote: ". . . distinctions are avoided in the *schema*, e.g., between religious institutes in which profession of solemn vows is made, and those in which simple vows are made. In the *schema* no mention is made since canonically both professions are equivalent." I.e. both are equally religious professions, although there may be differences because of the nature of the institutes and their traditions and norms. For some time it has been the practice of the Holy See to grant dispensations from solemn vows as well as simple vows.

directly treats exemption, and it merely states the principle that the pope may grant exemption to a religious institute for its welfare and the needs of the apostolate. Further determinations are left to particular law. As a general rule, wherever the 1917 Code had "exempt religious," the 1983 Code in the corresponding canon has "pontifical religious institutes." It was in this way that the Code Commission applied the principle that was established to guide its work:

> . . . At the same time the consultors of the study group considered it necessary to establish solidly *the principle of sufficient and equitable internal autonomy of each institute of consecrated life.*[32]
>
> . . . This means that exempt institutes, as far as the points mentioned above are concerned, are *in fact not exempt*. In other words since the celebration of the Council the exemption of an institute means little more than internal autonomy of life and government . . . because "exemption does not keep religious from being subject to the jurisdiction of the bishops in the individual dioceses according to the norms of the law . . ."[33]

An example of this can be seen by comparing two canons, one from each Code. First the 1917 Code has:

> Can. 344 — §2. The bishop is permitted to visit exempt religious only in the cases expressly stated in the law.

The corresponding canon in the 1983 Code is:

> Can. 397 — §2. The bishop may visit the members of religious institutes of pontifical right and their houses only in the cases stated in the law.

Just as the 1917 Code clearly recognized congregations with simple vows as true religious institutes and gave them a place in the general laws of the Church, the 1983 Code granted them juridical parity with the great orders with solemn vows.

Trend Toward Uniformity
in the Constitutions of Religious Institutes

The *Normæ* of 1901 were established to meet the needs of many recently founded religious communities. In some cases the founders, local ordinaries, and their advisors did not have the necessary canonical background to compose adequate constitutions. As an aid the second section of the *Normæ* contained

---

[32] *Communicationes*, 7 (1975), p. 85.

[33] *Communicationes*, 7 (1975), p. 88. The quote is from *Christus Dominus* no. 35, 3.

J. ROUSSEAU, O.M.I. suggested that the term *exemption* in reference to religious be eliminated, and that all religious be either pontifical or diocesan, and that the juridical distinctions concerning internal autonomy be based on that difference ("De relationibus iuridicis religiosorum cum sacra hierarchia recognoscendis," in *Apollinaris*, 60 [1967], pp. 215–263).

a "*Schema Constitutionum*," which is a detailed outline with 280 articles (art. 42–321) of what should be contained in the constitutions of an approved institute.[34]

From our post Vatican II perspective the *Normæ* sinned by insisting on the exclusion of spiritual elements from sources of revelation and the spiritual heritage of the particular institute, as well as the requirement of repeating norms of law contained elsewhere.

> 26. It is not permitted to have in the constitutions prefaces, introductions, forewords, historical notes, letters of encouragement or praise, save letters of praise and approval granted by the Holy See.
>
> 27. The quoting of texts of Holy Scripture, Councils, Fathers of the Church, of theologians, and of any book or author are to be excluded.[35]

In 1921 the Sacred Congregation for Religious published new *Normæ* which were hardly less restrictive than those of 1901. The above mentioned articles were repeated almost verbatim. The article concerning what is to be placed in the constitutions is very indicative of the official position at that time.

> 22. i) . . . since constitutions must contain only constitutive laws of a Congregation and directive laws for community activity, whether these pertain to government or to discipline and norms of life . . .[36]

The Sacred Congregation de Propaganda Fide published similar *Normæ* in 1940. An indication of both the need of the *Normæ* for many communities and the danger of them being practically copied can be seen in the *nota bene* that precedes them.[37]

> N.B. — This outline is not a *text* to be adopted as constitutions, but an *example* to be followed in drawing up Constitutions.

The purely juridical nature that constitutions were to have is seen again in this text:

> 12. The following are to be excluded from the text of constitutions:

---

[34] CONGREGATION OF BISHOPS AND REGULARS, *Normæ*, 1901, pp. 13–54.

[35] Ibid., p. 10.

[36] CONGREGATION FOR RELIGIOUS, *Normæ quas Sacra Congregatio pro Religiosis in novis congregationibus approbandis procedere solet*, March 6, 1921, in *AAS*, 13 (1921), pp. 312–317.

[37] CONGREGATION DE PROPAGANDA FIDE, *Normæ pro Constitutionibus congregationum iuris diocesani a S. Congregatione de Propaganda Fide dependentium*, Rome, Typis Polyglottis Vaticanis, 1940. It might be of interest to note that all three of these *Normæ* use feminine nouns and pronouns in referring to religious, although they apply to male religious as well. These *Normæ* for mission countries were especially needed for congregations founded by the local ordinaries with the encouragement of the Holy See.

a) prefaces, historical notes, letters of encouragement, and similar matters;

b) repetition of texts of Holy Scripture and of any book or author; . . .

The Sacred Congregation of Bishops and Regulars, and its successor the Sacred Congregation for Religious were very strict in the application of the *Normæ*. This resulted in a great similarity in the constitutions of very different communities. This was so much so that many, if not most institutes, had in their constitutions the same ends, works, kind of government, administration, etc.[38] The various communities were distinguished and kept their own identity by their customs, traditions, religious habit, particular devotions, and prayers.

Emphasis on the Particular Charism and Traditions of Each Institute

In *Lumen gentium* and *Perfectæ caritatis* the Fathers of Vatican II reaffirmed the ancient practice of giving religious institutes much greater latitude in composing their constitutions and rules. This was done in order that religious communities grow and flourish according to the spirit of their founders. The Council also affirmed that the sound traditions of each institute constitute its spiritual patrimony.[39] Paul VI in the motu proprio *Ecclesiæ Sanctæ* issued special norms for the implementation of the decisions of Vatican II and set new ground rules for the renewal of the constitutions of religious institutes.

12. The general laws of every institute (constitutions, typica, rules or whatever other name is given to these) must, generally speaking contain the following elements:

a) the evangelical and theological principles concerning religious life and its incorporation in the Church, and an apt and accurate formulation in which "the spirit and aims of the founder should be clearly recognized and faithfully preserved, as indeed should each institute's sound traditions, for all of these constitute the patrimony of an institute" (*PC*, no. 2, b)

---

[38] See X. OCHOA, C.F.M., "Patrimonium constitutionale institutorum perfectionis," in *Commentarium pro Religiosis*, 49 (1968). p. 98, note 2. Cf. also "Opera consultorum in apparandis canonum schematibus," in *Communicationes*, 5 (1973), p. 48: "Likewise, we tried prudently but with firmness to apply the principle of subsidiarity so that in the common law concerning institutes of perfection there would be only universal and flexible principles. This was done so that the quite harmful defect of the present legislation be corrected, and that fitting liberty be left to the individual institutes in applying the prescripts as the right means to fulfil their mission in the Church and for bringing about the continual renewal which was so encouraged by the council fathers."

[39] See *LG*, no. 45; *PC*, no. 2, b.

b) the juridical norms necessary to define the character, aims and means employed by the institute. Such rules must not be multiplied unduly, but should always be clearly formulated.

13. A combination of both elements, the spiritual and the juridical, is necessary, so as to ensure that the principal codes of each institute will have a solid foundation and be permeated by a spirit which is authentic and a law which is alive. Care must be taken not to produce a text either purely juridical or merely exhortatory.[40]

Paul VI emphasized that to a great extent it was up to each institute to bring about its own spiritual and apostolic renewal in light of Vatican II. He affirmed that this must not be left up to just the general chapters, but that all superiors and members must be involved in preparing the chapters and following through with the decisions of the chapters. This process was to include the study of and meditation on the Scriptures, and also an investigation and exposition of the theological, historical, and canonical aspects of religious life. Each institute was to pursue a study of its own original spirit, so that it could be faithfully preserved in making the necessary adaptation in freeing itself from foreign and obsolete elements.[41] It should be noted that nowhere did Paul VI or Vatican II call for a complete redrafting of constitutions. The call was for all these elements to be present in the constitutions.

This invitation of the pope was met with great enthusiasm by some religious, and with indifference or even resistance by others. The task of renewal by return to spiritual roots for greater service to the Church was more difficult than perhaps anyone realized at the time. With some it encountered inflexibility in maintaining that all the traditions of an institute were sacred, and with others an over eager tossing out of most of the past as obsolete and having no place in the *renewed* Church. Rewriting constitutions was a formidable task. Some went far beyond the call of Vatican II and Paul VI and drafted completely different constitutions which had little similarity with the text

---

[40] Paul VI, motu proprio, *Ecclesiæ Sanctæ II*, August 6, 1966, in *AAS*, 58 (1966), p. 777; trans. in *CLD*, vol. 6, pp. 286–287.

[41] See ibid., nos. 15–19. Many articles were written to aid religious in this task. Cf. J. Fuertes, C.F.M., "Charisma et vita religiosa," in *Commentarium pro Religiosis*, 59 (1978), pp. 211–227, 305–329; 60 (1979), pp. 3–26; A. Gutiérrez, C.F.M., "Constitutiones congruenter recognoscantur," in *Commentarium pro Religiosis*, 46 (1967), pp. 271–292; F. Jetté, O.M.I., "Le Retour au Fondateur," *La Vie des Communautés Religieuses*, 26 (1968), pp. 307–315; P. Molinari, S.J., "Renewal of Religious Life According to the Founder's Spirit," in *Review for Religious*, 27 (1968), pp. 796–806; X. Ochoa, C.F.M., "Modus determinandi patrimonium constitutionale cuiusque Instituti perfectionis proprium," in *Commentarium pro Religiosis*, 46 (1967), pp. 337–350; 47 (1968), pp. 97–111; E. O'Connor, "Vatican II and the Renewal of Religious Life," in *Review for Religious*, 26 (1967), pp. 404–423.

received from the founders. There was perhaps now the tendency of over-emphazing the theological and spiritual elements and of omitting the norms that are necessary for a code of law to govern a human society.

The essential task in all this was to express the spiritual patrimony of the institute in its constitutions or fundamental code of law. To do this the members had to have a clear grasp of their spiritual patrimony and to express it in words. Here existed the problem of finding the essentials, the timeless elements, without either falling into traditionalism or adopting all the fads of the moment. There was a particular problem for those institutes that did not have a charismatic founder who put his or her personal stamp on the institute.[42]

As an aid in the revision of the constitutions the Sacred Congregation of Religious and Secular Institutes compiled in 1974 a document with very general guidelines applying *Ecclesiæ Sanctæ*. Replying to the question of a superior general, the secretary of the Sacred Congregation stated that these were not new *normæ*.[43] In 1978 without the permission of the Sacred Congregation "Index articulorum pro redigendis constitutionibus" was published.[44] It contained a very general outline of subjects to be included in constitutions, and a brief annotation as to their content. In responding to an objection to this document, the secretary of the Congregation explained that it was a working document and not meant for publication, and that although the Congregation had thought of issuing official criteria for constitutions, it wanted to leave the institutes freedom in composing their own constitutions in following *Ecclesiæ Sanctæ*.[45]

---

[42] See E. Sastre Santos, c.f.m., "De normis ad codices congregationum religiosarum congruenter recognoscendos," in *Commentarium pro Religiosis*, 59 (1978), pp. 138–175. In particular pp. 141–143, note 19.

[43] See *Concilium "16"*, January 25, 1974, 3/74, p. 2, and the attached *Orientamenti per le Constituzioni*.

[44] See *Commentarium pro Religiosis*, 59 (1978), pp. 191–200.

[45] See *Concilium "16"*, 10/79 (February 23, 1979), pp. 2–6. For a reaction see *Commentarium pro Religiosis*, 61 (1980), pp. 144–145, and in particular note 3.

What is the best solution for this very real problem? Many institutes need assistance for the writing of their constitutions. Others want to know what *must* be in their constitutions to obtain approval from the Sacred Congregation. Should an institute be required to repeat in its constitutions what is already in the common law for all religious? Why repeat laws that are already in force? If there is not such repetition, is there not a danger that many religious, and even superiors, will not know the very basic elements of the common law that refer to them and their institutes? It would seem that no one wants new *normæ*. What criteria are the consultors of the Congregation to use in reviewing constitutions submitted for approval? Does much depend on which consultors

The commission for revision of the code of canon law set about its work by establishing principles to guide the revision. Two of the principles in particular shed light on the spirit guiding their work to incorporate the teaching of Vatican II in the revised law of the Church:

> 3. The sacred nature and organic construction of the ecclesial community shows that the juridical nature of the Church and all its institutions are directed toward furthering the supernatural life . . . For that reason the juridical order of the Church, its laws and precepts, the rights and obligations flowing from them must be in conformity with its supernatural end, for law in the mystery of the Church is a sacrament or sign of the supernatural life of the faithful, which it both signifies and fosters . . .[46]

> 5. What was just said pertains to the application of the *principle of subsidiarity* in canon law . . . The principle upholds legislative unity that must be preserved in the basic positions and in the more important pronouncements of the law of any society that is complete and coherent in its kind (*compactæ in genere suo*). It demonstrates the expedience and necessity of providing for the welfare especially of individual institutions by particular law made by them and by their having reasonable and recognized autonomy of executive governance . . .[47]

The study group for the law for religious refined further the general principles in order to more easily apply them in their task. They formulated four guiding principles based on *Perfectæ caritatis* and *Ecclesiæ Sanctæ* for their work in revising religious law:

> I. In the revision of the law for religious, the canons will be so drafted that it will appear that the juridical norms, although they are a treasure of grace for religious life, do not include everything, much less exhaust its riches, to promote God's gift of a religious vocation, assist the working of grace in souls dedicated to God to reach the perfection of charity and preserve them from dangers . . . With this guiding principle the group seeks to avoid on one hand an excessive number of norms which are better left to particular law, and on the other hand the idea, common even among some dedicated to seeking perfection, that formal and external observance of both common and particular law are sufficient for perfection . . .

> II. The canons that regulate religious discipline must promote the recognition of and the preserving of the spirit of the founder in each institute; help religious families to preserve their own patrimony, which consists in its own special nature, ends and sane traditions . . .

---

review a particular constitution? Are there objective norms?

[46] *Communicationes*, 1 (1969), p. 79.

[47] Ibid., pp. 80–81. Cf. comment by Paul VI on the application of this principle in the reform of the Code (ibid., p. 89).

III. While constitutive principles in religious life must be clearly stated and sanctioned—a proper flexibility in making disciplinary laws is to be maintained so that these can be easily adapted to different conditions and needs of the Church and of individuals . . . The group applied this principle extensively by formulating very general norms as a secondary principle and leaving a more specific determination to particular law, which as was stated above, will have great importance in the revised law . . .

IV. The canons that regulate governance and its exercise in religious institutes are to be so drafted that the conciliar principles of representation and cooperation of the members will be efficaciously put into practice . . . Religious institutes, or institutes of perfection, in general are above all else communities. For that reason they must not only live in a communitarian fashion, but also act as a community taking into account the nature, spirit, end of each institute . . .[48]

The text is burdened by these long quotations in order to show the determination of the study group to incorporate the council decisions in the revised Code. The revised canon law was not to be just the dry bones of law, but was to be fleshed out to make it a living reality in the Church.

Repeatedly in the reports of the study group are found references to these principles and the necessity of basing the new law on them.[49] The application of these principles pervades the whole section of the Code on institutes of consecrated life. They are particularly enshrined in three canons.

Can. 578 — The mind of the founders, and their dispositions concerning the nature, purpose, spirit and character of the institute which have been approved by the competent ecclesiastical authority, together with its sound traditions, all of which comprise the patrimony of the institute itself, are to be faithfully observed by all.

Can. 586 — §1. A true autonomy of life, especially of governance, is recognised for each institute. This autonomy means that each institute has its own discipline in the Church and can preserve whole and entire the patrimony described in c. 578.

Can. 587 - §1. To protect more faithfully the vocation and identity of each institute, the fundamental code or constitutions of the institute are to contain, in addition to those elements which are to be preserved in accordance with can. 578, basic norms about the governance of the institute, the

---

[48] *Communicationes*, 2 (1970), pp. 170–173.

[49] *Communicationes*, 5 (1973), p. 48. See ibid. pp. 56 and 67–68; and 2 (1970), p. 177, and 9 (1977), p. 55: "Thus, on the one hand a so-called levelling of institutes of consecrated life by excessive particular and minute juridical norms is avoided, and on the other hand institutes and their members are helped to find, through a true and fitting renewal, their own identity and own internal spirit if they have lost it, or to strengthen and preserve it."

discipline of the members, the admission and formation of members, and the proper object of their sacred bonds.

Clerical Religious Institutes

Although the first male religious, hermits and monks, were not priests, clerical religious institutes have had an important role in the Church for many centuries. Vermeersch summarized the relationship between priesthood and religious profession in various institutes in this way:

> Therefore the priesthood, which is something secondary for monks, for mendicants is equal in the intention with religious life. Priesthood for canons regular and clerics regular is in a certain way the principal thing intended, so that with them the religious life is added to the priesthood, rather than the contrary.[50]

Clerical religious congregations fit in this summary with the clerics regular, since they are similar in all except they make simple, not solemn vows.

The call of Vatican II to all religious to renewal has been the occasion for many members of clerical institutes to question whether or not priesthood is essential to their own institute. A number of different issues have contributed to this question. Many ministries are now open to the laity that in the past were de facto reserved to priests. There has been the desire to give lay religious, the brothers, full equality. How can this be done if the institute is clerical by definition and by law? There has been also a reaction to excessive clericalization in the Church, and to a ministry limited almost exclusively to the celebration of the liturgy and pious devotions.

The legal distinction between clerical and lay institutes in the 1917 Code was of little assistance in answering this problem. During the writing of the Code there was difficulty in finding the best formulation for this particular point, and it seems that the final text was an inadequate compromise. The 1912 draft of the Code had defined an institute as clerical in this way:

> A clerical religious institute is one which by its own end is directed to works that require the priesthood, or (aut) a notable part of the members are priests or preparing for the priesthood.[51]

---

[50] A. VERMEERSCH, S.J., and I. CREUSEN, S.J., *Epitome Iuris Canonici*, 7th ed., Malines, Dessain, 1949, vol. 1, no. 586. Many Franciscans (and perhaps others) might object to the accuracy of this statement in so far as it applies to their particular institute.

[51] A. LARRAONA, C.F.M., "Commentarium in partem secundam libri Codicis," *Commentarium pro Religiosis*, 2 (1921), pp. 284–285. The various draft texts of this canon in the preparation of the 1917 Code are reproduced there.

The 1914 draft substituted the word *et* (and) for *aut* (or), and thus required both elements. The 1917 Code itself dropped the first element, the end of the institute, and mentioned only the number of members who were priests.

> Can. 488 — 4°. A *clerical religious institute* is one in which a notable part of the members are priests; otherwise, it is a *lay institute*.

Thus, the distinction as presented in the law was based on something that could be very accidental and extrinsic to the nature of the institute. In fact, there could be and are clerical institutes that have more lay members than priests, e.g., the Viatorians and the Marianists. On the other hand, the determination by the end, as it was presented, seems inadequate since an institute with the end of christian education of youth could be either lay or clerical.[52]

Title I *De Institutis Religiosis*" in the 1977 *schema* (draft) had divided religious institutes into two categories—monastic and those dedicated to apostolic works. These latter were subdivided into canonical institutes, conventual institutes, and apostolic institutes. It was objected that the terminology *apostolic institute* was not precise since all institutes, even monastic, are apostolic.[53]

The *schema* also stated that monastic institutes are per se neither clerical nor lay (c. 100, §3); the canonical institutes are clerical (c. 112, §1); and nothing was said about the clerical or lay nature of conventual institutes. Apostolic institutes could be either clerical or lay, but no norm was given for determining which was which.

The study group in responding to the various suggestions revised the text to better respect the nature of the various institutes. The result was the method of treatment now found in the 1983 Code. This seems to respond better to the individuality of each type of institute. Religious institutes are not divided by type in the common law. Classifications other than clerical and lay, and pontifical and diocesan are left to particular law. Religious and secular institutes are treated separately after a common section under consecrated life, and societies of apostolic life have their own section with reference back to the parts applicable to them in the previous section (c. 732).

---

[52] See LARRONA, ibid. Commenting on this canon he said that the basis for the distinction of institutes is not directly the ministry of the members. However, he added, "Without a doubt the specific end of a religious institute generally indirectly determines the distinction as a clerical or lay institute. Thus, e.g., an institute of clerics regular or of missionaries, which has as its proper end apostolic ministry, certainly is clerical, for the end of itself necessary demands that the members become priests."

[53] See *Communicationes*, 10 (1978), p. 176.

This new approach appeared in the 1980 schema. It began the treatment of whether an institute was clerical or lay by stating:

Can. 516 — §1. Institutes of consecrated life, by their very nature, are neither clerical nor lay.[54]

The key words of this statement were originally found in the previous schema in canon 100:

§3. Monastic institutes are per se neither clerical nor lay.

As it stands this could be true of monastic institutes or for religious in the abstract, but hardly so for many existing religious institutes.[55] In speaking to the Jesuits in 1974 Paul VI said, "You are *priests*; that is an essential mark of the Company. . ."[56] This was clarified by the 1983 Code:

Can. 588 –§1. In itself, the state of consecrated life (*status vitæ consecratæ*) is neither clerical nor lay.

The religious state as such is neither lay nor clerical, although a particular institute may be lay or clerical by its very nature.

Because Paul VI touched this very point, it would be good to look more closely at his address to the XXXII General Congregation of the Society of Jesus in 1974. He spoke of the essential characteristics of the members of the Society—religious, apostles, priests especially united to the pope by vow:

Although the ancient practice of having brothers who do not become priests is not to be underestimated, for these worthy men have always performed an honorable and important work in your institute, you are *priests*; that is an essential mark of the Company. The priestly element was demanded by your lawgiver Father for all professed religious. He rightly did this for the priesthood is indeed necessary for the Order that he established in order that it especially care for the sanctification of the people by the divine Word and the sacraments. Your dedication to the exercise of the apostolic life—it is good to repeat it—is to be done in the fullest sense: by the charism of sacred orders by which a man is conformed to Christ sent by the Father. It is principally from this as a source that the apostolic nature of mission flows which you receive ex officio as sons of Ignatius.[57]

Thus, the pope affirmed that the Society of Jesus was by its very nature an institute of priests because of the intention of St. Ignatius as founder, and

---

[54] PONTIFICAL COMMISSION FOR THE REVISION OF THE CODE, *Schema Codicis Iuris Canonica (Patribus Commissionis reservatum)*, Vatican City, Libreria Editrice Vaticana, 1980. p. 125.

[55] See *Communicationes*, 15 (1983), p. 61.

[56] PAUL VI, allocution, "Sodalibus et Societate Iesu qui ad religiosæ suæ communitatis præsidium Cœtum Romam convenerunt," December 3, 1974 in *AAS*, 66 (1974), p. 717.

[57] Ibid.

from the very nature of their apostolic ministry which required priests for the celebration of the Word and the sacraments.

The marked change between the 1977 *schema* and the 1980 *schema* is evident. In the former the description of clerical and lay institutes was based on their works along with an exhortation to be faithful to them, and not to be lead away from them,

> Can. 117 — §1. Clerical Institutes will faithfully fulfill the ministry in exercising holy orders; other spiritual and corporal apostolic works, however, will be entrusted to other capable persons including the laity, unless the works are proper to the institute.
>
> Can. 118. Lay Institutes of both men and women fulfill the pastoral office of the Church through spiritual and corporal works of mercy and by serving people in various ways; wherefore they will remain faithful to the grace of their vocation.

It is not hard to see that a new approach was made taking into account *Lumen gentium*.[58] With stylistic changes the ideas of the council document are found in the revised Code. The Code Commission has admirably succeeded in incorporating the pastoral and theological teaching of Vatican II in the Church's law. The 1983 Code has:

> Can. 588 — §2. A clerical institute is one which, by reason of the end or purpose intended by the founder, or by reason of lawful tradition, is under the governance of clerics, presupposes the exercise of sacred orders, and is recognised as such by ecclesiastical authority.
>
> §3. A lay institute is one which is recognised as such by ecclesiastical authority because, by its nature, character and purpose, its proper role, defined by its founder or by lawful tradition, does not include the exercise of sacred orders.

This canon points out clearly the fundamental difference between clerical and lay institutions—the former presupposes the exercise of sacred orders, and the latter do not.[59] It is not the question of the individual members undertak-

---

[58] *LG*, no. 45; this text is found at the beginning of this chapter on page 123.

[59] It would be an unwarranted conclusion to say that it is inappropriate for monks to be ordained priests even though they may never assume pastoral ministry.

On April 18, 1971 Paul VI wrote to the minister general of the Carthusians: "From the very beginning of the Carthusian Order choir monks were either priests or religious preparing for the priesthood. There are some today who think that it is improper for those, who as monks or hermits will never exercise the sacred ministry, to be raised to the priesthood. As we said previously this opinion lacks a secure and solid foundation. For many saints and a great number of religious have united the profession of the monastic life, and even of the hermetical life, with the priesthood since they saw a fitting harmony between these two consecrations, that of the priest

ing the exercise of sacred orders, but of the institute as such. Does the institute have as its purpose the exercise of the ministerial priesthood or of only the common priesthood of the faithful?

The specific goal of priestly ministry is determined by the intention or purpose of the institute set by the founder, e.g., Ignatius in the case of the Jesuits, or by legitimate tradition, e.g., in the case of the Augustinians.[60] In a clerical institute the leadership is exercised by clerics (*sub modermine clericorum*).[61]

The other essential element is the particular type of approval given by the proper authority in the Church, i.e., by the Holy See or to the diocesan bishop. Without this approval the institute has no public juridical standing in the Church and no official role in the mission of the Church. No one, either an individual priest or an institute can legitimately exercise sacred orders without the authorization to do so from the Holy Father or the diocesan bishops who have the mission from Jesus to pasture his flock.[62]

The determination that an institute is clerical is not something extrinsic to it and imposed from the outside, but is based on its purpose to exercise the ministerial priesthood. This determination of its end is either from the founder or by the legitimate tradition of the institute. Consequently this canon is in

---

and that of the monk" (*AAS*, 63 [1971], p. 488).

On November 18, 1966 Paul VI said to the major superiors of Italy attending a congress in Rome: "If in fact the priesthood has been joined to monasticism, this has come about from the understanding of the harmony between the monastic and priestly consecrations . . . This harmony between the consecrated life through religious profession and sacerdotal consecrations, this special modelling of the religious priest to Christ, Priest and Victim, is realized in all other forms of clerical religious life. For in these there is a special link between the two consecrations. The special bond existing in these institutes between the religious profession and priestly ministry has as a consequence that 'the entire religious life of the members should be imbued by an apostolic spirit, and all their apostolic activity with a religious spirit' (*PC*, no. 8)" (*AAS* 58 [1966], pp. 1178–1182).

[60] See B. Rano, s.v. "Agostiniani," in *Dizionario degli Istituti di Perfezione*, Rome, Edizioni Paoline, 1974, vol. 1, p. 314.

[61] The question of brothers serving as superiors in clerical institutes with special reference to the Missionary Oblates of Mary Immaculate will be treated in chapter six.

[62] "In the eucharistic assembly the people of God are called together under the presidency of the bishop or of a priest authorized by him, who acts in the person of Christ" (c. 899, §2). ". . . priests and deacons, with the at least presumed consent of the rector of a church, have the faculty to preach everywhere, unless this faculty has been restricted or removed by the competent ordinary, or unless particular law requires express permission" (c. 764). "Apostolic action [of religious institutes] exercised in the name of the Church and by its command is to be performed in communion with the Church" (c. 675, §3).

complete conformity with the principle of subsidiarity and respectful of the legitimate autonomy of the institute.[63]

This determination by the institute itself is sanctioned by the proper Church authority through approval and, in the case of a clerical institute, the mission to exercise ordained priestly ministry, to share in the hierarchical service of preaching the Word and sanctifying its own members and the faithful by the celebration of the Eucharist and the other sacraments. Hence, this canon is also in complete conformity with the principles of ecclesiastical communion and canonical mission to exercise the pastoral ministry.

Summary

In the development of religious institutes and the laws governing them can be seen the Church as a divinely constituted human society. The working of the Holy Spirit appears not only in religious founders and their institutes, but also in the hierarchical Church guided by the same Spirit in testing, approving, guiding, and legislating for religious institutes and their activity. The human is very evident in the religious institutes as their members with lofty ideals face the reality of human frailty. The human is also seen in the hierarchical Church as it struggles to fulfill its mission in leading the faithful. This can be seen especially in the effort to legislate in a way that respects the freedom of the children of God while leading them on to live the demands of the Gospel that they have chosen to embrace more closely. This is a never ending task as people and times change and are led in new directions by the Holy Spirit. It is this precise task that was attempted in revising the Code of Canon Law. Even this very brief treatment of a few articles reveals the great progress that was made by the whole Church working together.

The canonical norms for religious are meant to be a means to help them live their vocation to holiness of life in honoring the Father and serving their brothers and sisters in imitation of Jesus. Just as this chapter began by quoting the Fathers of Vatican II on the place of religious in the Church, perhaps it can best be closed by quoting the challenge that they presented to religious.

Religious should try hard to ensure that through them the Church more effectively shows forth the real Christ—to believers and unbelievers—in prayer on the mountain, or announcing the kingdom of God to the crowds, or healing the sick and the wounded and turning sinners to a better life, or

---

[63] There is also a problem of semantics. The word *clerical* in some cultures has pejorative political and sociological connotations. It is evident that the word here is to be understood in its original and still legitimate theological and canonical sense.

blessing children and doing good to everybody, always, however, in obedience to the will of the Father who sent him. . . .

Let all, then, who have been called to the profession of the counsels make every effort to preserve and make greater progress in the vocation to which God has called them, for the richer holiness of the Church and the greater glory of the one and undivided Trinity, which in Christ and through Christ is the source and origin of all holiness.[64]

Having considered the foundation and juridical development of the Missionary Oblates of Mary Immaculate, as well as the juridical status of pontifical clerical religious congregations in general, we are ready to examine whether the Oblates are properly defined as a clerical religious institute, or whether such a denomination is—as some would suggest—an unjust imposition by the Holy See upon the society founded by Eugene de Mazenod.

---

[64] LG, nos. 46–47.

Chapter V
A Clerical Religious Institute

L ife is so multifaceted that it cannot be expressed adequately in words. For this reason every legislator faces the difficulty of drafting universal norms that respect all aspects of the people and institutions to be governed by law. Since every society must have laws, the legislator must do his best, while realizing that his efforts will present imperfect results—which consequently are open to criticism.

In the last chapter were seen the long struggles traversed before the present legislation for religious communities with simple vows was achieved and the similar exertion to describe adequately the distinction between clerical and lay institutes. Is the legislation perfect? Does it reflect satisfactorily the historical and charismatic reality of all religious institutes? Some religious may feel that their institute does not fit into the categories found in the law. Even the word *clerical* raises hackles. Unfortunately this term, which is used in a precise legal sense in c. 588, §2, also carries for some persons many unpleasant connotations. On the other hand, could more be expected? Is it not unrealistic to expect the perfect in this world?

A great step forward was made by the revised Code. By following the lead of *Lumen gentium*, it attempts to respect the individual intrinsic reality of each religious institute. This appears in the consideration of the end of the institute as determined by the founder and the institute's sound traditions as deciding factors in the juridical classification of an institute as clerical or lay.[1]

The present chapter is about one particular religious congregation, the Missionary Oblates of Mary Immaculate. First a few words will be said relative to the Oblates being a religious congregation. This is followed by the main subject of this chapter and of the dissertation—whether the description of clerical institutes as contained in c. 588, §2 is appropriate to it.

A Religious Congregation

Although his original intention was to found a house of diocesan missionaries, de Mazenod's society soon became a religious community. Since no one seems to question that the Missionary Oblates of Mary Immaculate is

---

[1] Supra pp. 140–145.

a religious congregation with simple vows, it will suffice to summarize here the data presented in chapter two which illustrate this fact.

De Mazenod had written Tempier in the fall of 1815 that the missionaries would not make vows,[2] and the first draft of the petition to the vicars general capitular of Aix for approval stated the same explicitly. Nevertheless the actual petition of January 25, 1816 did not even mention the question of vows.[3] Already in November 1817 de Mazenod in a letter to Tempier, concerning the novices, said that they must not forget that they belong to a congregation of *regular clergy*.[4]

The Constitutions adopted 1818 by the Missionaries of Provence included the vows of celibacy, obedience, and perseverance. Poverty was added in 1821.[5] At that time it was decided that the members of the society would henceforth be called *Father*—in conformity with the practice for religious priests—and no longer be addressed as *Monsieur*.[6] This was the customary title for the secular clergy and for priests who were members of institutes without public vows. It is clear that, although the society lacked ecclesiastical approval, de Mazenod and his associates considered themselves to be regulars or religious.

With the introduction of the Constitutions in 1818 a new vocabulary was also adopted—that of *oblate* and *oblation*. De Mazenod had translated *oblazione*, the word used by Alphonsus Liguori for religious profession.[7] Henceforth the members would make their *oblation* and become *Oblates*. First only the professed students were commonly called *simple Oblates* or *Oblates*. With time all professed members would be called *Oblates*, and speak of themselves as *the Oblates* or the *Oblate Fathers*, or the *Missionary Oblates*.[8]

On February 17, 1826 Leo XII approved both the institute as a congregation with simple vows and the new name of Missionary Oblates of Mary

---

[2] Supra p. 26.

[3] Ibid.

[4] Supra p. 28.

[5] Supra pp. 30–32.

[6] Supra pp. 32–34.

[7] Supra p. 34.

[8] In the 1826 Constitutions the noun *oblati* (*oblates* in English) is used 28 times; 15 times it refers to the professed students who are called once *scholastici oblati*, five times to the professed students and priests, and twice to all professed members of the Congregation. Once the expression *sacerdotes oblati* (oblate priests) is used. Religious profession is always spoken of as *oblation*.

Immaculate.[9] The Constitutions of 1853 added in the first article the expression "Religionis votis obligati" to the words "sacerdotes sæculares."[10] Until the pontificate of Leo XIII, members of institutes with simple vows were considered to be seculars, and not religious. Following the 1917 Code of Canon Law, the 1928 Constitutions dropped the word *sæculares*. The 1982 Constitutions state: "Elle groupe en communautés apostoliques des prêtres et des frères qui se lient à Dieu par les vœux de religion" (art. 1). The official English translation of the same article reads: "We come together in apostolic communities of priests and Brothers, united to God by the vows of religion."

De Mazenod's Intent and Purpose as Founder

The story of de Mazenod's vocation to the priesthood is long and circuitous. The first indications were seen during his exile in Venice as the disciple of Don Bartolo.[11] These went into eclipse during his forced sojourn in Naples and Palermo and also during the first years of his return to Aix. His main concern then was to restore the family finances through recovery of the property lost during the Revolution and of a fitting marriage.[12] A new period of religious fervor began and was marked by the experience of Good Friday 1807.[13] This was climaxed by his entering St. Sulpice Seminary and ordination to the priesthood.[14]

His personal history, as the heir of a noble family noted for its loyalty to Provence, the Bourbon royalty, and the Holy See, as well as being strongly anti-Jansenistic, set him apart from his fellow priests.[15] The vicars capitular general of Aix allowed him to choose his own ministry, and his zeal turned to those not reached by the parish clergy—the poor and servants, who did not understand French, the youth attending the achristian college, the prisoners, and dying. He preached at least one rural mission, and experienced the religious deprivation of the country people.[16]

---

[9] Supra pp. 47–49.

[10] Supra p. 66.

[11] Supra pp. 3–4.

[12] Supra pp. 5–6.

[13] Supra pp. 6–7.

[14] Supra pp. 7–8.

[15] Supra pp. 12–13.

[16] Supra pp. 12–18.

De Mazenod was confirmed in his decision to work in his native France and in particular in Provence by the reply of Pius VII to his long-time friend de Forbin-Janson, who wanted to go to China: "Especially to our brothers in faith."[17] In 1814 the latter founded with Rauzan the Missionaries of France, and pressed de Mazenod to join them. It was the following year that de Mazenod was moved by divine grace to found his own mission band for rural Provence, the Missionaries of Provence.[18]

De Mazenod and his companions embraced the tried and true apostolic method of bringing people back to the practice of their faith—extraordinary preaching leading to a reconversion, confession, and communion.[19] In addition to the missions, the society had as its ends the other ministries that de Mazenod had personally exercised as a priest—youth, prisoners, dying, and other extraordinary preaching, plus the replacement of the religious orders wiped out by the Revolution.[20] This latter responded to their desire to lead a regular community life. The intent and purpose of the Missionaries of Provence was the same as that of de Mazenod's personal call and charism—following the example of Jesus by holiness of life and the evangelization of the poor along with an intense prayer life.

This was stated very clearly in both the petition to the vicars general capitular of Aix and the first article of the Constitutions adopted in 1818.[21]

But who are we indeed that the good God should listen to our pleas? We are, or we ought to be, holy priests who consider themselves happy and very happy to devote their fortune, their health, their life in the service and for the glory of God. We are put on earth, particularly in our house, to sanctify ourselves while helping each other by our example, our words and our prayers. Our Lord Jesus Christ has left to us the task of continuing the great work of the redemption of mankind. It is towards this unique end that all our efforts must tend; as long as we will not have spent our whole life and given all our blood to achieve this, we have nothing to say; especially when as yet we have given only a few drops of sweat and a few spells of fatigue. This spirit of being wholly devoted to the glory of God, the service of the Church and the salvation of souls, is the spirit that is proper to our Congregation, a small one, to be sure, but which will always be powerful as long as it is holy. Our novices must steep themselves in these thoughts,

---

[17] Supra p. 19.

[18] Supra pp. 21–22.

[19] Supra p. 22.

[20] Supra pp. 17–18

[21] Supra pp. 25–26, and 30.

which must sink deep in them and be often meditated. Each society in the Church has a spirit which is its own; which is inspired by God according to the circumstances and needs of the times wherein it pleases God to raise these supporting bodies or rather it would be better to say these elite bodies which precede the main army on march, which excel in its bravery and which thus obtain the more brilliant victories.[22]

Perhaps this long paragraph should be summarized to emphasize the thoughts expressed by de Mazenod: each society in the Church has its own spirit, and the spirit of the Missionaries of Provence is that of a group of priests living in community in order to strive for personal holiness, continue the work of redemption, seek the glory of God, serve the Church, and obtain salvation of souls.

"Mission" and "Missionary"

De Mazenod gave no reason for choosing the name *Missionnaires de Provence*, and there was no need for him to do so. Everyone understood what was meant, and it was clear why the name was chosen. Rauzan and de Forbin-Jason had established the *Missionnaires de France*, a group of priests to conduct missions throughout France. De Mazenod and his companions were doing the same, but they would work in Provence. Perhaps there was another reason—the similar name could make easier an eventual joining of the two societies.[23]

Both the institute and residence were called *la mission*, and placed under the patronage of St. Vincent de Paul. The same was true of the church in Aix— it also was popularly called the church *de la Mission*.[24] The vigil of the feast of St. Vincent de Paul was to be preceded by a day of fast by the members of the community.[25]

---

[22] DE MAZENOD, to Tempier, August 22, 1817, *Oblate Writings*, vol. 6, no. 21, p. 35. Emphasis added.

[23] "However at this moment, as we begin, we must appear to have in common only the name, so as not to frighten both our superiors and the missionaries themselves who, with the exception of Deluy do not want to travel or work outside the diocese or who at the most [would go] into neighboring dioceses where they speak the Provençal tongue. Explain all that to M. Rauzan" (DE MAZENOD, to de Forbin-Janson, October 23, 1815, *Oblate Writings*, vol. 6, no. 5, p. 9). See also DE MAZENOD, to de Forbin-Janson, July–August 1816, *Oblate Writings*, vol. 6, no. 13, pp. 20–23.

[24] Supra p. 27. For examples of this: DE MAZENOD, to his mother, November 18, 1817: "It is necessary that my priest uncle take up residence at the Mission" (LM); Fortuné DE MAZENOD, to Eugene's father, August 16, 1818: "a deacon of the Mission" (FB); in *Missions O.M.I.* 84 (1957), p. 297.

[25] "Constitutions 1818," partie II, c. II, §2.

Although the first Christian missionaries were the Apostles, the word *mission* in the religious sense had its origin in the sixteenth and early seventeenth centuries.[26] It referred first to the sending of the Jesuits by the pope in virtue of their fourth vow. In France Pierre de Bérulle used in 1613 the word *mission* in the sense of extraordinary preaching to Catholics. Vincent de Paul in 1617 called his ministry of re-evangelization of the rural Catholics *mission*. The word was used in reference to the *sending* by the bishop for this work. In 1625 he established the *Congregation of the Mission*, or *Prêtres de la Mission*. Two contemporary groups adopted the name *Prêtres de la Mission*, but dropped it upon his insistence.

The various reference works consistently mention Vincent de Paul and the Congregation of the Mission, or Lazarists to use the common French term, in connection with the word *mission* and *missionary*.

By his adopting the words *mission* and *missionary* de Mazenod placed his society in the tradition of Vincent de Paul. If we are to understand what de Mazenod and his contemporaries meant when they employed these words, it is necessary to know exactly what they meant in nineteenth century France.

A dictionary printed in 1694 defined *missionnaire*: "Ecclésiastique [sic] qui est envoié pour catéchizer & pour prêcher."[27]p The eighteenth edition (1740) of the monumental dictionary of L. Moreri has: "Ecclésiastiques ou Religieux qui sont envoyez par le Pape ou par les Évêques, pour prêcher la foi aux Infidèles, ou pour réunir à l'Église les Hérétiques & les Schismatiques,"[28] and gives as examples the Jesuits, Carmelites, and the Capuchins.

Another dictionary that was printed two years after de Mazenod's death has: "Missionnaires, ecclésiastiques séculiers ou reguliers chargés de repandre la foi catholique parmi les hérétiques et les infidèles . . . En France le 1er établissement de missionnaires fut celui des Lazaristes, qui date de 1632 . . ."[29]

---

[26] See A. SEUMOIS, O.M.I., *Théologie Missionnaire*, 5 vols., Rome, Bureau de Presse O.M.I., 1973–1981), vol. 1, pp. 8-16; and id. *Teologia missionaria*, Bologna, Edizioni Dehonine, 1993, pp. 12–20 for an extended presentation of the beginning of and the development of the use of the word *mission* into the early seventeenth century.

[27] P. RICHET, *Nouveau Dictionnaire Français*, Cologne, Gaillard, 1694, s.v. "missionnaire."

[28] L. MORERI, *Le Grand Dictionnaire de l'Histoire*, 18th ed., Amsterdam, 1740, s.v. "missionnaires."

[29] Ch. DEZOBRY, and BACHELET, *Dictionnaire général de Biographie et d'Histoire*, Paris, Tandou, 1863, s.v. "missionnaire." In Italian the meaning was the same as in French. See R. MARONI, *Dizionario di Erudizione Storico-Ecclesiastico*, Venice, 1847, s.v. "Missionari—Ecclesiatici secolari o regolare che si dedicano alle *Missioni pontificie*, od alle Missione straniere . . ."

The terms were used in reference to both foreign missions and missions to separated Christians, whether Orthodox or Protestant, and to lapsed or tepid Catholics. An example of a book published for the latter is *Essai sur la Conduite, que peuvent se proposer de tenir les Prêtres appelés à travailler au rétablissement de la Religion Catholique en France*. It was written by a French priest in exile in Italy because of the Revolution, and given the alternate title of *Manuel des Missionnaires*. It is a complete handbook for use of missionary priests with both theological or motivational basis for this ministry and solutions for various moral cases. The author presents preaching as the fundamental means of conversion, "The absolutely necessary means to bring back our stray brothers is the preaching of the word of God."[30]

The following definitions found in standard reference works illustrate the lateness of the extension of the word *missionary* to persons other than priests:

Published in 1931: "Missionnaire — Prêtre employé aux missions (pour convertir infidèles)." (Missionary—Priest dedicated to the missions (to convert the infidels).

"Mission – maison habitée par une congrégation de prêtres qui s'occupent de missions. (Dans ce sens prend une majuscule.)" (Mission—a house that is the residence of priests who work on missions." [In this sense a capital letter is used.])[31]

Published in 1929: "Au sens rigoureux du mot, on réserve le nom de missionaires aux seul prêtres. Les frères, sœurs, medicins, catechistes, etc. sont des auxiliares" (In the strict sense of the word, the name of missionary is reserved just to priests. The brothers, sisters, doctors, catechists, etc. are auxiliaries).[32]

Published in 1957: "Le nom de missionnaires peu être donné à quiconque, clerc ou laïque, travaille en pays infidèle à la propagation de la foi. Plus strictement il est réservé aux prêtres affectés à ce ministère . . ." (the name of missionary can be given to whoever, cleric or lay person, who works in an infidel country for the propagation of the faith. More strictly it is reserved to priests who are attached to this ministry . . .).[33]

---

[30] M. COSTE, *Essai sur la Conduite* . . ., 3rd ed., (1801), p. 50. The translation of the title is "Essay on the Method for Priests to Use Who Are Called to Reestablish the Catholic Religion in France," and the alternate title is "Manuel for Missionaries."

[31] *Larousse du XXᵉ Siècle en six volumes*, Paris, Larousse, 1931, s.v. "mission."

[32] *Dictionnaire de Théologie Catholique*, s.v. "Missions, personnel étranger," J.-B. PIOLET.

[33] *Dictionnaire de Droit canonique*, s.v. "Missionaire," R. NAZ.

Published in 1983: "Prêtre des missions. *Un missionnaire catholique, protestant.*" (Priest of the missions. A Catholic missionary, a Protestant
missionary.)[34]

In his manual of missiology Paventi gives the theological juridical basis for
this limitation.

> Since, however, the main office confided to the missionary is a
> participation in ecclesiastical jurisdiction, it follows that in the juridical
> sense of the word, only the priest may be called a missionary because of his
> sacred ordination. Others, brothers and sisters, can merit this title only in
> a derived sense as cooperators—often irreplaceable cooperators."[35]

Lumen gentium both reflected an evolution in the theological thought on
the role of the laity in the mission of the Church and prompted its further
development.

> The apostolate of the laity is a sharing in the Church's mission of
> salvation and everyone is commissioned to this apostolate by the Lord
> himself through baptism and confirmation.[36]

This evolution in the understanding of the role of the non-ordained is reflected
in canon 225, §1 of the 1983 *Code of Canon Law* by its repetition of the above
text, and also in the section on the mission activity of the Church.

> Can. 784 — Missionaries, that is, those who have been sent by the compe-
> tent ecclesiastical authority to engage in missionary activity, may be chosen
> from the indigenous population or from others, be they secular clergy, or
> members of institutes of consecrated life or of a society of apostolic life, or
> other lay members of Christ's faithful.

Thus, the non-ordained members of the Church have not only an
evangelizing role,[37] an apostolate proper to their state in the Church, but they
can also be sent (*mittuntur*) by the competent ecclesiastical authority for a
mission task (*opus missionale*), and are truly missionaries.

---

[34] *Le Robert méthodique: dictionnaire méthodique du français actuel*, s.v., "missionnaire," Josette
REY-DEBOVE.

[35] S. PAVENTI, *La Chiesa Missionaria*, Rome, Unione Missionaria del Clero in Italia, 1949, p. 301.
Directly Paventi is speaking of the foreign missions but *mutatis mutandis* it applies to the home
missionaries.

[36] *LG*, no. 33; TANNER, p. 876. The Fathers of Vatican II used the word missionary in an all
inclusive way that included the non-ordained. *Ad gentes divinitus*, no. 26: "Therefore, all missionaries—priests, brothers, sisters and lay people—should be prepared and formed, each in accordance
with his or her particular state . . ." (TANNER, p. 1033).

[37] See *LG*, no. 35: "Therefore, even when occupied with temporal cares, the laity can and must
perform the valuable task of evangelizing the world" (TANNER, p. 878).

De Mazenod's Use of the Word "Missionary"

Since de Mazenod nowhere defined the word *missionary*, just as no one ordinarily defines the words that are used every day, and it is impossible to ask him to give us a definition, it is necessary to examine his writings to discover his meaning. Although his extant writings are indexed, the word *missionary* is not indexed. The reason is obvious—the word was used so often that it would have caused great difficulty to do so and the index would contain so many entries as to be practically worthless. The same is true of the 1928 Constitutions which have a twenty-four page index of 183 key words. The word *mission* is indexed, *missionary* is not. The listings would have been so many as to be almost useless.[38]

One cannot reasonably examine all his writings. What is to be done? Since the Constitutions are his major work, it will suffice to examine them minutely, and then see if the conclusions drawn are confirmed elsewhere. Most of the writings not mentioned in this dissertation are letters to family, friends, Oblates, fellow bishops, and of administration.

The 1826 *Constitutions and Rules* contain the word *missionary* seventy-six times. One finds that it is used ten times in the title of the Congregation or in a similar way, and consequently the context gives no indication as to its specific meaning. Thirteen times the use is all encompassing so as to include all the members (and even the novices). Except for once in the preface and once in the title of the section on the novitiate, all these passages are in the second part of the Constitutions.

1) Preface, "Pars secunda præscribit officia missionariis propria" (The second part deal with duty proper to the missionaries).

2) Chapter II, §2, art. 6, the missionaries will examine their conscience;

3) Chapter II, §3, art. 5, for breakfast the missionaries will have only bread;

4) Chapter II, §3, art. 8, the missionaries should have a hard bed;

5) Chapter III, §1, introduction, the missionaries will imitate the virtues of our Lord;

6) Chapter III, §1, art. 5, danger for missionaries who are not humble;

---

[38] F. JETTÉ points out that for de Mazenod "missionaries" and "apostolic men" were priests, that since his time the terminology has changed, and that today these "are equally applied to brothers and priests" (O.M.I., *The Apostolic Man, A Commentary on the 1982 Oblate Constitutions and Rules*, Rome, General House, 1992, p. 48.

In order to understand correctly de Mazenod's writings, we must keep in mind that these words had a different meaning for him, than they do for us.

7) Chapter III, §1, art. 6, the missionaries will be content with the last place;

8) Chapter III, §1, art. 7, the missionaries will be honored to perform humble tasks in the house;

9) Chapter III, §3, art. 5, the missionaries may not curl their hair;

10) Chapter III, §5, art. 3, the missionaries, when travelling, will follow the community schedule for religious exercises in so far as possible;

11) Chapter III, §5, art. 8, the missionaries, while travelling and dining with others, will be temperate in food and drink;

12) Chapter IV, §1, art. 1, when a missionary is ill, the superior will see that he has special care;

13) Pars III, chapter II, §2, the title, "De sacro novitiorum missionariorum militiæ tirocinio" (Concerning the sacred novitiate of the missionaries).

It could be argued that the references 6, 7, and 8 apply to the priests giving the missions and preaching, because of the insistence on humility. As was seen above, de Mazenod insisted on the great danger of pride for the missionaries from the success of their ministry.[39] Even though these references apply in a special way to the priests, it is evident that they refer to all the members, since they deal with the ascetical life to be practised by everyone.

Missionary occurs most frequently, forty-three times, in the first part of the Constitutions, that treats the end of the institute, missions, and other external ministry. Several examples can illustrate that in the context *missionary* means priest.

> Pars I, cap. I, art. 7. The missionaries will heal this deep and disgraceful wound (the fall of many priests from the fervor of their vocation) especially by prayer, good counsel, and example. Our houses will always be open to those whom God's grace leads to examine their conscience and to embrace a new life of penance and reparation.

> Pars I, cap. III, §2, art. 2. The missionary will, therefore, never refuse the aid of his ministry [as a confessor] to those who seek to go to confession, whether during the time of missions, or outside it.

> Pars I, cap. III, §5, art. 1. When those under the care of the missionaries fall sick, they should be prepared for the reception of the sacraments as soon as possible.

In the first part of the Constitutions the long chapter II "De Missionibus" uses the word *missionary* twenty-six times. There the word in some instances may include the professed students prior to their ordination as priests, for they

---

[39] Supra pp. 77–78.

could be used on the missions.[40] Since the students were ordained as soon as they were of canonical age, in practice this was the exception, and normally these Oblates would have been at least subdeacons: "Ordinarily novices will not be admitted to oblation unless they have received the subdiaconate."[41]

In the third part of the Constitutions the word *missionary* is used eight times:

1) Chapter I, §6, art. 9, when a canonical visitor has finished the visitation, he will return to the class of simple missionaries following his precedence in orders and oblation;

2) Chapter I, §11, art. 4, if the missionaries hear confessions after sunset . . .;

3) Chapter I, §11, art. 11, the prefect of the sacristy will assign the times for Mass for the missionaries;

4) Chapter II, §1, art. 18, the superior admits only those called by God, and in whom shine forth the qualities proper to an excellent missionary, *and* possessing the virtues forming priestly holiness;

5) Chapter II, §3, art. 8, a missionary designated by the superior general to receive vows;

6) Chapter II, §3, art. 17, Oblates, who are not yet priests, but have finished their studies, will attend the theological conferences of the missionaries;

7) Chapter II, §3, art. 22, upon ordination the missionary priests will assume their position of precedence according to the Constitutions;

8) Chapter II, §4, art. 1, the society approves the enrollment as sons men of good will, who not having the education necessary for missionaries, and not desiring to acquire it, want to save their souls in the institute performing the work that pertains to lay brothers in religious institutes.[42]

It can be concluded that in the 1826 Constitutions *missionary* in the strict sense means the priest members of the institute. These were the *missionaries,*

---

[40] *Constitutiones 1826*, pars III, cap. II, §3, art. 19.

[41] "Ordinarie ad oblationem non admittentur nisi novitii subdiaconatu insigniti" (ibid., pars III, cap. II, §3, art. 7).

[42] Ibid., pars III, cap. II, §4, art. 1, "Our Society also welcomes among her sons other men of good will who, though not having the education required for missionaries, and not desiring to acquire it, desire to labor for the salvation of their souls under the direction of the Rules of our Institute, in the performance of domestic duties as lay brothers (*religiosi famulantes*)." The Latin text uses indiscriminately *fratres laici* and *fratres famulantes*. These terms were translated in French first as *frères convers* and later as *frères coadjuteurs,* and in English as *lay brothers,* and later as *coadjutor brothers, oblate brothers, missionary brothers*. These expressions began to fall into disuse in the 1960s, and this was confirmed by a decree of the 1972 general chapter, "The term 'brothers' is applied to all Oblates who have made vows or promises according to the instruction *Renovatinis causam*, and are not ordained to the priesthood" (*Administrative Structures* 1972, p. 37, no. 36).

who were called to preach the Gospel. The simple Oblates, i.e., scholastics, were *missionaries* when they worked on the missions. Perhaps they could be called *missionaries* by vocation, i.e. they were called to become *missionaries*, and were preparing themselves to be *missionaries*, preachers of the Gospel. On the other hand, the brothers were not called directly *missionaries*, since they were not called or sent to preach. They were, however, full members of the Congregation, and were included when the word *missionary* referred to all the members of the Society. In this case they would be *missionaries* only indirectly and improperly.

The confirmation of this conclusion concerning de Mazenod's use of *missionary* can be seen in a letter that he sent to Tempier in 1821:

> They cannot be novices without taking the missionary habit (*l'habit missionnaire*). Their sojourn among the guests will have to be prolonged, that is to say, outside the novitiate, until they have their soutane, which will be given to them the day they enter the novitiate, if they arrived without it. When anyone seeks admission who already has his soutane, he should keep the rabat as long as he is with the guests and then put it aside the day of his entrance into the novitiate, because the missionary habit is the soutane without the rabat.[43]

The Constitutions spoke of the habit as *ecclesiastica talaris*, the cassock or soutane, and the large crucifix that was received at the time of oblation.[44] However, the brothers did not wear a soutane but *tunicella*, a tunic similar to a soutane but reaching somewhere below the knees, and a twelve centimeter crucifix.[45] Since they were not missionaries, they did not wear the same habit (*l'habit missionnaire*).

This conclusion is even more evident in light of the emphasis that de Mazenod placed on the crucifix, or *oblate cross*, as it came to be called, *ce signe de notre mission apostolique*.[46] Two quotes explain his insistence on wearing the crucifix. In 1816 he wrote de Forbin-Janson about the role it had already played in his own missionary experience.

---

[43] DE MAZENOD, to Tempier, January 18, 1821, *Oblate Writings*, 6, no. 59. pp. 73–74.

[44] See *Constitutiones 1826*, pars II, c. III, §3, art. 1–2. The cross is spoken of as the *instrumentum authenticum legationis*, credentials of the mission.

[45] See ibid., pars III, c. II, §4, art. 26–28; "Registre," 1843, p. 73; Pielorz, *Les Chapitres*, vol. 1, p. 192. The question of the habit of the brothers was frequently the subject of discussion at the general chapters. There was a strong resistance on the part of some priests into the twentieth century to the brothers wearing a habit. More about this in the next chapter, pp. 222–227.

[46] See DE MAZENOD, to Semeria, April 16, 1852, *Oblate Writings*, vol. 4, no. 27, p. 94: "This sacred sign of our apostolic mission."

While on this subject, I take the liberty of telling you that you would
have done well to adopt the crucifix, at least during the conducting of your
missions. You would hardly believe the effect it produces and how useful it
is. People accustomed to ecclesiastical attire are little impressed; but the
crucifix to them is awesome. How often have I seen, even among libertines,
some who, when they see it, cannot help removing their hats. It gives a
decided authority; it distinguishes the missionaries from other priests, and
that indeed is good because the missionary should be regarded as an
extraordinary man.[47]

The second written almost forty years later indicates the significance that
the cross had taken as part of the religious habit.

If necessary, it should be explained that with us the cross is an
essential part of our religious habit. We do not wear a hood or rosary
hanging from our belts, but the cross is given on the day of profession as
a distinctive sign of our ministry. We do not therefore wear it *ad libitum* as
other missionaries do.[48]

On December 11, 1825 de Mazenod asked Leo XII for a number of indulgences for the *missionaries*. One of them was; "A plenary indulgence to be gained by all the missionaries on the day of profession of vows and its anniversary."[49] The favor was granted by the rescript from Propaganda a week later:

A plenary indulgence to be gained by each missionary on the day of
his profession of vows, and its anniversary, if they contritely confess their
sins, celebrate Mass and recite prayers for the propagation of the faith, and
for the intentions of his Holiness.[50]

In 1851 de Mazenod petitioned Pius IX: ". . . since from the words of the
rescript the favor seems restricted to just the priests of the Congregation,
humbly requests that all the professed members may share the same favor."[51]

---

[47] DE MAZENOD, to de Forbin-Janson, October 9, 1816, *Oblate Writings*, vol. 6, no. 14, p. 24.

[48] DE MAZENOD, to Semeria, July 2, 1852, *Oblate Writings*, vol. 4, no. 30, p. 102.

[49] DE MAZENOD, to Leo XII, petition, December 11, 1825, Propaganda Archives, Aud. 65
(1825–2) 913 and 924; published in *Missions O.M.I.*, 79 (1952), pp. 448–449; *Écrits*, no. 4, pp. 38–40.

[50] CONGREGATION DE PROPAGANDA FIDE, rescript, December 18, 1825, Procurator's Archives O.M.I.,
XIV, no. 1; published in *Missions O.M.I.*, 79 (1952), pp. 445–446; *Écrits*, vol. 4, pp. 45–46.

[51] CONGREGATION DE PROPAGANDA FIDE, rescript, March 9, 1851, XIV, 2, Procurator's Archives
O.M.I.; published in *Constitutiones 1853*, p. 209; *Constitutiones 1894*, p. 209; *Règles et Constitutions à
l'usage des Frères Convers O.M.I.*, Marseille, 1859, the petition is explained as seeking the indulgence
"be extended to the lay brothers" because of a doubt. There is no mention of a doubt concerning
the inclusion of the simple Oblates, i.e., the scholastics, even though they could not celebrate Mass
as specified in the rescript.

Was de Mazenod's doubt about the meaning of the rescript, as to whether it applied to those who were not priests, based just on the condition of celebrating Mass? Until 1825 a number of simple Oblates had made their oblation, but no brothers had finished the novitiate and made their oblation. It seems that the doubt is based on the use of the word *missionary*. In the 1825 petition he had also requested:

> The indult for all the missionaries to bless crosses, crucifixes, holy medals, and rosaries and to attach the customary indulgences.[52]

Certainly he intended to request his particular privilege for just the priests. Evidently when he wrote *missionaries* in this case he meant exclusively the priests.

In 1851 de Mazenod wrote the president of the Central Council of the Society for the Propagation of the Faith in Lyon to thank him for an allocation of 10,000 francs for the new vicariate apostolic of Natal. He then took the opportunity to point out the sum was not sufficient to cover the expenses for the first year and the transportation. He asked that the amount be doubled to 20,000 and explained why the expenses were so great, "I must send there no less than three missionaries with the bishop, the Apostolic Vicar, who will be the head of the mission, and two brothers to serve them and act as catechists as needed."[53] A clear distinction is made between the missionaries and the brothers.

Confirmation can also be seen in the Instruction for the foreign missions. The only time the brothers are spoken of is where it is said if someone has to live alone, and there is no priest companion, that in so far as possible a brother should be with him order to fulfil the Rule.[54] The missionaries are also instructed to travel in so far as possible on a ship that has a Catholic captain "so that they may be able to fulfil the duties of both the priestly and the religious life."[55]

---

[52] CONGREGATION DE PROPAGANDA FIDE, rescript, December 18, 1825, Procurator's Archives O.M.I., XIV, no. 1; published in *Missions O.M.I.*, 79 (1952), pp. 445–446; *Écrits*, vol. 4, pp. 45–46.

[53] DE MAZENOD, to the president of the Central Committee for the Propagation of the Faith, Lyon, March 12, 1851, *Oblate Writings*, vol. 5, no. 124, p. 239. Cf. for similar usage, "El hermano que acompañará a los misioneros a las Misiones y pueblos ...," and "Al llegar en horas de silencio ó de descanso algún Misionero, Estudiante o Hermano de viage ..." ("Consueto Vicense, 1865," cited by S. SANTOS, C.F.M., "Los Hermanos Coadjutores en las Constituciones de P. Claret y una Consueta de la Casa de Vich," *Clarentianum*, 24 [1984], pp. 142 and 167).

[54] "Appendix de Externis Missionibus, Instructio," *Constitutiones 1843*, p. 173; *Constitutiones 1894*, p. 217; *Constitutiones 1910*, p. 206.

[55] "Instructio de Externis Missionibus," *Constitutiones 1853*, p. 176; *Constitutiones 1894*, p. 219;

De Maznod's original use of the word *missionary* was in conformity with the use by de Bérulle in 1613 and Vincent de Paul from 1617. Later he made the transition, just as Vincent de Paul had done before him, in using the same word in reference to the foreign missions. For him it never meant exclusively the latter. He followed a practice that had been in use for two hundred years.

It is to be noted that this double use is not the common practice of many institutes dedicated exclusively to the foreign missions, the *missiones ad gentes*.

Evangelizare Pauperibus Misit Me, Pauperes Evangelizantur

It seems that no study has been published on the origin of this motto that de Mazenod chose for his congregation. Cosentino's suggestion that it was adopted from the Vincentians appears most reasonable in light of de Mazenod's dependence on Vincent de Paul.[56] It should be noted, however, that the Vincentians have only the first part of the motto *He sent me to preach the Gospel to the poor*. The second portion, *The poor have been evangelized*, was part of the seal of the Missionaries of Provence in 1818. Both portions of the motto appear on the coat of arms printed on the title page of the 1827 Constitutions.

In recent years much time and energy, much of it very vocal and impassioned, have been spent proclaiming what it means to evangelize the poor. Many approaches can be taken. Currently the most popular is to take *poor* in a sociological sense as those who are materially deprived, with the more or less explicit implication that if this interpretation is not accepted, one is not for social justice. Such an interpretation is very facile. It is a fundamentalistic

---

Constitutiones 1910, p. 209.

[56] See Cosentino, *Histoire*, vol. 1, p. 152. Cosentino does not document his assertion. The folklore or oral tradition that de Mazenod was influenced by the Vincentian coat of arms found in the church of St. Sylvester al Quirinale (or in Monte Cavallo), where he lived (1825–1826) while awaiting the approbation of the Constitutions and the Congregation, must be judged in light of the fact that the seal of the Missionaries of Provence predates 1825. The embossed seal of the Missionaries of Provence is affixed to de Mazenod's oblation formula of November 1, 1818 (DM IX, 1). A picture of it is found in *Choix de Textes relatifs aux Constitutions et Règles O.M.I.*, Rome, 1983. Other than being oval rather than round, the basic form of the coat of arms is the same as in *Constitutiones 1827* with the inscription MP instead of OMI, and with only the last part of the motto "Pauperes Evangelizantur" on the upper edge of the seal.

For pious meditations and reflections not encumbered by historical documentation, see A. YENVEUX, O.M.I., *Les saintes Règles*, Paris: Procure Générale des Oblats, 1903, vol. 1, pp. 11–13; P. BOISRAMÉ, O.M.I., *Méditations pour tous les jours de l'année*, Tours, Mame, 1887, vol. 1, pp. 81–86; E. BAIJOT, O.M.I., "La devise des Oblats de Marie," in *Missions O.M.I.*, 50 (1926), pp. 313–316. See also G. COSENTINO, O.M.I., "Armoiries de la Congrégation," in *Études Oblates*, 24 (1965), pp. 59–61.

solution that puts the speaker on the side of the angels, and excuses from further research.

Another approach would be to go the hermeneutical route and seek the meaning in *Is* 61:1, *Lk* 4:18, and *Lk* 7:23. This method, although it is very scientific and erudite, misses the whole point.[57] It answers the wrong question. It interprets Holy Scripture, but does not tell us what de Mazenod meant.

The question is, "What did the motto mean to de Mazenod?" The only way to get the answer is to look to his writings and his practice. Any other method may give an emotionally or intellectually satisfying response, but it has no guarantee of accuracy. Just as de Mazenod did not have available the results of modern scriptural exegesis, he did not face the pastoral situations of the latter part of the twentieth century. It is one thing to speculate as to what he would do or say today, and a very different one to project anachronistically today's situations back on his time and affirm that he had today's pastoral concerns.

In his memoirs de Mazenod wrote that the principal end that he had in mind in establishing the Missionaries of Provence was the preaching of the Gospel, evangelization of the poor, prisoners and children.[58] Here again we run into the same problem as we did with the word *missionary*.

The meaning of *evangelization* was much more restricted than it is today. It was closely linked with its etymological origin, the Greek word for Gospel. All the reference works consulted give the same definition: "evangéliser— prêcher l'Évangile à . . ." (to preach the Gospel to . . .).[59]

The preaching of the Gospel was the ministry of the ordained. Even the word *ministry* in Catholic usage was restricted to the ordained clergy. Just as there was a theological development with Vatican II in the concept of who are

---

[57] In a paper presented at the XXIV Biblical Week of the Associazione Biblica Italiana, S. VIRGULIN concluded that although the *poor* (*anawim*) in Is 61:1 are indigent, their real poverty is in their spiritual stance—total openness to God, humility that is perfect in respect, obedience, and compunction—the perfection of faith. See "Gli 'Anawim' in *Is* 61, 1" (in *Evangelizare Pauperibus* Brescia, Paideia, 1978, pp. 229-236). It should be noted that the official Latin text (*Nova Vulgata Bibliorum Sacrorum Editio*, Vatican City, Typis Polyglottis Vaticanis, 1979) of Is 61:1 is: "ad annuntiandum læta mansuetis misit me." Neither of the traditional words *evangelizare* and *pauperes* is used. On the other hand the two citations from Luke that refer to Is. 61:1 are unchanged. See another paper given at the same congress by J. DUPONT, "Jesus annonce la bonne nouvelle aux pauvres" in *Evangelizare Pauperibus*, pp. 127-189 for a thorough treatment of the interpretation of the texts in Luke.

[58] Supra p. 25.

[59] See e.g., *Larousse du XXe Siècle* s.v. "evangéliser."

missionaries, there was a similar development in the role of the non-ordained in ministry and in evangelization. This development is based on their consecration in baptism and confirmation.[60]

What did de Mazenod mean by *preaching the Gospel*, evangelization? For an adequate answer it is necessary to examine not only his writings, but also his practice.

In the Preface of the Constitutions, de Mazenod presented the spiritual foundation for both the Congregation, and the Constitutions.[61] Here is seen clearly what he, as founder, had in mind:

> . . . if *priests* could be formed, afire with zeal for men's salvation . . . in a word, *apostolic men* . . . who would labor with all the resources at their command to convert others . . . striving solely for the glory of God, the good of the Church, and the growth and salvation of souls . . . men filled with zeal, ready to sacrifice goods, talents, ease, self, even their life, for the love of Jesus Christ, the service of the Church, and the sanctification of their brethren . . . ready to enter the combat, to fight, even unto death, for the greater glory of his most holy and sublime Name . . .
>
> We must spare no effort to extend the Savior's empire and to destroy the dominion of hell. We must lead men to act like human beings, first of all, and then like Christians, and, finally, we must help them to become saints . . . Such are the great works of salvation that can crown the efforts of *priests* whom God has inspired with the desire to form themselves into a Society in order to work more effectively for the salvation of souls and for their own sanctification . . .
>
> Wherefore, while pledging themselves to all the works of zeal which *priestly* charity can inspire—above all, to the work of the missions, which is the main reason for their union—these *priests* joined together in a society . . .[62]

Even a casual reading of the Preface reveals that de Mazenod intended the formation of a group of priests to follow the example of Jesus and the apostles to continue their work—the salvation of souls. They did in fact form the

---

[60] See LG, no. 35; PAUL VI, apostolic exhortation, *Evangelii nuntiandi*, December 8, 1975, in *AAS*, 68 (1976), pp. 1–96, nos. 47, 69, 70–71.

[61] Supra p. 54.

[62] *Constitutiones 1826*. Emphasis added. In "Constitutions 1818" an earlier formulation of the same matter was found in a long (120 lines of type) *nota bene* in a paragraph on the reform of the clergy (I partie, c. I, §3, Réformer le clergé). The Preface, which has always formed part of the Constitutions, is very clearly a document for a society of priests formed to exercise priestly ministry. For this reason, the general administration maintained that it was not necessary to state explicitly the clerical nature of the Congregation in the first article of the Constitutions. Supra p. 112.

the Missionaries of Provence "to devote themselves to all the good works that priestly charity can devise."

In the Constitutions these priestly works are spelled out. The end of the Congregation is stated in the first article, and then the various priestly ministries to accomplish this end follow:

Part I, c. I, a. 1. . . . devoting themselves principally to the preaching of the Gospel to the poor, and diligently striving to imitate the virtues and example of our Savior Jesus Christ.

Part I, c. I, a. 2. . . . every effort to provide spiritual aid especially to the country people, and to those in the towns and villages who have the greatest need . . . for all these they will break the bread of the divine word by means of missions, retreats, catechetical instructions, and other spiritual exercises.

Part I, c. I, a. 5. . . . one of our obligations is to instruct the young in their religious duties . . .

Part I, c. II, a. 22. . . . keep in mind the principal end of our Congregation, namely, that of laboring for the salvation of the most abandoned souls.

Part I, c. III, §I, a. 3. Since preaching and the wise administration of the sacrament of penance are most efficacious for the welfare of souls, all will strive to fulfil worthily these high and important offices.

Part I, c. III, §1, a. 5. We shall not obtain it . . . unless like the Apostle we preach "Jesus Christ and him crucified . . . not with pretentious speech, but in the demonstration of the Spirit . . ."

Part I, c. III, §2, a. 1. Hearts that have been moved by the words of the preacher are sanctified by the action of grace in the tribunal of penance. Preaching, indeed, has no other end than to lead sinners to the pool of salvation. What would become of those whom the Lord is drawing to Himself, if there were no friendly hand to plunge them into the healing waters, where their first innocence is restored . . . It is beyond all doubt that the hearing of confessions is to be preferred to preaching, when there is room for choice . . .

Part I, c. III, §4, a. 1. We are never to forget that the principal aim of our Institute is to help those souls whose need is the greatest. Hence the unfortunate inmates of prisons have a rightful claim on our charity.

In 1831 de Mazenod wrote a short commentary on part of the Constitutions. Rather than attempt a summary of these long citations concerning the end of the Congregation, here are his words that speak of the Oblate vocation and the end of Missionary Oblates of Mary Immaculate:

And this sublime vocation, shall we ever have an adequate conception of it? To arrive at this, one must comprehend how excellent is the end of our Institute. It is, undoubtedly, the most perfect that one can set before oneself in this world, for the end of our Institute is that which the Son of

God set before Himself when He came on earth, namely—the glory of his heavenly Father and the salvation of souls: "The Son of Man has come to search out and save what is lost." He went particularly to the poor—"He sent me to preach the Gospel to the poor," and we are established precisely to work for the conversion of souls, and particularly to preach the Gospel to the poor:

[He then quoted the first article of the Constitutions.]

The means which we use to attain this end, partake of the excellence of the end itself. They are, unquestionably, the most perfect means, for they are the very means used by our divine Savior, his Apostles and Disciples— the exact observance of the evangelical counsels, preaching, and prayer.[63]

The acceptance of the major seminary of Marseille in 1827 was the first of many seminaries for which de Mazenod took responsibility.[64] The 1853 Constitutions justified this ministry by saying that the missionaries would work in vain in calling sinners back from death, if there were not good priests in the parishes.[65]

Missionaries were sent to Corsica to save the "barbarians" that were a dismay. It was de Mazenod's intention to bring to this "half wild" island through the torch of an enlightened religion what civilization had failed to do.[66] They left Algeria because the bishop wanted to make them parish priests, and would not permit them to seek the conversion of the muslims.[67] In 1841 the first missionaries went to Canada to evangelize the whites and to bring the Gospel to the American Indians.[68] They went to England to convert the Protestants.[69] They were sent to Ceylon to instruct 150,000 Christians, and convert the million five hundred thousand gentiles.[70]

It was in 1852 that the first missionaries arrived in southern Africa. Unfortunately, de Mazenod had made the wrong choice in presenting Jean-François Allard to the Holy See to be vicar apostolic, and success was long in

---

[63] DE MAZENOD, "Nos saintes Règles," October 8, 1831, in *Circulaires Administratives*, vol. 1, p. 123.

[64] Supra p. 58.

[65] Supra p. 67.

[66] Supra pp. 59–60.

[67] Supra pp. 61–62.

[68] Supra p. 60.

[69] Supra p. 61.

[70] Supra p. 61.

coming. In this rather harsh letter to Bishop Allard, de Mazenod affirmed very clearly the purpose of the mission.

> There is matter for extreme concern in the lack of success of your mission to the Kaffirs. There are few examples of such sterility. What! not a single one of those poor infidels to whom you have been sent has opened his eyes to the truth you were bringing them! I have difficulty in consoling myself over it since you were not sent to the few heretics who inhabit your towns. It is to the Kaffirs that you have been sent, it is their conversion that the Church expects from the holy ministry she has entrusted to you.[71]

In the *Instructio* for the foreign missions the missionaries were told that the promotion of the material and social progress of the people was part of their mission work as a means for the greater success of their ministry. The brothers especially were to assume this role in helping the missionaries, and even replacing them. Schools were to be opened for the teaching of Christian doctrine along with the fine and practical arts necessary for good Christians and citizens. The missionaries were to instruct the people in the requirements of civil life that they might live in peace with each other and with other tribes. The converts were to be visited especially when ill in order to care for them spiritually and physically.[72]

Even as a septuagenarian, de Mazenod carried on a voluminous correspondence with his missionaries spread throughout the world. He complained when they did not write, and answered their letters with long detailed responses showing his personal interest in their spiritual welfare and ministry. His own letters reveal him as founder and spiritual father directing his sons in their life and ministry. They also throw light on his vision of the missions in the plan of salvation.

In 1851 he wrote these words to one of the missionaries in Oregon:

> Foreign missions compared to our missions in Europe have a special character of a higher kind, because this is the true apostolate of announcing the Good News to nations which have not yet been called to knowledge of the true God and of his son Jesus Christ . . . This is the mission of the apostles: "Euntes, docete omnes gentes!" this teaching of the truth must

---

[71] DE MAZENOD, to Allard, May 30, 1857, *Oblate Writings*, vol. 4, no. 26, pp. 205–206. It would be wrong, unjust, and anachronistic to judge harshly de Mazenod's use of the word *Kaffir*, which today is unacceptable.

[72] "Therefore in forming the workers, who are to be sent to the foreign missions, the superiors will see to it that there are one or more who are fit for this purpose, and give them companions from among the brothers, who are trained in the mechanical arts, that they may not only help the missionaries in such work, but also replace them" ("Instructio pro Externis Missionibus," in *Constitutiones 1853*, p. 179; *Constitutiones 1894*, p. 223; *Constitutiones 1910*, pp. 211–212).

penetrate to the most backward nations so that they may be regenerated in the waters of baptism. You are among those to whom Jesus Christ has addressed these words, giving you your mission as he gave their mission to the apostles, who were sent to convert our fathers.[73]

The Missionary Oblates of Mary Immaculate had been founded to preach the Gospel to the poor of Provence, and then extended their ministry to the neighboring parts of southern France. It was in the foreign missions that they began to preach the Gospel not only to Catholics, and Protestants as they had in England, but to those who had never heard the Good News. A whole new kind of missionary activity was opened to them. Both in Europe and in the foreign missions the goal was that which was very clearly stated in the Preface, "We must lead men to act like human beings, first of all, and then like Christians, and finally, we must help them to become saints."

Just as de Mazenod had fought the remnants of Jansenism in Provence with the introduction of the moral theology of Alphonsus Liguori to bring the people to the reception of the sacraments and holiness of life, he encouraged a similar approach to the foreign missionaries.

Bishop Grandin wrote that because of the customs of polygamy and divorce among the North American Indians the missionaries had admitted to communion only a few of the old converts:

I heard Archbishop Taché say that when he was with our venerated founder, the latter asked him this question: "Have you many communicants among your Christians?" "Monseigneur," answered the young bishop [he was 28 at the time], "so far we have not dared to give Communion except to a few old people." "What are you saying!" the superior general of the Oblates retorted with astonishment, "You have not dared give Communion except to a few old people and you think that you can christianize those people! Don't count on it without the holy Eucharist . . ."[74]

Thus, it is evident that for de Mazenod, *"evangelizare," "évangéliser,"* meant to bring people to a full Christian life and holiness through the priestly ministry of preaching the Gospel, and the administration of the sacraments. He founded a society of priests precisely to do that. The ministry of ordained priests is so essential to his notion of evangelization that his Congregation could not exist

---

[73] DE MAZENOD, to Ricard, December 6, 1851, *Oblate Writings*, vol. 2, no. 157, pp. 19–30.

[74] V. GRANDIN, O.M.I., *Quelques notes sur Monseigneur Taché, o.m.i.*, Postulation Archives O.M.I. (typed copy), vol. 5 (there are no page numbers); also quoted by P. Benoît, *Vie de Mgr Taché* Montréal, Beauchemin, 1904, vol. 1, pp. 333–334. Taché was the first Oblate bishop in western Canada. Grandin was 28 at the time of his appointment as Taché's coadjutor.

without ordained priests and their priestly ministry. Without the ministerial priesthood it would be an essentially different society with its members exercising the ministry of the common priesthood of the faithful received through baptism and confirmation—not the Missionary Oblates of Mary Immaculate established by de Mazenod.

Another question that, although not of importance in determining its canonical status, is of great significance for a real understanding of the Missionary Oblates of Mary Immaculate is what he meant by "pauperes." Here again it is imperative to look both at what de Mazenod wrote, and what he did.

Before looking at his writings it is necessary to consider the meaning of the French word *abondonné(e)* because it occurs often, perhaps even more frequently, than the word *pauvres* (the poor). The natural tendency for an English speaking person is to translate it as *abandoned*. In some contexts it does mean *abandoned*; that, however, is not so in the cases that will be examined.

The older and as well as the more recent French dictionaries give basically the same meaning. One example will suffice to show the meaning in the context used by de Mazenod.

> *abandonner* — laisser sans secours, délaisser entièrement.
> Un père *abandonne* un fils qui le déshonore.
> Un médecin *abandonne* un malade.
> *abandonné, ée* — adj. et part. pass. d'*abandonner*
> Le voyez-vous seul, *abandonné*?
> La veuve *abandonnée*, et ses enfants orphelins ont souffert la faim dans une cruelle solitude.[75]

It thus is seen that *abandonné(e)* in some contexts means to leave someone without help, assistance, aid. A person is in need and no one comes to his or her assistance. No one English word adequately translates *abandonné(e)* in these cases. It is often best translated by a phrase such as *completely* or *most neglected*. *Les âmes abandonnées* are those persons (souls) who are completely neglected; they have no one to help them.

---

[75] M. BESCHERELLE, *Dictionnaire National*, Paris, Simon, 1849, vol. 1, p. 7. The official French text of the 1982 *Constitutions et Règles O.M.I.* uses the word *délaissé* in C. 5, but has in R. 2 *abandonné*. "C. 5. Son premier service dans l'Église est de faire connaître aux plus délaissés le Christ et son Royaume." "R. 2 ... la fin principale de la Congrégation: l'évangélisation des plus abandonné." It should be noted that the English text in these two instances uses *abandoned*. It is the opinion of the author that it would have been better rendered by saying *most neglected*.

When speaking of the persons to be ministered to de Mazenod used the word *pauvres* (the poor) with the word *évangéliser* (to preach the Gospel), otherwise he usually spoke of *les âmes abandonnées*. Some examples that have already been used will illustrate this.

When the Bishop of Metz, the vicar capitular of Aix, asked de Mazenod what ministry he wanted, the reply was that his ambition was to consecrate himself to the service of the poor (*pauvres*) and the young.[76] In his lenten conferences in 1813 at the Madeleine in Aix he addressed the servants and workers with the words:

> All you poor (*pauvres*) of Jesus Christ, you afflicted, unfortunate, suffering, infirm, diseased . . . You are the children of God, the brothers and sisters of Jesus Christ . . . the cherished portion of his inheritance.[77]

He gave de Forbin-Janson as his reason for not joining forces with the Missionaries of France that the people of Provence were without anyone to help them, that there was hope for their conversion, and if he left them they would be completely neglected (*abandonner*).[78] He asked Tempier to join him because it was only by missions that the people, who were completely neglected (*abandonnée*), could be brought back to the faith.[79]

Later de Mazenod wrote that the Congregation was founded: "for the greater glory of God, to serve the Church for the sanctification *of the most neglected souls,* and the education or reform of the clergy .. ."[80] In the French draft of his petition for the papal brief of approval he wrote the Congregation was established that they might devote themselves "à la plus grand gloire de Dieu, au salut *des âmes les plus abandonnées* et au service de l'Église."[81]

The Preface of the Constitutions gives an insight into de Mazenod's view of the situation of the Church and the faithful in post-revolutionary France. This is the background of his decision to form a society of missionaries to preach the Gospel to the poor, and to come to the aid of the most neglected:

---

[76] Supra p. 13

[77] Supra pp. 15–16.

[78] Supra p. 20.

[79] Supra p. 22.

[80] [Toussaint] RAMBERT, *Vie de Monseigneur Charles-Joseph-Eugène de Mazenod, évêque de Marseille,* 2 vols., Tours, Mame et fils, 1883, vol. 1, p. 161.

[81] *Écrits,* vol. 4, p. 58; *Missions O.M.I.,* 79 (1952), p. 458. The official petition in Latin reads: "quidquid majorem gloriam Dei, quidquid animarum imprimis derelictarum salutem et Ecclesiæ utilitatem efficacius promovere posset" (*Écrits,* vol. 4, p. 148; *Missions O.M.I.,* 79 (1952), p. 549).

"évangéliser *les pauvres* et de venir au secours *des âmes les plus abandonnées.*"[82]
These two, *the poor* and *the most neglected people,* are frequently linked. In the
Preface he wrote:

> The Church, that glorious inheritance purchased by Christ the Savior
> at the cost of his own blood, has in our days been cruelly ravaged. The
> beloved spouse of God's only-begotten Son is torn with anguish as she
> mourns the shameful defection of the children she herself bore. Christians,
> but apostates, and utterly mindless of God's blessings, they provoke divine
> justice by their crimes. And did we not know that the sacred deposit of
> faith is to be preserved intact to the end of time, we would hardly be able
> to recognize the religion of Christ from the few remaining traces of its past
> glory that lie scattered about. Such is the state of things brought about by
> the malice and corruption of present-day Christians that it can be truly said
> that the greater number of them are worse off now than was the gentile
> world before its idols were destroyed by the Cross. . . .

> How vast the field that lies before them! How worthy and holy the
> undertaking! The people are caught up in crass ignorance of all that pertains
> to their salvation. The consequence of their ignorance has been a weakening
> of the faith and a corruption of morals with all the licence which that
> inevitably entails. Thus, it is supremely imperative, that we lead the
> multitude of lost sheep back to the fold, that we teach these degenerate
> Christians who Jesus Christ is, that we rescue them from Satan's power and
> show them the way to eternal life. We must spare no effort to extend the
> Savior's empire . . .

> Wherefore, while pledging themselves to all the works of zeal which
> priestly charity can inspire—above all, the work of the missions, which is the
> main reason for their union—these priests, joined together in a society,
> resolve . . .

Although de Mazenod's pastoral concern was for the poor and the
neglected, for him it was not a narrow principle that was interpreted in an
absolute way. This can be seen already in the words of the Preface "pledging
themselves to all the works of zeal which priestly charity can inspire." On the
other hand it would be a mistake to use this statement to say that he included

---

[82] *de Mazenod,* to the Bishop of Limoges, October 24, 1847(?), cited by Rambert, *Vie.* vol. 2,
p. 255. Cf. E. Lamirande, "Les pauvres et les âmes les plus abandonnées," in *Études Oblates,* 20
(1961), pp. 3–19 for a thorough treatment of this subject. He concludes: "In reference to the
question [who are the *pauvres,* the poor] that we are presently considering, it seems to us that
above all the idea of *abandon* (neglect) is most fundamental. The Founder was moved by the distress
of the Church and of souls. Those who are most destitute of spiritual help, these are the poor, the
little people; it is these above all that the Congregation cares for. It will be first of all attentive to
spiritual distress, but it will not forget that the disinherited in any way have a preferential right to
its solicitude . . ."

all priestly ministry. He called back his men from Algeria because the bishop would not let them be missionaries.[83] They were not to be *just* parish priests, although de Mazenod had accepted six parishes—four in France and two in Canada.[84]

He said that they were consecrated *principalement*[85] (principally) for the instruction of the people, they were dedicated *surtout*[86] (above all, especially), *spécialement*[87] (especially), *de préférence*[88] (by preference) to the little people and the most neglected souls.

With this as the guiding principle for the apostolic work of the Missionary Oblates of Mary Immaculate:

—he formed the youth organization of Aix for the religiously neglected secondary school students, many of whom were the sons of the *best* families (the economically poor did not attend secondary school);[89]

—he accepted the direction of five major seminaries to prepare priests for the people who had been evangelized;[90]

—he accepted the ministry of seven Marian shrines both to evangelize the pilgrims and to deepen their faith;[91]

—he would have assigned priests as navy chaplains, if they had not been so young and inexperienced;[92]

—he authorized ministry to communities of women religious, and gave his approval for Oblates to found such institutes;[93]

—he agreed that institutions for teaching of youth overseas were not contrary to the spirit of the institute;[94]

---

[83] Supra pp. 61–62.

[84] See J.FABRE, report to the Holy See, December 10, 1862, CICLSAL Archives, M. 29.

[85] DE MAZENOD, to Rauzan, October 30, 1818, LM; DE MAZENOD, to Leo XII for approval of Congregation, December 8, 1825, *Écrits*, vol. 4, p. 58.

[86] DE MAZENOD, to Fortuné de Mazenod, fall 1823, cited by RAMBERT, *Vie*, vol. 1, p. 382; DE MAZENOD, to Tempier, March 20, 1826, *Oblate Writings*, vol. 7, no. 231, p. 63.

[87] DE MAZENOD, to the vicar general of Grenoble, June 17, 1828.

[88] DE MAZENOD, to Merlin, September 10, 1852, LM.

[89] Supra pp. 17 and 56,

[90] Supra pp. 58–59.

[91] Supra p. 63.

[92] Supra p. 64.

[93] Supra pp. 65 and 72.

[94] Supra p. 59.

—he directed his missionaries to care for the Italian and German immigrants in Marseilles.[95]

For de Mazenod the determination of who were the poor and the neglected souls was not an intellectual or speculative question, but a practical one. His vision was anything but myopic in deciding whether this or that work would be for the poor and neglected.

In two letters to Honorat, the first superior in Canada, one can see the motives that lead him to make concrete decisions.

> I am not well enough informed to decide the question of New York for the reason that I have just given you. How can you impoverish yourselves to the extent of depriving yourselves of the services of Father Telmon? And what ministry do they propose at New York? Is it not to take charge of a parish in that city? What then will happen to the missions? I was never in favor of establishing ourselves in the United States because it seemed to me there were nothing but parishes there and the project of New York seems to be nothing more than that.[96]
>
> . . . I would insist that we establish ourselves at Quebec and Montreal. I am certainly of your opinion that there is too much talk of projects and even as you say, that too many of them have been formed; that is why I have not favored the projects of Toronto, of New York. If we do not do this ourselves, others will not delay in doing so. And beware especially lest you be outsmarted . . . You say to me: that is not where the most neglected souls are. True, but in establishing yourselves there, you provide yourselves with the means to come to the aid of those most neglected souls, without taking into account that you will also do much good to many who, while not most neglected, are nonetheless in need.[97]

To bring this part to closure, it can be said that de Mazenod's pastoral dedication as founder was for those who had no one to minister to them. The *paupers*, the *pauvres*, are those who are *les âmes abandonnées*, the completely neglected. They are in spiritual need, and there is no one else to come to their rescue. It is especially to them that his Missionary Oblates will bring the Good News of salvation and the sacramental means to lead a full Christian life.[98]

---

[95] Supra p. 60.

[96] DE MAZENOD, to Honorat, January 17, 1843, *Oblate Writings*, vol. 1, no. 15a, pp. 34–35.

[97] DE MAZENOD, to Honorat, October 7, 1843, *Oblate Writings*, vol. 1, no. 27, p. 64.

[98] Cf. A. D'ADDIO, O.M.I., *Cristo Crocifisso la Chiesa Abbandonata, Eugenio de Mazenod: un apassionato di Cristo e della Chiesa*, Frascati, Scolasticato O.M.I., 1978, p. 179: "After all is said the poor are those who cannot hear the Word of God."

The Oblates are not just priests; they are missionaries. Theirs is a specialized ministry to the most needy—the country people who lack priests, especially priests who speak their language, immigrants in a foreign land, young men preparing for the priesthood, neglected youth in an achristian environment, the young who have no one to give them a proper human education, those in the military with all its spiritual dangers, the sick and dying whom the parish clergy cannot care for, religious women who need specialized pastoral ministry, prisoners, especially those condemned to death, the pilgrims seeking renewal at Marian shrines. These are frequently the materially poor. They are the needy and those in distress, and there is no one else to preach to them "Jesus Christ and him crucified," no other "friendly hand to plunge them into the healing waters."

No Identity Crisis

De Mazenod and the first generation of Oblates had no doubts about what they were or who they were. To use modern terminology, they did not have an identity crisis.[99] De Mazenod's position on this is clear from the previous presentation. The rank and file members of the institute did not differ from him in this. They called themselves *missionaries* because they were priests dedicated to the specialized ministry of conducting missions, and later of working in the foreign missions whether in England or overseas. At that time only priests were called missionaries, as was seen above in this chapter.

From the beginning of the institute the members added to their names an abbreviation for *missionary* and *priest*. There were variations of this for those not yet ordained to the priesthood.[100] The word missionary was not used in reference to the brothers. After the approval by Leo XII and the changing of the name of the Congregation there was a gradual adoption of an abbreviation for Oblate of Mary Immaculate.

The word *Oblate* was introduced to affirm the new identity of religious with the acceptance of the first Rule in 1818 and the profession of vows.[101] In 1821 they began calling themselves *père* (*Father*) instead of *monsieur*, and even the professed students were called *Father*.[102]

---

[99] This was a very popular expression in the 1970s, when many questioned the nature and the ministry of ordained priests.

[100] Supra p. 34.

[101] Supra p. 34.

[102] Supra p. 33.

When a brother candidate applied for admission to the novitiate the words "en qualité de frère convers" (as a lay brother) were added to the standard formula.[103] A clear distinction was made between those entering to become priests and the brothers.

The understanding of the members of the Congregation can be seen from a discussion that took place at the 1831 general chapter. Twelve of the twenty-two professed priests were members of the chapter. The question was raised as to how the spiritual conference, commonly called *coulpe* or chapter of faults, was to be conducted with reference to the brothers. It was unanimously decided that the brothers would first accuse themselves of infractions of the Rule and be accused by the others, and then retire before the exercise was to be continued for the other members of the community.

> The Chapter based its decisions on the fact that the Congregation is a society of priests, and not of brothers as, for example, the Franciscans. The lay brothers must always take their place after the principal members of the society, even if the latter are only simple novices and not yet tonsured.[104]

The conviction by all the members of the Congregation from 1826 until 1866 that they enjoyed the privilege of exemption is an indication that they considered themselves to be a clerical community.[105] The privileges that they were most concerned about were things that pertained to holy orders or the exercise of orders—the right to grant dimissorial letters, to be ordained *ad titulum mensæ communis*, to administer viaticum and extreme unction to their own members, the faculty to administer the sacrament of penance to their own members without having jurisdiction from the diocesan bishop.[106]

Similar Institutes

On March 9, 1826 de Mazenod wrote that the Oblates were a Congregation in the Church just as the Lazarists (Vincentians), the Passionists, the Liguorists (Redemptorists), etc.[107] All three of these societies were clerical communities. In fact, their very names at that time indicated that they were such. Vincent de Paul's Congregation of the Mission was commonly called *Prêtres de la Mission* (*Priests of the Mission*), and he insisted on exclusive use of that

---

[103] Supra p. 35.

[104] "Registre," 1831, vol. 1, p. 39; PIELORZ, *Les Chapitres*, vol. 1, p. 107.

[105] Supra pp. 78–84.

[106] *Circulaires*, June 29, 1866, no. 17, vol. 1, pp. 153–167.

[107] Supra p. 50.

name.[108] The official name of the Passionists was *Congregatio Clericorum Excalceatorum Sanctissimæ Crucis et Passionis Domini Nostri Jesu Christi* (Congregation of Disclaced Clerics of the Most Holy Cross and of the Passion of Our Lord Jesus Christ).[109] The name of the Liguorists or Redemptorists was *Congregatio presbyterorum (sub invocatione) Sanctissimi Redemptoris (Salvatoris)* (Congregation of Priests [with the title] of the Most Holy Redeemer [Savior]).[110] All three had in their name a word that identified them as priests.

The same could be said of the *Missionary Oblates of Mary Immaculate* since at that time *missionary* referred only to priests dedicated to the missions. It should be noted that *missionnaires* in French is a noun, and not an adjective as *missionary* is in the English name.

Propositions of Union

In 1816 two miracles were performed at Aix through the intercession of Alphonsus Liguori, and de Mazenod wrote up an account of them. He sent it along with a monetary gift to help with the canonization expenses to the major rector of the Redemptorists in Rome. The latter in his letter of thanks suggested that the Missionaries of Provence join his society.[111] No documentation of de Mazenod's response to the invitation exists.

De Forbin-Janson's request that de Mazenod join forces with the Missionaries of France, and the reasons for declining were treated above in chapter one.[112]

Because of his desire to have a foundation in Italy de Mazenod took the initiative in seeking union with three other groups of missionaries established in Italy. First, in 1825 on his way to Rome he tried to get Pio Bruno Lanteri to unite the Oblates of the Blessed Virgin with his Congregation.[113] On his return from Rome in 1826 he made a special trip to Chambéry in order to investigate

---

[108] Supra p. 152.

[109] *Regulæ et Constitutiones Congr. Ss.mæ Crucis et Passionis D.N.J.C.*, Rome, Fontes Historicæ Congregationis Passionis, 1958, vol. 1, pp. 2–3.

[110] BENEDICT XIV, apostolic letter, *Ad pastoralis*, February 25, 1749: *Benedicti XIV Acta*, ed. R. DE MARTINIS, Naples, Artigianelli, 1894, vol. 2, pp. 41–43; also *Codex Regularum et Constitutionem Congregationis SS. Redemptoris*, Rome, Cuggiani, 1896, p. 3.

[111] REY, vol. 1, pp. 197–198.

[112] Supra p. 20.

[113] Supra pp. 42–43.

the possibility of a merger with Joseph-Marie Favre, a well-known missionary of that diocese.[114]

Less known is his meeting with Gaspar del Bufalo in April 1826 and again in 1832. The obstacle to union with the Congregation of the Most Precious Blood was the difference over the question of religious vows. De Bufalo's opposition to having vows was just as strong as de Mazenod's insistence on them.[115]

The common element in all these institutes is that they are societies of priests dedicated to missions, clerical communities.

In 1842 while Aubert was seeking to establish the Congregation in Ireland, he became acquainted with the Brothers of Saint Patrick whose motherhouse was at Tullow, County Carlow, Ireland. The brothers showed interest in joining the Oblates as a means of obtaining pontifical status. However, the project was rejected by the bishop of Kildare and Leighlin, who opposed the brothers being withdrawn from his jurisdiction.[116]

One could speculate as to what status these brothers would have had in the Congregation if a merger had taken place. It would, however, be a mistake to spend much time on the proposed union since the talks never really got off the ground. The bishop's opposition nipped it in the bud as soon as it was mentioned to him.

An indication of the probable solution can be seen in discussion at the 1856 general chapter. A number of missionaries had requested brothers to be catechists and school teachers, and a proposal was made to form a group of *frères catéchistes*. Because there was general agreement that this would be inopportune because of the great difficulties that there would be in the relationship of such brothers with the *frères convers proprement dits* (the lay brothers in the strict sense), and the serious troubles that such problems could cause. Consequently the proposition was not brought to a vote.[117] No mention was

---

[114] DE MAZENOD, to Honorat, May 28, 1826; to Tempier, May 29, 1826, May 30, 1826, June 10, 1826, *Oblate Writings*, vol. 7, nos. 244–246, pp. 102–108, pp. 110–114. For more information concerning Joseph Marie Favre (1791–1838) see: *Dictionnaire d'histoire et de géographie ecclésiastique*, Paris, Letouzey et Ané, 1967, vol. 16, p. 765.

[115] F. CIARDI, O.M.I., "Un projet de fusion avec les Missionnaires du Précieux Sang," in *Vie Oblate Life*, 37 (1978), pp. 65–70. Cf. "Lettre de M<sup>gr</sup> de Mazenod au Chanoine del Bufalo," ibid., pp. 70–71.

[116] Cf. T. ORTOLAN, O.M.I., *Les Oblats de Marie Immaculée*, vol. 1, pp. 521–522; DE MAZENOD, to C. Aubert, December 25, 1842, in *Oblate Writings*, vol. 3, no. 3, p. 4.

[117] "Registre," vol. 1, p. 160; PIELORZ, *Les Chapitres*, vol. 2, p. 77. Earlier during the chapter Semeria, coadjutor vicar apostolic of Jaffna and vicar of missions of Ceylon, said in his report: "It is not only missionaries that are requested, but also brother catechists who can help the fathers

made of possible difficulties with the scholastics or the priests. Can there be any doubt that such brothers would not have belonged in the ranks of the clerics, but would have been a different type of brother?

In all instances, except one, considerations of union with another institute were with societies of priests, i.e., clerical institutes. The exception was the Brothers of Saint Patrick, a lay community. However in this case it was not a question of changing the nature of the Oblates, but of the other institute joining them in order to have papal approval. The advantage to the Oblates would have been twofold: a toehold in Ireland and a group of brothers to complement the priests by their teaching.

Tradition

An attempt will be made to show briefly the continuation of this conviction that the Missionary Oblates of Mary Immaculate are a clerical congregation. The word *clerical* is a canonical term, and it would be a mistake to look for it in common usage within the Congregation. However, the reality is expressed in different ways as will be shown.

Shortly after Fabre was elected as de Mazenod's successor, he wrote his first circular letter in which he said, "We are priests, we are religious . . ."[118] In this statement he made no special reference to the fact that many were not priests. Why? The society as such was for priests and those who helped them.

Confirmation of this can be found in the necrology notice of Brother Victor Hourdier who died in July 1898. After the death of both his parents he was raised by an uncle. In the evenings a cousin read aloud to him the *Annales de la Propogation de la Foi*, and good books. He was deeply impressed and decided that he wanted to go to the missions. One day he approached his pastor and said:

    —Father, I would like to be a missionary.

    —Missionary? Do you know what you are saying, my son? You can't read or write, and you want to be a missionary?

    —It's true, Father. I don't know the ABCs, and I am too old to begin now. Couldn't I go with the missionaries on their apostolic journeys and serve them in all their needs?

---

in teaching the adults and the direction of schools for the children" ("Registre," vol., p. 155; PIELORZ, *Les Chapitres*, vol. 2, p. 68). Note again the word *missionary* applies only to priests.

[118] J. FABRE, March 21, 1862, no. 11, *Circulaires*, vol. 1, p. 3 [77–79]; supra p. 75, note 80.

—Ah, do that, yes. You could do that. What society of missionaries do you want to join? There are many of them.[119]

In 1896, Soullier, the third superior general, addressed a circular "To All the Religious, Priests or Aspiring to the Priesthood, in the Congregation of Missionary Oblates of Mary Immaculate" with the title "The Studies of the Missionary Oblate of Mary Immaculate."[120] Although no one today would have any difficulty with the superior general addressing a letter on studies to the priests and the students for the priesthood, everyone would find it incomprehensible to give the letter a title that implicitly affirms that it is for all Missionary Oblates of Mary Immaculate.

The second part of this sixty page circular has the title, "L'Étude et le Missionnaire." The beginning of this section reveals the understanding at that time of the nature of the Congregation.

> Jesus Christ, the founder of the Church, is also the one who governs it. The most characteristic element of His form of government is that it is a method of setting apart. We are trying to say that Jesus exercises over the multitude of faithful, who constitute the Church, a series of progressive choices.

> "*Set apart for me,*" He says to His representatives on this earth. Behold some emerge from the common multitude of faithful and attach themselves to Jesus Christ by the triple bonds of poverty, chastity and obedience—these are the religious.

> "*Set apart for me,*" Jesus Christ says again. Behold some men step out of the ranks of the simple religious and climb to the altar—these are the religious priests.

> "*Set apart for me,*" He says for the third time. "*Set apart Barnabas and Saul for me to do the work for which I have called them*" (*Acts* 13:2). Behold the religious set apart to preach the Gospel. "*Set apart to proclaim the gospel of God*" (*Rom* 1:1). Behold the missionary religious priests.[121]

Alfred J.B. Yenveux (1843–1903) spent almost twenty–five years studying the writings of de Mazenod, and was commissioned by Fabre to write a commentary on the Constitutions and Rules. He spoke of de Mazenod as the

---

[119] *Notices Nécrologiques O.M.I.*, vol. 7, p. 348. Victor Hourdier (1846–1898) made his first oblation in 1865 and perpetual oblation in 1872 after serving in the Franco-Prussian War. He spent his whole religious life at the general house in Paris. According to his necrology notice, he worked and prayed too hard. His devotion as infirmarian to the sick was limitless.

[120] *Circulaires*, December 8, 1896, vol. 2, no. 61, p. 1.

[121] *Circulaires*, December 8, 1896, vol. 2, no. 61, pp. 31–32.

founder of a Congregation of *Prêtres Missionnaires* (missionary priests).[122] In listing the distinctive characteristics of the Congregation, he wrote:

> They must be *Sacerdotes, priests*; they are not simple *brothers*. The laymen who join the society, while truly being part of the Congregation, will nevertheless have the title *Fratres Famulantes, lay brothers*[123]

In 1949, questionnaires were sent to all the novice masters of both the scholastic and brother novices. In his report and analysis of the responses, the director general of studies presented two items that manifest the tradition of the Congregation. The first concerns the scholastic novices who numbered 215.

> The young men entering the novitiate are for the most part attracted by the ideal of the priesthood and of being missionaries, often they have not even dreamed about the religious life in a really precise way.[124]

At that time a separate formation was given to the 76 brother novices. Their formation was in accord with their position in the Congregation.

> The brother is a member of the Congregation and not a servant. An effort is made in many ways to get them to really understand this by explaining to them that they are just as truly religious and Oblates as the priests, that they are associated with the priests in the same work of salvation of souls, that they cooperate in this effectively by their life of work and prayer. Insistence is placed on the position they occupy in the Mystical Body because of their vows. One report presents the co-priestly vocation of the brother in this way, "The best place of the brother is at the altar near the priest when he presents to the priest the matter of the sacrifice of the altar and unites himself with him during the important moments of the Mass."[125]

> To the extent that they are conscious of the co-priestly aspect of their vocation, they are led also to discover its missionary character. Insistence is placed on the missionary value of their life of prayer and work. This is the sense of the majority of reports.[126]

On August 15, 1951, Deschâtelets, superior general, sent to the Congregation a ninety-one page circular, "Our Vocation and Our Life of Intimate Union with Mary Immaculate"[127]. He ordered that it be read publicly as soon as

---

[122] A.J.B. Yenveux, o.m.i., *Les Saintes Règles de la Congrégation des Missionnaires Oblats de Marie Immaculée, expliquées d'après les Écrits, les leçons et l'esprit de Mgr Charles-Joseph-Eugène de Mazenod*, 2 vols., Paris, Procure des Oblats, 1903, vol. 1, p. 26. In addition to the two published volumes there are 7 mss. volumes. It seems that since only the Holy See could interpret the Constitutions, it was thought that it was not permitted to publish a commentary on them.

[123] Ibid., p. 31, emphasis in original text.

[124] Daniel Albers, o.m.i., "Compte Rendu des rapports sur les noviciats de la Congrégation," in *Études Oblats*, 10 (1951), p. 168.

[125] Albers, "Compte Rendu," pp. 224–225.

[126] Ibid., p. 226.

possible after reception, and during each annual retreat until the 1953 general chapter. The purpose of the letter was to stimulate the fervor of religious life and to foster a deep and filial devotion to Mary Immaculate.[128]

In treating "the unique character of our Oblate way of life: its characteristic elements," he stated:

> First and foremost, we are—*priests*. "Art. 1. The end of this humble Congregation . . . is that *priests*, living together . . . in community . . ." Priests among countless other priests, but priests with a special inspiration which gives a particular outline to the priesthood of an Oblate . . .[129]
>
> It is true that we are religious as well as priests, but even our religious mentality itself is conditioned by priestly charity to such an extent that the Oblate who would subordinate sacerdotal grace to the grace of his religious vocation would falsify his Oblate life. The Oblate is, and ought to remain, both priest and religious. Neither status can be separated from the other if he wishes to remain a true Oblate of Mary Immaculate.[130]

At first reading this paragraph may seem to some to be an exaggeration or even untrue. It is, however, based on de Mazenod's clear intention as demonstrated by what he did in founding an apostolic community and the name he chose for it.

What did he understand by that name? *Missionnaires Oblats de Marie Immaculée, Missionarii Oblati Mariæ Immaculatæ*, is more accurately translated into English as *Oblate Missionaries of Mary Immaculate*, and not Missionary Oblates of Mary Immaculate. In French and in Latin, *missionaries* (*missionaires, missionarii*) is a noun that meant for de Mazenod *priests dedicated to the missions*, and is modified by the adjective *oblats* (*oblati*), which meant for him *religious*. He founded a group of missionary priests, who became religious, religious missionaries, i.e., Oblate Missionaries. Thus, the name he elected corresponded exactly to the society he founded. Although his community was not composed exclusively of priests, the name for him was not a problem, because it was primarily a community of ordained priests.

To the last paragraph of the previous quotation, Deschâtelets added a footnote in order to explain how it applies to the brothers.

---

[127] *Circulaires*, August 15, 1951, no. 191, vol. 5, pp. 298–386, An official English text was published with the page numbers 1–91. It is this text that is quoted.

[128] Ibid., pp. 3–4.

[129] Ibid., pp. 8–9, emphasis in original text.

[130] Ibid., pp. 19–20.

Let us remark, in passing, that this shows that, in order to be truly Oblate, our lay brothers must live in a very intimate union with the Oblate priestly life. Here is a mystique, a spirituality which must vitalize the religious and missionary life of our brothers.[131]

The self-understanding of the Congregation's tradition as a clerical institute is evidenced by the immediate implementation of the pontifical rescript *Cum admotæ* that was addressed to the superiors general of pontifical clerical religious institutes and presidents of monastic congregations. The rescript was issued on November 6, 1964 and the following December as soon as he had a final version, Deschâtelets sent a copy to all provincials and vicars of missions and subdelegated to them all the faculties that he could.[132] Although the rescript was addressed only to clerical institutes, no Oblate has ever questioned its applicability to the Congregation.

On February 18, 1966 an unofficial consultation was made at the Sacred Congregation of Religious in order to aid the general chapter that was in the process of a complete revision of the Constitutions. Although the responses received were unofficial, they guided the chapter in its work, and thus influenced the 1966 Constitutions *ad experimentum*. The capitulants were given the responses in the form of questions and answers. Concerning the question at hand the following is of particular interest and importance.

Question: We intend to introduce into the first article of our Rules mention of the brothers. In order to avoid any doubt on [sic] the nature of our Congregation (clerical) as a result, should we insert a special article on the (clerical) nature of the Congregation?

Reply: You may do so, if you wish. But it appears clearly in the Constitutions, in the point dealing with the Government, since the brothers have no part in the government. Nevertheless, you may indicate this, if you wish. The clerical nature of the Congregation must not be left in any doubt.[133]

In his presentation of the 1966 Constitutions *ad experimentum* to the Congregation, Deschâtelets said that the text seeks

---

[131] Loc. cit., note 17.

[132] Paul VI, pontifical rescript, *Cum admotæ*, November 6, 1964, in *AAS*, 59 (1967), pp. 374–378; trans. *CLD*, vol. 6, pp. 147–152. Deschâtelets, to all provincials and vicars of missions, December 28, 1964, copy in General Secretariat O.M.I., file polycopie, juillet 1964–octobre 1965. Cf. also, *Circulaires*, March 25, 1967, no. 235, vol. 8, pp. 65–86.

[133] A. Guay, o.m.i., procurator general, and F. Sackett, o.m.i., "Études en marge du Chapitre Général de 1966 (Position Papers)," General Archives O.M.I. The name of the person giving the responses is not given. It is the last document in the volume, p. 3.

to describe its characteristic as a clerical Institute. Even though some of its members are not priests, all have the same religious and missionary obligations as cooperators with Christ, the Savior . . ."[134]

In the petition to the Sacred Congregation of Religious for permission to implement the 1966 Constitutions *ad experimentum*, it was affirmed that the structure of the Congregation was basically unchanged.[135]

A congress on "The Charism of the Founder Today" was held at the General House in Rome from April 26 to May 14, 1976. In the "Final Declaration of the Congress" it was noted that there was hesitation on the part of some to consider *priesthood* an essential characteristic of the Congregation.

The *priesthood*, essential element of the Congregation: (20 in favor, 6 against, 2 abstaining) some had reservations because the Institute comprises brothers; a certain number of young Oblates are slow to accept ordination without specific community service; and finally because of the difference in perspectives between the Founder's time and our own time.[136]

The background to this can be seen in the summary on the "Fundamental Values of the Congregation."[137]

In the mind of Eugene de Mazenod, the celebration of the eucharistic sacrifice and the announcing of God's word were closely connected with the effectiveness of evangelization and the conversion of souls. One could not exist without the other.

Eugene de Mazenod was convinced that, in the Congregation, the evangelization of the poor and abandoned could not be an aim in itself but must lead sinners to the sacraments of reconciliation and the Eucharist, and must lead pagans to baptism. In this total missionary outlook the ministerial priesthood appears as not merely useful but essential for the Oblate Congregation as such. In this perspective it is easy to understand why the Founder placed formation and sanctification of the clergy as the second aim of the Congregation . . .

---

[134] *Circulaires*, April 12, 1966, no. 227, vol. 7, p. 356; the text is cited supra p. 102.

[135] O'Reilly, to Holy Father, July 9, 1966, copy of original in Procurator's Archives O.M.I.; *Circulaires*, September 8, 1966, no. 233, vol. 7, pp. 426–428.

[136] "Acta of the Congress, the Charism of the Founder Today," in *Vie Oblate Life* (formerly *Études Oblates*), 36 (1977), p. 287.

[137] M. Zago, o.m.i., "Some Insights on the Fundamental Values of the Congregation of the Missionary Oblates of Mary Immaculate" (ibid. pp. 253–283). This paper is a compilation of the various values agreed upon along with note taken of the different positions of various individuals.

Some Oblates do not consider the priesthood necessary for the accomplishment of their mission.[138] Does this not in any way lessen the sacerdotal charism of the Congregation?

Since the Congregation is made up of brothers and priests it is not possible to force any member to direct his steps towards the priesthood. Individual choice must be respected as is clearly indicated in the 1966 Constitutions which abolishes the distinction between "scholastics" and "coadjutor" brothers.[139]

---

[138] In his report to the 1972 chapter Deschâtelets said: "Many scholastics delay, sometimes indefinitely, their call to holy orders. Some do not even foresee being ordained, unless it becomes an immediate ecclesial need. They are no longer exceptions; from a trend which is finding its way and consists in stressing the 'missionary-religious' rather than the 'missionary-religious-priest,' they will soon become an active element within the Congregation" (*Circulaires*, April 11, 1972, no. 247, vol. 8, p. 419).

It is the policy of the general administration to give a scholastic who does not choose to be called to the priesthood an *obedience* as a brother transferring him from the category of scholastics. Permanent deacons within in the Congregation are considered to be brothers and not scholastics, even though they are clerics.

The phenomenon of scholastics not requesting ordination to the priesthood, which was not as general as Deschâtelets's report would seem to indicate, seems to have been peculiar to the late 1960s or early 1970s. Around that time about ten scholastics made such a decision. During the ten years 1974–1983 only nine scholastics became brothers for various reasons, but twenty-eight brothers became scholastics in order to be ordained priests; in the years 1984–1994 seventeen brothers became scholastics and nineteen scholastics became brothers (files of the General Secretariat O.M.I.).

[139] This is a rather unusual statement not based on the text of the 1966 Constitutions *ad experimentum*. Cf. Pars III, cap. IV, art. 88–104, "De Scholasticorum Institutione et Præparatione ad Sacros Ordines" (The Education and Preparation of Scholastics for Holy Orders) and cap. V, art. 105–112, "De Institutione Fratrum post Novitiatum" (The Training of Brothers after the Novitiate). C. 126 granted active vote in the election for delegates to the general chapter to the priests who had completed their theological studies on the day the general chapter was convoked, and to the brothers who had made perpetual vows on that day. It was not granted to scholastics who had perpetual vows, even if they were ordained, and had not completed their theological studies. Even article 1 spoke of "sacerdotes cum laicis coadunati," and does not mention scholastics. The latter are not mentioned since it is not a permanent state in the Congregation, but a transitory one in preparation for the priesthood. The 1966 Constitutions *ad experimentum* explicitly distinguished between scholastics and brothers not preparing for ordination as priests.

As superior general, Zago addressed directly the question of the nature of the Congregation in a message to Oblates in first formation in "The Priestly Character of the Congregation," January 25, 1992, in *OMI Documentation*, no. 185 (April 1992), pp. 1–18. Because of the importance of this document it is repeated in its entirety in Appendix I, infra pp. 269–280. In this letter Zago stated: "A person who had intended the priesthood may discern a call to the brotherhood, and someone who wanted to consecrate himself as a brother may discern a call to the priesthood. This openness to making a change prior to perpetual vows reflects the present situation . . . Perpetual oblation ought to mark the conclusion of one's choice, an option that should never be made lightly (infra, p. 280).

This, however, does not weaken the priestly character of the Congregation which must be understood in the light of Vatican II and of present-day theology.[140]

Fernand Jetté, superior general (1974–1986), was asked to speak to the Congress of European Oblate Scholastics in Vermicino, Italy on July 16, 1979, and to present his expectations of formation in the Church today and the expectations of the Congregation today for scholastics. The fifth of the six points he developed was:

> 5. *Men who have chosen to serve the poor in a way that is clearly related to evangelization and which tends always*—even if it cannot be done immediately—*toward the explicit preaching of Jesus Christ* and the celebration of salvation in the ecclesial community and by means of the sacraments . . .[141]

The subject of the clerical nature of the Congregation was mentioned only twice during the plenary sessions of the 1974 and 1980 general chapters. At the beginning of the 1974 general chapter the various commissions were given the opportunity to recommend topics for consideration by the entire chapter. The sixth commission (German language) suggested that the character of the Congregation be considered. It asked whether the Congregation was priestly, or a community of brothers, or an association of persons dedicated to the mission with the poor, and what was the predominant characteristic and the *conditio sine qua non* to be a member?[142] The question was one of many not placed on the agenda and was not considered.

---

[140] ZAGO, "Some Insights," in *Vie Oblate Life*, 36 (1977), p. 279.

Thus, it is seen that some of the participants in the congress did not distinguish between the nature of the Congregation and the particular charisms of the individual members. They had difficulty in seeing how the brothers could be fully members, if the Congregation is clerical. True, de Mazenod lived in a different age, and his theology of priesthood was that of his age, and the role of the laity in ministry has evolved, but still this was not a problem for him. Even though the name *missionary* did not include the brothers, he did not hesitate to say that they were *sons* of the Society (*Constitutions 1826*, pars III, cap. II, §4, art. 1). Not all members of the Congregation are called to the same kind of ministry or work. Each member shares in his own way in the community charism, without one being more a member than another. Perhaps one could make a comparison with membership in the Church. Bishops, priests, deacons, and simple faithful are equally members of the Church. To affirm that the ordained have a different ministry than the nonordained is not a belittling of the latter.

The assertion that many priests do not understand and appreciate the role of the laity in evangelization and ministry is just a confusion of the issue. The question is not the intellectual and psychological position of an individual priest or lay person who does not have a correct understanding of the Church's teaching.

[141] *Documentation O.M.I.*, 100/81, May 1981, p. 7.

[142] "Registre," 1974, p. 48.

During the 1980 general chapter the question was asked by one of the members if the Congregation was clerical, and what were the consequences of being a clerical institute. Michael O'Reilly, procurator general, answered the question and it was not brought up again.[143]

In an explanation to the Congregation the procurator general commented on the various modifications that the Sacred Congregation of Religious and Secular Institutes requested in the Constitutions before giving its approbation. In addressing the insistence by the Sacred Congregation that the phrase "a clerical Congregation of pontifical right" be added to the first article he wrote:

> In all previously approved texts of the Constitutions, Article 1 spoke of a Congregation of priests, and the Founder's Preface left no room for doubt as regards the nature and identity of the Congregation.
>
> In our discussions with the Sacred Congregation we emphasized the point that the Preface forms an integral part of the Constitutions and that the priestly nature of the Oblate congregation was clearly indicated there.[144]

The constant Oblate tradition and understanding of the priestly nature of the Congregation, which has taken into account the developments since Vatican II, is summarized in the second basic principle of the "General Norms for Oblate Formation":

> *The ministerial priesthood is an essential element of the Oblate Congregation. There is a fundamental unity in Oblate formation.*
>
> "The sight of these evils has so touched the hearts of certain priests . . ." (Preface). Blessed Eugene de Mazenod's response to the Church's urgent appeals was inseparably linked to the grace of the ministerial priesthood.
>
> In fidelity to the Founder's charism, the priesthood remains an essential element of the Congregation, since the principal goal of its mission is full evangelization: witness, proclamation of God's Word, implanting and building up the Church, celebration of the sacraments, especially of reconciliation and of the Eucharist. As priests and brothers, Oblates have complementary responsibilities and roles in evangelizing (cf. C. 7 and Rules 3 and 7). The Oblate religious missionary life and the mission of both the priests and the brothers are inseparably linked to the ministerial priesthood.
>
> Oblate formation is fundamentally one. For both priests and brothers, it is formation in one and the same charism. For both it shows, in ways appropriate to each group, the inseparable relationship to the ministerial priesthood. Oblate formation assists all candidates to achieve the proper

---

[143] "Registre," 1980, p. 129.

[144] M. O'REILLY, O.M.I., "The Approval of the 1980 Constitutions and Rules by the Holy See," *Documentation O.M.I.*, 124/84, March 1984, p. 8.

appreciation, unity and harmonious development of the religious and priestly elements of our missionary vocation . . .[145]

On January 25, 1992, Marcello Zago, superior general, in preparation for the XXXII general chapter addressed a letter to the Oblates in first formation, which he entitled "The Priestly Character of the Congregation." He explained:

> The Oblate charism is a gift that the Spirit has transmitted through a concrete person, Eugene de Mazenod. The Lord prepared this gift through the Founder's personal experience, one that was marked by the vocation to the priesthood.[146]

> The Church's mission is carried on in many manners and ways, as the missionary encyclical of John Paul II reminds us.[147] All Christians are coresponsible for the mission and make their contribution according to each one's state and charism.[148] The missionary priority assigned to our Congregation is priestly, precisely because it is oriented to proclaiming the Good News and to establishing Christian communities. As Oblates our particular and primary—though not exclusive—contribution to the Church's mission is "principally the evangelization of the poor."[149]

The ministry of ordained priests is so central to the Congregation, that it could not be understood without it. Without ordained priests and their ministry of preaching the Word of God and celebrating the Eucharist and sacraments one would have a completely different society with an essentially diverse apostolate. It is simply impossible to imagine the Oblates without priests and their ministry.

---

[145] *General Norms for Oblate Formation*, Rome, Missionary Oblates of Mary Immaculate, 1984. This document was unanimously approved on May 5, 1983 at the plenary session of the General Council, *Procès Verbaux*, April 11–May 6, 1983, p. 20.

During the 1980 general chapter Jetté, the superior general, was asked the question, "How can the Institute's orientation to missionary life be reconciled with *personal charism*?"

He responded: "We must respect personal charisms in the measure in which they can be integrated into the charism of the Congregation. If such an integration is impossible, we have to conclude that the vocation is not Oblate. Thus the necessity to discern the issue of vocation during the period of formation, the need for dialogue between the members of a Province. There is an Oblate mission where there is an Oblate or an Oblate community doing Oblate work . . . If this is not the case, we have only personal work being done" (*Information O.M.I.*, 168/80, November 1980, p. 4.

Cf. M. GILBERT, O.M.I., "Brèves réflexions sur le caractère sacerdotal de la Congrégation selon le Fondateur et la tradition oblate," in *Vie Oblate Life*, 39 (1980), pp. 93–101.

[146] ZAGO, "The Priestly Character of the Congregation," p. 3; infra Appendix I, p. 270.

[147] JOHN PAUL II, encyclical, *Redemptoris missio*, December 7, 1990, in *AAS*, 83, (1991), pp. 249–340, nos. 41–60.

[148] Ibid., no. 61–86.

[149] ZAGO, "The Priestly Character," p. 5; infra Appendix I, pp. 271–272.

The Holy See's canonical recognition of the Congregation as a clerical institute is based on this inherent reality which is rooted in de Mazenod's intention as founder and confirmed by the constant tradition of the Missionary Oblates of Mary Immaculate.[150]

Proportion of Clerics

According to c. 488, 4° of the 1917 Code of Canon Law, which was in force until November 27, 1983, a clerical religious institute was one in which a notable part (*plerique*) of the members were raised to the priesthood.[151]

It might seem that this was a very material and even arbitrary consideration, but it often has a basis in the understanding and intentions of members of their institute, and of those seeking membership. If the greater part of the members joined a religious society with the intention of becoming priests, it is an indication that they considered the society to be priestly or clerical at the time they joined and that they were acquiring a certain "right" to be ordained. If they in fact were ordained and exercised the ministry of the ordained priesthood as the work of their religious family, it is also an indication that at least most of them considered that the institute itself has as its purpose the ministry of the ordained priesthood.

It has been the constant practice from the beginning of the Missionary Oblates of Mary Immaculate for a person joining to express his intention of studying for the priesthood or becoming a brother, and the person belonged to the category that he had chosen.[152] The novitiate for one category was not sufficient for the other until 1969.[153] The fact that a scholastic with perpetual vows did not continue on to ordination for one reason or another was sufficient reason for a dispensation from his vows, since they were considered to be made in view of becoming a priest.

---

[150] The assertion that the Holy See's requiring that the first of article of the Constitutions say that the Congregation is clerical is "a canonical imposition" (René Motte and Alfred Hubenig, "Saint Eugene de Mazenod," Ms. [1994], p. 29) seems to imply that the clerical nature of the Congregation is an imposition from without, which is not in conformity with de Mazenod's intention and the Congregations sound traditions. Such an implication could not be further from the truth.

[151] Supra p. 141.

[152] Supra p. 35.

[153] Congregation for Religious, instruction, *Renovationis causam*, January 6, 1969, in *AAS*, 61 (1969), p. 116, no. 27 (*CLD*, vol. 7, p. 503–504) abolished the requirement of *CIC¹*, c. 558 requiring special novitiates for different categories of religious.

In fact the majority of men joining the Congregation have done so to become priests as can be seen from the following statistics.

Professed Oblates

year	priests	scholastics	brothers	total	percent clerics[154]
1826	15	7		22	100%
1831	22	10	2	34	94%
1843	44 (2)[155]	13	11	68	84%
1861	273 (6)	53	88	414	79%
1873	378 (8)	48	100	520	81%
1879	434 (12)	67	214	715	70%
1893	658 (10)	201	352	1211	71%
1898	758 (14)	227	398	1427	72%
1904	1028 (13)	310	349	1777	80%
1907	1182 (11)	250	485	1917	75%
1924	1479 (13)	487	554	2520	78%
1936	2288 (17)	1399	1016	4703	78%
1942	3003 (22)	1211	1188	5402	78%
1954	4137 (32)	1285	1219	6641	82%
1967	5298 (31)	975	1267	7540	83%
1972	5286 (36)	581	1143	7010	84%
1983	4395 (42)	424	786	5605	86%
1987	4156 (43)	554	726	5436	87%
1995	3990 (44)	546	673	4973	87%

N.B. Priests who had not completed their theological course were counted among the scholastics until they finished their studies and received their first obedience.

year	priests	First Vows scholastics	brothers	percent clerics
1980		80	15	84%
1982	2	112	9	93%
1983		112	12	90%
1993	3	144	7	95%
1994		115	7	94%

---

[154] Including all scholastics, even though they became members of the clerical state only with the reception of the tonsure (*CIC¹*, c. 108, §1) prior to 1969, and since then with the reception of the diaconate (see PAUL VI, *motu proprio, Ministeria quædam*, August 15, 1972, in *AAS*, 64 (1972), p. 531, no. I) since they pertained to the category of clerics.

[155] The number of cardinals, archbishops, and bishops included in the number of priests.

Governed by Clerics

Prior to the 1966 Constitutions *ad experimentum,* the brothers had no role whatsoever in the government of the Congregation. The Constitutions always stated explicitly that the superiors were priests.[156] Although the Constitutions did not mention the requisite of priesthood for provincial consultors, local assistants, treasurers, etc., this was understood by all and never called into question. Corroboration of this is seen in the decision of the 1966 general chapter, which will be seen shortly, permitting brothers to hold a number of offices which previously were not open to them.

An example of the understanding of how absolute this exclusion was can be seen in the minutes of the 1904 general chapter. It will be recalled that at that time the scholastics had a consultative vote in the local chapters choosing the delegates to the provincial chapter in preparation for the general chapter. The scholastics would vote during the chapter, their votes would be counted, and announced. Once this was done, the priests who had finished their course of theology would elect the delegate to the provincial chapter.[157] The only item of business, unless the superior general requested that something be discussed, was the election of the delegate. Once this was done, the chapter adjourned.

There were three irregularities in the election of Ignace Watterott, superior of St. Charles Juniorate, Netherlands, a house of the German province. He had been elected to represent the vicariate of missions of Cimbebasia (Windhoek, Namibia). Eleven lay brothers had assisted at the election in a consultative fashion, the minutes of the meeting did not state how many votes Watterott received, and they were not signed by all the priests who were present for the election.

However, the minutes did state that the election was conducted according to the prescriptions of the Rules. Since the Rules did not permit the brothers to vote, it was certain that they did not participate in the same way as the priests did. Because it was evident from the minutes that the brothers did not actually vote, and that the vicar of missions had seen this abuse of allowing the brothers to be present for a chapter in a house of the Congregation, he was excused. There was also the extenuating circumstance of the war of the Hereros that prevented all except four priests from being present. The general

---

[156] Supra p. 56.
[157] Supra p. 56.

chapter declared that the brothers must never be permitted to be present, even for consultation. Watterott's election was accepted as valid.[158]

Toward the end of the chapter someone asked if it was certain that the brothers could not assist at any chapter, local or provincial. The committee on discipline responded affirmatively, and the chapter ratified the response.[159] It was proposed in the 1906 general chapter that the brothers have a consultative vote in the local chapters. The chapter rejected the proposition.[160]

While the brothers had no role whatsoever in the government of the Congregation, the bishops had, if not by virtue of being bishops, an extensive one in fact. The practice was for a vicar apostolic to be named also vicar of missions, the equivalent of provincial.[161] This usage, which ceased only in the middle of the twentieth century, gave many bishops the right to attend the general chapters.[162] As long as the general house was in France, the two Oblate bishops residing France, Guibert and Balain, were routinely invited to be members of the chapter, if they had not been elected as delegates of one of the vicariates of missions.

Although the 1906 general chapter rejected a proposal that all Oblate bishops, even if they were not vicars of missions, be members of the chapters, the mere proposal of such a motion is an indication of the attitude toward the position of bishops within the Congregation. No doubt this resulted from de Mazenod's long tenure as both superior general and bishop of Marseille, and his principle that in mission territory assigned to the Congregation the vicar or prefect apostolic should also be the religious superior.

There are other signs of this tendency. At the chapter following de Mazenod's death, Guibert felt it necessary to speak on behalf of all the bishops present to urge the capitulants not to elect a bishop as superior general. When Dontenwill saw that he was about to be elected superior general in 1908, he protested saying that he should have taken the same steps that Bishop Legal had taken in 1906 to ward off being elected.[163]

A movement set in to eliminate bishops from any role in government, and this culminated in the 1972 general chapter when bishops and ecclesiastical

---

[158] "Registre," 1904, pp. 3–4.

[159] Ibid., p. 47.

[160] Ibid., 1906, pp. 94–95.

[161] Supra pp. 69–70.

[162] Supra pp. 70–71.

[163] "Registre," 1908, p. 159.

superiors (vicars and prefects apostolic, and apostolic administrators) were the only Oblates in perpetual vows excluded by particular law from passive voice in the election of delegates for the general chapter.[164] This exclusion was removed by the 1974 general chapter.[165]

Following the lead of *Perfectæ caritatis*[166] which encouraged that brothers be more closely associated with the life and work of religious communities, the 1966 general chapter granted the brothers in perpetual vows the right to vote for the delegates to general chapters, and to make suggestions for the appointment of provincials. It likewise recommended that technical duties be confided to brothers to free the priests for the works of the ministry. It also stated that brothers could be appointed treasurers.[167]

The 1972 general chapter implemented the decree *Clericalia instituta*[168] by not only allowing brothers to be members of the general chapter but requiring that at least six brothers be named capitulants with the right to vote, giving brothers in perpetual vows active and passive voice, saving special canonical requirements for certain offices, and also stating explicitly that they could be local assistants, provincial consultors, and members of the general council.[169] Finally it said that a brother in perpetual vows could be named local superior with the necessary indult.[170] All these norms were an application of the above-mentioned decree of the Sacred Congregation given in response to questions concerning which offices brothers could hold *salva Instituti natura et indole clericali* (with due regard to the clerical nature and character of the institute).

The 1982 Constitutions include the same norms. Although C. 82, which was required by the Sacred Congregation, specifies that superiors, their vicars and replacements be priests, Rule 90 does allow a brother in perpetual vows to be appointed superior of a local community with the necessary indult from the Holy See. In his explanation of the approval of the 1982 Constitutions to the Congregation the procurator general wrote:

---

[164] *Administrative Structures*, 1972, pp. 15–16, no. 6.

[165] *Acts of the General Chapter 1974*, p. 34, no. 6.

[166] VATICAN II, decree on the up-to-date renewal of religious life, October 28, 1965, *Perfectæ caritatis* [=PC], in *AAS*, 58 (1966), pp. 702–712, no. 15.

[167] *Circulaires*, May 1, 1966, no. 230, vol. 7, p. 410.

[168] SCRIS, decree, *Clericalia instituta*, November 27, 1969, in *AAS*, 61 (1969), pp. 739–740; *CLD*, vol. 7, pp. 468–469.

[169] *Administrative Structures*, pp. 12–13, 38–39.

[170] Ibid., p. 39.

Since the Congregation is a clerical Congregation, it is required that superiors and their vicars be priests (art. 82). This has been the long-established tradition in the Church . . . The chapter of 1980 was aware of the canonical norms and delicately referred to them in Rule 101 of the chapter text. In suitable cases, where special circumstances warrant, the S.C. grants an indult allowing a brother to be a local superior, as is mentioned also in Rule 90 of the final text.[171]

The provisions of the 1982 Constitutions and Rules were drafted in conformity with *Clericalia instituta*. Article 82, which was added upon the insistence of the Sacred Congregation, merely repeats and specifies the universal norm by stipulating that superiors must be priests. Rule 90 provides for the special circumstances when it is opportune for a brother to be named superior by reiterating the universal norm that an indult is required from the Holy See. Thus, Rule 90 is not in conflict with the requisite of c. 588, §2 which requires that governance is by clerics, but is a provision for seeking a dispensation from that norm when appropriate.[172]

Approval by the Holy See as a Clerical Institute

Since a religious institute receives its juridical personality from its formal approval by the competent ecclesiastical authority, such approval is of paramount importance. It not only gives the institute official standing in the Church, but also determines its particular classification as clerical or lay.

As was seen in chapter four, this classification is not something arbitrary, but is based on the spiritual patrimony and nature of the particular institute.[173] Consequently, in light of de Mazenod's intention of founding a society of missionary priests, and the constant tradition that priestly ministry is essential to the nature of the Congregation, it is not surprising that the Holy See has

---

[171] O'REILLY, "Approval" 10. It would seem that the *questions* concerning the clerical status of the Congregation are based not so much on whether or not the ministry of the ordained priesthood is essential to the Congregation, but rather on de Mazenod's intention of founding a missionary institute, on who are missionaries today in light of Vatican II, and on the consequence of brothers being excluded as superiors because of the canonical status of the Congregation as a clerical institute. Is this restriction arbitrary, discriminatory against the brothers, and contrary to the modern understanding of the basic equality of all persons? This question will be considered in Chapter VI.

[172] "The very organizational structure of the Congregation is influenced by its clerical character but those in charge are to be priests. This is obligatory for major superiors whereas on the local level someone who is not ordained may be a superior with the permission of the Holy See" (ZAGO, "The Priestly Character," p. 7; infra Appendix I, p. 273).

[173] Supra pp. 140–145.

always recognized the Missionary Oblates of Mary Immaculate as a clerical institute.

The Sacred Congregation insisted that the first article of the 1982 Constitutions contain the expression "clerical Congregation of pontifical right."[174] Although this precise canonical terminology was not in previous Constitutions, the concept is nothing new since the first article of all previously approved texts spoke of the Oblates as a community of priests,[175] and the inclusion of the papal briefs of approval in all printed texts was to indicate that the Congregation was of pontifical right.

Some members of the province of Canada had suggested in 1926 that the first article of the Constitutions name along with the priests both the scholastics and the brothers. The reason given for mentioning the latter was because of their importance both in numbers and by their work.[176] This suggestion was rejected. Later in his commentary on the Constitutions, Villeneuve, who had been the delegate from that province, wrote concerning the decision:

> The chapter did not agree. It must be recognized that the institute is a clerical institute which accepts brothers as auxiliaries—the present text notes that clearly.[177]

Thus, it is seen that the members of the chapter in 1926 did not accept the suggestion precisely because the mentioning of just the priests was an affirmation of the canonical clerical status of the Congregation. This was the same preoccupation in 1966, when an official of the Sacred Congregation was asked if it was necessary to insert a special article stating the clerical nature of the Congregation since the brothers were to be mentioned in the first article.[178] Hence the members of both the 1926 and the 1966 general chapters had no doubt about the recognition of the Congregation by the Holy See as a clerical institute.

---

[174] O'Reilly, "Approval," p. 8.

[175] Supra pp. 55, 67, and 94.

[176] Cf. Suggestions for the revision of the Constitutions, General archives O.M.I., CC et RR 1926, Cong. Gen., Canada.

[177] J-M. Rod. VILLENEUVE, O.M.I., "Étude analytico-synthétique de nos Règles des Miss. O.M.I. etc.," (1929), General Archives O.M.I.

Joseph RESLÉ, O.M.I. commented on article 1 of the 1928 Constitutions by stating: "The Congregation is a priestly institute, under the leadership of priests, destined for the formation of priests, directed toward priestly work, so that all, even the lay brothers in their own way dedicated themselves to the priestly life and ministry. Thus, the Congregation is a *clerical religious institute* ([*CIC¹*], c. 488, 4°)" (*Commentarium privatum Constitutionum et Regularum*, Ottawa, Études Oblates, 1958, first part, p. 25).

[178] Supra p. 181.

From its very beginning the Congregation was considered by the hierarchy as a society of priests. It would be superfluous to repeat what has already been said about the accepted meaning of the word *missionary* at that time, and to show how this word was constantly used in official documents in reference to the Missionaries of Provence, the Oblates of Saint Charles, the Missionary Oblates of Mary Immaculate.

The recognition of the nature of the society can also be seen from other expressions found in official documents. In the *celebret* given de Mazenod by the vicars capitular general of Aix in 1817, they speak of him as "a priest of this city of Aix and also superior of the Congregation of priests of the Mission of Provence."[179]

On December 5, 1817 Pius VII in a brief granted a plenary indulgence requested to "our beloved son and priest Eugene de Mazenod, superior, and the other secular priests of the community or society of Missionaries of Provence"[180] who were conducting missions.

The seven diocesan bishops who gave de Mazenod letters of recommendation to the Holy See for the Oblates of Saint Charles and their Constitutions mentioned the priestly ministry of the missions, and three of them explicitly spoke of them as priests:

> . . . of the Constitutions of the Oblate priests of Saint Charles . . .[181]
> . . . wherever the Oblate priests of Saint Charles are sent to evangelize the people.[182]
> . . . the statutes of the society of Oblate priests of Saint Charles, who are called the Missionaries of Provence . . .[183]

Even a very casual look at Leo XII's brief *Si tempus unquam* shows that he was approving a society of priests.

> If there ever was a time when this Apostolic See endeavored to encourage and support by every means at its command the zeal of those

---

[179] BEYLOT and GUIGOU, *celebret*, July 9, 1817, DM VII; *Écrits*, vol. 3, pp. 120–121; *Missions O.M.I.*, 79 (1952), pp. 120–121.

[180] PIUS VII, apostolic letter, *Cælestium munerum thesauros*, December 5, 1817, Procurator's Archives O.M.I., XIX, 1; *Écrits*, vol. 3, pp. 71–72; *Missions O.M.I.*, 79 (1952), pp. 71–72. N.B. The ms. has *munerum* and not *numerum* as in the published text.

[181] Fortuné DE MAZENOD, bishop of Marseille, September 26, 1825, Vatican Archives, Congregation of Bishops and Regulars, Marseille, 1846, 2119/2–4993–2; *Constitutions 1827*, 190–191; *Écrits*, vol. 4, pp. 12–13; *Missions O.M.I.*, 79 (1952), pp. 412–413.

[182] P.F. DE BAUSSET-ROQUEFORT, archbishop of Aix, October 23, 1825, ms. and printed references same as in previous note.

[183] C.-A. DE RICHERY, bishop of Fréjus, November 1, 1825, ms. and printed references same as above in note 180.

priests, who, burning with the fire of holy love, preach the Gospel throughout the whole world . . .

Pius VII, who guided back to port the storm tossed vessel of the
Church, . . . stated that, due to the disorders of the Church and State in
France, preachers of the Gospel were needed for the work of recalling to
the right path . . . A short time afterwards a small band of priests was
formed in the diocese of Aix, in Provence, in southern France, to undertake
this sacred ministry. The astonishing success, however, with which Divine
Goodness was pleased to crown their efforts could not long remain hidden
. . . [The Congregation's ministries requiring ordained priests are mentioned
here.]

When, indeed, the great benefits flowing from this Society were
perceived by all, its priests soon came to be spread far and wide . . .

In conclusion, We firmly hope that the members of this holy Family,
who are employed in the ministry of the Word of God under Rules so well
fitted to form hearts to piety, and who claim as their patroness, the Virgin
Mother of God conceived without sin, will strive with all their strength and
especially by their example, to bring back to the bosom of the Mother of
Mercy those men and women, whom Jesus Christ on His Cross willed to
give her as sons and daughters.[184]

In the brief *Quam multa sit mensis* approving the changes in the Constitutions, Gregory XVI twice spoke of the Oblates as a Congregation of priests:

We have seen recently an auspicious event in the Church, since a new
Congregation of priests was established, who bearing the name of Missionary Oblates of the Most Holy and Immaculate Virgin Mary have propagated
the Word of God especially among the simple people . . .

As is only proper we bestow merited praise on this Congregation of
priests, ratify and confirm it by the sanction of our apostolic authority with
this present letter.[185]

Seven years later in the brief approving the modifications of the Constitutions introduced the 1850 general chapter, Pius IX used twice the expression
congregatio presbyterorum (congregation of presbyters or priests) and twice
spoke of the members of the Congregation as priests:

. . . the priests of the Congregation fighting the good fight, spread
everywhere the glory of the divine Name . . . The ardor of their great
charity, which inflames the priests of the aforementioned Congregation to

---

[184] LEO XII, apostolic letter, *Si tempus unquam*, March 21, 1826, MD XII 2b; printed in *Bullari
romani continuatio*, Prati: Aldina, 1854, vol 16, pp. 413b–415a; *Constitutiones 1827*, pp. 173–180;
Constitutiones 1853, pp. 183–188; *Constitutiones 1894*, pp. 189–194; *Constitutiones 1910*, pp. 164–168;
Constitutiones 1928, pp. 188–193.

[185] GREGORY XVI, apostolic letter, *Quum multa sit messis*, March 20, 1846, MD XII 3; printed in
Constitutiones 1853, pp. 189–192; *Constitutiones 1894*, pp. 195–198; *Constitutiones 1910*, pp. 169–171.

their very marrow, could not be contained by the boundaries of Europe. Not deterred by the difficulty and hardship of any journey they have reached the most remote regions of Asia, America, and Africa . . . For these reasons Leo XII approved this saving Congregation of Priests so worthy of praise by the Church, and then Gregory XVI confirmed it . . .

Therefore We, wanting to provide for the welfare and increase of this Congregation of Priests . . . ratify by the sanction of our Apostolic authority and confirm . . .[186]

In the brief conferring the pallium on de Mazenod and his successors as bishop of Marseille, Pius IX spoke of him as the "founder and superior of a congregation of priests with the title Oblates of the Blessed and Immaculate Virgin Mary."[187]

The Holy See in its relationship with the Missionary Oblates of Mary Immaculate has always treated it as a clerical congregation. A clear example of this was seen in the question of exemption in the 1860s and the subsequent granting of the faculties requested so that the Oblate superiors would not have to have recourse to the diocesan bishops for various internal matters.[188] These faculties, which referred to things pertaining to reception of or the exercise of holy orders, were renewed regularly until they were made obsolete by the pontifical rescript *Cum admotæ* in 1964. As was said above, no one has ever questioned that the rescript, which was only for clerical institutes, applied to the Congregation.

Just as Pius IX in *Quum nullo unquam tempore* made specific mention of the foreign missions, Pius X in *Decessorum Nostrorum vestigiis* spoke of the great expansion of the Congregation in the missions and said that fourteen vicariates apostolic were confided to it.[189] Pius XI in *Mirabili plane modo* also drew special attention to the foreign missions.[190]

This is another example of the Holy See treating the Missionary Oblates of Mary Immaculate as a priestly institute and implicitly confirming the clerical

---

[186] Pius IX, apostolic letter, *Quum nullo unquam tempore*, March 28, 1851, DM XII 4; printed in *Constitutiones 1853*, pp. 193–197; *Constitutiones 1894*, pp. 199–202; *Constitutiones 1910*, pp. 172–175.

[187] Pius IX, apostolic letter, *Romani Pontifices*, April 1, 1851, printed in *Procès-Verbal de la remise faite par Monseigneur l'Évêque de Marseille entre les mains du Conseil Municipal de Bref de N.S.P. Le Pape qui lui confère le Pallium*, May 9, 1851, Marseille, Barile, 1851.

[188] Supra pp. 83–84.

[189] Pius X, apostolic letter, *Decessorum Nostrorum vestigiis*, September 7, 1910, in *AAS*, 2 (1910), pp. 901–903; General Archives O.M.I.; printed in *Constitutiones 1910*, p. vi.

[190] Pius XI, apostolic letter, *Mirabili plane modo*, May 21, 1928, in *AAS*, 20 (1928), pp. 341–344; General Archives O.M.I.; printed in *Constitutiones 1928*, p. 9.

nature of the Congregation. The Holy See simply took for granted that the Congregation is a clerical institute in *entrusting* or *confiding* to it responsibility for mission territories almost equal in size to all of Europe from the Atlantic Ocean to the Urals. In 1950 the Congregation still had *confided* to it more than 9,400,000 square kilometres.[191] By that time a number of dioceses in the southern part of western Canada had been transferred to the responsibility of secular diocesan bishops.

Although today the Congregation has only four vicariates apostolic[192] and one prefecture apostolic,[193] many of the former vicariates, which are now dioceses, still have Oblate bishops, and the greater part of their clergy are Oblates. Some twenty-five years ago the bishop of Copenhagen gave the Oblates the pastoral responsibility of the handful of Catholics in Greenland which alone is more than four times the size of Spain, and a few years later the bishop of Stockholm placed the Oblates in charge of the northern half of Sweden, some 200,000 square kilometres.

The Holy See and the bishops have entrusted the Congregation with the priestly ministry in these huge areas in order to establish the Church, care for the faithful by the celebration of the Eucharist and the administration of the sacraments, to preach the Gospel to those who do not know Jesus and bring them to baptism and membership in the Church.

In a word, the Holy See has always recognized the Congregation as composed principally of priests dedicated to the ministry by their ordination as priests. Thus, in 1827 the Holy See approved it as a clerical institute. When the Oblate superiors are asked to take responsibility for a territory, it is that priests be sent there either to establish the Church or to minister primarily as ordained priests to the faithful. When they are asked to assume the spiritual care of a parish or other institution, it is precisely the ministry of ordained priests that is requested. This is not to say that other apostolic works that may be done by the laity, as well as by priests, are not included, but that primarily the preaching of the Word of God and the sacramental ministry proper to ordained priests is intended.

---

[191] See J. DESPONT, *Nouvel Atlas des Missions*, Paris Œuvre de la Propagation de la Foi, 1951. *Annuario Pontificio*, Roma, Libreria Vaticana, 1951.

[192] Vientiane, Laos; Pilcomayo, Paraguay; Jolo, Philippines; and Rundu, Namibia.

[193] Sahara Occidental.

Summary

Under the leadership of Eugene de Mazenod a group of secular priests founded the Missionaries of Provence to preach missions for the spiritual renewal of Provence and the other priestly works undertaken by de Mazenod in Aix. Within a few years of their foundation they made religious vows and received papal approval in 1826 as a congregation of secular priests with religious vows. With the acceptance of foreign missions to care for Catholics without priests and to preach Christ to the "gentiles" a rapid growth began in their membership as well as in their field of ministry. With the canonical evolution of the standing of such societies they became a clerical religious institute with simple vows.

The Oblates have always been considered as a society of priests even though brothers formed an important part of the community almost from the beginning. Their role historically was considered as that of auxiliaries to the priests. The priests have always shouldered the responsibility of the internal government of the society. The priests and scholastics preparing for the priesthood have always comprised a sizable majority of the members. At the present time approximately 90% of those making first vows are either priests or desire to become priests.

The striving for greater internal unity and brotherhood within religious communities and the development of the apostolate of the laity with Vatican II brought about a corresponding evolution in the place of the brothers within the Congregation and in their external apostolic activity. Since 1966 they have had a role in the government of the Congregation within the limits of common law for clerical institutes, or in special circumstances with an indult from the Holy See granting a restricted variance to the common norm for clerical institutes.

The growth in the understanding of the laity's place the in the apostolate of the Church has lead to the brothers taking active roles in pastoral activity, and they have become true missionaries. This has in no way lessened the ministry of the priests as ordained ministers of the Word and the sacraments. The constant tradition since de Mazenod is that priestly ministry is essential to the mission of the Congregation.

Since the ministerial priesthood is essential to the Congregation, "the Oblate religious missionary life and ministry of both the priests and brothers are inseparably linked to the ministerial priesthood."[194] The Missionary Oblates

---

[194] *General Norms for Oblate Formation*, pp. 7–8, second basic principle.

of Mary Immaculate cannot be imagined without priests—without priests it would be an essentially different society with an essentially diverse ministry.

Both the diocesan bishops and the Holy See have always acknowledged the priestly nature of the Congregation by entrusting it with ministry and pastoral responsibilities that required the exercise of the powers received from sacerdotal ordination. The priestly nature of the Congregation is not something that was imposed by the Sacred Congregation of Religious and Secular Institutes, but is based on de Mazenod's intention as founder. This is confirmed by constant tradition—both within and without the Congregation. From the first papal approbation the Congregation has been formally constituted and canonically recognized as a clerical religious institute.

The general chapters, superiors general, and other major superiors of the Congregation both in their official documents and way of governing have always acted as superiors of a clerical religious institute.

Religious institutes are either lay or clerical, and the distinguishing note is the inclusion of the exercise of sacred orders in the nature and end of the particular institute.[195] Since the evangelization of the poor by the Word, the celebration of the Eucharist and in the sacrament of reconciliation, is essentially linked with the exercise of the ministerial priesthood, the Congregation is properly considered canonically as a clerical institute.

---

[195] See c. 588, §§2–3.

Chapter VI
The Brothers

Since the Missionary Oblates of Mary Immaculate were founded as a community of priests to exercise specialized priestly ministry, and the status of the brothers has always been distinct from that of the priests and those preparing for the priesthood, this special position of the brothers deserves particular consideration.

This will be done within the perimeters of this dissertation. Consequently the history and dedicated service of the some two thousand living and deceased Oblate brothers will be touched upon only insofar as required for an understanding of their juridical status and its evolution.[1]

Sons of the Congregation

From the very beginning, de Mazenod established as the purpose of his group of missionaries not only priestly ministry but also the practice of the religious virtues for the sanctification of the members.[2] As was seen in the second chapter the evolution of the institute from that of a society of diocesan

---

[1] See the articles of Jean-Marie LAROSE on the brothers for a mine of information on the history of the brothers in the Congregation: "Étude sur l'origine des frères convers chez les Oblats (1815–1961)," in *Études Oblates*, 12 (1953), pp. 65–126; "Les sources des articles des Règles concernant les frères coadjuteurs," in *Études Oblates*, 14 (1955), pp. 210–244, 278–301; "Les travaux des frères," in *Études Oblates*, 17 (1958), pp. 119–151; "Les écoles pour futurs Frères Oblats," in *Études Oblates*, 21 (1962), pp. 184–188; "La place des Frères coadjuteurs dans la Congrégation," in *Études Oblates*, 24 (1965), pp. 131–152.

It seems that Larose, at times, is moved by his love for the brothers to write in a way that some may find a bit strange for rigorously scientific work. In a few instances, his conclusions seem to this author to be forced, and not based on solid proof, e.g., the influence of Brother Maur, de Mazenod's companion upon returning to Aix, as having a great role in the decision to have brothers in the Congregation (*Études Oblates*, 12 (1953), pp. 66–69). He does not document such an influence on de Mazenod's decision. The same could be said of his questioning that the brothers are "*conversi*" as set out in the 1917 Code of Canon Law (*Études Oblates*, 24 [1965], pp. 149–151).

See I. TOURIGNY, O.M.I., "Le Frère oblat selon le Fondateur et la tradition oblate," in *Vie Oblate Life*, 39 (1980), pp. 45–63. Like Larose, in this fine article Tourigny seems at times to be moved in his conclusions more by esteem for the brothers, than by documentary evidence.

For a juridical treatment of the status of the brothers from the beginning of the Congregation through *Constitutiones 1928* see the excellent study by G. COSENTINO, o.m.i., *Histoire de nos Règles*, 6 vols., Ottawa, Éditions des Études Oblates, 1955, vol. 3, pp. 168–177; vol. 5, pp. 226–242; vol. 6, pp. 22–29, 305–309.

[2] Supra p. 25.

missionaries to that of a religious community was very rapid. Already in 1817 de Mazenod wrote that they were a congregation of regular clergy.[3] The first Constitutions with vows of celibacy and obedience were adopted in 1818,[4] and the vow of poverty was added in 1821.[5]

Following the long tradition of clerical religious communities,[6] de Mazenod already in the 1818 Constitutions foresaw a special class of members known as "*frères convers*," lay brothers.

In the introduction to the first Constitutions he wrote that there would be a section on the brothers and left two blank pages at the appropriate place in the manuscript for it.[7] The fact that no one had joined the community as a brother and also because Alphonsus Liguori did not have a special section on the brothers explain his not writing the section at that time.

Before proceeding further it would be good to examine the various names for the brothers used in the beginning of the Congregation. In the 1818 Constitutions there are only five references to the brothers and the following words are used: *frères*,[8] *frère laïque*,[9] and *frères servants*[10] each once. Twice *frères convers* is employed.[11]

---

[3] See DE MAZENOD, to Tempier, November 4, 1817, *Oblate Writings*, vol. 6, no. 29, p. 45; cited supra p. 28.

[4] Supra p. 29.

[5] Supra pp. 30–32.

[6] Cf. T.A. BROCKHAUS, O.S.B., *Religious Who are Known as Conversi, A Historical Synopsis and Commentary*, Washington, Catholic University of America Press, 1946, for a historical-juridical study of brothers through the 1917 Code of Canon Law and a very complete bibliography.

[7] *Constitutiones 1818*, pp. 53–54, Postulation Archives O.M.I., DM XI 1; printed in *Missions O.M.I.*, 78 (1951), p. 93; *Écrits*, vol. 1, p. 93.

[8] *Constitutiones 1818*, II partie, chapitre I, Des autres principales observances; *Missions O.M.I.*, 78 (1951), p. 59; *Écrits*, vol. 1, p. 59.

[9] Loc. cit.

[10] Ibid., II partie, chapitre I, §1; *Missions O.M.I.*, 78 (1951), p. 48; *Écrits*, vol. 1, p. 48.

This particular article, which refers to the income of each house, is a translation from Alphonsus Liguori, who used the expression *Fratelli servienti*. See Cosentino, *Histoire*, vol. 1, pp. 87–89.

An English-speaking person needs to be on guard lest the French word *servant* be taken as the equivalent of *servant* in English. The meaning in French in this context is the same as that of *frère convers*. Cf. M. BESCHERELLE, *Dictionnaire National*, Paris, Simon, 1849, s.v. "servant": "**Frères servants**. Dans quelques communautés, les frères convers employés aux œuvres serviles du monastère." Other standard dictionaries give similar definitions.

[11] Ibid., Preface, in *Missions O.M.I.*, 78 (1951), p. 12; *Écrits*, vol. 1, p. 12; and ibid., II partie, chapitre I, Des autres principales observances, in *Missions O.M.I.*, 78 (1951), p. 57; *Écrits*, vol. 1, p. 57.

In the final French text of 1824 or 1825 upon which the Latin translation of 1825 was based the same words are used, except *frère laïque* becomes *frère lai*[12] and *frères servants* was changed to *frères servans*.[13] This latter change may have been a mistake in copying the text. In addition to the five references mentioned in the previous paragraph a section was added on the spiritual prefect of the brothers in which *frères convers* is used five times.[14] In the special section on the brothers in the third part of the Constitutions *frères convers*[15] is used eight times and *frères*[16] is used four times.

The official Latin text of 1826 translates these various names indiscriminately as either *fratres laici* or *fratres famulantes*. Also *religiosi famulantes* and *famulantes* are each used once. There is no apparent pattern for choosing one expression or the other, v.g., in the section on the spiritual prefect of the brothers the French text uses only the expression *frères convers*, which is translated twice by *fratres famulantes* and thrice by *fratres laici*.[17] On the other hand the special section on the brothers has five times *fratres famulantes*, four times *fratres laici*, twice *novitii famulantes*, and once each *religiosi laici* and *famulantes*.[18] The Latin text never uses the expression *fratres conversi*. It is to be noted that the translation was not made by de Mazenod but by Albini and Courtès.[19]

Because of the prevailing use in the French texts of *frères convers* and the indiscriminate translation of the various French expressions for the brothers as either *fratres famulantes* or *fratres laici*, there is no basis for concluding that there is any special significance to be seen in the use of the Latin word *famulantes*.[20] This is especially so, since there is no evidence to indicate that de

---

[12] "Saintes Règles, texte français définitif (1824–1825), sur lequel a été faite la version latine," II partie, c. II, §3, DM XI 4, Postulation Archives O.M.I., DM XI 4.

[13] Ibid., II partie, c. I, art. 43.

[14] Ibid., III partie, c. I, §10.

[15] Ibid., III partie, c. II, §4.

[16] Loc. cit.

[17] *Constitutiones 1927*, pars III, c. I, §10.

[18] Ibid., pars III, c. II, §4.

[19] See COSENTINO, *Histoire*, vol. 2, pp. 38–40.

[20] Larose and Tourigny see very different implications in the use of the word *famulantes*. Commenting on *Constitutiones 1928* replacing *laicus* by *famulantes* wherever the former was used in previous editions of the Constitutions, Larose says: "'Laicus' is distinguished from 'sacerdos' (priest); this is in the sphere of the Church, which is proper in religious life. But 'famulantes' (servant) is distinguished from 'dominus' (master): this is on the level of social class, which is offensive within a family . . ." (*Études oblates*, 24 [1965], p. 143).

Mazenod was responsible for choosing one Latin word over another. In any case, the everyday name was *frères convers*.

The most important article concerning the brothers in the 1928 Constitutions is the first in the section entitled "De fratribus famulantibus," i.e., lay brothers:

> Art. 1. The Society welcomes as sons men of good will, who, though not possessed of the knowledge necessary for missionaries, and even declining to attain it, desire, however, to labor for their own salvation under the guidance of the Rules of our Institute, while employed in duties which pertain in religious institutes to lay brothers.[21]

An analysis of this article separates a number of elements: 1) the Congregation accepts as members men who do not intend to become missionaries; 2) either because they do not have the necessary education or do not wish to acquire it; 3) who seek their own salvation by following the Constitutions of the Congregation; and 4) they will do the traditional work of lay brothers in religious institutes.

It should be recalled that the popular understanding of the word *missionary* included only priests, and that the technical meaning was expanded to include others only very recently.[22] No doubt, it is superfluous to point out that this article was written long before the age of universal education. This explains article eight of this section, which presupposes that some of the candidates will not be able to read and write.

However, the brothers are not to be considered as servants, but as *veri Societatis filii* (true sons of the Society), who are responsible for the domestic tasks for the common benefit of the Society and of the Church, while others are responsible for greater duties (art. 11). Consequently, they share the same dining room and religious exercises, in so far as compatible with their duties and education, with the rest of the community (art. 12). Because of their other duties, they were exempt from divine office, but were to recite a certain number of Our Fathers, Hail Marys and Glory Bes (art. 19–21).

Instead of making perpetual vows at the end of the novitiate, as was the case with priests and students for the priesthood, the brothers made their

---

Tourigny sees the word in a very different light: "[The Latin text of 1826] does not use the name *convers* or *servants* as in other institutes, but that of FAMULANTES. It underlines that they are truly part of the 'family.' This reduces the above-mentioned situation of separation between the fathers and the brothers . . ." (*Vie Oblate Life*, 39 [1980], p. 50).

[21] *Constitutiones 1927*, pars III, c. II, §4.

[22] Supra pp. 151–161, 178, and 181.

oblation for one year, and at the end of one year for five years (Art. 15). Then they may make their perpetual vows.

Particular note should be taken of the fact that the temporary profession of the brothers was also called *oblation* (art. 15–18). This was the same word used for the perpetual vows of the members of the institute, and the origin of the name Oblate. Although the brothers were not missionaries, they were equally members of the family as Oblates, religious. This is clear from the expression *ceterorum Oblatorum* (other Oblates) (Art. 15). This is pointed out here because at that time the scholastics were generally called *oblats* or *simples oblats* when distinguishing them from the fathers and the brothers.[23]

The other members received with their oblation, which was always perpetual, the large cross to be worn as part of their habit as missionaries.[24] The brothers with their temporary oblation received a smaller cross without the corpus as part of their habit (art. 27–28). Their habit was not the regular cassock of the missionaries, who belonged to the clergy, but rather a shorter cassock (art. 26). However, while working they could wear ordinary clothes (art. 29).

De Mazenod and the Brothers

It would seem that some of the priests did not have de Mazenod's appreciation for the role of the brothers in the Congregation, and in spite of the clear prescriptions of the Constitutions treated them as hired servants. This judgment is based on de Mazenod's correspondence. In 1842 he wrote the novice master:

> I reply that I have always considered it an injustice to make men, who have joined us to become religious, work from morning to night.
>
> Without a doubt they have to work, but they must also pray, and they have to learn the duties of the religious life. They are not hired hands, they cannot be treated as paid servants who are given a wage to work all day long.[25]

The letter continues with detailed specifics as to how the brothers are to be present for the community prayers and meals, and are to be given the regular spiritual conferences prescribed by the Constitutions.

In a 1853 letter to the superior in Oregon, who wrote complaining of the

---

[23] Supra p. 34.

[24] Supra pp. 158–159.

[25] DE MAZENOD, to Vincens, December 8, 1842, LM.

lack of religious spirit among the brothers, de Mazenod advised:

> Try to make them understand this without offending them because they are complaining that they are being treated too harshly, that they have been made into slaves, and that nobody cares for their spiritual welfare, which is serious, for this is a right that nobody can deny them, and I must ask you to provide for them in this matter so as to acquit yourself of an obligation from which you cannot be dispensed. Also, their load of work must be decreased: this is a duty in charity and justice.[26]

De Mazenod's concern for the brothers was not limited to their spiritual life. He did not hesitate in insisting that their talents be respected and used in such a way to benefit both the Congregation and the human growth of the individual. His insistence on true respect for the individual brother can be seen in the letter recommending a new postulant.

> I don't have the time to recommend to you the postulant novice that I am sending you. He is a man of good will, capable of great sacrifices for the good Lord, for whom he gives up all the advantages that he could have in the world. I bring to your attention that he should not be assigned to heavy work. He should not be used on the farm or in the garden. He has other talents that should be used in the Congregation, perhaps in some educational institution. He has excellent penmanship; it would be difficult to find a better master. I give you this advice, so that you do not make a mistake. It is a question of forming him to the religious life, to develop in him the germ of the virtues that the Lord has placed in his heart, along with good measure of good will and perfect devotion. Make of him a good religious and ask of him only that which he is capable of and for which he is made. I repeat, he is for light and artistic work, if necessary . . . It may happen that outside the novitiate they complain that we have not placed a pickaxe in his hands, but I repeat it again, I am not sending him to you for that purpose.[27]

The acceptance of foreign missions in 1841 opened a whole new apostolic field not only for the fathers, but even more so for the brothers. There were nine professed brothers at the time, and two of them were in the first group leave for Canada. Brothers, who had until then performed only "the traditional work of lay brothers in religious institutes," would quickly become also teachers and catechists in Canada, England, Ireland, the United States, southern

---

[26] DE MAZENOD, to Ricard, May 12, 1853, *Oblate Writings*, vol. 2, no. 177 p. 56.

In 1849 two brothers in Oregon were ready to leave with six horses for California to prospect for gold in order to support the mission, when the plan was halted (see É. Lamirande, "Project de Fondation en California [1849–1853]," in *Études oblates*, 22 [1963], pp. 18–20).

[27] DE MAZENOD, to Vandenburghe, December 6, 1852, LM.

Africa, and especially in Ceylon. Even before the Constitutions were changed in 1853 to recognize officially this new apostolate, de Mazenod would speak of them as catechists.[28]

Louis Soullier, who during his twenty-five years as assistant general and later as superior general (1893–1897) was visitor of practically the whole Congregation, was guided by the same principles as de Mazenod.

> Our principle of government is that subjects be used according to their abilities. Just as among the ordained, some have more aptitude for preaching, and others for teaching—differences that we are happy to take into consideration, without nevertheless establishing categories among our priests; thus, among the lay members, some have more aptitude for education, others for manual work, this permits us to satisfy the various needs without creating honorific distinctions or privileged situations.[29]

Instruction of Poor Children

The 1850 general chapter recognized the need of some of the brothers being teachers and catechists and approved that the Constitutions should be amended to include such work by the brothers.[30] In conformity with this decision the first article on the brothers was modified by the addition of the words, "and also in the instruction of poor children, when judged expedient."[31]

Although the apostolate of teaching was officially open to the brothers with the 1853 Constitutions, this in itself did not fill the need for teachers. There simply were neither enough brothers nor sufficient brothers who were prepared to teach. At subsequent general chapters the question was raised

---

[28] See DE MAZENOD, to Propagation of the Faith, Lyon, October 14, 1847, *Oblate Writings* vol. 5, no. 109, p. 213; December 14, 1847, *Oblate Writings*, vol. 5, no. 110, p. 216; April 17, 1852, *Oblate Writings*, vol. 5, no. 135, p. 252; December 27, 1853, *Oblate Writings*, vol. 5, no. 149, p. 264; April 5, 1860, *Oblate Writings*, vol. 5, no. 183, pp. 303–304; April 10, 1861, *Oblate Writings*, vol. 5, no. 187, p. 311; DE MAZENOD, to Barnabò, prefect of the Congregation de Propaganda Fide, September 13, 1860, *Oblate Writings*, vol. 5, no. 71, p.146.

[29] L. SOULLIER, Act of Visitation of the British Province 1893, cited by LAROSE in "La place des Frères coadjuteurs" in *Études oblates*, 24 (1965), p. 142. Commenting on this text Larose states: "It must be admitted that these broad views of the Founder and Father General Soullier were not, as it were, known outside the English-speaking brothers." To substantiate his assertion he mentions the fact that the vernacular summaries of the Constitutions and Rules for the brothers added a special section on the principal jobs of the brothers—sacristan, infirmarian, porter, wardrobe-keeper, cook, refectorian, and gardener, but only the English edition contained the instruction for the foreign missions.

[30] See "Registre," 1850, p. 108; PIELORZ, *Les Chapitres*, vol. 1, p. 299.

[31] *Constitutiones 1853*, pars III, c. II, §4, art. 1.

repeatedly under different forms. Since there were few, if any, schools in the missions, the need was great to found new schools and enlarge the existing ones. To fill this need it was proposed that a separate category of teaching brothers be founded within the Congregation.

This was rejected by the 1856 chapter because such a special class of brothers could have great difficulties in their relationship with the lay brothers in the strict sense.[32] The 1861 chapter strongly encouraged the preparation of brothers for teaching, but insisted that they would not form a distinct category within the Congregation.[33] The 1879 chapter again rejected a proposal for a separate class of brothers after the intervention of Cardinal Guibert who maintained that troubles would be caused by the ambition of such brothers to become priests, and their temptation to scorn (*mépriser*) the fathers.[34]

At the 1887 chapter a proposal was adopted to establish an apostolic school to prepare teaching brothers for the missions, even though it was pointed out that there could be the danger of schism within the Congregation as there was with the Marist (sic) Brothers and the Brothers of Charity.[35] However, such a school was not in fact begun.

Seven years later it was the danger of the brothers wanting to become priests and of internal dissension with the consequent lessening of religious spirit that were pointed out. Still the 1893 chapter voted to form teaching brothers for work both in the missions and "apud domesticos fidei magis excultos," among the faithful. They would not, however, be a separate category.[36] Evidently the majority of the chapter was more impressed by the apostolic needs, than by the "danger" of having educated brothers. The 1904 chapter insisted that the provincials should do everything possible to develop the natural talents of the brothers.[37]

---

[32] See "Registre," 1856, p.160; PIELORZ, *Les Chapitres*, vol. 2, p.77. COSENTINO quotes this text and the following ones concerning teaching brothers (in *Histoire*, vol. 6, pp. 24–29). Cf. supra p. 176.

[33] See "Registre," 1861, p. 12; PIELORZ, *Les Chapitres*, vol. 2, pp. 173–174. On this occasion the newly elected superior general Joseph Fabre lamented the fact that the number of brothers was "decreasing each day." In fact, in 1856 there were 60 brothers and in 1861, 88—an increase of 45% in a period of a little over five years (see PIELORZ, *Les Chapitres*, vol. 2, pp. 23 and 140). Would that we had such "decreases" today!

[34] See "Registre," 1879, p. 237.

[35] See "Registre," 1887, p. 295.

[36] See "Registre," 1893, p. 80.

[37] See "Registre," 1904, p. 52.

Even though the number of brothers, who were teachers, was always the minority, the official position of the Congregation was constant: to meet the needs, especially in the missions, brothers were to be formed as teachers without, however, forming a distinct category of brothers. This was in accord with de Mazenod's principle that each man should be employed in accord with his talents and the needs of the Church and Congregation.

Extended Apostolic Role

The 1928 Constitutions not only transferred the first article on the brothers to the first chapter of the Constitutions but it also omitted the expression that the brothers did not have the knowledge to be missionaries. This was no longer the case, and many found it objectionable. It also changed the last part of the article to read, "vel etiam auxilium missionariis præstando prout Superioribus opportunum visum fuerit" (or also rendering such other assistance to the missionaries as may judged opportune by superiors).[38] This more supple wording recognized that the teaching brothers were a minority, and at the same time opened to the brothers other occupations not requiring ordination.[39]

It was the 1966 general chapter that sought to integrate the brothers as closely as possible in the community and apostolate of the Congregation.

> The Chapter has considered the vocation of the brothers, in its baptismal richness and specifically religious character, rather than in relation to the priesthood, since both the fathers and the brothers are associated with the mission of the Congregation, each according to his proper function in the Church.[40]

This found its expression in a number of articles in the 1966 Constitutions *ad experimentum*. For the first time the particular law of the Congregation

---

[38] *Constitutiones 1928*, art. 9.

[39] See COSENTINO, *Histoire*, vol. 6, p. 29. It seems evident that the brothers' auxiliary role to the priests is to be so understood as auxiliaries to the priests not as individuals, but as missionaries, i.e., in and for the mission of preaching the Gospel and celebrating of the Eucharist and the sacraments. Cf. "One cannot fully understand the vocation of a lay brother without the Mass of the Missionary Oblate priest. The most perfect concept of our community life as Missionary Oblates, implies that lay brothers unite themselves with the priests at Mass, humbly serving Mass, participating in the Sacrifice of Jesus on the altar for the salvation of the world. This is, we believe, the sublime vocation of a lay brother" (L. DESCHÂTELETS, *Circulaires*, November 1, 1947, no. 181, vol. 5, p. 154 [27]). Although this would not be expressed in the same words today, it would seem that the concept is still valid. Cf. supra pp. 184–186, and 198.

[40] L. DESCHÂTELETS, *Circulaires*, May 1, 1966, no. 230, vol. 7, p. 407 [3].

proposed a truly adequate picture of the field of apostolic labors opened to the brothers. The more important articles are quoted here because of their influence on the evolution of and greater understanding of the role of the brothers in the work of the Congregation.

C. 1. . . . priests in union with brothers (*laicis*),[41] bound by religious vows and living together as brothers, closely cooperating with one another in Christ the Savior, devote themselves principally to the preaching of the Gospel to the poor.

5 C. . . . priests and brothers (*laicis*) will work with one heart, each in his own ministry and in his won field, for the advancement of the Kingdom of God.

R 15. The brothers have an important missionary role to play everywhere, but especially where the Church is being established. Their work often places them in close contact with the everyday life of the people. They are thus called to give special witness of a life inspired by the Gospel.

This allows them to exercise a very fruitful apostolate, complementary to that of the priests of their community.

R. 16. Moreover, because of their special competence, they can cooperate efficaciously in the technical development of the region. In this manner they will show forth the effectiveness of their love for men, in pursuit of their missionary apostolate.

R. 17. They will share in certain pastoral works such as catechizing, teaching, formation, social works and actively participating in the celebrating of the liturgy, assuming the roles proper to them.

R. 18. As a result of community solidarity, they share in the life and apostolate of their house simply by carrying out faithfully those charges which are entrusted to them according to their respective aptitudes, whether of an intellectual, technical or manual nature.

Since article 9 of the 1928 Constitutions had already extended to the brothers apostolates not requiring ordination, one might ask what juridical change did the 1966 Constitutions *ad experimentum* make in their work. Perhaps one could say that the 1928 Constitutions contained the germ of what was to

---

[41] "The title lay, kept in the Latin text despite many interventions against it, only follows the juridical language of the Holy See, which distinguishes clerics and laymen, even though both may or may not be religious" (L. DESCHÂTELETS, *Circulaires,* May 1, 1966, no. 230, vol. 7, p. 408).

While this statement is true, the tone seems to be too apologetic and to give the impression that the distinction between clerics and lay persons is merely juridical. Of course, this is not the case since it is based on the essential difference between the ministerial priesthood of the ordained and the common priesthood of the faithful. This traditional teaching of the Church was clearly proclaimed in *Lumen gentium* (no. 10). See also *Lumen gentium* (nos. 17 and 28).

Since some of the brothers are now deacons and thus clerics, today the word laymen (*laici*) would not include all the brothers.

be written in 1966. Certainly there is a logical development of the tradition of the brothers performing the apostolates for which they were qualified.

The basis for an adequate response is that the whole question is not so much juridical but rather historical, theological, and psychological. First of all the world of 1928 was very different from that of 1966. Vatican II accelerated the theological understanding of the role of the laity in the Church. Because of this, religious were psychologically ready to see the implications of these developments in their lives and apostolate. The above quoted articles from the 1966 Constitutions and Rules *ad experimentum* could not have been written in 1928, and if they had been written, they could not have been understood at that time.

The 1982 Constitutions broke from the tradition of previous Constitutions by not naming and describing various apostolic works.[42] The work of the Congregation is described as the evangelization of the poor without mentioning specific ministries of either the fathers or the brothers.

> C. 1. . . . We come together in apostolic communities of priests and brothers, united to God by the vows of religion, cooperating with the Savior and imitating his example, we commit ourselves principally to evangelizing the poor.
> C. 5. We are a missionary Congregation. Our principal service in the Church is to proclaim Christ and his Kingdom to the most abandoned . . .
> C. 7. As priests and brothers, we have complementary responsibilities in evangelizing. We will spare no effort to awaken or to reawaken the faith in the people to whom we are sent, and we will help them to discover "who Christ is." Our mission puts us on constant call to respond to the most urgent needs of the Church through various forms of witness and ministry, but especially through proclaiming the Word of God which finds its fulfilment in the celebration of the sacraments and in service to others . . .
> C. 38. Obedience and charity bind us together, priests and brothers, keeping us interdependent in our lives and missionary activity . . .

In his presentation to the Congregation of the proposed text for the Constitutions and Rules to be considered by the 1980 general chapter the president of the commission that prepared the text wrote:

> In the spirit of the Council documents and according to the expressed desire of many, the distinction between fathers and brothers has been considerably toned down. The text proposes a special article on the broth-

---

[42] Supra p. 116. Cf., however, Rule 2: "Preaching missions at home and sending missionaries abroad have been traditionally central to our apostolate . . ."

ers in the First Part, and some articles on formation specific to them in the Third Part.[43]

Among the recommendations concerning the proposed text was the suggestion that there be no special article on the brothers since such an article would signify a distinction between the priests and the brothers.[44] The article that had been proposed for the Constitutions was dropped, but one was placed in the Rules.

This is Rule 3 which was composed by the brothers who were members of the chapter, and approved on their recommendation. For that reason, it has special significance.[45]

---

[43] *Constitutions and Rules of the Congregation of the Missionary Oblates of Mary Immaculate, Proposed Text Prepared by the Revision Commission for the General Chapter of 1980,* Rome, 1979, p. vi.

[44] "Réactions sur le projet des Constitutions et des Règles—1980," I, C. 8, nos. 24, 47, 54, 61, and 67, General Archives O.M.I.

[45] Both the French and English texts of Rule 3 are printed here for easy comparison. Both are official texts of the Congregation, and did not have to be approved by the Holy See. The difficulty of drafting a legal text in two languages can be seen here. One can also see the almost impossible and thankless task given a committee to revise a text.

First of all, the adjectives *professionnel* in French and *professional* in English do not have exactly the same meaning. E.g., *professional services* require a university education. Such is not the case for *services professionnels.* An *école professionnelle* is where one receives training for a trade (cf. *Petite Larousse illustré, 1984,* s.v. *professionnel).* While a *professional school* is an institution preparing persons for a highly specialized field in the liberal arts or sciences, e.g. medicine, law, theology.

Attention should be called to the first sentence of the first paragraph. The French text is the same as that approved by the chapter ("Chapitre Général 1980, Const. et Règles," 13a, General Archives O.M.I.). The English text approved by the chapter read, "in the one priesthood of Christ" ('General Chapter 1980, Const. and Rules,' 10a, General Archives O.M.I.), the same as the French text. This was revised by the post-capitular commission to the present reading: "the common priesthood."

The commission was within its authority granted by the 1980 chapter ("Registre" 1980, p. 233) to improve the formulation, if necessary, as far as style and grammar.

The first sentence of Rule 3 is based on *Lumen gentium,* no. 10, "The common priesthood of the faithful and the ministerial or hierarchical priesthood, though they differ in essence and not simply in degree, are nevertheless interrelated: each in its own particular way shares in the one priesthood of Christ" (emphasis added).

The present English text merely states that the brothers share in the common priesthood of the faithful, while the French text states that both the priests and the brothers share in the same priesthood, even though in an essentially different way.

The other editions follow the French: "I Fratelli oblati partecipano dell'unico sacerdozio de Cristo;" "Unsere Brüder haben teil an dem einen Priestertum Christi;" "Los Hermanos oblatos participan del único sacerdocio de Cristo."

R. 3 Les Frères oblats participent à l'unique sacerdoce du Christ. Ils sont appelés à collaborer à leur manière à la reconciliation de toutes choses en Lui (cf. *Col* 1:20). Par leur consécration reglieuse, ils témoignent d'une vie tout inspirée de l'Évangile.

Les frères ont partout un rôle missionnaire important à jouer dans la construction de l'Église, mais spécialement là où est proclamée pour la première fois la Parole de Dieu. Leurs services d'ordre technique, professionnel ou pastoral, leur donnent souvent l'occasion d'exercer un ministère fructueux en des milieux que ne sont pas toujours accessibles aux prêtres.

R.3 Oblate brothers share in the common priesthood of Christ. They are called to cooperate in their own way reconciling all things in him (cf. *Col* 1:20). Through their religious consecration, they offer a particular witness to a life inspired by the Gospel.

Brothers have an important missionary role to play in building up the Church everywhere, but especially in those areas where the Word is first being proclaimed. Through their technical, professional or pastoral service they are often able to exercise a fruitful ministry in situations not always open to the priest.[46]

The full participation of the brothers in the whole life and ministry of the Congregation is very emphatically asserted by the 1984 "General Norms for Oblate Formation."

In fidelity to the Founder's charism, the priesthood remains an essential element of the Congregation, since the principal goal of its mission is full evangelization: witness, proclamation of God's Word, implanting and building up of the Church, celebration of the sacraments, especially of Reconciliation and of the Eucharist. As priests and brothers, Oblates have complementary responsibilities and roles in evangelizing (cf. C. 7 and Rules 3 and 7). The Oblate religious missionary life and the mission of both priests and brothers are inseparably linked to the ministerial priesthood.[47]

---

[46] The last sentence was amended by the 1986 general chapter to read: Missioned by the Church, their technical, professional or pastoral service, as well as their witness of life, constitute their ministry of evangelization" ("Changes to the Constitutions and Rules as approved by the General Chapter of 1986," p. 2).

[47] *General Norms*, pp. 7–8.

Cf. "The Oblate Brother, Replies to a questionaire," *Documentation O.M.I.*, 126/84, May 1984 and 128/84, August 1984. In this survey of the responses of 350 of the 786 brothers (44.5%), are revealed the deepest thoughts of many brothers concerning their own vocation, life, and work.

The following is a testimony of a group of brothers as to how they saw their vocation and its priestly dimensions. In their preparation for the 1966 chapter the brothers of Bolivia meeting in a special congress said: "The brothers are unanimous in saying that they joined the Congregation of the O.M.I.s because they saw the possibility of working directly with the oblate priest: to replace the priest in temporal tasks, so that he could be one hundred percent pastor of souls; to be a real companion, a support, a confidant of the oblate priest. Because of this close relationship with the priesthood, *the oblate brother has truly a priestly vocation*, which the teaching and nursing brothers

They (the brothers) also share, by reason of belonging to a Congregation whose identity is marked by priestly ministry, in a particular relationship to the ordained priesthood.

With the riches proper to their vocation, the Oblate brothers share
actively in the community life and works of the Province. Their vocation
does not separate them from their fellow Oblates either in their living or
working situations. The tasks assumed by the brothers in service of the
mission depend on the life and options taken by each Province; the range
of these tasks is very broad and should always remain open.[48]

Oblates and Missionaries

The brothers are true Oblates and true missionaries. Why state the
obvious? Because some have not in the past understood that the brothers are
full members of the Congregation, and even today some may not realize that
now they are truly missionaries.

De Mazenod in parallel texts used the same expression for clerical
candidates and brother candidates seeking to join the Congregation. In both
cases the words used are "in filios adscribere" (to be enrolled as sons).[49] Thus
all the members are sons of the Congregation, and true members of the family.

De Mazenod used the same word for the religious profession of the
brothers and the other members–*oblation*.[50] By making their profession all
became Oblates.

This is confirmed by Deschâtelets: ". . . the Oblate vocation is the same
for the fathers as well as for the brothers."[51] This constant tradition is the basis
of the following statements found in the "General Norms for Oblate Formation"

From the very first years of the Congregation, brothers joined priests
in order to live the religious missionary charism of the Blessed Eugene de
Mazenod.[52]

Oblate formation is fundamentally one. For both priests and brothers,
it is formation in one and the same charism. For both it shows, in ways

---

do not have" ("Congrès des Frères Oblats de Marie-Immaculée, Bolivie," June 4–5, 1965, Bolivie,
Frères Coadjuteurs, General Archives O.M.I., emphasis in text).

[48] *General Norms*, p. 72.

[49] See *Constitutiones 1826*, pars III, C. II, §1, art. 1, general article concerning persons seeking
admission, and pars III, c. II, §IV, art. 1, for men seeking to become brothers. The handwritten text,
DM XI Ms VI (exemplar authenticum 1826), has "adscribi" and not "abscribi" as in the printed text.
Clearly the latter is a typographical error.

[50] Supra p. 205.

[51] *Circulaires*, May 1, 1966, vol. 7, no. 230, p. 407.

[52] *General Norms*, p. 71.

appropriate to each group, the inseparable relationship to the ministerial priesthood.[53]

It would be superfluous to repeat what was said above concerning the evolution of the meaning of the word *missionary*.[54] There is no doubt, as the word is accepted today both by hierarchical Church and in common usage, that the brothers are missionaries.

The 1982 Constitutions speak twice of all Oblates as missionaries. The first time is in article 32 in reference to prayer life, "It is as missionaries that we worship, in the various ways the Spirit suggests to us. We come before him bearing with us the daily pressures of our anxiety for those to whom he has sent us (cf. *2 Cor* 11:28)." The second is in article 65. Here the young Oblates, scholastics and brothers, are instructed to prepare themselves for perpetual oblation by continuing to assimilate the Oblate charism, ". . . they will gradually become men of God, missionaries rooted in Christ, who are ready to give themselves totally through their perpetual oblation."

Any remaining doubts that may have possibly existed as to whether the brothers are missionaries should have been laid to rest by the statement of the norms for formation:

> The brothers are missionaries by the same title as are all the members of the Oblate Congregation, but they share in the pastoral responsibility of the Church by works proper to them. They also share, by reason of belonging to a Congregation whose identity is marked by priestly ministry, in a particular relationship to the ordained priesthood.[55]

In this context what does the expression "by the same title" mean? It signifies unequivocally that the brothers, just as all other Oblates, are missionaries by virtue of their oblation and consequent membership in the Missionary Oblates of Mary Immaculate, a missionary institute.[56]

---

[53] *General Norms*, p. 8.

[54] Supra pp. 151–154. It would seem that the first official statement that the word "missionary" could be used for the brothers was in 1953. The general chapter held that year said: "It also favors the appellation . . . 'Missionary Oblates' to include brothers . . ." (*Circulaires*, December 8, 1953, vol. 6, no. 203, p. 125).

[55] *General Norms*, p. 72.

[56] Of course a brother, just as an Oblate priest or scholastic, can be a missionary also by another title, e.g., by being assigned to a mission or mission work by a competent ecclesiastical authority (cf. c. 785, §1). The word *missionary* is not an univocal term. This is even more so since Vatican II. V.g., a prefect or vicar apostolic; a foreign priest evangelizing in the missions "ad gentes" or the unchurched in his own country; a religious man or woman dedicated to teaching, nursing, or otherwise helping the poor in a mission country, or one's own country; a short term lay volunteer in a mission; a priest preaching missions; a member of an institute dedicated to the

5. We are a missionary Congregation. Our principal service in the Church is to proclaim Christ and his Kingdom to the most abandoned . . . These are the poor with their many faces; we give them our preference.[57]

---

missions, who has never been to the missions; etc. . . . are all rightfully called missionaries. However, the term is verified in a different way in each case.

It would seem that a group of brothers of the vice-province of Bolivia in an open letter "Todos somos Misioneros" (in *Chasqui*, 12 (1983), pp. 10–11, November 1983) were rather simplistic in their use of the word *missionary*. To present a line of argumentation with the principle that all Oblates are missionaries: "Todos somos Misioneros, *cada uno segùn su carisma* [emphasis added] . . . we are all missionaries, each one according to his charism," and to reach a conclusion without taking into account the particular charism of each is to set oneself up for an illogical conclusion. In reading this letter one needs to recall that a missionary charism is a gift bestowed by God for the building up of the Christian community, the Church and all charisms are not of equal rank (cf. 1 Cor 12–14; Eph 4:7–13). *Missionary* is an analogous term, what is true of one missionary is not necessarily true of every missionary. They seem to put on the same level of missionary activity, pastoral ministry and work of development and promotion of the standard of living of the poor and the struggle for justice, without taking into account any hierarchy of importance. Do they see that the missionary ministry of preaching the Gospel and celebrating the Eucharist and sacraments has a primacy over working as a carpenter or economist? True, the latter may be necessary in certain situations, but even there, to be truly missionary such activity has to be directed ultimately toward proclaiming the Gospel and Eucharist. Jesus preached the Gospel and also healed the sick and fed the hungry. Does anyone deny that justice is integral to the preaching of the Gospel? But evangelization is above all the preaching of the Gospel leading to faith in Jesus, the Eucharist and the other sacraments.

Fallacies are to be found also in the description of the founding charism of de Mazenod and the consequent denial of the clerical nature of the Congregation. One might well ask what they understand by evangelization.

The present author found especially objectionable their attack on F. Jetté, the superior general, and the members of the general council for calling an international meeting of brothers in 1985. In their view such a meeting is an anachronism and implies a lack of understanding of the charism of the Founder, and the questionnaire sent to all the brothers did not reflect the 1982 Constitutions (7 and 38) and Rules (3). They asserted: "La organizaciòn de una sesiòn internacional sòlo para los Hermanos y la encuesta que parece suponer que muchos no son felices por ser Hermanos (no màs), que ellos 'piensan un poco' (no màs) y que ellos tienen solamente 'trabajos encomendados' y 'responsabilidades confiadas' (para los Padres), es màs bien un paso atràs." Perhaps the one redeeming factor of this temerarious attack is that the English translation that was published toned down the demeaning and sarcastic language of the original text (see *Newsletter*, Missionary Oblates of Mary Immaculate, St. Paul, Minnesota, no. 206, 14–15, January 1984).

In a letter to the Congregation, Jetté, the superior general quoted a brother, and continuted: "'I am happy to be a brother. And with God's grace, I would choose this vocation today.' This affirmation is found again and again in a very large number of the 350 letters received . . . Reading these letters has been for me one of the most exciting experiences of my term as superior general" ("Twenty-first letter of the Superior General," in *Communique O.M.I.*, 35/84, Appendix, January 1984). It would seem that these 350 brothers found no objection to the questionnaire.

[57] *Constitutions 1982*.

The Name "Brother"

The 1953 general chapter devoted considerable time to various questions concerning the brothers—their formation, replacement of the traditional office, Masses to be said for the intentions of the brothers, and ten secondary questions.[58] the first of these was the name or appellation to be used for the brothers. The following are the French and English versions of the as presented to the chapter:[59]

1. APPELLATION: "Frères Convers": on demande de remplacer le Latin "famulans" par "coadjutor" et le français "frère convers par frère coadjuteur or auxiliaire or simplement frère oblat." LE COMMISSION EMET LE VŒU que l'on généralise l'habitude de dire non plus frère convers mais coadjuteur et qu'on emploie l'expression missionnaires oblats à la place de Pères oblats pour ne pas exclure les Frères. Pour les textes de nos Stes Règles "famulans, famulantes," la Commission renvoie la question à la Commission préparatoire."

1. APPELLATION: "Frères Convers": it is requested that the Latin "famulans" be replaced by "coadjutor" and the French " 'frère convers' by coadjutor or auxiliary or simply oblate brother." THE COMMITTEE PROPOSES that the custom be generalized of saying no longer "frère convers," but coadjutor and that the expression Missionary Oblates be used in place of Oblate Fathers in order not to exclude the brothers. For the text of our Holy Rules "famulans, famulantes," the committee refers the question to the preparatory commission.

The proposal was approved by the chapter,[60] and presented to the Congregation in these words:[61]

[Le Chapitre] favorise aussi l'appellation de "coadjuteur" au lieu de convers, celle de "Missionnaires Oblats" pour y inclure les Frères . . .

[The Chapter] also favors the appellation of "coadjutor" instead of "lay," that of "Missionary Oblates" to include brothers . . .

---

[58] "Chapitre Général 1953, Cong. Gén., Frères coadjuteurs (1)," Propositio 97, General Archives O.M.I.

[59] Ibid.

[60] "Registre," 1953, p. 237.

[61] *Circulaires*, December 8, 1953, vol. 6, p. 125, in both the French and English editions.
Note in the English edition of the circular letter: "What was actually proposed was using the French term 'frère coadjuteur' instead of the French term 'frère convers.' The members were invited to suggest a corresponding English term to use instead of 'lay brother.' Hence it is in order to suggest an appellation which might prove to be more widely preferred than that of 'coadjutor brother.'"
In the Central U.S. Provice, it was decided to use the expression *oblate brother(s)*.

The use of the terms *frère convers* and *lay brother* has gradually diminished since the 1953 chapter. It would seem that the second part of the proposal approved by the chapter was not expressed clearly in the circular letter. In any case, it was not understood by many, and *Oblate Fathers* is still frequently used to mean the Congregation or its members. It would be interesting to poll the Oblates today in order to find out how many of them know that a general chapter officially encouraged the use of the name *Missionary Oblates*.[62]

The 1966 Constitutions and Rules *ad experimentum* employed the word *laici* twice in referring to the brothers and the rest of the time the word *frater*.[63] In the two instances where the Latin text had *laici* the French, German, Spanish, and Italian semi-official translations had *laïcs, laien, laicos,* and *laici*. On the other hand the English translation used the word *brothers*.

In his presentation of the chapter to the Congregation, Deschâtelets gave as one of the chapter's guiding principles:

> 2) The capitulants preferred to indicate the positive aspects rather than the negative ones of the life of the brothers. There is no more question of lay brothers or coadjutor brothers, but simply brothers.[64]

But it is quite evident that by this last sentence Deschâtelets was speaking about the name to be used for the brothers, and not an elimination of the distinction between the brothers and the scholastics, i.e., professed students for the priesthood. This is very clear from the context in the 1966 Constitutions and Rules *ad experimentum*.[65]

The 1972 chapter explicitly considered the name to be used for the brothers. The following proposal was approved:

> **36—Brothers**
>
> The term "brothers" is applied to all Oblates who have made vows or promises according to *Renovationis causam*, and are not ordained to the priesthood.[66]

---

[62] Anyone disconcerted by the non-implementation of this chapter proposal could with profit consider *Jn* 8:7 together with his own observance of other general chapter decisions.

The January 1995–1996 Bell telephone directory for Ottawa-Hull has "PÈRES OBLATS" for the institutions of St. Joseph Province and "OBLATES OF MARY IMMACULATE" for those of St. Peter's Province. The Montreal Bell telephone directory for 1994-1995 has "Pères Missionnaires Oblats de M.I." for the houses of St. Joseph Province.

[63] Supra p. 210.

[64] *Circulaires*, May 1, 1966, no. 230, vol. 7, p. 407.

[65] Supra on p. 183 was considered the most unusual statement ". . . the 1966 Constitutions which abolishes the distinction between *scholastics* and *coadjutor* brothers." Its falsity is evident from articles 1, 5, 48, 85, 88–104, 105–112, and 126.

[66] It is very clear from the second sentence that the first sentence refers *only* to the question

Brothers who are in the period of explicit preparation for the priesthood are called "scholastics." A period of regency (*stage*), even if it interrupts the regular course of studies, is to be considered as part of such explicit preparations.[67]

With time this official policy has become in fact a general practice within the Congregation.[68] Although it must be admitted that old habits die hard. In

---

of name, and not to a denial of a distinction between scholastics and brothers not preparing for the priesthood.

It is difficult, if not impossible, to understand how one author, commenting on this article could say, "The distinction between the *coadjutors* of former times and the **scholastics** is again lessened. From now on only two general categories of members are recognized in the Congregation—the religious who are priests and those who do not accede to the priesthood. The question of the possibility of two "categories" of brothers, tossed about since the time of the Founder, is definitively closed; there is only one category of brothers, whether they are destined for the priesthood or not" (I. TOURIGNY, O.M.I., "Le Frère oblat selon le Fondateur et la tradition oblate," in *Vie Oblate Life*, 39 (1980), pp. 59–60).

The first sentence is true—both the non-ordained members are to be known as *brothers*. The second sentence is also true, but it is nothing new—the students for the priesthood, even those not in orders, have always been considered as clerics and forming part of the same category as the priests, and the brothers belonging to the other category of members. The question of two categories of brothers alluded to was not in question at the 1972 chapter; it had been resolved negatively for many decades. It had always been a question of lay brothers in the strict sense, i.e., brothers dedicated principally to manual labor, and not a special category of teaching brothers distinct from the lay brothers (supra p. 176–177). The last clause of the quotation is completely inaccurate. If it were true, why did the author in the first sentence say that the distinction was diminished, and not eliminated? The reality of the distinction appears from the next paragraph where scholastics in perpetual vows are granted only active voice in elections, and all other members have both active and passive voice, "saving special canonical requirements for certain offices" (*Administrative Structures O.M.I.*, no. 37). Ibid., no. 39: "A brother in perpetual vows, and provided he is not a scholastic may be named Superior of a local community . . . with the necessary indult."

[67] *Administrative Structures O.M.I.*, no. 36

Since the 1826 chapter scholastics, professed students for the priesthood, have been called "brother." Supra p. 34. In those provinces where German, Dutch, Flemish, and Polish are spoken the Latin *frater* and not the vernacular for brother has been used in contrast to the other languages. This difference may be explained by the use of the latin *pater* in addressing the priests in those languages rather than the vernacular word for father, and the practice of other religious institutes. The vernacular word for brother has always been used in all provinces for the non-clerical brothers.

In *Personnel O.M.I. 1973, Personnel O.M.I. 1977, Personnel O.M.I. 1981, Personnel O.M.I. 1987*, and *Personnel O.M.I. 1993* the scholastics and other brothers are distinguished by an appropriate abbreviation, e.g., in French f., sc., or scol., and in English Bro. and Schol and Sc.

The use of the word *scholastic* seems to be recent in the Congregation. Its first appearance in the Constitutions was in those of 1910 in article 796.

[68] To rightly understand this statement, one must keep in mind the contemporary practice of informality that exists in many places, i.e., most priests, brothers, and scholastics are frequently—

the 1982 Constitutions and Rules the word *brothers* is used only for those not preparing for the priesthood. This is consistent with previous Constitutions, although since 1826 professed students for the priesthood officially have also been called *brother*.

Oblation

To simplify the presentation and provide for easy comparison, the evolution of the principal norms for oblation for priests and scholastics will be considered first. Then those for the brothers will be presented.

Following the general practice of religious institutes of that time, de Mazenod in the first Constitutions prescribed that perpetual vows were to be made at the end of the novitiate.[69] However, ordinarily a novice was not to be admitted to oblation until he was a subdeacon.[70] This meant that ordinarily no scholastic would make his perpetual oblation before he was twenty-one.

These norms were maintained in the 1826 Constitutions.[71] The 1853 Constitutions dropped the latter provision, but stated that the novitiate could be extended for those who were not subdeacons, if it was opportune.[72] In such a case the novice, after a year in the novitiate, went to the scholasticate to begin his studies while continuing to be novice. He would make his oblation there.

The 1867 general chapter was faced with the necessity of the novices living in a novitiate approved by the Holy See, and the undesirability of the scholastic novices either making their perpetual oblation after one year of novitiate or of postponing their studies. The solution was to introduce temporary vows for one year for novices not in sacred orders.[73] However, they

---

if not almost always—addressed by their given name without a title or honorific.

[69] See "Constitutions 1818," III partie, c. II, §3; *Missions O.M.I.*, 78 (1951), pp. 91–92; *Écrits*, vol. 1, pp. 91–92.

[70] See ibid. The Council of Trent required as the minimum age for ordination to the subdeaconate twenty-two years begun, i.e., the person had to be twenty-one (sess. XXIII, de ref., c. XII).

[71] See *Constitutiones 1826*, pars III, c. II, §III, art. VII and X.

[72] See *Constitutiones 1853*, pars III, c. II, §II, art. II.

[73] See *Circulaires*, August 1, 1871, no. 22, vol. 1, p. 13; this change is found in *Constitutions 1894*, pars III, c. III, §III, art. V. Cf. *Circulaires*, June 29, 1866, no. 17, vol. 1, p. 159; CONGREGATION OF BISHOPS AND REGULARS, 15°, January 5, 1866, II-1, Procurator's Archives O.M.I.

Just a few years prior to this the norm requiring three years of temporary vows prior to solemn vows in regular orders of men was enacted (CONGREGATION OF BISHOPS AND REGULARS, *Neminem latet*, March 19, 1857, in GASPARRI, *Fontes*, vol. 4, no. 1976, p. 960; PIUS IX, encyclical letter, *Amantis-*

were not to receive the oblate cross until their perpetual oblation.[74]

The 1910 Constitutions conformed to the "Normæ" of 1901 and required that all priests and scholastics make annual profession for three years prior to perpetual oblation.[75] This provision was repeated by the codes of 1917 and 1983, and all subsequent editions of the Constitutions.[76]

When de Mazenod added to the Constitutions the section on the brothers, he provided that they would make temporary vows for six years prior to perpetual oblation.[77] One of the cardinals who studied the Constitutions in view of papal approval objected to this, and de Mazenod argued as to the wisdom of this provision citing the practice of the Brothers of the Christian Schools.[78] He also prescribed that ordinarily the brothers would not make vows before they were twenty-one.[79]

According to the 1826 Constitutions they were to make first annual vows for a year, and then five year vows prior to perpetual vows.[80] This was changed in the 1910 Constitutions to follow the same provision as for the priests and scholastics of annual vows for three years, but this was to be followed by three year vows, keeping six years of temporary profession before perpetual oblation.[81] This edition of the Constitutions also changed the minimum age for vows for the brothers to seventeen.[82] The 1966 Constitutions *ad experimentum*

---

simus, April 8, 1862, in GASPARRI, *Fontes*, vol. 2, no. 533, pp. 955–961).

[74] See ibid.

[75] See *Constitutiones 1910*, art. 771; "Normæ," no. 104.

[76] See *CIC¹*, c. 574; *CIC*, c. 658 2°; *Constitutiones 1928*, art. 734; *Constitutions 1982*, C. 60.

[77] See *Constitutiones 1826*, pars III, c. II, §IV, art. XV.

[78] See DE MAZENOD, to Pedicini, February 14, 1826, Congregation of Bishops and Regulars, Marseille, 1846 2119/2–4993/2, Vatican Archives; *Écrits*, vol. 4, p. 114; *Missions O.M.I.*, 79 (1952), p. 514; Cosentino, *Histoire*, vol. 1, pp. 176–177.

[79] See *Constitutiones 1826*, pars III, c. II, §IV, art. 16. Clement VIII had established for regular orders the minimum age of twenty for reception as a novice for *conversi* (lay brothers) (constitution, *Cum ad regularem*, March 19, 1603, in GASPARRI, *Fontes*, vol. 1, no. 189, §4).

[80] See *Constitutiones 1826*, pars III, c. II, §IV, art. XV and XVIII.

[81] See *Constitutiones 1910*, art. 771. The *Normæ* required three years of temporary profession prior to perpetual vows (nos. 103–105).

[82] See *Constitutiones 1910*, art. 808. According to the *Normæ* a person less than seventeen could make first vows (nos. 61 and 65).

In 1861 Fabre, the superior general, declared: "The lay brothers, who live in places that do not have a law of military conscription, can make their oblation before they are 20 years old. Since it is because of such laws that the Rule does not permit the lay brothers to make their vows before that age" ("Registre," 1861, p. 18). This text is quoted by PIELORZ, *Les Chapitres*, vol. 2, p. 181.

required that the brothers make annual vows for six years before perpetual profession.[83]

The 1917 Code completely reorganized the legislation for vows, and imposed the same requirements for clerical and lay religious. The 1928 Constitutions adopted for everyone the minimum ages of the 1917 code of fifteen years completed for beginning novitiate and twenty-one years completed for perpetual profession.[84]

The 1982 Constitutions for the first time established uniform norms for length of temporary vows for all Oblates—priests, scholastics, and brothers. All are required to make annual profession for a minimum of three years prior to perpetual oblation.[85] The minimum age for profession is not mentioned and consequently is that of the common law—eighteen and twenty-one years completed for first and perpetual oblation respectively.[86]

Religious Garb

The Missionaries of Provence kept the cassock, which they had worn as secular priests, but ceased wearing the *rabat,* the clerical neckpiece common in France at that time, as their habit. De Mazenod spoke of their dress as the *habit missionnaire* (the missionary habit).[87] With oblation they received a large cross which they wore hanging around their necks at all times.[88] This was incorporated in the Constitutions.

> Art. 1. They will have no other habit than the cassock (*ecclesiastica talaris*), which they wear even when travelling, except in the cases of longer journeys, when a coat (*tunica brevior*) is worn.
>
> Art. 2. Their only distinctive mark will be the crucifix, which for the convenience of their ministry, they will wear upon their breast, inserted in the cincture and hanging from a cord around their neck. This crucifix will serve as the credentials of the mission to be carried to different peoples.[89]

---

[83] See *Constitutiones 1966,* art. 85.

[84] See *CIC¹*, cc. 555, §1, 1° and 573; *Constitutiones 1928,* art. 686 and 734. The 1966 Constitutions did not specify the minimum age. Consequently it was that of the 1917 Code of Canon Law.

[85] See *Constitutiones 1982,* C. 60.

[86] See *CIC,* cc. 656, 1° and 658, 1°.

[87] Supra p. 158.

[88] Supra pp. 158–159.

[89] *Constitutiones 1826,* pars II, c. III, §3. N.B. Journeys at the time were on foot or by means of horses.

It is not hard to understand the reasons leading de Mazenod to adopt a different garb for the brothers. They were not clerics, which explains why they did not wear the *ecclesiastica talaris* (clerical cassock or soutane). They were not missionaries, hence neither the missionary habit nor the large cross of the missionaries. However, they were religious and had to be given an appropriate religious habit.

Art. 26. The dress of the lay brothers is a simple wool tunic (*tunicella*), which they wear upon beginning the novitiate.

Art. 27. When they make annual vows, they receive a plain cross.

Art. 28. With perpetual vows, they receive the corpus of Christ crucified.

Art. 29. During their work, the lay brothers may wear ordinary clothing.[90]

These articles underwent but very minor modifications in the various editions of the Constitutions until 1910. In spite of this, there were, it would seem almost continuous questions, problems, diversity, and even harsh words concerning the brothers' manner of dressing.[91]

De Mazenod had in 1843 determined the brothers' habit would be similar to that of the fathers, but shorter, in conformity with the practice of other religious communities and that the size of their cross was to be twelve by six centimetres.[92] It would seem that some of the French brothers wore cassocks almost as long as those of the priests, and because of "ambitious pretensions" they had even begun to wear crosses almost as large as those of the fathers. In 1867 insistence was placed on returning to the length of the cross set by de Mazenod.[93] The 1879 chapter decided that the size was to be sixteen centimetres by eight.[94]

There was great diversity as to when the brothers were to wear their habit, and much was left up to the provincials. Many of the brothers were very unhappy with the short cassock prescribed for them. In France they wore outside the house either lay clothes or a cassock about as long as that of the fathers. With persecution of the Congregation in France in 1880 the brothers

---

[90] *Constitutiones 1826*, pars III, c. II, §4.

[91] See COSENTINO, *Histoire*, vol. 5, pp. 231–242, and 321–322 for a very thorough treatment of the brothers' habit along with the quotation of the pertinent texts. This work has everything up to its publication in 1955.

[92] See "Registre," 1843, p. 73; PIELORZ, *Les Chapitres*, vol. 1, p. 192.

[93] See "Registre," 1879, p. 226.

[94] See ibid.

ceased wearing a habit, even in the novitiate. The 1903 persecution confirmed this practice.[95]

Many of the brothers, especially those in Italy, were discontented with this situation. Word of this must have gotten to Esser, who wrote in his *votum* of 1907:

> The poor brothers, for example, do not have a clearly set habit. Except in the German province (if I am well informed), they do not ever go out in their religious habit, but in lay clothes. Within the house itself, there is great difference according to the houses: in some the habit is worn only for Communion, in others not even then; in other houses it is used for all the community exercises.[96]

The capitulants in 1908 agreed that the cassock had become the regular religious garb of the brothers, and that the new edition of the Constitution should describe it as well as the cloak. The latter was to differ so as to be distinguished from that of the priests. The provincial could with the consent of his extraordinary council decide what other garb the brothers would wear

---

[95] De Mazenod was following the practice of other religious institutes when he wrote: "They cannot be novices without taking of the habit of missionary . . ." (de Mazenod to Tempier, January 18, 1821, *Oblate Writings*, vol. 6, no. 59, p. 73). This ancient practice had been confirmed by the Council of Trent (sess. XXV, *de regularibus*, c. 15) and Clement VIII (constitution, *Cum ad regularem*, March 19, 1603, in GASPARRI, *Fontes*, vol. 1, no. 189, §7, p. 359) for regular orders. *CIC¹*, c. 553 stated that the novitiate was to begin by the reception of the habit or in another way prescribed by the Constitutions.

SCRIS in the instruction *Renovationis Causam*, January 6, 1969, specified: "It belongs to the general chapter to decide matters relative to the habit of novices and other candidates for religious life" (*AAS*, 61 (1969), 118, no. 33). The Sacred Congregation of Worship in *Ordo professionis religiosæ* prescribed "The rite of first profession provides for the handing over of the habit and the other insignia of religious life in accordance with the very ancient custom of giving the habit when the time of probation has been completed; the habit is a sign of consecration" (Vatican City, Typis polyglottis vaticanis, 1970). SCRIS in a private response affirmed the competency of the general chapter to determine the habit for novices (SCRIS, response, June 8, 1970, in X. OCHOA, *Leges Ecclesiæ*, 6 vols. Rome, Commentarium pro Religiosis, 1966–, vol. 4, no. 3864).

Neither the 1972 nor the 1974 general chapter discussed or made any regulations concerning the habit, although the 1972 chapter decreed the implementation of *Renovationis causam* (see "Text on Formation of the 1972 Chapter," *Acts of the General Chapter 1974*, p. 71). Nevertheless in many provinces about this time the habit ceased to be given to the novices at the beginning of the novitiate and was not given at the time of profession.

[96] ESSER, votum, May 20, 1907, M. 29, CICLSAL Archives.

It is well to recall that in 1907, there were only four provinces on the European continent; the two of France with no houses open in France because of the persecution, the German province founded in 1895, and the Belgian province founded in 1905. All the houses in Italy, with the exception of the Roman Scholasticate, were part of the first province (Midi) of France.

when according to the circumstances they did not wear the cassock.[97]

> 820. The habit of the lay brothers will be like that of the priests, with this difference that the cassock, from the cincture upwards, is fastened with concealed hooks-and-eyes going in a row toward the left shoulder, that the cincture is of plain wool and the cross is smaller . . .[98]

Unfortunately, whoever wrote this article made a mistake, which was not caught by anyone prior to approval by the Holy See. The brothers' cassock had always had the opening from the cincture toward the right shoulder, and not the left shoulder. This caused great consternation among the brothers because their cassock had always buttoned to the right, and only women buttoned to the left. The 1938 chapter noted that this matter had been considered in 1926 while revising the Constitutions but the change was not made.[99] The committee found the objections of the brothers understandable, and said that one should not insist on the observance of the article. It also suggested that epicheia could rightly be applied in this case. This was approved by the chapter along with the recommendation that provincials and superiors see to it that the brothers have a proper religious garb for their protection outside the community.[100]

The 1966 Constitutions *ad experimentum* did not mention the habit, but in article 41 stated that the crucifix received on the day of perpetual oblation was to be the only distinctive sign of the Oblates. This was but a paraphrase of all the previous editions of the Constitutions.

However, Rule 207, 2° established that the provincial could, "determine the proper attire (*habitum*) for the brothers outside the house," only after he

---

[97] See "Registre," 1908, p. 243; *Constitutiones 1910*, art. 821.
The "Normæ" prescribed that there not be great disparity in the habits of different categories of members (§68).

[98] *Constitutiones 1910*.

[99] See "Registre," 1938, p. 49.

[100] See "Registre," 1938, pp. 155–157. In his report to the Congregation on the work of the general chapter, Labouré, superior general, wrote: ". . . one could very well be, at least in our opinion, an excellent religious and save one's soul, even if one's cassock is buttoned to the left instead of to the right. Our decision was not accepted, and the question was brought to the chapter. The chapter also declared that it had neither the power to change article 781 of the Rule, nor the desire to request the Holy See to change it. Nevertheless, out of respect for human weakness, which thus finds a stumbling block there where it should see only an occasion of merit by the practice of obedience and denial of one's own will, the chapter advises the superiors not to insist on this point of the Rule and to allow the lay brothers to continue according, as they desire, to button their cassock to the right" (*Circulaires*, March 19, 1939, vol. 4, no. 164. p. 355). It would seem that these words reflect more Labouré's own attitude than that of the chapter.

had consulted his council. It would seem that this article presupposes that the brothers would wear a habit.

The 1980 general chapter treated the question of habit with benign neglect. In fact, it was not even considered, and there was nothing in the Constitutions or the Rules as approved by the chapter about the habit. The procurator general in his article presenting the process of approval of the Constitutions said:

> We were asked to mention in the Constitutions the Oblate habit. Basing ourselves on the text of Canon 669 and on the Founder's statement, "their only distinctive mark will be the crucifix," we presented the text of Art. 64, which was accepted.[101]

Even a casual reading of article 64 reveals its conformity with the tradition of the Congregation and the previous approved editions of the Congregation, in that it specifies the garb as the same as that of the secular clergy.

> C. 64. The Oblate habit is the same as the clerical dress in which we live. When we wear a cassock, our only distinctive sign is the Oblate cross.

This article makes no distinction between the dress of the brothers and the priests. Consequently both are to wear the same religious garb. The comment of one author on the Code clearly expresses the principle, which is in question here, and its application.

> Those, that have their own religious habit, are obliged to wear it. Others must dress as the diocesan priests, following the instructions that the bishops' conference has given for the diocesan priests (c. 669, §2). It is the task of the particular law to establish whether a community has its own religious habit, or the garb of the diocesan priests was always up to now to be worn. In this case it must be concluded that also the members who are not priests are to wear the same garb as the priests.[102]

It follows that the religious garb for all Oblates—priests, scholastics, and brothers is the same, i.e., that of the secular clergy of the particular place where they are living and working at a given moment.[103]

---

[101] O'Reilly, M., "Approval," p. 9.

[102] P. ZEPP, "Überblick über das Religiosenrecht des CIC 1983," in Ordens-Korrespondenz, 25 (1984), pp. 17–18.

[103] Can there by any doubt that this prescription also applies to brothers that are permanent deacons? Canon 288 states that c. 284, to which c. 669, §2 refers, does not apply to permanent deacons, unless particular law establishes otherwise. Certainly c. 288 does not refer to permanent deacons who are members of a religious institute. If it did, brothers who are not deacons would be required to dress as the diocesan priests, but the brothers who are permanent deacons would wear lay garb.

What about the size of the oblate cross? The 1982 Constitutions do not touch this question. The first sentence of article 64 speaks only of the habit, and not of the cross, which is treated in the second sentence. In all previously approved editions of the Constitutions the habit, i.e., the cassock, and the cross were treated as separate questions in distinct articles. The 1966 Constitutions *ad experimentum* did not touch the question of habit, but only that of the cross as the distinctive sign. Although from the beginning the brothers wore a smaller cross, it was only in the 1910 and 1928 Constitutions that it was spelled out that their cross was to be smaller than that of the other Oblates.

A number of perpetually professed brothers have requested and received from their major superior a large oblate cross, which they now wear when in cassock. This seems to be in accord with the principle enunciated in the 1982 Constitutions:

C. 71. United as brothers in one apostolic community, we are all equal before God our Father who distributes charisms and ministries so that we can serve his Church and its mission . . .

Because of the equality of all members, it is logical that only such differences and distinctions exist among Oblates that are based on the particular charisms and ministries within the Congregation and Church. It would seem that ordinarily today these differences would not require that there be a difference in the size of the priests' and scholastics' cross and that of the brothers. This certainly appears to be true where the cassock and cross are rarely, if ever, worn. However, the situation might be very different in those places where the cassock and cross are the ordinary daily dress. If in such situations, the same sized cross for all would cause pastoral problems among the people, the demands of the ministry would certainly suggest the difference be maintained. De Mazenod insisted upon the cross as a help in the ministry.[104] It is not difficult to draw conclusions from that principle.

On the other hand, many brothers prefer to continue to wear the smaller cross that they received on the day of their oblation. This is certainly in accord with the letter of article 41 of the 1982 Constitutions. How could anyone say that it is contrary to the spirit of the Constitutions or the Church, which leaves so much to the free choice of individuals?

---

[104] Supra pp. 158–159.

Formation

Because of the great emphasis placed today on both spiritual formation and formation for a person's work as a missionary and a religious, one might be lead to believe that it is something new. Without exaggeration it can be said that a major concern of every religious community has to be the formation of its members. Without a proper formation, the community's charism will not become incarnate in an individual, and he will not be able to contribute fully toward the fulfilment of the institute's life and goals. Although one would look in vain for the word *formation* in the earlier Constitutions and other documents, the reality is clearly there.

As with all religious the most intensive period of religious formation for Oblates as outlined in the first Constitutions was the novitiate. The continued spiritual formation of all the members consisted in the observance of the vows, the daily spiritual exercises, reception of the sacraments, annual and monthly retreats, and a monthly personal spiritual conference with the superior concerning one's own progress as a religious.[105]

Of course the scholastics and priests followed the course of studies prescribed by canon law for ordination. In addition to this the Constitutions required that the missionaries, i.e., the priests, after the mission season were to return to their community to meditate on the divine law and devote themselves to the study of holy scripture, the Church Fathers, dogmatic and moral theology, and the other branches of ecclesiastical sciences, and to prepare new material for the next missions.[106] Once a week the priests and scholastics were to meet with the superior to consider together better methods in conducting missions and the mistakes to be avoided and the most suitable means to be used to fulfil the end of the Congregation, the salvation of souls.[107] Later the frequency of these meetings was changed to "from time to time during the year," but the discussions were broadened to include not only the missions but also other similar works.[108] Only the experienced missionaries were permitted to preach without having written out their sermons, having them corrected and committed to memory. Even they were required to speak from a well prepared outline.[109]

---

[105] See *Constitutiones 1826*, pars II; *Constitutiones 1928*, art. 176–307.

[106] See *Constitutiones 1826*, pars II, c. III, §I, art. 10; *Constitutiones 1928*, art. 297.

[107] See *Constitutiones 1826*, pars II, c. II, §IV, art. 16.

[108] See *Constitutiones 1928*, art. 282.

[109] See *Constitutiones 1826*, pars I, c. III, §1, art. 6–9; *Constitutiones 1928*, art. 99–102.

De Mazenod recognized that these provisions did not meet the particular needs of the brothers, many of whom had very little if any formal education, and whose work as religious was very different from the clerics. For this reason he prescribed that in each house there would be a spiritual prefect of the brothers. While the local bursar was responsible for their work, the spiritual prefect was charged with their continued spiritual formation. The Constitutions spelled out his duties in working with the brothers for their continual growth as Christians and religious:

> Art. 6. Each Sunday the spiritual prefect will give the brothers a simple conference, after the manner of a catechetical instruction, on the teaching of Christ and the duties of religious life. He will be equally zealous in giving them all the needed instruction on the fruitful, fervent, and frequent reception of the sacraments, and the right fulfilment of all their own special duties.
>
> Art. 7. He will instruct them in the method of mental prayer, often ask them unexpectedly to give an account of their prayer. He will also question them on what they read, so as to know what profit they are deriving from it.[110]

It would seem that in some places these prescriptions were not always observed with the consequent spiritual neglect of the brothers. This was frequently brought up at general chapters, and the response was a call to the observance of the Constitutions.[111]

Since the brothers were not being prepared for a precise goal with a clearly defined plan of required studies, the needs of the moment, the lack of resources and personnel, and the small number of young brothers in some provinces and missions explain the lack of a systematic program in a number of places. Notable exceptions were Germany and Eastern Canada that had large numbers of vocations to the brotherhood, and were able to establish quality programs for both their spiritual and vocational training. During the later 1940s and the 1950s there was a concerted effort throughout the Congregation to upgrade formation programs for brothers. Unlike that of scholastics, the formation of the brothers has varied considerably within the Congregation at any given moment.[112]

---

[110] See *Constitutiones 1826*, pars III, c. I, §X; *Constitutiones 1928*, art. 624–625.

[111] See "Registre," 1856, p. 146; 1879, pp. 233–234; 1904, p. 47; 1932, p. 495.

[112] See Daniel ALBERS, O.M.I., "Compte Rendu des rapports sur les noviciats de la Congrégation, Deuxième partie: Les noviciats de Frères Convers," in *Études oblates*, 10 (1951), pp. 213–248; J.M. LAROSE, O.M.I., "Les écoles pour futurs Frères Oblats" in *Études oblates* 21 (1962), pp. 184–188.

The *General Norms for Oblate Formation* very delicately allude to the danger of shortchanging a formation that has few in it: "Whether the candidates are many or few, priests and brothers are equally entitled to an adequate formation" (p. 8).

The 1966 Constitutions *ad experimentum* devoted a whole chapter with eight articles to the formation of brothers after the novitiate.[113] Emphasis was placed both on the spiritual and technical or vocational formation as well as the development of an apostolic spirit. There was no mention in the Constitutions of a spiritual prefect of the brothers. However, the Rules provided that the provincial "audito consilio" could name a moderator of brothers, where necessary or useful (R. 207, 2°).

In conformity with the principle established of brevity for the 1982 Constitutions, the same ideas are contained in one article written specifically for the brothers.

C. 67. During the years after the novitiate, the brother grows in appreciation of his special vocation. With this in mind, professional training prepares him for his specific role. His doctrinal and pastoral education is adapted to his work and ministry. Thus, in his own community as well as outside it, the brother can give witness of solid faith and of service that is competent and selfless.

However, one must not conclude that the formation of the brothers is neglected by having only one article. Without exaggeration it can be said that the Preface of the Constitutions as well as the first part, "The Oblate Charism," constitute the content of the integral formation for all Oblates.

The Rules place upon the individual brother's provincial the obligation, "to have a planned program for the brother's Christian, religious and professional formation" (R. 66).

Neither the 1982 Constitutions nor Rules make any mention of a spiritual prefect or moderator of the brothers. It would seem that this is an application of the principle of unity in the oblate community.[114]

Diaconate

Acting consistently with the tradition in the Congregation, which had its origin with de Mazenod, of employing all in accordance with their personal talents, vocation, and the needs of the Church and Congregation, the 1972 general chapter approved:

. . . the introduction of the Permanent Diaconate in the Congregation for those brothers who are suitably qualified, and who have a vocation for this form of ministry.[115]

---

[113] See *Constitutiones 1966*, art. 105–112.

[114] See *Constitutions 1982*, cc. 37, 38, and 81. Cf. *PC*, no. 15.

[115] See *Administrative Structures*, no. 40. Supra p. 108.

The Rules adopted by the 1980 general chapter incorporate and spell out more clearly both the personal call of a brother to the permanent diaconate and the motivation for such a call.

R. 67. If a brother in perpetual vows discerns that, in response to apostolic needs, the Lord is calling him to the permanent diaconate or to the priesthood, the provincial in council may admit him as a candidate after having been authorized to do so by the superior general in council.[116]

Two different questions are treated in this article—the call of a brother to the diaconate and the call to the priesthood. This latter question will be considered separately shortly.

The call to receive holy orders is twofold—an interior call from God and an external call from the Church made through one's superior with hierarchical authority. The interior call by God is recognized by the spiritual discernment of the individual working with his spiritual advisors and superiors. This particular article of the Rules insists that the call is in response to apostolic needs, i.e., dictated by the role the individual is to exercise in the mission of the Congregation in the Church. In other words the call to diaconate is a call to serve in a particular way. In discerning whether or not he has an interior divine call to diaconate, a brother has to reflect with the aid of his spiritual director on how he can best evangelize the poor and his own motivation.

Why must the provincial be authorized by the superior general to permit a brother to begin serious preparation for diaconate, when such authorization is not required for a scholastic? The answer is that a scholastic entered the Congregation and was accepted for oblation with holy orders in view. When the provincial with the approval of his council requested the superior general to confirm the call of a scholastic to perpetual vows, the superior general with the consent of this council gave the approval of the Congregation for the scholastic to continue his preparation for holy orders and at least implicitly judged that he was qualified for ordination. Such was not the case when he confirmed the call of a brother for perpetual oblation. The latter's aptitude for ordination was not a question at that time. This is what is to be judged when approval is given for a brother to begin serious preparation for ordination.[117]

---

[116] *Constitutions 1982.* It would seem that the words of the other official version of the Rules, i.e., the French text: "à la suite d'un discernement spirituel adéquat," are stronger than the English "discerns that."

N.B. "When the expression 'superior general in council' or 'provincial in council' is used, it means the superior general or provincial with the consent of his council" (C. 83).

[117] Abstractedly it would be possible for a man to join the Congregation with the permanent diaconate in mind, and for his provincial to accept him for oblation while considering him a

Brothers who are candidates for the permanent diaconate or have been ordained deacons are and remain brothers, i.e., they do not thereby become members of the category of scholastics and priests. At the same time they do not form a separate category of brothers within the Congregation. Recall the move in the nineteenth century to have a separate category of teaching brothers.

Besides affecting their work and study assignments the practical consequences of their belonging to the category of brothers are two. First of all, a permanent deacon may be called to the general chapter by the superior general, as one of the six brothers that he is to name capitulars (R. 112). Secondly, the rules also provide that a brother in perpetual vows may be appointed with the necessary indult local superior (R. 90). A scholastic is not eligible to be one of the six brothers named by the superior general as capitulars, and the Rules make no mention of the possibility of a scholastic to become a local superior.

Change of Category

Prior to Clement VIII there was no universal norm governing the transfer of a religious from one category to another within the same institute. Because of abuses and the transfer of unqualified lay brothers to the class of clerics within their order and subsequent ordination, Clement VIII in "Cum ad regularem" forbade the practice.[118] Consequently, for a professed brother in a regular order to become a cleric an indult from the Holy See was necessary. There was no universal norm concerning a transfer from the category of clerics to that of lay brothers. Although there was no universal norm for institutes with simple vows, the praxis of the Holy See was contrary to such transfers.

The *Normæ* of 1901 confirmed this practice.[119] This was incorporated in the 1917 Code:

---

candidate for the permanent diaconate. In such a case, in light of Rule 67 this information would have to be presented to the superior general when requesting approval for the call to perpetual oblation. Rule 67 is written with the supposition that it is a brother who already has perpetual vows who wishes to be ordained.

[118] See GASPARRI, *Fontes*, vol. 1, no. 189. Cf. A. PUGLIESE, "De Mutatione Classis apud Religiosos," in *Monitor ecclesiasticus*, 87 (1962), pp. 498–514; A. LARRAONA, "Consultationes," in *Commentarium pro religiosis*, 3 (1922), p. 11; idem, "Commentarium Codicis," in *Commentarium pro religiosis*, 23 (1942), pp. 182–186.

[119] *Normæ*: "After profession, there is no transfer from the first class to the second class, or vice versa."

Can. 558 — In religious institutes in which there are two classes of members, the novitiate made in preparation for membership in one class is not valid for membership in the other class.

This norm that applied to all religious institutes was modified by *Renovationis causam*:

27 — In Institutes having different novitiates for different categories of religious, and unless the Constitutiones stipulate otherwise, the novitiate made for one category is valid likewise for the other . . .

Until the 1980 general chapter the particular law of the Missionary Oblates of Mary Immaculate did not mention the transfer of an Oblate from one category to another. The universal norms were followed. Consequently, prior to *Renovationis causam* an individual wishing to change his category had to either make a new novitiate or obtain an indult from the Holy See dispensing him from making a novitiate for the new category.

There were in the past cases of scholastics who, for one reason or another, were not ordained. Some became brothers; others remained scholastics until their death. Of course, this was an abnormal situation, since being a scholastic is meant as a temporary state in preparation for priesthood. Scholastics are members of the same category as the priests.

The Rules enacted in 1980 provide for both eventualities—a scholastic becoming a brother and a brother becoming a scholastic, i.e., a student for the priesthood. Rule 67, which was already quoted, provides for the case of a brother desiring to be ordained a priest.[120] The provincial with the consent of his council, after having obtained the authorization of the superior general with the consent of his council, may permit him to become a candidate for the priesthood. Thus, with this authorization he would change category and become a scholastic. On the other hand, Rule 64 provides for the case of a scholastic, who ceases to be a candidate for the priesthood.

R. 64. At the end of the formal scholasticate training, Oblates take up their ministry as priests. If a scholastic discerns that he is not called to the priesthood but intends to remain an Oblate, he asks the superior general for an obedience to begin his mission as a brother.[121]

Rule 64 seeks rather delicately to eliminate the anomaly of a person being a permanent scholastic. A scholastic who has finished his theological studies is either to request ordination, or an obedience to be a brother, or a dispensation from his vows.

---

[120] Supra p. 230.

[121] *Constitutions 1982.*

In his message to Oblates in first formation, Marcello Zago addressed the question of an individual changing from one category to another:

> In both vocations an eventual change of choice is foreseen: a person who had intended the priesthood may discern a call to the brotherhood, and someone who wanted to consecrate himself as a brother may discern a call to the priesthood. This openness to making a change prior to perpetual vows reflects the present situation which foresees a common novitiate for the two states of life, during which the common aspects of the charism and dimensions of religious life are stressed. This is also due to the fact that a choice is made more gradually and a greater discernment is required. Perpetual oblation ought to mark the conclusion of one's choice, an option that should never be made lightly.[122]

Brothers as Superiors

In *Perfectæ caritatis*, the decree on the renewal of religious life, Vatican II spoke of the spirit of unity and charity among the members of an institute. As a means to achieve this goal it insisted:

> In order to strengthen the bond of brotherhood between the members of an institute, those who are called lay brothers, cooperators, or some such name should be associated more closely with the life and work of the community.[123]

---

[122] Marcello ZAGO, "The Priestly Character of the Congregation," January 25, 1992, *OMI Documentation*, no. 185 (April 1992), p. 18; Appendix I, infra pp. 269–280.

[123] *PC*, no. 15. For a correct understanding of the last paragraph of no. 15, it should be recalled that it was a separate article (no. 32) in the previous draft of the text (see *Schema*, April 22, 1963, *Acta Synodalia Sacrosancti Concilii Oecumenici Vaticani II*, vol. 3, pars 7, p. 774, and vol. 4, pars 3, pp. 524–525). Nos. 30, 31, and 32 were joined and expanded to form the present no. 15.

The last paragraph refers to non-clerical institutes that are "non mere laicalia," i.e., not entirely lay, e.g., some recent and some ancient monasteries, and some modern institutes such as the Little Brothers of Jesus (cf. A. GUTIÉRREZ, "Consultationes," in *Commentarium pro religiosis* 46 (1967), p. 378). That it does not refer to clerical institutes is confirmed by the response given to a suggestion that the paragraph be dropped (*Acta Vaticani II*, vol. 4, pars 3, p. 567).

It seems that the fact that the last paragraph of no. 15 does not refer to clerical institutes but to institutes that are "not entirely lay" is overlooked and, in fact, the contrary is implied in a memorandum sent to the Holy Father by the Council of the Union of Superiors General. In the section "Brothers in Clerical Institutes" it stated: "This restriction (concerning brothers being superiors) appears to many religious throughout the world to go against the directives of the Vatican Council who saw the only difference between clerical and lay members as one of Sacred Order (*PC*, no. 15)" (*USG Communicatio Sanctæ Sedis*, no. 1/83, p. 9). This statement is not factual insofar as it refers to *Perfectæ caritatis*, no. 15 and the directives of Vatican II.

One author quoted the last paragraph of no. 15 and omitted the words "which are not entirely lay . . . of their very nature." He wrote: ". . . the Council suggested the possibility that . . . 'men's institutes . . . can . . . admit clerics and lay men, in accordance with their constitutions, on

Paul VI with his *motu proprio Ecclesiæ Sanctæ* issued norms for the implementation of several Vatican II decrees including *Perfectæ caritatis*. In reference to the sentence just quoted, he said:

27. General chapters and synaxes must study the manner in which religious who are called lay brothers, cooperators or any similar name, may, gradually, obtain an active voice in specified community activities and in elections, and for some offices obtain a passive voice. They will thus become more directly involved in the life and activities of the community and the priests will have greater freedom to perform those ministries which are reserved to them.[124]

A number of clerical institutes asked what could be done in applying this norm, while not changing the "finis, natura, indoles," the purpose, nature, character, of their institutes as also demanded by *Ecclesiæ Sanctæ*.[125] In response to this the Sacred Congregation of Religious and Secular Institutes issued the decree *Clericalia instituta* to clarify the question. The first three points of the decree list the roles and offices that general chapters may allow the nonclerical members to exercise or hold. The last number states which offices they may not hold:

4. On the other hand, nonclerical members will not be able to assume the office of superior or of vicar, general, provincial or local.[126]

The 1972 general chapter in virtue of the authority granted by the above mentioned documents approved the following:

(*Note*: brothers who are not clerics may not serve as the official replacement for the Superior. Decree S.C. Rel. Nov. 27, 1969)

39—A brother in perpetual vows, and provided that he is not a scholastic may be named Superior of a local community in certain circumstances when this is desirable, and with the necessary indult.[127]

---

an equal footing and with equal rights and obligations, apart from those arising out of sacred orders'" (Paul BOYLE, C.P., "Attention to the Person and to Present-Day Sensitivity," in *USG Conventus Mensilis* February 10–12, 1982, p. 16 [Italian ed., p. 21]). One reading his article could easily be led to believe that the quote applies to all men's institutes, which is not the case.

Cf. William H. WOESTMAN, O.M.I., "De institutis clericalibus vitæ consecratæ et superioribus non clericis," in *Monitor Ecclesiasticus*, 110 (1985), pp. 411-420.

[124] PAUL VI, apostolic letter *motu proprio, Ecclesiæ Sanctæ II*, August 6, 1966, in *AAS*, 58 (1966), p. 780, no. 27; trans. *CLD*, vol. 6, p. 290. Cf. also the last paragraph SCRIS, decree, *Clericalia instituta*, November 27, 1969, in *AAS*, 61 (1969), pp. 739-740; trans. *CLD*, vol. 7, pp. 468-469.

[125] *Ecclesiæ Sanctæ II*, no. 6.

[126] *Clericalia instituta*.

[127] *Administrative Structures*, p. 39.

The Constitutions as approved by the 1980 chapter did not mention any necessary requisites for an individual to become superior. In other words, it added no requisites that were not norms of universal law. The Rules, however, stated:

R. 101. Any Oblate whose first formation is completed and who is perpetually professed may be appointed local superior provided the norms of law are fully observed.[128]

This article added to the common law the requirement that for an individual to be appointed local superior he must have perpetual vows and have finished his first formation, and explicitly stated that universal law had to be observed. Since the latter required that superiors in clerical institutes be clerics, it recognized that the nonclerics could not be superiors.

This was in accord with the principle used in drafting the Constitutions of not repeating universal laws which already have normative force for the Congregation. The repetition of a universal norm in particular law does not make it any more obligatory than it was already.

The Congregation of Religious and Secular Institutes requested that the Constitutions specify that superiors had to be priests,[129] and determine a length of time after perpetual profession for a person to be eligible to be a major superior. This was done in article 82.

C. 82. An Oblate appointed or elected superior, vicar or replacement of a superior, must have finished his first formation, taken perpetual vows and been ordained a priest . . .

The content of the above-quoted Rule 101 was reworked, and what was implicit was made explicit. It is basically the same text as approved by the 1972 chapter and is now part of the final text.

R. 90. An Oblate brother in perpetual vows may, in certain circumstances and with the necessary indult, be appointed superior of a local community.

---

[128] GENERAL CHAPTER OF 1980, *Constitutions and Rules of the Congregation of the Missionary Oblates of Mary Immaculate*, Rome, 1981. The text had two official versions—English and French. Following the norm of *Ecclesiæ Sanctæ II*, no. 6, this text was promulgated and was the "Constitutions" until *Constitutions 1982* were approved by the Sacred Congregation and promulgated.

[129] "L'incise 'les normes du droit étant respectées' est insuffisante; écrire: 'une fois ordonné prêtre.' Après 'supérieur local' ajouter: 'ou vicaire local,'" (PERONIO, to Jetté, "Observations du *Congresso*," March 25, 1982, General Secretariat O.M.I.). Need it be pointed out that the SCRIS decree of November 27, 1969 had "Sodales non clerici," which in 1969 included the tonsured, etc. and since 1972 includes deacons? Supra p. 112.

Is the requirement that an Oblate be a priest in order to be appointed superior a discriminatory limitation imposed by the Sacred Congregation for Religious and Sacred Institutes?[130] One author put it in this way:

> Distinctions within the religious family which do not flow from the charism of the institute or which are not clearly seen as intrinsically flowing from and essentially connected with sacred orders are viewed by modern man as arbitrary, restrictive and discriminating . . .

> This decree *Clericalia instituta* and the legislation on this point proposed for the new Code of Canon Law are certainly not perceived as being just.[131]

What is to be said of this contention?

The Sacred Congregation issued a declaration that was distributed to the major superiors in the United States which gave the background of the decree *Clericalia instituta* and the reasoning upon which it was based. The declaration is too long to quote in full. However, the core of the explanation for the decision is:

> The conclusions reached by the plenary meeting of the Sacred Congregation were not motivated by any considerations of excessive "clericalism," nor on any supposed principle that no priest member of a religious institute can be subject to a lay religious in what pertains to the religious life. There are concrete cases to the contrary. Neither was any important role played by canon 118 of the Code of Canon Law, which demands clerical status for the exercise of ecclesiastical jurisdiction.

> The basic consideration was that although both clerical and lay religious are equally members of their respective institute and thus, as religious, can enjoy the same rights and be bound by the same obligations, nevertheless a new element comes into the picture in clerical institutes. In such institutes, superiorship on any level involves in varying degrees the direction and supervision of the priestly ministry. Because of the particular obligations entailed by the administration of the sacraments, especially the celebration of the Eucharist, the official preaching of the word of God, etc. the priestly ministry calls for special competence and preparation, plus the particular ministerial grace which is one of the main fruits of the sacrament of orders.[132]

---

[130] The group of brothers of the vice-province of Bolivia spoke of "Las limitaciones que pone la 'Congregaciòn de los Religiosos'" ("Todos somos Misioneros").

[131] Paul BOYLE, C.P., "Attention to the Person," in *USG Conventus Mensilis*, February 10–12, 1982, p. 17 (Italian ed., p. 22).

[132] SCRIS, declaration, N. 1511/59, distributed by the apostolic delegate to the United States, April 17, 1970, N. 811/70, in *CLD*, vol. 7, pp. 469–471.

In 1974 the United States Conference of Major Superiors of Men passed a resolution which stated, "The Conference of Major Superiors of Men USA requests the Sacred Congregation for Religious and Secular Institutes to reconsider its previous decisions which excluded lay brothers who are members of clerical societies from holding the office of superior."[133] A paper entitled "Who should be superior?" was prepared for the resolution. The bases for argument for the resolution of the Conference of Major Superiors are:

> 1. The ministry of the superior within a religious institute is that of maintaining and promoting the fidelity of the institute to its charism and the adaptation and renewal of the institute in order to actualize its charism more fully. The most fundamental qualification of the superior, therefore, should be his ability to stimulate and actualize the efforts of the members to live out their charism . . .

> 4. . . . . the qualifications for being a religious superior derive from the charism of the institute rather than from any relationship to the sacrament of orders of the power of jurisdiction . . .[134]

> 5. The role of the priest-members of such institutes, as priests, is concerned with the official tasks of ordained ministry in the church. As such they have an additional preoccupation, in no way contrary to, but sometimes in creative tension with, the particular charism of the institute . . .

> 6. The vocation of lay members of religious institutes is derived from the charism of the institute and is not mixed with a vocation to share in the official ministry of the hierarchy. Because of the greater clarity of the charismatic vocation of the institute in their lives, they may sometimes be especially qualified for leadership in the living out of this charism. . .[135]

The key element in this author's argumentation is that a religious superior has the responsibility of maintaining and promoting the particular charism of

---

[133] *Origins*, 5 (1976), no. 44, p. 695.

[134] Of course the Congregation in the declaration giving the background for *Clericalia Instituta* had said that the jurisdiction and the fact of ordination were not the bases for saying that brothers could not be superior in clerical institutes. The paper was on this point repeating to the Congregation what it had already said.

However, the question of jurisdiction was understood by another writer to play such a role in the Congregation's dealing with the Missionary Oblates of Mary Immaculate, "Finally, it seems that because of the implications regarding the ecclesiastical jurisdiction, the 'clerical' nature of the Institute (C. 1) restricts brothers in the exercise of juridical authority: an indult from the Holy See is needed to appoint a brother as superior of a community (R. 90)." (F. JETTÉ, O.M.I., "Twenty-First Letter of the Superior General," in *Communiqué O.M.I.*, 35/84, Appendix, p. 2). The writer did not explain the basis of his opinions.

[135] David A. FLEMING, S.M., "Who should be superior?" in *Origins*, 5 (1976), no. 44, pp. 693–699.

his institute. This line of reasoning is solidly based on *Lumen gentium* (no. 45) and *Perfectæ Caritatis*. The latter clearly enunciated the importance of the elements proper to each institute and the obligation of nurturing and furthering them for the welfare of the Church.

> b) It is to the Church's great advantage that each religious foundation has its particular spirit and function. Each must, therefore, reverence and embrace the genius and directives of its founder, its authentic traditions, the whole heritage, indeed, of the religious body.[136]

In chapter four it was seen how the Commission for the Revision of the Code deliberately incorporated this Vatican II teaching concerning the spiritual patrimony of religious institutes into the 1983 Code.[137] The result of this solicitude is found especially in cc. 578, 586 §1, and 587 §1. Can there be any doubt that the spiritual patrimony of each institute is considered by the Church to be paramount? Without it an institute would cease to be true to its basic nature— would, in fact, lose its own particular identity, and become handicapped and ultimately frustrated in fulfilling its proper mission in the Church. In these canons is found a prime example of the Church's hierarchy making wise laws in order to pasture the People of God in accord with the promptings of the Holy Spirit.[138]

Can there be any doubt about the positive element found in the statement "the qualifications for being religious superior derive from the charism of the institute"? For an individual to be a good religious superior, it is not sufficient for him/her to be talented, prayerful, filled with apostolic zeal, a good administrator, have good judgement, skilled in dealing with other persons. A superior must be permeated with the particular spirit of the institute—must understand and treasure its spiritual patrimony. The particular charism must be incarnated in him/her. Otherwise there is the danger of having a good manager, who is appreciated and like, but who does not really contribute to the development and flourishing of the institute according to the spirit of the founder and its sound traditions.

In paragraphs 5 and 6 quoted from the paper submitted by the American Conference of Major Superiors of Men is reflected the author's own particular perspective, which is based on his experience as a Marianist. His religious

---

[136] *PC*, no. 2; TANNER, p. 940.

[137] Supra pp. 135–140.

[138] See *Lumen Gentium*, no. 45.

community, which has as its purpose the education of youth and less than one-third of whose members are priests, is hardly what would be called a typical clerical institute.[139]

He introduced his paper by pointing out that a number of institutes with both priest and brother members have brothers as local and major superiors and gave as examples the Marianists, the Congregation of the Holy Cross, the Hospitallers of St. John of God, various groups of Franciscans.[140] Is it necessary to point out none of these institutes are typical clerical communities?

This list illustrates a point made by the secretary of the Congregation:
> There is discrimination when some arbitrary action is performed, not when a decision is based on equitable reasons. There must be a certain amount of flexibility, because in "clericality" and "laicality" there is always a margin either way. In this sense, SCRIS has shown itself sympathetic to requests for permission. But one has to admit that in some institutes in which priestly activity occupies a position that is important and even preponderant, the religious-priest is particularly suited for the role of superior, father and director. . .[141]

A careful reading of points 5 and 6 reveals that the argumentation presented may easily be applicable to a community such as the Marianists, but it is by no means valid for an institute whose goal is priestly ministry. In fact, for such a community the opposite is true.

In chapter four it was seen that the classification of a religious institute is not something arbitrary, but is based on the spiritual patrimony and nature of the particular institute.[142] The Missionary Oblates of Mary Immaculate have always considered themselves to be a clerical congregation.[143] The same is true

---

[139] The Marianists are also called the Brothers of Mary. Their founder Chaminade wanted to unite priests and brothers as perfect equals. See *New Catholic Encyclopedia*, s.v. "Marianists," by G.J. RUPPEL.

   One cannot logically use the practice and particular law of the Marianists as precedents applicable to a clerical institute whose nature, character, spiritual patrimony etc. are very different. The Marianists are much less "priestly" in their ministry, and consequently less "clerical" than most clerical institutes.

[140] FLEMING, "Who should be superior?"

[141] A. MEYER, O.S.B., quoted in, "Conclusions," *USG Conventus Mensilis*, Feb. 10–12, 1982, p. 19 (Italian ed., p. 27).

[142] Supra pp. 141–145.

[143] Supra pp. 173–174, 177–186, 197–199.

   This assertion refers to all official statements as documented in chapter five. It is said in spite of a few discordant voices that have been raised in recent years, since the contrary opinion is in opposition with the constant tradition of the Congregation and has no solid basis in tradition or law.

of bishops and the Holy See.[144] This is based not on some external consideration or decree, but on the intrinsic nature of the Congregation. It is a clerical
religious congregation because it is a priestly religious institute.

> In fidelity to the Founder's charism, the priesthood remains an
> essential element of the Congregation, since the principal goal of its mission
> is full evangelization: witness, proclamation of God's word, implanting and
> building up the Church, celebration of the sacraments, especially of
> Reconciliation and of the Eucharist . . . The Oblate religious missionary life
> and the mission of both priests and brothers are inseparably linked to the
> ministerial priesthood.[145]

There can hardly be an objection to the requirement that the particular
law of a society state the basic requisites for persons holding office. The
problem is how this is to be done, and what requisites are to be specified.

St. Thomas' classic definition affirms that law is an ordinance of reason.[146]
Consequently, a law must be just and respect the rights and dignity of all
persons. In order to be reasonable the legislator must consider what happens
commonly and in the majority of cases, and make the law accordingly.
Otherwise, the law would no longer be a universal norm. However, since a law
is universal, it cannot foresee every individual case, and there may be circumstances where the application or the observance of the law would be unreason-
able. In such instances there are grounds for an exception to the law, and a
dispensation should be sought and granted.[147]

Although an individual priest may not for various reasons have the
personal aptitude to be superior, the priest-members have a background—
formation, education, priestly ministry, personal charism to priestly ordination,
and sacramental grace flowing from the sacrament of holy orders, that prepare
them for the role of spiritual leader, father, director of their fellow religious.
The priestly component of their own personal charism and experience is most
important since the ministerial priesthood is an essential element of the
Congregation, and an Oblate superior is responsible for his brother religious
in promoting the mission of the Congregation. Since the lay members of the
Congregation are not normally prepared by their education, formation, and
apostolic ministry and do not have a personal vocation to the ministerial

---

[144] Supra pp. 192–197.

[145] *General Norms for Oblate Formation*, pp. 7–8, second basic principle.

[146] See I–II, q. 90, a. 4.

[147] See I–II, q. 96, a. 6; I–II, q. 97, a. 4; II–II, q. 147, a. 4.

priesthood, it is less likely that they are prepared to be the spiritual fathers of their fellow religious and leaders in the mission of the Congregation.

A law that respects this reality is far from being arbitrary, much less an unjust limitation imposed from on high. The requirement that all superiors of the Missionary Oblates of Mary Immaculate be priests is a perfectly reasonable norm, based on the very nature of the Congregation and the prevalent qualification of its members—both priests and brothers.[148] This is seen from a consideration of the principal duties of a superior.

His role is to aid and support his community and its individual members to live fully the Oblate life in order to experience in a concrete way:

> The call and the presence of the Lord among us (which) bind us together in charity and obedience to create anew in our own lives the Apostles' unity with him and their common mission in his Spirit.[149]

Thus, the insistence of the Congregation of Religious and Secular Institutes that the Constitutions state that superiors be priests is sound and good law—it respects the nature, traditions, the spiritual patrimony of the Missionary Oblates of Mary Immaculate, and it also respects the usual aptitudes of the individual Oblates, priests and brothers, to fulfil the office of superior.

In addition, it is not just a repetition of the common law, which requires that superiors of clerical institutes be clerics. This specifying of the universal norm is in complete conformity with the spiritual patrimony of the Congregation. Permanent deacons as members of the category of brothers have the same formation and basic education as the other brothers. As a whole they have not been educated and formed to be spiritual leaders and fathers of their

---

[148] While the author of this dissertation was a member of the U.S. Conference of Major Superiors of Men (1975–1981) and of its national board (1977–1980), he personally held and supported the conference's position on brothers as superiors in clerical institutes. His own position on this question evolved and changed during the process of researching and writing this dissertation. His stance is now based on the role that the spiritual patrimony must play in the life of each religious institute.

One must distinguish between types of clerical institutes. Some are essentially very priestly, such as clerics regular and those similar to them, e.g., the Missionary Oblates of Mary Immaculate. It is the author's opinion that a lay member of such an institute would usually not be personally qualified to be a superior, because of the reasons given in the text—especially since he lacks the personal charism of ministerial priesthood, which is essential to his institute. Consequently, the law for such institutes should recognize this. Whether the lay members of a clerical institute that is not so priestly in its nature are normally qualified to be superiors is a different question.

[149] *Constitutions 1982*, C. 3.

fellow Oblates—priests and brothers. In addition, they do not have the benefit of the experience of the ministerial priesthood.

Would it not be better to state implicitly, as the 1980 general chapter did, that only priests are to be superiors by referring to the requisites of common law and not mentioning priestly ordination? Would this not be more considerate than pointing out, as it were, in bold type a difference between the various members of the Congregation?

The answer to both questions is *yes*, if one does not mind lack of clarity for those who do not know the universal law and the consequent danger of misunderstanding. It is *no*, if one thinks that law should be clear and readily understood by all. Is it not better for a man joining the Congregation as a brother to understand clearly that normally he will not be called to shoulder the burdens of being superior?

The procurator general, in commenting on the reactions of the Congregation of Religious to the proposed text as a whole, said:

It can be readily admitted that some of the suggestions made by the Sacred Congregation clarified or even improved the text . . .[150]

Just as the insistence that the first article of the Constitutions state that the Missionary Oblates of Mary Immaculate are a clerical Congregation of pontifical right[151] clarified what was stated more indirectly, and removed any possible misinterpretation, article eighty-three now unequivocally states that superiors are to be priests who have made their perpetual oblation. This is both a clarification and an improvement.

At the same time, Rule 90 recognizes that there will be cases when, for various reasons, the most qualified individual to be superior will be a brother. It is written in the particular law of the Congregation that a brother may be appointed local superior with an indult. This specification by Rule 90 is important, because it plainly affirms that the general norm must be adapted, when it would not meet the needs of a particular community.

Between the 1972 general chapter's approval of the naming of a brother as a local superior with the required indult and 1984, approximately ten brothers were named superior. Since then a number of others have received

---

[150] O'REILLY, "Approval," p. 11.
[151] Supra pp. 112–113 and 184–186.

a similar appointment. Each time an indult was requested from the Holy See it was granted. This is a clear example of flexibility on the part of the Sacred Congregation adapting the law to the concrete situation.[152]

Summary

Already in 1818 de Mazenod's vision of his missionary society included, along with priests, consecrated laymen, who would dedicate their lives in the service of the mission. They were "to be sons of the family," to take the same vows, and form part of the same community as the priests by sharing the same dining room and spiritual exercises.

The spirit of fraternal unity and charity that he envisioned for his religious community is seen in the prayers that they were to recite together at noon each day.

> To Your servants, O Lord, gathered together in Your Name, and partaking of one bread, grant to be of one mind towards another, and to consider one another to provoke unto charity and good works, so that, by the holiness of their lives, the good odour of Christ be shed abroad throughout the world.

> O God of love, grant that we, Your children, who eat at Your table, may bear one another's burdens in charity unfeigned, so that Your blessed peace, which surpasses all understanding, may keep our hearts and minds in Christ Jesus, our Lord, in the unity of the Holy Spirit, one God, world without end. Amen.[153]

Although initially the work of the brothers was limited to the traditional work of lay brothers in religious institutes, this rapidly changed with the acceptance of foreign missions. Even though they were not at that time called missionaries, their contribution to the preaching of the Gospel reached within a few years in North America from the Saint Lawrence to the Pacific Ocean and from the Arctic to the Gulf of Mexico and the Rio Grande. During de Mazenod's lifetime the brothers accompanied the priests to southern Africa, first to Natal and then to Basutoland. Perhaps it was the missionary bishops and priests in Ceylon who appealed to him most urgently for brothers to share in their mission.

The foreign missions opened not only new territory to the brothers, but even more significantly extended the field of their service to that of builders

---

[152] See Appendix III, p. 287, for an example of such an indult.

[153] COSENTINO, G., *Exercises de Piété de l'Oblat*, Ottawa, Éditions des Études Oblates, 1962, p. 140. These two prayers along with the one immediately preceding them were used in the Congregation from its beginning. The origin of these prayers is uncertain. See op. cit. 139.

of churches and schools. They became, along with the Oblate missionary bishops and priests, co-founders of new churches. At the same time, many of them were given a directly apostolic charge as catechists and teachers of the children and also of trades. The unity of the Oblate community was especially shown by a brother accompanying a priest to the isolated mission posts in order to form together a religious community.

This development was based on the principle of employing each person, insofar as the mission of the Congregation permits, according to his own talents and aptitudes. This evolution was officially recognized in 1853 by appropriate modifications of the Constitutions.

During the latter half of the twentieth century, this tradition built on the theological and juridical development of the mission of the laity in the Church. The 1966 chapter opened new works to the brothers and gave them a share in the government of the Congregation with the right to vote. The 1972 chapter continued in the same line by opening to them a number of offices including that of local superior, when special circumstances warrant it, and the approval of the permanent diaconate.

A group of secular priests joined forces to become missionaries, and within a few years they became the Missionary Oblates of Mary Immaculate, a religious community with a priestly mission, and were so recognized by the Holy See. This constant tradition was expressed by the 1980 general chapter in this way, "There is no ministry, however, which is foreign to us, provided we never lose sight of the Congregation's primary purpose: to evangelize the most abandoned."[154]

It was immediately after these words that the 1980 general chapter, at the request of the brothers who were capitulars, added a special article to express explicitly that they as sharers in the one priesthood of Christ, "are called to cooperate in their own way in reconciling all things in him."[155]

De Mazenod bequeathed a third prayer to be recited just before the two quoted above. It is a prayer for personal holiness of those consecrated as priests and for a fruitful ministry.

> O God, our High Priest and Victim, who with Your own body and blood refresh the ministers, which you have consecrated to yourself, grant, we beseech you, that we, as sharers of your priesthood, may walk worthy of the vocation to which we are called, and may zealously feed your people

---

[154] *Constitutions 1982*, R. 2.
[155] *Constitutions 1982*, R. 3.

both by word and example.[156]

Although originally this prayer referred only to ordained priests, today there is no difficulty in understanding it analogously in light of the common priesthood shared by all the faithful. However, the Oblate brothers, in addition to sharing in the one priesthood of Jesus by their baptism and confirmation, are united intimately to the priestly mission of the Congregation by their religious consecration and also by their close union with their ordained brothers. Thus, we have summed up the very life of the Congregation—priests and brothers united by religious vows and priestly consecration, each in his own way, as brothers to preach the Gospel to the poor and bring them to the fullness of life in Jesus through the Eucharist and other sacraments.

---

[156] N.B. This is a revised translation of this prayer. The earliest English translation found (and it is also in all subsequent prayer manuals) omitted the words "ministros," "ministers," and "ut tui sacerdotii consortes," "sharers of Your priesthood," found in the original Latin text. Was this done out of "sensitivity" for the brothers? See *Manual of Prayers for the Use of the Fathers and Brothers Oblates of Mary Immaculate*, London: R. & T. Washbourne, 1915, p. 40.

Epilogue

Nota bene. What more sublime purpose than that of their Institute? Their founder is Jesus Christ, the very Son of God; their first fathers are the apostles. They are called to be the Savior's co-workers, the co-redeemers of mankind; and even though, because of their present small number and the more urgent needs of the people around them, they have to limit the scope of their zeal, for the time being, to the poor of our countryside and others, their ambition should, in its holy aspirations, embrace the vast expanse of the whole earth.[1]

When de Mazenod wrote these words for the first Constitutions, the Missionaries of Provence numbered six priests and three students in minor orders, plus a handful of candidates. Although his zeal was without bounds, little could he have imagined the growth and expansion of his society that was on the verge of opening its second house.

In fact it was because of this second foundation that all agreed that he should compose constitutions to assure unity within the society. He expressed it in this way:

> The example of the saints and reason itself make it amply clear that the success of such a holy undertaking as well as the maintenance of discipline in any society make certain rules of life absolutely necessary for unity of thought and action among the members. Such unity is a body's strength, keeping up its fervor and insuring that it lasts.[2]

Clearly, de Mazenod saw the Constitutions and Rules not as an end in themselves, but as a necessary means to reach the goals of his little group of missionaries—their personal growth in virtue and the preaching of the Gospel to the poor. He insisted on the observance of the Constitutions because without it unity of spirit and action would be mere pipe dreams.

Having built the Missionary Oblates of Mary Immaculate upon a solid foundation and having sent his missionaries to the four corners of the world, he expressed his dying wish for his sons.

> Practice among yourselves charity . . . charity . . . charity . . . and without, zeal for the salvation of souls.[3]

In 1982 Fernand Jetté, superior general, presented to the Congregation the Constitutions approved by the Sacred Congregation of Religious and

---

[1] "Constitutions 1818," I partie, c. I, §3; *Constitutions 1982*, p. 12.

[2] "Constitutions 1818," Avant-propos; *Constitutiones 1826*, Preface; *Constitutions 1982*, Preface.

[3] *Circulaires*, May 26, 1861, no. 9, vol. 1, p. 9 [63].

Secular Institutes. He echoed de Mazenod's words written to Tempier on February 18, 1826 immediately after the first approval of the Constitutions, pointing out their dignity and importance because of the official approval of the Church.[4] Jetté then added his own reflections expressing the place of the Constitutions in the lives of de Mazenod's sons.

It is the Church therefore that "constitutes" us what we are. She vouches to the faithful for the Gospel authenticity of the life-project we offer them.

With this approbation, one more step is taken in committing ourselves to a new phase and moving resolutely toward the future. The time of discussing the letter of the law is over; it is now time to act, "the time to apply calmly and perseveringly the revised and approved Constitutions is at hand."[5]

Strengthened by this approbation, let us all renew ourselves in the spirit of our vocation, "a spirit of total dedication to the glory of God, the service of the Church and the salvation of souls".[6] Let us head into the future filled with great desires, with unshakable hope and courage, eyes fixed on the vastness of the apostolic field opening up before us.

May Blessed Eugene de Mazenod, our Founder and Father, obtain this grace for us![7]

---

[4] See DE MAZENOD, to Tempier, February 18, 1826, *Oblate Writings*, vol. 7, no. 226, pp. 41–42.

[5] JOHN PAUL II, address to the major superiors of religious of France, June 2, 1980, in *ORe*, June 23, 1980, p. 15.

[6] DE MAZENOD, to Tempier, August 22, 1817, *Oblate Writings*, vol. 6, no. 21, p. 35.

[7] Fernand JETTÉ, O.M.I., *Letters to the Oblates of Mary Immaculate*, Rome, General House, 1984, pp. 120–121.

Sources and Select Bibliography[1]
I — Ecclesiastical Sources

Acta Apostolicæ Sedis, Commentarium Officiale. Rome: 1909–

Acta Sanctæ Sedis. Rome, 1865–1908.

Acta Synodalia Sacrosancti Concilii Oecumenici Vaticani II. 4 vols. (25 parts) Vatican City: Libreria Editrice Vaticana, 1970–1978.

Analecta Juris Pontificii. Rome: 1852–1891.

BENEDICT XIII. Apostolic Constitution, *In Apostolicæ dignitatis solio*, January 26, 1725. In *Recueil des Bulles, Brefs, et Rescripts accordés par le Saint-Siège à l'Institut des Frères des Écoles Chrétiennes*. Rome: l'Institut Pie IX, 1907.

Benedicti XIV Acta. Ed. R. Martinis. Vol. 2. Naples: Artigianelli, 1894.

Benedict XIV. Apostolic Letter, *Ad Pastoralis dignitatis fastigium*, April 18, 1746. *Acta Congregationis SS. Crucis et Passionis D.N.J.C.* Vol. 12.

Bullarii Romani Continuatio. Vol. 16. Prato: Typographia Aldina, 1864.

Bullarium, Diplomatum et Privilegiorum Sanctorum Romanorum Pontificum Tauriensis editio. 25 vols. Turin: Franco et Dalmazzo, 1857–1872.

Canones et Decreta Concilii Tridentini ex editione Romana MDCCCIV Repetiti. Ed. A.E. Richter. Leipzig: Bernhard Tauchnitz, 1853.

Canon Law Digest. Ed. T.L. BOUSCAREN and J.I. O'CONNOR. 6 vols. Milwaukee: Bruce, 1934–1969. 3 vols. Mundelein, Illinois: Canon Law Digest, 1975–1983.

Codex Iuris Canonici Pii X Pontificis Maximi iussu digestus Benedicti Papæ XV auctoritate promulgatus. Ed. Petrus Card. GASPARRI. Rome: Typis Polyglottis Vaticanis, 1917 (reprint 1927).

Codex Iuris Canonici, auctoritate Ioannis Pauli PP. II promulgatus. Vatican City: Libreria Editrice Vaticana, 1983.

Codicis Iuris Canonici Fontes cura Emi Card. Gasparri editi. 9 vols. Rome (later Vatican City): Typis Polyglottis Vaticanis, 1923–1939. (Vols. 7–9, ed. Emus. Iustinianus Card. SERÉDI).

Collectanæ in usum Secretariæ Sacræ Congregationis Episcoporum et Regularium. Ed. A. BIZZARRI. Rome: Typographia Polyglotta, 1885.

---

[1] Limited to those sources and works consulted during the research for and writing of this dissertation.

Communicationes. PONTIFICIA COMMISSIO CODICI IURIS CANONICI RECOGNOSCENDO. Vatican City: 1969– .

Corpus Iuris Canonici. Ed. Lipsiensis 2ª, ed. Aemilius Friedberg. Leipzig, 1879–1881. Reprint ed. Leipzig: Officina Berhardi Tauchnitz, 1928.

Leges Ecclesiæ post Codicem iuris canonici editæ. Xaverius OCHOA. 6 vols. Rome: Commentarium pro Religiosis, 1966–1987.

Ordo Professionis Religiosæ. Editio typica. Vatican City: Typis Polyglottis Vaticanis, 1970; reprint 1975.

PIUS IX. Apostolic Letter *Romani Pontificis*. April 1, 1851. In *Procès-verbal de la remise faite par Monseigneur l'Évêque de Marseille entre les mains du Conseil Municipal du Bref de N.S.P. le Pape qui lui confère le Pallium*. (May 9, 1851) Marseille: Brile, 1851.

PONTIFICIA COMMISSIO CIC RECOGNOSCENDO. *Schema Codicis Iuris Canonici (Patribus Commissionis reservatum)*. Vatican City: Liberia Editrice Vaticana, 1980.

PONTIFICIA COMMISSIO CIC RECOGNOSCENDO. *Schema Canonum de Institutis vitæ consecratæ per professionem conciliorum evanglicorum*. Vatican City: Typis Polyglottis Vaticanis, 1977.

SACRED CONGREGATION OF BISHOPS AND REGULARS. *Normæ secundum quas S. Congr. Episcoporum et Regularium procedere solet in approbandis novis institutis votorum simplicium*. Rome: Typis S.C. de Propaganda Fide, 1901.

SACRED CONGREGATION DE PROPAGANDA FIDE. *Normæ pro Constitutionibus congregationum iuris diocesani a S. Congregatione de Propaganda Fide dependentium*. Rome: Typis Polyglottis Vaticanis, 1940.

SACRED CONGREGATION OF RELIGIOUS. *Normæ da tenersi presenti dai RR.mi Consultori nella revisione delle Costituzioni conformate al Codice*. N. 1343/23. October 28, 1922. Rome, 1922.

Rome. Procurator's Archives O.M.I.
Contains originals or copies of papal rescripts and other documents concerning the Missionary Oblates of Mary Immaculate.

Rome. Sacred Congregation of Religious and Secular Institutes Archives. M 29. For photocopies of pertinent documents: Rome. General Archives O.M.I.; for printed text see Georges COSENTINO, *Histoire de nos Règles*.

TANNER, Norman P., S.J. Ed. *Decrees of the Ecumenical Councils*. Original languages and English trans. 2 vols. Georgetown, Georgetown University Press, 1990.

Vatican City. Vatican Secret Archives.
For pertinent documents: *Écrits du Fondateur*, vols. 3 and 4. Ed. P.E. DUVAL.

Rome: Maison Général O.M.I. 1952. In *Missions O.M.I.*, 79 (1952), pp. 1–135, 401–580.

II — Oblate Sources and Select Bibliography
1. Charles Joseph Eugene de Mazenod

Handwritten Sources

Rome. Postulation Archives O.M.I.
The Postulation Archives of the Missionary Oblates of Mary Immaculate contain the bulk of de Mazenod's handwritten papers. Copies of the balance of his writings are also conserved. All these documents are classified as follows:

DM — Documents of de Mazenod. (Includes class notes, retreat notes and resolutions, conference notes, writings concerning the Congregation, etc.). In chronological order according the the literary form. Nineteen dossiers.

JM — Journals of de Mazenod. (Relatively small sections are preserved). Eleven dossiers.

LM — Letters to and from de Mazenod. (Catalogued alphabetically according to the correspondent). Forty-three dossiers.

FB — Fonds Boisgelin. De Mazenod's only sister, Charlotte-Eugènie-Antoinette, married Marquis Armand de Boisgelin, and all of the papers preserved by the family became, on the death of de Mazenod and his sister, the property of the Marquis' descendants and heirs. Of these the Oblates have secured all those documents which touch on de Mazenod and his uncle, Bishop Charles-Fortuné. Eight dossiers.

Les Saintes Règles, expliquées d'après les écrits les leçons et l'esprit de Mgr Charles-Joseph-Eugène de Mazenod. Ed. A.J-B. Yenveux. 2 vols. Paris, 1903. Ms. 7 vols. 1878–1903. Fragments of de Mazenod's writings arranged in order corresponding to the articles of the Constitutions. Many of the original documents used are no longer extant.

In addition, all of de Mazenod's writings from whatever sources, both primary and secondary, have been carefully transcribed, with source cited, and bound in chronological order. 32 vols. These have been indexed on filing cards according to names and subjects.

Évêché de Marseille. *Mandements, Lettres pastorales, Ordonnances, Circulaires de Monseigneur Charles-Fortuné de Mazenod, Évêque de Marseille. 1823–1837.* One bound volume.

Évêché de Marseille. *Mandements, Lettres pastorales, Ordonnances, Circulaires, Discours de Monseigneur Charles-Joseph-Eugène de Mazenod, Évêque de Marseille.* 1837–1861. One bound volume.

"Insinuations." Five registers of official acts of the bishops of Marseille between 1823 and 1861. Postulations Archives O.M.I. bound photocopies of the originals. 10 volumes.

"Registre Lettres Administratives." Seven registers of administrative letters of the bishops of Marseille between 1823 and 1865. Postulation Archives O.M.I. bound photocopies of the originals. Eight volumes.

Rome. Archives (international) of the Holy Childhood Pontifical Work. De Mazenod to Charles de Forbin-Janson. 1814–1817.
These letters contain details about the founding of the Congregation not found elsewhere. The Holy Childhood Archives were transferred from Paris to Rome in October 1983.

Printed Sources

DE MAZENOD, Charles-Joseph-Eugène. "Antécédents de la première approbation pontificale des Constitutions et Règles des Missionnaires Oblats de Marie Immaculée," ed. P.E. DUVAL. Vol. 3. *Écrits du Fondateur.* Rome, 1952. In *Missions O.M.I.*, 79 (1952), pp. 1–135.

———. "Appendix de Externis Missionibus, Instructio," *Constitutiones 1853,* 167–182; *Constitutiones 1894,* 211–226; *Constitutiones 1910,* 201–214.

———. *Choix de Textes Relatifs aux Constitutions et Règles O.M.I.* Ed. Paul SION. Rome, 1893.
Selected Texts Related to the O.M.I. Constitutions and Rules. Ed. Paul SION, O.M.I. Trans. Bastiampillai RAYAPPU, O.M.I. Rome, 1984.

———. "Circulaire de Mgr Charles-Joseph-Eugène de Mazenod (le 2 février 1857)." In *Circulaires Administratives,* vol. 1, pp. 121–130.
"Circular Letter of Mgr. Charles Joseph Eugene de Mazenod (February 2, 1857)." Trans. in *Mission O.M.I.*, 77 (1950), pp. 127–142.

———. "Constitutions et Règles." Infra under heading Constitutions.

———. *Écrits Oblats.* Ed. Yvon BEAUDOIN, O.M.I. Rome: Postulation générale O.M.I., 1977– .
Vol. 1: *Lettres aux correspondants d'Amérique, 1841–1850.* 1977.
Vol. 2: *Lettres aux correspondants d'Amérique, 1851–1860.* 1977.
Vol. 3: *Lettres et documents concernant l'Angleterre et l'Irlande, 1842–1860.* 1978.

Vol. 4: *Lettres aux correspondants de Ceylan et d'Afrique, 1847–1860.* 1979.

Vol. 5: *Lettres à la S. Congrégation et à l'Œuvre de la Propagation de la foi, 1832–1861.* 1981.

Vol. 6: *Lettres aux Oblats de France, 1814–1825.* 1982.

Vol. 7: *Lettres aux Oblats de France, 1826–1830.* 1983.

Vol. 8: *Lettres aux Oblats de France, 1831–1836.* 1984.

Vol. 9: *Lettres aux Oblats de France, 1837–1842.* 1985.

Vol. 10: *Lettres aux Oblats de France, 1843–1849.* 1986.

Vol. 11: *Lettres aux Oblats de France, 1850–1855.* 1987.

Vol. 12: *Lettres aux Oblats de France, 1856–1861.* 1987.

Vol. 13: *Lettres à divers correspondants sur la Congrégation des O.M.I., 1815–1861,* 1989.

Vol. 14: *Écrits spirituels (1794–1811).* 1991.

Vol. 15: *Écrits spirituels (1812–1856).* 1991.

————. *Oblate Writings.* Ed. Yvon BEAUDOIN, O.M.I. Rome: General Postulation O.M.I., 1978–

Vol. 1: *Letters to North America, 1841–1850.* Trans. John Witherspoon MOLE, O.M.I. 1978.

Vol. 2: *Letters to North America, 1851–1860.* Trans. 1979.

Vol. 3: *Letters and Documents Concerning England and Ireland, 1842–1860.* Trans. John Witherspoon MOLE, O.M.I. 1979.

Vol. 4: *Letters to Ceylon and Africa, 1847–1860.* Trans. 1980.

Vol. 5: *Letters to the Sacred Congregation of Propaganda Fide and to the Society of the Propagation of the Faith, 1832–1861.* Trans. Peter. C. FARRELL. 1982.

Vol. 6: *Letters to the Oblates of France, 1814–1825.* Trans. John Witherspoon MOLE, O.M.I. 1984.

Vol. 7: *Letters to the Oblates of France, 1826–1830.* 1985. Trans. John Witherspoon MOLE, O.M.I. 1985

Vol. 8: *Letters to the Oblates of France, 1831–1836.* Trans. Michael HUGHES, O.M.I. 1985.

Vol. 9: *Letters to the Oblates of France, 1837–1842.* Trans. Bastiampillai RAYAPPU, O.M.I. 1986.

Vol. 10: *Letters to the Oblates of France, 1843–1849.* Trans. Lionel DESJAR-DINS, O.M.I. and George CAPEN, O.M.I. 1986.

Vol. 11: *Letters to the Oblates of France, 1850–1855.* Trans. John Witherspoon MOLE, O.M.I. et al. 1991.

Vol. 12: *Letters to the Oblates of France, 1856–1861.* Trans. John RHEIDT, O.M.I. 1989.

———. "Extraits du Journal du Mgr Ch.-Jos.-Eug. de Mazenod (1837–1838)." In *Missions O.M.I.*, 12 (1874), pp. 153–216.

———. "Journal d'une Mission (novembre–décembre 1816)." In *Missions O.M.I.*, 4 (1865), pp. 276–286, 418–430.

———. "Journal du Révérendissime Père Charles-Joseph-Eugène de Mazenod durant son séjour à Rome (1825–1826)." In *Missions O.M.I.*, 10 (1872), pp. 335–472.

"First Roman Journal (1825–1826)." Trans. John Witherspoon MOLE, O.M.I. In *Missions O.M.I.*, 79 (1952), pp. 197–366.
The English text is complete, i.e., it contains passages in the original mss. not included in the published French text.

———. "Lettre-Circulaire de Mgr Charles-Joseph-Eugène de Mazenod (le 2 août 1853)." In *Circulaires Administratives*, vol. 1, pp. 108–113.

"Circular Letter of Mgr. Charles Joseph Eugene de Mazenod (August 2, 1853)." Trans. in *Missions O.M.I.*, 77 (1950), pp. 120–127.

———. "Nos Saintes Règles." In *Circulaires Administratives*, vol. 1, pp. 121–130.

"Our Holy Rules." Trans. R.F. CORMICAN, O.M.I. In *Missions O.M.I.*, 77 (1950), pp. 362–379.

———. "Voyage en Afrique de Mgr Ch.-Jos.-Eug. de Mazenod, à l'occasion de la translation des reliques de Saint Augustin, en 1842." In *Missions O.M.I.*, 12 (1874), pp. 417–457.

"African Journey of Mgr. Charles J. Eugene de Mazenod (Translation of the relics of St. Augustine) 1842." Trans. R.F. CORMICAN, O.M.I. In *Missions O.M.I.*, 81 (1954), pp. 91–130.

———. "Voyage à Rome du Révérendissime Père Charles-Joseph-Eugène de Mazenod, Fondateur et Premier Supérieur Général de la Congrégation des Oblats de Marie Immaculée (1825–1826)." In *Missions O.M.I.*, 10 (1872), pp. 153–332.

"Journey to Rome of the Most Reverend Father Charles Joseph Eugene de Mazenod, Founder and First Superior General of the Congregation of the Oblates of Mary Immaculate (1825–1826)." Trans. John Witherspooon MOLE, O.M.I. In *Missions O.M.I.*, 77 (1950), pp. 380–402; In *Missions O.M.I.*, 78 (1951), pp. 199–275, 712–795.

———. "Voyage à Rome de Notre Vénéré Fondateur en 1854 pour la définition du dogme de l'Immaculée Conception." In *Missions O.M.I.*, 11 (1873), pp. 5–67.

"Second Roman Journal, Bishop de Mazenod's Diary of his visit to Rome for the Definition of the Dogma of the Immaculate Conception." Trans. R.F. CORMICAN O.M.I. In *Missions O.M.I.*, 79 (1952), pp. 698–759.

2. Constitutions and Rules of the Missionary Oblates of Mary Immaculate

Rome. Postulator's Archives. DM XI.

Ms. I, "Constitutions et Règles de la Société des Missionnaires de Provence" (Premier manuscrit français).

This ms. in Paul-Émile Duval, ed. *Écrits du Fondateur*, vol. 1. In *Missions O.M.I.*, 78 (1951), pp. 11–97.

Mss. II, IIbis, III, IV, V.

Ms. VI. "Constitutiones, Regulæ et Instituta Societatis Missionariorum Oblatorum Sanctissimæ et Immaculatæ Virginis Mariæ, Gallo-Provinciæ nuncupatorum." "Exemplar authenticum." Rome, February 17, 1826.

Constitutiones et Regulæ Congregationis Missionariorum—Oblatorum Sanctissimæ et Immaculatæ Virginis Mariæ. A Sanctissimo in Christo Patre et Domino, Domino Nostro Leone Papa XII una cum Instituto in forma specifica approbatæ. Gallipolis, 1827.

"Constitutiones, Regulæ et Instituta Societatis Missionariorum Sanctissimæ et Immaculatæ Virginis Mariæ." In Paul-Émile Duval, ed. *Écrits du Fondateur*, vol. 2, pp. 21–154. In *Missions O.M.I.*, 78 (1951), pp. 340–474.

Constitutiones et Regulæ Congregationis Missionariorum Oblatorum Sanctissimæ et Immaculatæ Virginis Mariæ, a Leone Papa XII una cum Instituto in forma specifica approbatæ, a Gregorio XVI confirmatæ, Et juxta Pii IX apostolicas litteras editæ. Marseille: Marius Olive, 1853.

Constitutiones et Regulæ Congregationis Missionariorum Oblatorum Sanctissimæ et Immaculatæ Virginis Mariæ, a Leone Papa XII una cum instituto in forma specifica approbatæ a Gregorio XVI confirmatæ, Et juxta Pii IX apostolicas letteras editæ. Tours: Typis A. Mame, Typographi, 1894.

Constitutiones et Regulæ Congregationis Missionariorum Oblatorum Sanctissimæ et Immaculatæ Virginis Mariæ, a Leone Papa XII una cum instituto in forma brevis approbatæ, a Gregorio XVI et Pio IX confirmatæ et juxta Pii X apostolicas litteras editæ. Rome, 1910.

Constitutiones et Regulæ Congregationis Missionariorum Oblatorum Sanctissimæ et Immaculatæ Virginis Mariæ, a Leone XII una cum Instituto primum adprobatæ postque Codicis Juris Canonici promulgationem a SS. D. N. Pio Papa XI in forma specifica confirmatæ. Rome, 1928.

Translations were published in French, English, German, Italian, Polish, Dutch, Swedish, and Japanese.

Constitutiones et Regulæ Congregationis Missionariorum Oblatorum Sanctissimæ et Immaculatæ Virginis Mariæ a Capitulo Generali XXVII Exaratæ. Rome, 1966. This text *ad experimentum* was published with French, English, German, Italian, Spanish, and Polish translations.

The General Chapter of 1980. *Constitutions and Rules of the Congregation of the Missionary Oblates of Mary Immaculate.* Rome, 1981. The English and French texts were official. Versions were also published in German, Spanish, and Italian. This text was promulgated and was the official text until the text approved by the Holy See was promulgated.

Constitutions et Règles de la Congrégation des Missionnaires Oblats de Marie Immaculée. Rome, 1982.
This is the official text of the Constitutions approved by the Sacred Congregation of Religious and Secular Institutes, and of the Rules approved by the 1980 general chapter.
Translations have been published in German, Dutch, Spanish, Italian, Polish, Japanese, Portuguese, Sesotho, and Bahasa Indonesia .

Constitutions and Rules of the Congregation of the Missionary Oblates of Mary Immaculate. Rome, 1982.
The Rules are the official text approved by the 1980 general chapter. The Constitutions are a translation of the approved French text.

Règles et Constitutions à l'usage des Frères Convers de la Congrégation de la Très-Sainte Vierge Marie, imprimées par ordre du Révérendissime Supérieur-Général Charles-Joseph-Eugène de Mazenod, Évêque de Marseille, etc. Marseille, 1859.
This and the other "Rules" for the brothers are summaries of the Constitutions prepared for the brothers, who could not the printed Latin texts.

Règles et Constitutions à l'usage des Frères Convers de la Congrégation de la Très-Sainte et Immaculée Vierge Marie. 2nd edition. Paris, 1877.

Rules and Constitutions for the use of the Lay Brothers of the Congregation of the Most Holy and Immaculate Virgin Mary, printed originally in French by the order of the Most Reverend Superior-General and Founder, Charles Joseph Eugene de Mazenod, Bishop of Marseilles, &c., and now Translated into English and printed by order of the Very Rev. Father Joseph Fabre, Superior-General. London, 1864.

Regeln und Einrichtungen zum Gebrauche der Laienbrüder der Kongregation der Oblaten der unbefleckten Jungfrau Maria. Lüttich, 1889.

Costituzioni e Regole della Congregazione dei Missionari Oblati di Maria Immacolata approvate insieme all'Istituto dal Papa Leone XII e dopo la promulgazione del

Nuovo Codice di Diritto Canonico riapprovate in forma specifica dalla Santità del Papa Pio XI. (Ad uso dei Fratelli Conversi). Naples, 1930.

Libellus de Instituto, Regulis et Constitutionibus Congregationis Missionariorum —Oblatum Sanctissimæ et Immaculatæ Virginis Mariæ, Candidatis Tradendus. Marseille, 1853.
This is a summary of the Constitutions for the use for candidates prior to beginning their novitiate.

Textus Constitutionum Congregationis Missionariorum Oblatorum Sanctissimæ et Immaculatæ Virginis Mariæ a Commissione Post-Capitulari de Mandato Capituli Generalis anno 1959 Celebrati a Rev.mo Patre Generali Instituta Revisus et Emendatus Capituli Generalis Proxime Venturi Approbationi Subiiciendus, una cum Regulis Capitularibus. Rome, 1966.
This is the famous *Textus Revisus* that was rejected by the 1966 general chapter.

Constitutiones et Regulæ Congregationis Missionariorum Oblatorum Sanctissimæ et Immaculatæ Virginis Mariæ, Textus renovatus et accomodatus iuxta sacrosancti Concilii Vaticani Secundi præscripta, nonnullis Congregationis sodalibus diligentur exaratus, et Capitulo Generali reverenter propositus. Rome, 1971.

Constitutions and Rules of the Congregation of the Missionary Oblates of Mary Immaculate, Proposed Text by the Revision Commission for the General Chapter of 1980. Rome, 1979.
This proposed text was published also in French, German, Italian, Spanish, and Polish.

Rome. General Archives O.M.I. Constitutions et Règles.

3. General Chapters and General Administration

Handwritten and Typed Sources

Rome. General Archives O.M.I.

"Registre des Délibérations des Chapitres Généraux de la Société des Missionnaires dits de Provence." "Actes des Chapitres Généraux de la Congrégation des Oblats de Marie Immaculée." "Chapitres Généraux." And other similar titles. 15 vols. 1818– .
The text is printed for the chapters until 1862 by Pielorz, *Les Chapitres Généraux au temps du Fondateur.*

"Procès Verbaux des Conseils Généraux de la Congrégation des Missionnaires Oblats de Marie Immaculée." 22 vols. (Vols. 16–22 are in the General Secretariat O.M.I.). 1844– .

Printed Sources

Acta Capitulorum Missionariorum Oblatorum Sanctissimæ et Immaculatæ Virginis Mariæ. 5 vols. Paris, 1867–1899. Liege (?), 1904. Rome, 1906–1949.

1972 General Chapter. *Administrative Structures*. Rome, 1972.

1972 General Chapter. *Missionary Outlook*. Rome, 1972.

Acts of the general chapter 1974. Rome: O.M.I., 1976.

Necrologium Patrum et Fratrum Congregationis Missionariorum Oblatorum B. Mariæ Virginis Immaculatæ. Rome, 1983.

General Norms for Oblate Formation. Rome: Casa Generalizia O.M.I., 1984.

JETTÉ, F., O.M.I. *Lettres aux Oblats de Marie Immaculée*. Rome: Maison Générale, 1984.
Letters to the Oblates of Mary Immaculate. Trans. of the preceding. Rome: General House, 1984.

Most of these letters of the superior general were previously published in either *Acta Administrationis Generalis O.M.I.* or in *Information O.M.I.*

Discontinued Series

Circulaires Administratives des Supérieurs Généraux aux Membres de la Congrégation des Missionnaires Oblates de M.I. 8 vols. (vols. 5–8 are double volumes —French and English). Marseille, 1850–1862. Paris, 1863–1904. Liege, 1904–1905. Rome, 1906–1972.

Missions de la Congrégation des Missionnaires Oblats de Marie Immaculée [=*Missions O.M.I.*]. 98 vols. Marseille, 1862. Paris, 1863–1902. Liege, 1903–1905. Rome, 1906–1971.
Not published 1915–1918, 1941–1946.
Letters of missionaries, superiors of missions, information of special interest to Oblates. In later years, official acts of the superior general, and of the Holy See affecting the Oblates.

Notices Nécrologiques des Membres de la Congrégation des Oblats de Marie Immaculée. 8 vols. Paris, 1868–1888. Bar-le-Duc, Belgium, 1899. Rome, 1939.

Current Publications

Acta Administrationis Generalis O.M.I. Rome, 1972– .

Communiqué O.M.I. Rome, 1972– . Issues number consecutively.

Official publication of the O.M.I. General Council's reports on its plenary sessions. Published in French, English, German, Italian, Polish, and Spanish.

Documentation O.M.I. Rome, 1968– . Issues numbered consecutively.
Monthly publication in six languages of matters of interest to Oblates.

Information O.M.I. Rome, 1967– . Issues number consecutively.
Monthly newsletter of the Congregation, published in six languages.

Personnel O.M.I. 22 vols. Marseille, 1854. Paris, 1880–1895. Liege, 1905. Rome, 1910– .

4. Books and Articles on the Missionary Oblates of Mary Immaculate[2]

ALBERS, Daniel, O.M.I. "Compte Rendu des rapports sur les noviciats de la Congrégation." In *Études Oblates*, 10 (1951), pp. 153–248.

BAIJOT, E. ,O.M.I. "La devise des Oblats de Marie." In *Missions O.M.I.*, 50 (1926), pp. 313–316.

BOBICHON, Marius, O.M.I. "Holy Scripture in the Revised Text of the Constitutions and Rules." In *Documentation O.M.I.*, 90/80 (June 1, 1980), pp. 1–7.

BOISRAMÉ, Prosper, O.M.I. *Méditations pour tous les jours de l'année à l'usage de la Congrégation des Missionnaires Oblats de Marie Immaculée.*, 3 vols. Tours: Mame et Fils, 1827.

BOUCHER, Alban, O.M.I. *Provinciaux et Vicaires des Missions dans la Congrégation des Missionnaires Oblats de Marie Immaculée 1841–1948.* Ottawa: Éditions des Études Oblates, 1949.

BOUDENS, Robrecht, o.m.i. *Mgr Ch.-J.-E. de Mazenod, Évêque de Marseille (1837–1861), et la Politique.* Lyon: Éditions du Chalet, 1951.

CARRIÈRE, Gaston, O.M.I. *Le Père du Keewatin.* Montréal: Rayonnement, 1962.

CHAMPAGNE, Claude, O.M.I. "Instruction de Monseigneur de Mazenod relative aux missions étrangères." In *Kerygma*, 9 (1975), pp. 164–177.

CIARDI, Fabio, O.M.I. "Fisonomia e natura della communità oblata nel periodo di fondazione (1815–1818)." In *Clarentianum*, 16 (1976), pp. 173–275.

———. *I fondatori uomini dello spirito, per una teologia del carisma di fondatore.* Rome: Città Nuova, 1982.

---

[2] A most thorough bibliography of de Mazenod, as founder and as bishop of Marseille, is found in each volume of Leflon's *Eugene de Mazenod*.

————. "Un projet de fusion avec les Missionnaires du Précieux Sang." In *Vie Oblate Life*, 37 (1978), pp. 65–71.

COSENTINO, Georges, O.M.I. "Armoiries de la Congrégation." In *Études Oblates*, 24 (1965), pp. 59-61.

————. "La cinquième édition des Règles (1928)." In *Études Oblates*, 12 (1953), pp. 166–182.

————. *Exercices de Piété de l'Oblat*. Ottawa: Éditions des Études Oblates, 1962.

————. "Existence juridique de notre Congrégation pendant ses dix premières années (1816–1826)." In *Études Oblates*, 12 (1953), pp. 3–24.

————. "Un formateur: le P. Maunier (1769–1844)." In *Études Oblates*, 13 (1954) pp. 219–269.

————. "La forme d'approbation de nos Règles en 1826." In *Études Oblates*, 12 (1953), pp. 234–265.

————. *Histoire de nos Règles*. 6 vols. Ottawa: Éditions des Études Oblates, 1965. A most thorough study of the Constitutions through the 1928 edition. In addition to a detailed history of all modifications, there are extensive citations of the various official texts and other pertinent documents in the original languages.

————. "Un inconnu: le P. Icard, (1790–1835)." In *Études Oblates*, 16 (1957) pp. 321–346.

————. "Un inconstant: le P. Deblieu (1789–1855)." In *Études Oblates*, 17 (1958) pp. 152–179.

————. "L'introduction des vœux dans notre Congrégation." In *Études Oblates*, 13 (1954), pp. 287–308.

————. "Notre Congrégation a-t-elle été fondée le 25 janvier 1816?" In *Études Oblates*, 15 (1956) pp. 148–158.

D'ADDIO, Angelo, O.M.I. *Cristo Crocifisso la Chiesa Abbandonata, Eugenio de Mazenod: un apassionato di Cristo e della Chiesa*. Frascati: Scolasticato O.M.I., 1979.

DOYON, Bernard, O.M.I. *The Cavalry of Christ on the Rio Grande*. Milwaukee: Bruce, 1956.

DROUART, Jean, O.M.I. "The Place Given to the Founder's Thought and Texts in Drafting the Constitutions and Rules." In *Documentation O.M.I.*, 94/80 (May 1, 1980), p. 2.

DUMAS, Auguste, O.M.I. "Galliopolis." In *Études Oblates*, 6 (1947), pp. 209–210.

GILBERT, Maurice, O.M.I. "Brèves réflexions sur le caractère sacerdotal de la Congrégation selon le Fondateur et la tradition oblate." In *Vie Oblate Life*, 39 (1980), pp. 93–101.

———. Oblate Life, Some Reflections on the New Constitutions. Trans. Frederick SACKETT, O.M.I. Ottawa, 1967.

Originally published as "Réflexions sur la vie oblate à la lumière des nouvelles Constitutions." In *Études Oblates*, 25 (1966), pp. 273–355.

GRATTON, H. "La dévotion salvatorienne du Fondateur." In *Études Oblates*, 1 (1942), pp. 157–178.

GUTHANS Jean-Baptiste, O.M.I. "Quelques réflexions sur les 'Constitutions et Règles nouvelles'." In *Études Oblates*, 28 (1969), pp. 201–218.

JEANCARD, [Jacques]. *Oraison funèbre de Monseigneur Charles-Joseph-Eugène de Mazenod, évêque de Marseille; prononcée le 4 juillet 1861, dans l'Église Saint-Martin (cathédrale provisoire) à Marseille.* Marseille, 1861. In *Missions O.M.I.*, 17 (1879), pp. 112–135.

JETTÉ, Fernand, O.M.I. Review of "La vie spirituelle d'Eugène de Mazenod," by Jósef PIELORZ, O.M.I. In In *Études Oblates*, 20 (1961), pp. 87–91.

———. *O.M.I., The Apostolic Man, A Commentary on the 1982 Oblate Constitutions and Rules.* Rome; General House, 1992.

LAFONTAINE, Paul-Henri, O.M.I. "Nature de l'approbation de nos Règles." In *Études Oblates*, 6 (1947), pp. 91–116.

LAROSE, J.M. "Les écoles pour futurs Frères Oblats." In *Études Oblates*, 21 (1962), pp. 184–188.

———. "Étude sur l'origine des frères chez les Oblats (1815–1861)." In *Études Oblates*, 12 (1953), pp. 65–126.

———. "La place des Frères coadjuteurs dans la Congrégation." In *Études Oblates*, 24 (1965), pp. 131–152.

———. "Les sources des articles des Règles concernant les frères coadjuteurs." In *Études Oblates*, 14 (1955), pp. 210–244, 278–301.

———. "Les travaux des frères." In *Études Oblates*, 17 (1958), pp. 119–151.

LAMIRANDE, E. "Les 'deux parts' dans la vie de l'homme apostolique d'après Mgr de Mazenod." In *Études Oblates*, 25 (1966), pp. 177–204.

———. "Les pauvres et les âmes abandonnées." In *Études Oblates*, 20 (1961), pp. 3–19.

LEFLON, Jean. *Eugène de Mazenod, Évêque de Marseille, Fondateur des Missionnaires Oblats de Marie Immaculée (1782–1861)*. 3 vols. Paris: Plon, 1957–1965. *Eugene de Mazenod, Bishop of Marseille, Founder of the Oblates of Mary Immaculate*, trans. Francis D. FLANAGAN, O.M.I. 4 vols. New York: Fordham University Press, 1961–1970.

LEVASSEUR, Donat, O.M.I. *A History of the Missionary Oblates of Mary Immaculate; Toward a Synthesis*. Trans. John RHEIT, O.M.I. and Aloysius KEDL, O.M.I. 2 vol. Rome, General House, 1985 and 1989.

———. *History of the Oblate Congregation*. Ottawa: Éditions des Études Oblates, 1959.

MITRI, Angelo, O.M.I. *Blessed Eugene de Mazenod, His Life and Work, His Beatification Cause*. Rome: Postulation O.M.I., 1979.

MOOSBRUGGER, Robert, O.M.I. *The Spirituality of Blessed Eugene de Mazenod, Founder of the Missionary Oblates of Mary Immaculate, from the Beginning of the Congregation (1818) until He Takes Possession of the Diocese of Marseille as Bishop (1837)*. Rome: Catholic Book Agency, 1981.

MORABITO, J. *Je serai prêtre*. Ottawa: Éditions des Études Oblates, 1954; In *Études Oblates*, 12 (1954), pp. 1–204.

MORRISEY, Francis G., O.M.I. "The Juridical Situation of Oblate Bishops in the Congregation." In *Vie Oblate Life*, 54 (1995), pp. 65–81.

MOTTE, René, O.M.I. and Alfred HUBENIG, O.M.I. "Saint Eugene de Mazenod." Ms. [1994].

O'REILLY, Michael, O.M.I. "The Approval of the 1980 Constitutions and Rules by the Holy See." In *Documentation O.M.I.*, 124/84 (March 1984), pp. 1–12.

ORTOLAN, Théophile, O.M.I. *Les Oblats de Marie Immaculée*. 2 vol.

PELLETIER, Paul-Émile, O.M.I. "The Church in the World and our New Constitutions." In *Études Oblates*, 26 (1967), pp. 254–272.

PIETSCH, J. O.M.I. "Notre Fondateur et les communautés religieuses de Marseille." In *Études Oblates*, 6 (1947), pp. 157–182; 7 (1948), pp. 211–228, 263–286.

PIELORZ, Józef, O.M.I. "À propos du F. Maur." In *Études Oblates*, 13 (1954), pp. 248–249.

———. *Les chapitres généraux au temps du Fondateur*. 2 vols. Ottawa: Éditions des Études Oblates, 1968.
Contains the text of all the general chapter minutes through 1861.

———. "Nouvelles recherches sur la Fondation de notre Congrégation," In *Études Oblates*, 83 (1956), pp. 192–253; 84 (1957), pp. 111–166.

————. "Nouvelles recherches sur notre premier Chapitre Général." In *Études Oblates*, 21 (1962) pp. 22–40.

————. "Premières missions des Missionnaires de Provence (1816–1826)." In *Missions O.M.I.*, 82 (1955), pp. 549–561; 641–655.

————. "Les rapports du Fondateur avec les curés d'Aix (1813–1826).œ In *Études Oblates*, 19 (1960) pp. 147–171; 328–367.

————. "Le séjour du Fondateur à St-Laurent et la rédaction de nos Règles (août–octobre 1818)." In *Missions O.M.I.*, 84 (1957) pp. 297–322.

————. "La vie spirituelle de Mgr de Mazenod, fondateur de la Congrégation des Missionnaires Oblats de Marie Immaculée, première partie: 1782–1812, étude critique." S.T.D. dissertation, Pontifical Gregorian University, 1954.

————. *La vie spirituelle de Mgr de Mazenod, 1782–181, étude critique.* Ottawa: Éditions des Études Oblats, 1956.

————. "Le rôle du Fondateur danx les six premiers Chapitres généraux." In *Études Oblates*, 24 (1965) pp. 267–288; 341–367.

RAMBERT, [Toussaint], O.M.I. *Vie de Monseigneur Charles-Joseph-Eugène de Mazenod, Évêque de Marseille, Fondateur de la Congrégation des Missionnaires Oblats de Marie Immaculée.* 2 vols. Tours: Mame et fils, 1883.

RESLÉ, Joseph, O.M.I. *Commentarium privatum Constitutionem et Regularum.* 5 vols. Ottawa: Études Oblats, 1956–1963.

REY, Achille, O.M.I. *Histoire de Monseigneur Charles-Joseph-Eugène de Mazenod, Évêque de Marseille, Fondateur de la Congrégation des Missionnaires Oblats de Marie Immaculée.* 2 vols. Rome: Maison Générale, 1928.

SCHARACH, P., O.M.I. *Geschichte der Kongregation der Oblaten der Unbeflekten Jungfrau Maria.* 3 vols. St. Karl: 1947–1953.

TACHÉ, Alexandre, O.M.I. "1980 Constitutions and Rules Project, Principles Underlying the Drafting of the Revised Text." In *Documentation O.M.I.*, 97/80 (September 1, 1980), p. 2.

————. "La vie spirituelle d'Eugène de Mazenod, Fondateur des Missionnaires Oblats de Marie Immaculée aux origines de la société (1812–1818)." S.T.D. dissertation. Gregorian University, 1960.

————. *La vie spirituelle d'Eugène de Mazenod, Fondateur des Missionnaires Oblats de Marie Immaculée, aux origines de la Société (1812–1818), étude historico-doctrinale.* Rome: Gregorian University, 1963.

THIEL, Joseph, O.M.I. "Relations du Fondateur avec P. Lanteri." In *Études Oblats*, 12 (1946) 129–142.

TOURIGNY, I. , O.M.I. "Le Frère oblat selon le Fondateur et la tradition oblate." In *Vie Oblate Life*, 39 (1980) 45–63.

TRUSSO, F., O.M.I. *Corso di Exercizi sulla nuova Regola*. Marigliano: Piccola Opera dell Redenzione, 1977.

VILLENEUVE, J.-M.-R., O.M.I. "Étude analytico-synthétique de nos Stes Règles des Miss. O.M.I. avec comparison des diverses éditions et rapprochements des décisions capitulaires, actes de visites et traditions de famille en guise de commentaires." 3 vols. Ottawa, 1929. (Typewritten).

WOESTMAN, William H., O.M.I., "De Mazenod and Military Chaplaincy," in *Vie Oblate Life*, 47 (1988), pp. 41-43.

5. Encyclopedia, Reports, and Other Publications

"Comparative Statistics 1980–1982." In *Information O.M.I.*, 195/83 (February 1983), p. 1.

The Congregation Renewed. Rome: The General House, 1968.

"The Congress on the Charism of the Founder Today." (Rome: 26 April – 14 May 1976), *Documentation O.M.I.*, 65/76, pp. 1–14.

Dizionario degli Istituti de Perfezione. S.v. "Oblati de Maria Immaculata," by Fabio CIARDI, O.M.I.

Études de la Province de Saint-Joseph sur le projet de revision des Constitutions et des Regulæ Capitulares paru dans "Missions," Nos 317 et 317bis. Montréal: Maison Provinciale, 1965.

Études Oblates. Since 1974 *Vie Oblate Life*. 43 vols. Ottawa, 1942– .
Trimestral review published by the Oblates of St. Joseph's Province, Canada. Founder Maurice GILBERT, O.M.I..
All Oblates have a debt of gratitude to Gilbert, G. Carrière, his sucessor, and Romuald Boucher, o.m.i., present editor, and their collaborators for the multitude and value of the research sponsored, articles published, and books reviewed.

1980 General Chapter. "From the Capitulars to all their Oblate Brothers." In *Information O.M.I.*, 171/80 (December 1980), pp. 1–2.

"The Oblate Brother, Replies to a Questionnaire." In *Documentation O.M.I.*, 126/84, pp. 1–12, 128/84, pp. 1–12 (May and August 1984).

Rapport sur les Provinces et Vicariats 1932. Rome: 1932.

Sociological Survey for the 1972 Chapter. Rome: 1972.

"Todos somos Misioneros." In *Chasqui*, 12 (November 1983), pp. 10–11. Trans. *Newsletter* (Missionary Oblates of Mary Immaculate, Saint Paul, Minnesota) no. 206, pp. 14–15 (January 1984).

III — Other Canonical, Historical, and Theological Works
1. Books and Articles

ANDRÉS GUTIÉRREZ, D.X., C.M.F. "Constitutiones congruenter recognoscantur." In *Commentarium pro Religiosis*, 46 (1967), pp. 270–292.

————. "Participatio laicorum in regimine religionis clericalis." In *Commentarium pro Religiosis*, 46 (1967), pp. 377–387.

————. "Innovationes in Parte III libri II novi Codicis, quæ est De institutis vitæ consecratæ et de societatibus vitæ apostolicæ." In *Commentarium pro Religiosis*, 64 (1983), pp. 5–72.

BOYLE, Paul, C.P. "Attention to the Person and to Present-Day Sensitivity." In *USC Conventus Mensilis*, 10–12 February 1982, 16–17.

BROCKHAUS, T..A., O.S.B. *Religious Who Are Known as Conversi, A Historical Synopsis and Commentary.* Washington: Catholic University of America Press, 1946.

CAPPELLO, F.M., S.J. *Summa Iuris Canonici in usum scholarum concinnata.* 3 vols. 4th ed. Rome: Gregorian University, 1945.

COSTE, M. *Essai sur la Conduite que peuvent se proposer de tenir les Prêtres appelés à travailler au rétablissement de la Religion Catholique en France.* 3rd. ed. 1801.

CREUSEN, I., S.J. "De iuridica status religiosi evolutione brevis synopsis historica." In *Periodica*, 31 (1941), pp. 143–155, 216–241.

DESPONT, J. *Nouvel Atlas des Missions.* Paris: Oeuvre de la Propagation de la Foi, 1951.

FANFANI, L.I., O.P. *De Iure Religiosorum ad Normam Codicis Iuris Canonici.* 3rd. ed. Rovigo: Istituto Padano di Arti Grafiche, 1949.

FLEMING, D.A., S.M. "Who should be superior?" *Origins, NC Documentary Service*, 5 (April 1976), pp. 694–699.

FUERTES, J. , C.M.F. "Charisma et vita religiosa." In *Commentarium pro Religiosis*, 59 (1978), pp. 211–227, 305–329; 60 (1979), pp. 3–26.

————. "Commentarium in Rescriptum Pontificium 'Cum admotæ,' Facultas n. 13." In *Commentarium pro Religiosis*, 45 (1966), pp. 52–69.

GUTIÉRREZ, Anatasius. "Canones circa instituta vitæ consecratæ et societatis vitæ apostolicæ vagantes extra earum partem." In *Commentarium pro Religiosis*, 64 (1983), pp. 73–96; 65 (1984), pp. 7–22; 207–222; 315–325.

HAYES, Carlton J.H. *A Political and Cultural History of Modern Europe*. 2 vols. 1939 edition. New York: Macmillan, 1951.

HOSTIE, R. *Vie et Mort des Ordres Religieux*. Paris: Desclée de Brouwer, 1972.

JETTÉ, Fernand, O.M.I. "Le retour au Fondateur." In *La vie des Communautés Religieuses*, 26 (1968), pp. 307–315.

LARRAONA, A., C.M.F. "Commentarium in Partem Secundam libri Codicis, quæ est: de Religiosis." In *Commentarium pro Religiosi*, 1 (1920), pp. 16–21, 45–50, 133–140, 171–177, 209–211; 2 (1921), pp. 273–287; 23 (1942), pp. 182–186.

————. "Consultationes." In *Commentarium pro Religiosis*. 3 (1922), pp. 10–13.

————. "Questio Canonica." In *Commentarium pro Religiosis*, 4 (1923), pp. 113–119.

LATREILLE, A. et al. 3 vols. *Histoire du Catholicism en France*. Paris: Éditions Spes, 1957.

LEFLON, Jean. *La crise révolutionnaire (1789–1846)*. Fliche-Martin, no. 20. Paris: Bloud et Gay, 1949.

LESAGE, Germain, O.M.I. *L'Accession des Congrégations à l'État religieux canonique*. Ottawa: Éditions de l'Université d'Ottawa, 1952.

MOLINARI, P. , S.J. "Renewal of Religious Life according to the Founder's Spirit." In *Review for Religious*, 27 (1968), pp. 796–806.

OCHOA, X., C.M.F. "Modus determinandi patrimonium constitutionale cuiusvis instituti perfectionis proprium." In *Commentarium pro Religiosis*, 48 (1967), pp. 337–350; 49 (1968), pp. 97–111.

O'CONNOR, Edward, C.S.C. "Vatican II and the Renewal of Religious Life." In *Review for Religious*, 26 (1967), pp. 404–423.

ONSTENK, Nicolaus, S.V.D. "De Constitutione S. Pii V 'Circa pastoralis' super clausura monialium et tertiariorum." In *Periodica*, 40 (1951), 210–230.

PAVENTI, S. *La Chiesa Missionaria*. Rome: Unione Missionaria del Clero in Italia, 1949.

PUGLIESE, A. "De Mutatione Classis apud Religiosos." In *Monitor Ecclesiasticus*, 87 (1962), pp. 498–514.

ROUSSEAU, Joseph, O.M.I. "De Relationibus Iuridis Religiosorum cum Sacra Hierarchia Recognoscendis." In *Apollinaris*, 60 (1967), pp. 215–263.

SASTRE SANTOS, Eutimio, C.M.F. "De normis ad Codices Congregationum religiosarum recognoscendos." In *Commentarium pro Religiosis*, 59 (1978), pp. 128–175.

———. "I fratelli laici nei nostri istituti." In *Commentarium pro Religiosis*, 66 (1985), pp. 289–305.

SEUMOIS, André, O.M.I. *Introduction à la missiologie*. Schöneck-Beckenried, Switzerland: Neue Zeitschrift für Missionswissenschift, 1952.

———. *Théologie Missionnaire*. 5 vols. Rome: Bureau de Presse O.M.I., 1973–1981.

———. *Teologia missionaria*. Bologna: Edizioni Dehonine, 1993

SEVRIN, E. *Les missions religieuses en France sous la Restauration (1815–1830)*. 2 vols. Paris: Procure des Prêtres de la Miséricorde, 1948; Libraire Philosophie Vain, 1959.

TERZI, I. "Brothers in Clerical Institutes." In *USG Conventus Mensilis*, 10 February 1982, pp. 14–15.

THOMAS AQUINAS, *Summa Theologicæ*. Ed. P. Carmello according to the Leonine Edition. Turin: Marietti, 1952.

VERMEERSCH, A., S.J. and I. CREUSEN, S.J. *Epitome Iuris Canonici*. 3 vols. 5th. ed. Malines: Dessain, 1933.

ZEPP, P. "Überblick über das Religiosenrecht des CIC 1983." In *Ordens-Korrespondenz*, 25 (1984), pp. 6–30.

2. Encyclopedia, Reports, and Other Publications

"Les Congrégation Séculières," In *Analecta Juris Pontificii*, 3 (1861), pp. 52–103, 147–217.

"Brothers in clerical Institutes." In *USG Communicatio Sanctæ Sedis*, circ. 1/83 (January 15, 1983), pp. 8–9.

"Brothers and Priests in the Same Institute, Conclusions." In *USG Conventus Mensilis*, 10–12 February 1982, pp. 19–20.

The Catholic Encyclopedia. S.v. "Sodality," by J. HILGERS.

"Constitutions—leur rédaction—leur approbation." In *Consilium "16"* (Unione Internazionale delle Superiore Generali), Circ. 10/79 (23 February 1979), pp. 2–6.

Dictionnaire de Droit Canonique. S.v. "Congrégation Religieuse," by J. Creusen.

Enciclopedia Cattolica. S.v. "Congregazione Mariana," by E. Villaret.

"Index articulorum pro redigendis constitutionibus." In *Commentarium pro Religiosis*, 59 (1978), pp. 191–200; 61 (1980), pp. 144–145.

"Orientations pour les Constitutions." In *Concilium "16."* (Unione Superiore Generali). Circ. 3/74 (25 January 1974), pp. 1–3; E. Gamberi. "Annexe au Conseil '16' du 25 January 1974." pp. 1–7.

Appendix I

To Oblates in First Formation
The Priestly Character of the Congregation

Dear Brother Oblates:

This letter of communication comes to you at an important moment in the Congregation's journey, for it is preparing for the general chapter. Every chapter leaves its mark on the Congregation's life. If we are properly prepared and open to the inspiration of the Holy Spirit, a chapter is a moment of grace, unity, and religious apostolic renewal for the worldwide Oblate community.

A number of reasons have influenced me to choose the topic of this letter, the 1990 Synod of Bishops on the formation of priests for today's Church and world and the post-synodal exhortation of John Paul II are the ecclesial context. It is the Oblate charism, however, and the manner of living it that suggest and prompt this reflection on an aspect of every Oblate's life.

Some sectors of the Congregation know only the Oblate priest, so much so that our community is referred to in an erroneous way. In other sectors we find a tendency to deny our priestly character, and this in the name of our evangelizing mission or because all of our members are equal. In other instances we have lost the sense of evangelization as the proclaiming of Jesus Christ and the forming of Christian communities and that precisely because this aspect of our vocation has remained obscure.

In point of fact, the Congregation of the Missionary Oblates of Mary Immaculate founded by Eugene de Mazenod includes priests and brothers and is by its very nature priestly and clerical.

The Preface of the Constitutions and Rules recalls the fact that the apostolic men called to respond together with Eugene de Mazenod to the missionary challenges facing the Church were priests: "The sight of these evils has so touched the heart of certain priests, zealous for the glory of God, men with an ardent love for the Church, that they are willing to give their lives, if need be, for the salvation of souls. They are convinced that if priests could be formed, afire with zeal for men's salvation, priests not given to their own interests, solidly grounded in virtue—in a word, apostolic men . . ., there would be ample reason to believe that in a short while people who have gone astray might be brought back to their long-unrecognized responsibilities."

269

In the new Constitutions, the Holy See wanted the priestly character of the Congregation to be mentioned in the very first article, even though this was expressed in equivalent terms in Constitution 7.

This dimension of our charism is not something that is secondary, something linked to the founding of the Institute and to the passing of needs of that time: it is something that is of the essence and therefore a permanent aspect of our vocation. This dimension affects all our members, be they priests or brothers; it qualifies the purpose and missionary priority of the Institute; and has its repercussions on the latter's structures and even more on its spirituality.

Our charism is modeled on Eugene de Mazenod's experience

The Oblate charism is a gift that the Spirit has transmitted through a concrete person, Eugene de Mazenod. The Lord prepared this gift through the Founder's personal experience, one that was marked by the vocation of the priesthood.[1]

After hearing in his childhood the call to the priesthood, Eugene in his youth followed other ideals, a refusal that he thereafter looked upon as a state of sin.[2] His conversion experience of Good Friday in 1807 bore its full fruit in his choosing the priesthood at time when the Church was being persecuted and abandoned. While a seminarian in Paris, he wrote to his mother on June 29, 1808: "What the Lord wants of me is to do is that I renounce the world . . . that I most especially dedicate myself to his service in order to strive to reawaken the faith that is dying out among the poor; in a word, that I am disposed to carry out all the orders he may wish to give me for his glory and the salvation of souls whom he has redeemed by his precious blood."[3] The formation he received at Saint-Sulpice deeply marked Eugene's life and spirituality,[4] and that in continuity with the Good Friday experience wherein he had discovered the crucified Christ as his Savior and the Savior of all mankind.

---

[1] I. TOURIGNY, "Le charisme sacerdotal du bx Eugène de Mazenod," in *Vie Oblate Life*, 36 (1977), pp. 151–172.

[2] See Y. BEAUDOIN, Introduction to *Blessed Eugene de Mazenod: Spiritual Writings*, Oblate Writings, 14, 1804–1811, Rome, 1991, pp. xvi–xxvi.

[3] Ibid., p. 63.

[4] J. MORABITO, *"Je serai prêtre"; Eugène de Mazenod de Venise à Saint-Sulpice (1794–1811)*, Ottawa, 1954.

The first years of his ministry were dedicated to young people for whom he founded an association, to workers in the city, and to prisoners: preaching and Christian formation in their regard was his primary concern. The evangelization needs of the rural population, the limits of individual pastoral activity, and the search for a holy, exemplary priestly life impelled him to found a community of priests who were true missionaries and committed to their own sanctification.

The Rules drawn up in 1818 as well as those approved by Leo XII in 1826 and revised in 1853, reflect the priestly ideal and apostolic experience of Eugene and his companions. The Preface and some of the more significant texts are quoted in the new Constitutions. They speak of zealous priests who are sent out to conquer the world, who are ready to sacrifice everything "for the love of Jesus Christ, and the sanctification of their brethren . . ."; priests who are committed "to all the works of zeal which priestly charity can inspire, above all to the work of the missions"; "holy priests who, filled with the Holy Spirit and striving to walk in the footsteps of the divine Shepherd, feed with watchful and constant care the sheep that have been led back to him."[5]

This ideal, put into practice by the Founder and by so many Oblates, has called forth apostolic initiatives and commitment to holiness. Side by side with Oblates known throughout the Congregation for their zeal, such as Fathers Gérard and Albini for example, each one of us knows other fellow Oblates who are truly animated by priestly charity in evangelizing and serving the poorest of the poor. I think one could comment on the Constitutions and Rules not only by means of selected texts of the Founder, but by means of the life lived by so many Oblates in every part of the world.

The evangelizing purpose that flows from our priestly character

Evangelizing the poor (C. 1), proclaiming the Good News to those who have not yet heard it or to those who are beyond the reach of ecclesial structures (C. 5), the evangelizing creativity of awakening or reawakening the faith, making known who Christ is especially through proclaiming God's Word which finds its fullness in the celebration of the sacraments and in serving one's neighbor (C. 7), are equivalent descriptions of the priestly purpose that is part and parcel of the Oblate charism.

---

[5] Preface of the Constitutions and text on p. 74.

The Church's mission is carried on in many manners and ways, as the missionary encyclical of John Paul II reminds us.[6] All Christians are coresponsible according to each one's state and charism.[7] The missionary priority assigned to our Congregation is priestly, precisely because it is oriented to proclaiming the Good News and to establishing Christian communities. As Oblates our particular and primary—not exclusive—contribution to the Church's mission is "principally the evangelization of the poor."

Since the 1966 chapter, the Constitutions and Rules distinguish ministries from purpose. The purpose of evangelizing the poor can be achieved through different ministries according to places and needs. The evangelizing purpose is no longer identified with the ministry of parish missions, as it was in the first Rule, even though a significant historical value is attached to it (see R. 2). Thus there is unity in the purpose of the various forms of the apostolic activity that we carry on in areas of a Christian tradition or in mission territories (see C. 5).

The priority given by our Oblate tradition and our present Constitutions to proclamation is in line with the missionary mandate reaffirmed in the encyclical *Redemptoris missio* and constitutes the great ecclesial challenge in a pluralistic world, often indifferent and to a great part non-Christian.

Proclamation is the permanent priority of mission. The Church cannot elude Christ's explicit mandate, nor deprive men and women of the "Good News" about their being loved and saved by God. "Evangelization will always contain—as the foundation, center, and at the same time the summit of its dynamism—a clear proclamation that, in Jesus Christ . . . salvation is offered to all men, as a gift of God's grace and mercy (*Evangelii nuntiandi*, no. 27[8]). All forms of missionary activity are directed to this proclamation, which reveals and gives access to the mystery hidden for ages and made know in Christ (cf. *Eph* 3:3–9; *Col* 1:25–29), the mystery which lies at the heart of the Church's mission and life, as the hinge on which all evangelization turns.

In the complex reality of mission, initial proclamation has a central and irreplaceable role, since it introduces man "into the mystery of the love of God, who invites him to enter into a personal relationship with himself in Christ" (*Ad gentes*, no. 13[9]) and opens the way to conversion. Faith is born of preaching,

---

[6] See JOHN PAUL II, encyclical letter, *Redemptoris missio*, December 7, 1990, in *AAS* (1991), pp. 24–340, nos. 41–60

[7] Ibid., nos. 61–86.

[8] PAUL VI, apostolic exhortation, *Evangelii nuntiandi*, December 8, 1975, in *AAS*, 68 (1976), pp. 5–76.

[9] VATICAN II, decree on the Church's missionary activity, *Ad gentes*. December 7, 1965.

and every ecclesial community draws its origin and life from the personal response of each believer to that preaching (see *Evangelii nuntiandi*, nos. 13–15). Just as the whole economy of salvation has its center in Christ, so too all missionary activity is directed to the proclamation of this mystery.[10]

There is a deep syntonic resonance between our Constitutions and Rules and the missionary encyclical in regard to the priority of proclamation or evangelization.[11] For us the priority of proclamation is a consequence that flows from the priestly character of the Congregation, according to the manner and example of the Apostles whom the original Rule presents as our first fathers. Through the activity of the Spirit and its acceptance in faith, the Word constitutes Christian communities and attains its fullness in the celebration of the Eucharist. Establishing and caring for Christian communities are not opposed to evangelization but are a consequence thereof. As missionaries, however, we must make these communities missionaries in turn in regard to the persons and culture of the environment in which they live.[12]

The very organizational structure of the Congregation is influenced by its clerical character but those in charge are to be priests. This is obligatory for major superiors whereas on the local level someone who is not ordained may be a superior with the permission of the Holy See.

A charism with a priestly spirituality

The priestly character of the Congregation also affects our Oblate spirituality. Christ is perceived as Savior, as he who out of love has redeemed us and the whole of mankind by his blood. He is not only the object of our ministry but also the model of its execution.

The Eucharist is the very center of our personal and community existence. In Christ present in the Eucharist Oblates find the source of their unity and communion, even when circumstances of their missionary commitment keep them at a distance from each other. Constitution 33 well expresses the centrality of the Eucharist as the source and summit of the Church's life:

> We will live such lives as to be able to worthily celebrate it every day. As we participate in its celebration with all our being, we offer ourselves with Jesus the Savior; we are renewed in the mystery of our cooperation with him, drawing the bonds of our apostolic community ever closer and opening the horizons of our zeal to all the world.

---

[10] Ibid., no. 44.

[11] Ibid., nos. 2, 20, 23, 31, 34, 44, and 58.

[12] Ibid., nos. 20, 26, 27, 48, 49, 51, and 53.

What the Founder lived during his entire lifetime is what he wrote in 1812 on the occasion of his ordination:

> Please God that my whole life be dedicated to this sublime ministry. I will convert a greater number of souls through my diligence at the altar than with the preaching that I might do.

For many Oblates the Eucharist is not only the source of their life but also the only form of their ministry. In the Sahara and other places where there is no Christian community, they find in the celebration of the Eucharist the ultimate motive for their presence and the strength of their gratuitous witness. We ask ourselves the same question as did Brother Gabriel Tessier, forty years a missionary in Cameroon (he died on April 23, 1991), who wrote in his notes:

> Does the Mass make me a sower of joy, a bridge between God and my brothers? Does my life at every moment reflect faith, hope, and trust in God? May the Mass make me a builder of hope amid those around me, may my life as a Christian and a religious make me a living Gospel, a bearer of the Good News.

All of our prayer is marked by our missionary being; that is why "we come before him bearing with us the daily pressures of our anxiety for those to whom he sends us" (C. 32). Because of this apostolic spirituality, our prayer contemplates the Lord not only in himself but also in his mystery of love and of salvation for persons, cultures, and religions, whereby it adapts itself to different spiritual traditions and makes them into an Areopagus of evangelization.[13] The very events of our lives and ministry itself are avenues of encounter with the Lord (see CC. 31, 33, and 56).

Praying the divine office is not only a duty that the Church lays upon her ministers and a way of continuing the tradition of the monastic orders, but also a way of carrying out our Oblate mission.[14]

Ministry in regard to priests

The Founders' ideal and the goal of our founding was to provide the Church with priests who evangelize and who are holy; this is rather strongly expressed in the Preface, the result of a Gospel reading of the situation and the response to be given thereto. Oblates are called to be these evangelizing priests and holy priests. If we are not, that would mean that we are unfaithful to the charism of our vocation in the Church.

---

[13] Ibid., no. 38.

[14] See C. 53; cf. *Redemptoris missio*, no. 20; and N. SCHAFF, "La Psalmodie divin en commun," in *Études oblates*, 9 (1950), pp. 115–128.

The Founder quickly became aware that the Congregation had to try and transmit such a priestly ideal to those outside her ranks by means of giving example, promoting welcome and animation and taking on seminary formation. Thus formation of the clergy became one of the Congregation's ends. This too remains for us a challenge and a criterion for evaluating our performance. Are we an example, an attractive and constructive force for a clergy that evangelizes and is holy? An answer requires more finesse than simply counting the number of seminarians whom we animate and the number of Oblates involved in clergy formation. Such self-examination is ever more necessary today in a crisis situation that affects us at least as much as it does other priests.

Ministry promoting the formation of the clergy does not start with a special obedience or once we are involved in ministry. Eugene de Mazenod wanted scholastics to be an example to the seminarians with whom they were studying and were in contact. Today such opportunities of contact are even more frequent, for most of you are taking your studies together with other seminarians. We do not need to adopt the attitude of being others' teachers; nevertheless our authentic witness can affect others. Furthermore, such a duty begins within our Oblate communities in regard to our fellow brothers, for whom we are responsible by virtue of our religious commitment and a specific vow (C. 29).

An outstanding witness

Father Deschâtelets, superior general from 1947 to 1972 , underlined in his circular letter no. 191 of 1951 the characteristic traits of the Oblate vocation and its originality. He wrote:

First and foremost, we are *priests* . . . Priests among so many other priests, but priests with a special inspiration which give a particular outline to the priesthood of an Oblate. We are priests so that we may restore to the priesthood all its glory, all its prestige, and, by the example of our lives, carry along with us all those who, like ourselves, are signed with the sacred character of holy orders. In laying the foundations of his Institute, our Founder did indeed plan to work for the conversion of the masses, but he also had in mind the reform and sanctification of the clergy. It was for this reason that, from the beginning, he demanded that his disciples follow so high, so perfect a standard of priestly life . . .

We know that emphatic insistence upon the necessity of sanctity in the priest is no new thing within the Church. On this, as on many other points, Father de Mazenod is in perfect accord with all the great apostles of the priesthood. . . . Let us try, dear Oblates, to grasp the full import of our Founder's message. Let us be priests in the very front rank of the Church's priests. Let us not be mere mediocrities, priests whom our Founder described as "common goods of little value"; he did not want such men as his associates. That we may attain the standard he desired, let our spiritual life be firmly based upon the richest elements of a priestly life which draws forth from the sacrament of orders a most intense vitality. . . .

. . . Priestly charity should saturate our lives, it should be the motive of all our actions, it should be the very air that we breath . . . Even our religious mentality itself is conditioned by priestly charity to such an extent that the Oblate who would subordinate sacerdotal grace to the grace of his religious vocation would falsify the basic orientation of his Oblate life. The Oblate is, and ought to remain, both priest and religious. Neither status can be separated from the other if he wishes to remain a true Oblate of Mary Immaculate.

. . . The Oblate may not be as other priests, he must be the model priest. The grace of his special vocation sweeps him upwards to the very heights, it calls on him to set the standard and to assist in the formation of a worthy priesthood. . . . The Preface is indeed the synthesis of the Rule. Moreover, it reminds us in terms which admit no ambiguity of our obligation to priestly holiness—*verbo et exemplo*—so that whenever the priesthood falls into a feeble state, we may be able to restore it.[15]

A charism shared by priests and brothers

Our priestly purpose and spirituality have never excluded the presence of brothers in the Congregation and the full sharing of the same charism; I would say that the brothers help the Congregation better to live this dimension of its vocation.

The modality of relationships between priests and brothers and the forms of ministry carried out by the latter have varied according to times and places. The name was changed from lay brother to coadjutor brother. The brother's activity was often seen as a support to that of the priest; rather, it is complementary.

It would certainly be impossible to grasp the organization and development of our missions *ad gentes* without the presence and work of the brothers. The Oblate presence among the Amerindians of Canada, among the Africans of Lesotho and of Namibia would have been substantially different if they had not been there. The ecclesial and even the civil structures of various countries are the result of the brother's activity. Their influence, however, has been more radical than the fruit of their labors. They have wielded an influence through their being and example not only through their work. They have transmitted

---

[15] Léo DESCHÂTELETS, "Our Vocation and Our Life of Intimate Union with Mary Immaculate," *Circulaires*, August 15, 1951, no. 191, vol. 5, pp. 298–386; an official English text was published with the page numbers 1–91; the reference are to this booklet; pp. 8–9, 19–20, 14, and 15.

important Gospel values, such as the meaning of work in societies that despised the same, the worship of God in the ordinary things of life, the gratuitousness of the religious life, the sense of prayer, simplicity, and closeness to people.

What is even more impressive to me is the fact that the brothers have been very much aware of the priestly character of the Oblate charism. I have met brothers who have deeply affected my Oblate life and that of others in formation houses and in our apostolic communities. Some brothers who are more known in the Congregation are noteworthy for their contribution to the vocation and perseverance of priests, their sense of priesthood, their spirituality.

Brother Anthony Kowalczyk, whose cause for beatification is introduced in Rome, has always been referred to as a pillar in the apostolic school of Edmonton and in the provinces of Western Canada. Many attribute their growth and fidelity in their priestly vocation to the influence of this Servant of God, to his prayer, word and example. Several have testified that they overcame trials and temptations thanks to his word and prayer, not only during the period of their first formation but also when they were already engaged in in ministry.

In regard to Brother Ernest Gauthier, the doorkeeper at the University Seminary in Ottawa, a number of people have stated that they had recourse to him in their difficulties and that his influence was more decisive for them than that of the professors and formators they had been assigned. These and other brothers did not claim for themselves roles that pertain to others; rather they fully lived out their own specific Oblate vocation.

The presence of brothers in a clerical Congregation reminds us that our specific mission is entrusted to the community before it is to persons. To carry out its mission a community needs different and complementary contributions. Their presence reminds us that the mission depends on our being, first of all, more than on what we do. The quality of our life wields its influence not only through example but also by means of our collaboration in the saving work of Christ.

Complementarity in the same charism

"We come together in apostolic communities of priests and brothers, united to God by the vows of religion" (C. 1). Not only the religious life but all the elements of our charism are shared by the brothers and priests who incarnate two vocations within one and the same charism. In this full sharing of the charism by two distinct vocations there are complementary ways of living it. I will treat of only two values more pertinent to our topic, namely our priestly and our Marian character.

The double manner of participating in the one and only priesthood of Christ makes the presence of priests and brothers complementary. The ministerial priesthood reminds us that the Church is a gift of God, that the sacraments are not realities that the community gives to itself but which it received from Christ's mercy. The common priesthood allows us to receive the sacraments and makes the whole of one's life a worship of God, a witness to people. Basically speaking, the common priesthood reminds us and brings it about that our ordinary life is transformed by God and becomes a cult addressed to him and a witness and service to our neighbor.

Hence, there is complementarily between the two forms of sharing Christ's one and only priesthood even within a clerical Congregation. The priests consecrate the Eucharist and administer the sacraments; the brothers are a reminder that the whole of life ought to be a worship acceptable to God, the eucharist of all that is created and of our whole existence. While the ministerial priesthood underlines God's gift, the common priesthood requires response and acceptance of this gift on our part. All of us come together in the one and only eucharistic sacrifice so that our whole life may be acceptable to God and of benefit to this Church.

The role of Mary illustrates in another way the place of the brother within the Congregation. All of us ought to have a tender devotion towards our Mother and to find in her the model of our consecrated life. The brother in the community, however, represents Mary in a special way. Mary is not a ministerial priest. And yet she gave birth to Jesus the priest, educated Jesus for his mission, and accompanied him especially in the supreme act of salvation by means of the cross: *stabat*, John says. And she accompanied the Apostles, from Cana where they began to recognize Christ's divinity to the Cenacle where she was present while they were waiting for the Holy Spirit and at the outset of the mission.

In a clerical Congregation the brother takes Mary's place: he is a presence of Mary, a discreet role and presence, important and necessary. Concretely this often takes on the form of simple services, such as Mary provided at Nazareth; on other occasions it means taking part in community and apostolic activities; always it is a following of Christ and a cooperating by means of one's being even unto the cross and apparent defeat like on Calvary; more often it means taking part in prayer as in the Cenacle.

The brother is a great gift to the Congregation, a Marian presence in view of achieving the same common mission of evangelizing the poor. Can we conceive the mission of Jesus without Mary? Can we think of the Oblate mission without the brothers?

I believe Blessed Eugene de Mazenod would agree with these reflections of mine: he sensed the beauty of the religious vocation thanks to a brother with whom he lived during his first years as a priest. This contact with a brother was not irrelevant to our founding.

Living the priesthood within the charism

If all Oblates are called to live the priestly character of the Congregation, this is true for the person who has the specific vocation and the ministerial priesthood. Every Oblate must exercise and live his priesthood within the Oblate charism. The Oblate priest is not a diocesan priest. He is to live out his missionary quality in whatever ministry assigned to him: he is to give priority to evangelizing the poor, those who are far away, those who are beyond the reach of Church structures or have never been Christian (see C. 5). He is to develop apostolic creativity and courage (see C. 8) and effect an integral evangelization that promotes all the aspects of the person and society (see C.9). He is to be engaged in establishing Christian communities that are missionary in their own milieu and open to the world at large. For this too he is to be a man of community and communion with the Congregation that lives out the mission in so many contexts.

In the graced moment in which the Church and world live today, missionary challenges are not lacking. Today we need to commit ourselves to evangelizing Christian communities that are to live and radiate their own faith in a new context. Above all we need to commit ourselves to a new evangelization of those who are no longer Christian and to be available and active in evangelizing those who have never been Christian. This triple commitment addressed to the entire Church[16] is a renewing challenge to our Congregation whose end is the evangelization of the poor.

If every priest today is invited to discover the missionary dimension of his vocation, this is all the more true for us Oblates. The Congregation does not prepare an Oblate to carry out a personal mission and to be loaned to a local Church. He carries out his apostolate as an Oblate who integrates the various aspects of our charism. "Oblates are committed to the missionary work as members of the Congregation and of their respective provinces" (R. 1). Our charism ought to imbue the Congregation's priests with a particular style and dynamism.

---

[16] See *Redemptoris missio*, nos. 32–34.

Common and differentiated formation

The Constitutions and Rules have a section that is rather elaborated on formation after the novitiate: it is divided into three parts, one that is general, one for those going on to the priesthood, and another for those oriented to the life of a brother (cf. CC 65-67). The period in temporary vows is to be seen as a time of initial formation for all. Practices and places of formation vary according to Provinces and countries. In an ever growing number of cases formation is in common even though programs may be distinct. This can be beneficial for the future life in common and for an adapted insertion into the Church of today when theological formation is being given to more and more laity. However, there must also be a specific formation both for those who are preparing to be priests and for those who are preparing themselves as brothers. Besides being a means of making it a reality, commitment to an adequate formation is a sign of the authenticity of one's vocation.

In both vocations an eventual change of choice is foreseen: a person who had intended the priesthood may discern a call to the brotherhood, and someone who wanted to consecrate himself as a brother may discern a call to the priesthood. This openness to making a change prior to perpetual vows reflects the present situation which foresees a common novitiate for the two states of life, during which the common aspects of the charism and the dimensions of religious life are stressed. This is also due to the fact that today a choice is made more gradually and a greater discernment is required. Perpetual oblation ought to mark the conclusion of one's choice, an option that should never be made lightly.

A prayer as a wish and a greeting

In the *Oblate Prayer* book, we find after the midday examen, two or three prayers (depending on the language editions): one focuses on our ministerial priesthood and the other on fraternal charity. May these prayers be lived realities for each one of us. The one which speaks of the priestly character is also my wish for you:

> O Lord, our High Priest and Victim,
> You refresh with your own Body and Blood
> those who are consecrated to you and your service.
> Grant that we who share in your priesthood
> may walk worthy of the vocation to which we are called,
> and may ever nourish your people
> both by word and by example.

Rome, 25th January 1992   Marcello Zago, O.M.I.
                                           Superior General

Appendix II
John Paul II Addresses Relgious Men

Religious Life Can Greatly Assist Priests[1]

1. There are deep affinities between the priesthood and religious life. Actually, down the centuries the number of religious priests has increased. In most cases these are men who, having entered a religious institute, were ordained priests within it. Less frequent, but still numerous, are the cases of priests incardinated in a diocese who subsequently join a religious institute. Both cases show that in male consecrated life the vocation to a religious institute is very frequently associated with a vocation to the priestly ministry.

2. We can ask ourselves what the religious life contributes to the priestly ministry and why, in God's plan, so many men are called to this ministry within the framework of religious life. Let us answer that, if it is true that priestly ordination itself entails a personal consecration, entering religious life predisposes the subject to accept the grace of priestly ordination better and to live its requirements more completely. The grace of the evangelical counsels and of community life has been shown to foster the acquisition of the "holiness" required by the priesthood because of the priest's function with respect to the Eucharistic and Mystical Body of Christ.

Furthermore, the striving for perfection that marks and characterizes religious life encourages the ascetic effort to make progress in virtue, to grow in faith, hope and especially charity, and to live a life that conforms to the Gospel ideal. To this end, institutes offer formation so that religious may be firmly guided from their youth in a life of holiness and acquire solid convictions and habits of life that are evangelically austere. In these spiritual conditions, they can draw greater benefit from the graces which accompany priestly ordination.

3. Nevertheless, before religious vows become obligations assumed in connection with Holy Orders and the ministry, they have an inherent value as a response of oblative love to the One who with infinite love "offered himself freely" for our sake (cf. Is 53:12; Heb 9:28). Thus the commitment to celibacy is not primarily a requirement for the diaconate or the priesthood, but adherence to an ideal that requires the total gift of self to Christ.

---

[1] JOHN PAUL II, address at general audience, February 15, 1995, in OR, February 16, 1996; Eng. trans. in ORe, February 22, 1995, p. 11.

Let us add that with this commitment prior to ordination, religious can help diocesan priests to understand better and further appreciate the value of celibacy. It is to be hoped that, far from casting doubt on the validity of such a decision, they will encourage diocesan priests to be faithful in this area. This is a beautiful and holy ecclesial role carried out by religious institutes outside their confines for the benefit of the entire Christian community.

Belonging to a religious institute enables the priest to live evangelical poverty more radically. Indeed, it is community life that permits the members of an institute to give up their personal belongings, while the diocesan priest normally has to provide for himself. Thus an increasingly visible witness of evangelical poverty is to be hoped for and expected from religious priests, which, in addition to sustaining them on their way to the perfection of love, can encourage diocesan priests to seek practical ways of living a life of greater poverty, especially by pooling some of their resources.

Religious recognize in Pastors expression of divine authority

Lastly, the vow of obedience taken by religious is intended to exercise a beneficial influence on their attitude in the priestly ministry, spurring them to submission towards the superiors of the community helping them, to communion in the spirit of faith with those who represent God's will for them, and to respect for the authority of the bishops and the pope in the fulfilment of their sacred ministry. From religious priests, therefore, not only is formal obedience to the Church's hierarchy expected and hoped for, but also a spirit of loyal, friendly, and generous co-operation with it. By their formation in evangelical obedience, they can more easily overcome the temptations of rebellion, systematic criticism, distrust, and can recognize in the Pastors the expression of divine authority. This is also a useful aid that, as we read in the decree *Christus Dominus* of the Second Vatican Council, religious priests can and must bring to the sacred pastors of the Church, today as in the past and even more in the future, "in view of the more pressing needs of souls ... and in view of the growing needs of the apostolate" (*CD*, no. 34).

4. And again: religious priests can show through their community life the charity which must motivate the presbyterate. According to the intention expressed by Christ at the Last Supper, the precept of mutual love is linked to priestly consecration. In relations of communion established in view of the perfection of love, religious can witness to the fraternal charity that binds those who, in Christ's name, exercise the priestly ministry. Clearly, this fraternal love should also characterize their relations with diocesan priests and with members of institutes other than their own. This is the source of that "organized co-operation" recommended by the Council (*CD*, no. 35, 5).

Religious must preserve spirit of their institute

5. Again according to the Council, religious are more deeply committed to serving the Church by virtue of their consecration based on the profession of the evangelical counsels (cf. *LG*, no. 44). This service consists above all in prayer, in acts of penance and in the example given by their own life, but also in their participation "in the external works of the apostolate, with due consideration for the special character of each religious institute" (*CD*, no. 33). By their participation in the care of souls and the works of the apostolate under the authority of the sacred pastors, religious priests "thus ... may be said in a certain sense to belong to the diocesan clergy" (*CD*, no. 34), and must therefore "exercise these duties in such a way as to be the auxiliaries of the Bishop" (*CD*, no. 35, 1), while at the same time preserving "the spirit of their own institute" and remaining faithful to the observance of their rule (*CD*, no. 35, 2).

It is to be hoped that through the work of religious priests, the unity and harmony Jesus requested for all those who agree to be, like him, "consecrated in the truth" (*Jn* 17:19) will become more and more a reality in the dioceses and in the whole Church, and thus radiate the *imago Ecclesiæ Caritatis* (the image of the Church of charity) throughout the world!

Role of Lay Religious in the Church[2]

1. In religious institutes which consist mainly of priests, there are many "brothers" who are fully-fledged members although they have not received holy orders. They sometimes have the title of "co-operators," or an equivalent term. In the ancient mendicant orders they were generally known as "*lay* brothers." In this expression, the term "brothers" means "religious" and the qualification "lay" means "those not ordained priests." If it is then considered that in several of the ancient orders such religious were called "*conversi*," it is easy to perceive in most cases the history to their vocation—in other words, with reference to the *conversion* which originally impelled them to give themselves completely to God in service to the "priest brothers," after years of life spent in various secular careers: administrative, civil, military, commercial, etc.

---

[2] John Paul II, address at general audience, February 22, 1995, in *OR*, February 23, 1995; Eng. trans. in *ORe*, March 1, 1995, pp. 11.

However, the words of the Second Vatican Council remain decisive. They state that the "lay religious life . . . is a state for the profession of the evangelical counsels which is complete in itself" (*PC,* no. 10). Commitment to the priestly ministry is not required by the consecration which is proper to the religious state, and therefore even without priestly ordination a religious may live his consecration to the full.

Lay religious life is a way of perfection

2. In looking at the historical development of consecrated life in the Church, a significant fact is clear: the members of the first religious communities were called "brothers" without distinction, and the great majority of them did not receive priestly ordination because they did not have a vocation to the ministry. A priest could join these communities but could not claim privileges because of holy orders. When priests were needed, one of the "brothers" was ordained in order to meet the community's sacramental needs. Over the centuries, the proportion of monks who were priests or deacons in comparison to the number of those who were not priests continued to grow. Gradually a division was established between clerical members and lay "brothers" or *conversi.* The ideal of a consecrated life without the priesthood lives on in St. Francis of Assisi, who did not feel personally called to the priestly ministry, although he later agreed to be ordained a deacon. Francis can be considered an example of the holiness of a "lay" religious life. His witness demonstrates the perfection that can be reached by this way of life.

3. Lay religious life has continued to flourish down the centuries. In our age too it has endured and has developed in two directions. On the one hand, we have a certain number of lay brothers who have joined various *clerical* institutes. With regard to them, the Second Vatican Council makes one recommendation: "In order to strengthen the bond of brotherhood between the members of an institute, those who are called lay brothers, co-operators or some such name should be associated more closely with the life and work of the community" (*PC,* no. 15).

Then there are *lay* institutes which, recognized as such by the authority of the Church, have their own proper role by virtue of their nature, character and aim. This is defined by their founder or by a legitimate tradition, and does not include the exercise of holy orders (*CIC,* c. 588, §3). These "institutes of brothers," as they are called, do indeed carry out a precise function which is valuable in itself and particularly useful in the Church's life.

4. The Second Vatican Council was thinking in particular of these lay[3] institutes when it showed its appreciation for the state of lay religious life: "The holy Synod holds it in high esteem, for it is so useful to the Church in the exercise of her pastoral duty of educating the young, caring for the sick, and in other ministries. It confirms the members in their vocation and urges them to adapt their life to modern requirements" (PC, no. 10). The Church's recent history confirms the important role played by the religious who belong to these institutes, especially in educational or charitable works. It can be said that in many places it is they who have given the young a Christian education, founding schools of every kind and for all levels. Again, it is they who have created and administered institutions offering social assistance to the sick and the physically and mentally handicapped, for whom they have also provided the necessary buildings and equipment. Thus their witness to the Christian faith, their dedication and their sacrifice should be admired and praised, while it is to be hoped that the aide of benefactors—in the best Christian tradition—and subsidies provided by modern social legislation may increasingly enable them to care for the poor.

The "great esteem" expressed by the Council shows that the Church's authority highly appreciates the gift offered by the "brothers" to Christian society through the ages, and their collaboration in evangelization and in the pastoral and social care of peoples. Today more than ever, we can and must recognize their historical role and their ecclesial function as witnesses and ministers of Christ's kingdom.

5. The Council made provision for brothers' institutes to benefit from the pastoral ministry necessary for the development of their religious life. This is the meaning of the statement which resolved a problem frequently discussed inside and outside these worthy institutes: "there is nothing to prevent some members of institutes of brothers being admitted to holy orders—the lay character of the institutes remaining intact—by provision of their general chapter and in order to meet the need for priestly ministration in their houses" (PC, no. 10). This is a possibility to be evaluated in accordance with the needs of time and place, but in harmony with the most ancient tradition of monastic institutes, which are thus able to flourish. The Council recognized this possibility and stated that there was no impediment to its implementation: but it lets the highest governing assembly of these institutes—the general chapter—decide, without offering explicit encouragement in this regard, precisely

---

[3] The Italian text has the word *laicali*, unfortunately the English translation in *ORe* renders it with the word *secular* and not lay, and changes the meaning of the phrase.

because it is concerned that these institutes of "brothers" continue in line with their vocation and mission.

May Church be enriched with vocations to the brotherhood

6. I cannot bring this discussion to a close without stressing the rich spirituality suggested by the term "brothers." These religious are called to be *brothers of Christ*, deeply united with him "the firstborn among many brothers" (*Rom* 8:29). *Brothers to one another*, in mutual love and working together in the Church in the same service to what is good. *Brothers to every man*, in their witness to Christ's love for all, especially the lowliest, the neediest; *brothers for a greater brotherhood in the Church*.

Unfortunately in recent times a decreased number of vocations to the lay religious life is becoming apparent in both clerical and lay[4] institutes. A new effort must be made to foster these important and noble vocations so they may thrive anew: a fresh effort to promote vocations, with a new commitment to prayer. The possibility of a *lay* consecrated life must also be presented as a way of true religious perfection in both the old and new male institutes.

At the same time, it is most important that in clerical institutes whose members also include *lay* brothers, the latter should play a suitable role so as to co-operate actively in the institute's life and apostolate. Then there is a need to encourage lay institutes to persevere on the path of their vocation, adapting to a changing society, but constantly retaining and deepening the spirit of total self-giving to Christ and to the Church as expressed in their individual charism. I ask the Lord that an ever growing number of brothers may enrich the Church's holiness and mission.

---

[4] Here again the Italian text has the word *laicali*, and unfortunately the English translation in ORe renders it with the word *secular* and not lay.

Appendix III

Indults Permitting
Brothers to Be Appointed Superior

Congregatio pro Religiosis et Institutis Sæcularibus[1]

Prot. No. 20030/87

Most Holy Father:

The superior of the Most Holy Rosary Province of Canada of the Congregation of Oblates of Mary Immaculate requests from your Holiness the faculty of naming—for the reasons presented—Brother Emelien Nadeau to the office of superior of the house "Saint-Louis" in Sainte-Foi.

And God, etc. . . .

Having considered the explanation of the procurator general, the Congregation for Religious and Secular Institutes grants the petition, excluding any power comprising ecclesiastical jurisdiction, everything else in law being observed.

Not withstanding anything to the contrary.

Given in Rome, March 1, 1986.

+ V. Fagiolo
Secretary

Jesus Torres, C.M.F.
Under Secretary

---

[1] Unofficial translation.

Congregatio pro Religiosis et Institutis Sæcularibus[2]

Prot. No. 20030/87

Most Holy Father:

The provincial superior of the Central United States Province of the Congregation of Oblates of Mary Immaculate requests from your Holiness the faculty of naming—for the reasons presented—Brother Francis Xavier Sullivan, a non-cleric, to the office of superior of the Southern Illinois District.

And God, etc. . . .

Having considered the explanation of the procurator general, the Congregation for Religious and Secular Institutes grants the favor according to the petition, excluding any power connected with holy orders, everything else in law being observed.

Not withstanding anything to the contrary.

Given in Rome, February 2, 1987.

+ V. Fagiolo
Secretary

Jesus Torres, C.M.F.
Under Secretary

---

[2] Unofficial translation.

Index

Aa 9, 15

abandonner 168

Ad pastoralis dignitatis fastigium 127

Adinolfi, Archpriest 44, 46, 47

Administrative Structures 71, 106, 107, 109, 157, 191, 219, 230, 235

administrators apostolic 107

Africa 62, 70, 165, 196, 207, 244

Aix 2, 3, 5, 6, 11-15, 17, 18, 20-23, 25, 27-29, 37-40, 42, 43, 46, 49, 60, 86, 148-151, 169, 171, 175, 194, 195, 197, 201

Albini, Charles 42, 60, 203

Algeria 61, 62, 69, 165, 171

Allard, Jean-François 62, 66, 69, 165, 166

Alphonsus Liguori, Saint 29, 30, 34, 37, 44, 55, 127, 148, 167, 175, 202

apostles, 22, 25, 54, 77, 107 142, 152, 163, 165-167, 247, 273, 275, 278

apostolic men 117, 155, 163

apostolic communities 112, 117, 149, 211

apostolic role 209

Apostolic See 48, 194

Apostolicæ dignitatis solio 126, 127

Arctic 85, 244

Ascendente Domino 126

Association of Christian Youth 17

Augier, Cassien 85, 87

Augustine, Saint 51

Augustinians 144

Avezzano 86

Baffie, Eugène 87, 90, 95, 96

Balain, Mathieu 71, 190

Barnabites 3

Basil, Saint 51

Belgium 64, 74, 85, 86, 118

Belmont 86

Benedict, Saint 51

Benedict XIII 126, 127

Benedict XIV 127-129, 175

de Bérulle 152, 161

Bishops and Regulars, Congregation of 44, 50, 52, 65, 72, 78-83, 85, 87, 89, 90, 97, 100, 119, 128, 129, 134, 135, 194, 220, 221

Boniface VIII 124

Bourget, Ignace 60

Brothers of Saint Patrick 176, 177

Bytown 61, 95

Cadieux, Vincent 71

Canada 61, 62, 69, 70, 72, 74, 84-86, 95, 165, 167, 171, 172, 193, 197, 206, 229, 276, 277

cassock 158, 205, 222-227

Castiglione, Cardinal 46

category 52, 183, 187, 188, 208, 209, 219, 232-234, 242

Cazebon, Gilles 118

Ceylon 61-63, 66, 74, 165, 176, 207, 244

chapter of faults 57, 174

charism of the Founder 116, 182, 216

Cimbebasia 189

Circa pastoralis 125

clerical 45, 80, 85, 102, 103, 108, 112, 113, 120, 121, 269, 273, 277, 284, 286 clerical congregation 113, 185, 192, 193, 196, 240, 243, 277, 278

clerical institute 102, 112, 143-145, 181, 182, 185, 187, 192, 193, 197, 197, 240, 242

Clericalia instituta 108, 113, 191, 192, 235, 237, 238

clericalism 237

clerics 28, 67, 113, 123, 127, 140, 141, 143, 144, 175, 177, 183, 187-189, 192, 210, 219, 223, 229, 232, 234-236, 242

coadjutor 63, 157, 167, 176, 183, 217, 218, 276

Collège Bourbon 2, 17

Colombo 74

Conditæ a Christo 129

Conference of Major Superiors of Men (U.S.A.) 238, 239

Constitutions—1818 34, 42, 76, 202,

Constitutions—1826 52, 54, 148, 155, 157, 220, 221

Constitutions–1928 96, 149, 155, 193, 204, 209, 210, 222, 227

Constitutions—1966 *ad experimentum* 54, 72, 98, 103-107, 110, 115, 117, 121, 181-183, 189, 209-211, 218, 221, 225, 227, 230

Constitutions—1982 36, 54, 71, 88, 110–117, 120–122, 149, 155, 168, 191–193, 210, 214, 216, 219–221, 226, 229, 230, 232, 235, 241, 244, 247, 270, 274, 275, 277, 279, 280

consultor 82, 89, 90, 97, 105, 108, 119

Copenhagen 197

Corijn, Daniel 118, 119

Corsica 59, 60, 165

coulpe 57, 174

cross 6, 12, 22, 158, 159, 170, 175, 195, 205, 221-223, 225-227, 240, 278

crucifix 22, 158, 159, 222, 225, 226

Cum admotæ 84, 130-132, 181, 196

Decessorum nostrorum vestigiis 93, 196

Deschâtelets, Leo 60, 69, 97, 101-103, 106, 109, 179, 180, 181, 183, 209, 210, 214, 218, 275, 276

diaconate 108, 188, 230-232, 245, 281

Doctrinaires 2, 3

Dontenwill, Augustin 71, 87, 90, 93-97, 190

ecclesiastical superiors 65, 107, 191

Ecclesiæ Sanctæ 103, 104, 107, 108, 112, 121, 135-138, 216, 235, 236

Emery 9, 10

Esser, Tomasso 89-92, 97, 100, 119, 224

Evangelica testificatio 1

evangelization 55, 63, 102, 118, 122, 150, 152, 162, 163, 167, 182, 184-186, 199, 211, 213, 216, 241, 269, 271-274, 279, 285

exemption 78-80, 82, 83, 130, 132, 133, 174, 196

Fabre, Joseph 57, 70, 71, 73-84, 95, 171, 177, 178, 208, 221

Favre, Joseph-Marie 81, 176

de Forbin-Janson, Charles 6-8, 15, 18-21, 23, 27, 28, 150, 151, 158, 159, 169

foreign missions 9, 59, 60, 63-65, 68, 69, 74, 78, 85, 92, 93, 95, 96, 153, 154, 160, 161, 166, 167, 173, 196, 198, 206, 207, 244

formation 51, 73, 113, 114, 117, 140,

163, 179, 182-186, 193, 210, 212-215, 217, 224, 228-230, 234, 236, 241, 242, 269-271, 275-277, 280, 281, 282

Fortin, Gérard 99, 104

France 3, 5, 6, 8, 9, 13, 17-22, 27, 31, 33, 37, 39, 44-47, 63-65, 73, 74, 78, 84-86, 88, 90, 120, 128, 150-153, 167, 169, 171, 175, 190, 195, 222-224, 248

Francis of Assisi, Saint 18, 51, 71, 78, 109, 284

Franciscans 18, 58, 140, 174, 240

fratres laici 157, 203

fratres famulantes 157, 179, 203, 204

Fréjus 32, 40, 42, 59, 194

frère 33, 35, 174, 201-203, 217-219

frère convers 14, 35, 157, 159, 174, 176, 201–204, 217, 218, 229

fundamental values 121, 122, 182

Gallicanism 47

Galveston 61

Gap 46, 47

Gaspar del Bufalo, Saint 176

George, Francis 109

Germany 64, 74, 86, 229

Good Friday 1807 6, 7, 22, 149, 270

governed by clerics 189

government 10, 17, 36, 38, 39, 51, 54, 56, 59, 64, 65, 68, 69, 85, 86, 95, 101-103, 107, 117, 128, 130-135, 178, 181, 189, 190, 198, 207, 245

Grandin, Vital 70, 167

Greenland 197

Gregory XIII 125, 126

Gregory XVI 65, 195, 196

Guibert, Joseph–H. 63, 70, 71, 73, 84,

190, 208

Guigou, Vicar Capitular 27, 38, 194

Guigues, Joseph-Eugène 69, 70, 95

Gulf of Mexico 244

habit 125, 135, 158, 159, 205, 222-227

Hanley, Richard 109

Holy See 10, 39-41, 45, 46, 51, 52, 59, 70, 78, 83, 84, 87, 89-92, 94, 103, 108, 109, 111, 113, 118, 121, 122, 124, 126, 128, 129, 132, 134, 144, 146, 149, 165, 171, 179, 185, 191-194, 196-199, 210, 212, 220, 225, 232, 233, 238, 241, 244, 245, 270, 273

Honorat, Jean-Baptiste 60, 61, 81, 172, 176

Hospitallers of St. John of God 240

Hünfeld 86

Icosia 59

Ignatius of Loyola, Saint 142, 144

immigrants 60, 172, 173

in forma specifica 52, 80, 89, 91, 97, 112

Ireland 61, 85, 86, 96, 176, 177, 206

Italy 22, 64, 74, 85, 144, 153, 175, 184, 224

Jaffna 62, 63, 69, 71, 176

Jansenism 6, 167

Jansenist 1, 6, 37

Jersey 85

Jesuit(s) 2, 7-9, 112, 124-126, 142, 144, 152

Jetté, Fernand 14, 20, 109, 111, 112, 136, 155, 184, 186, 216, 236, 238, 247, 248

Julius III 124

juridical status 55, 123, 124, 146, 201

Labouré, Theodore 97, 225

Lanteri, Bruno 42, 43, 175

Laos 72, 76, 110, 118, 197
Lavillardière, Auguste 86, 87, 90
lay institute 141, 143
Lazarists 50, 152, 174
legitimate autonomy 145
Lemius, Joseph 90, 91, 95
Leo XII 42-50, 52, 53, 58, 80, 81, 83,
    89, 91, 120, 148, 159, 171, 173,
    195, 196,271
Leo XIII 95, 129, 149
Liège 85, 86
Longeon, general econome 85
Lubricum vitæ genus 125
Lumen gentium 123, 135, 143, 146,
    147, 154, 163, 210, 212, 239,
    283
Luxembourg 85
manu militari 85
Marianists 141, 240
Marie-Rose 2
Marseille 2, 10, 16, 17, 37, 39, 41, 42,
    50, 58-60, 65, 66, 73, 81, 86,
    159, 165, 169, 190, 194, 196,
    221
de Mazenod, Charles-Antoine 2, 3
de Mazenod Charles-Auguste-André 4
de Mazenod, Charles Joseph Eugene
    (The references are too numeous
    to indicate.)
de Mazenod, Charles-Louis-Eugène 2
de Mazenod, Charles-Fortuné 2, 10,
    21, 36, 37, 39, 42, 59, 150, 151,
    171, 194
Mexico 61, 244
Miller, William 87
Ministeria quædam 131, 188
Mirabili plane modo 97, 196
Missionaries of France 6, 19, 150,
    169, 175
missionary role 210, 213
missionary institute 192, 215
missionary habit 158, 222, 223
Missionary Outlook 106, 107, 182
Montreal 60, 61, 70, 71, 101, 167, 172,
    218
Namibia 189, 197, 276
Napoleon 9, 10, 13, 14, 17-20
Natal 61, 62, 66, 69, 70, 160, 244
Netherlands 64, 74, 189
New York 2, 29, 37, 61, 172
Nice 2, 3, 42, 45, 71, 82
Normæ 82, 85, 89, 90, 92, 129, 131,
    133-135, 137, 221, 225, 232
North America 61, 64, 96, 244
North American Indians 167
Notre-Dame-du-Laus 28
O'Reilly, Michael 182, 185, 192, 193,
    243
oblate charism 117, 186, 215, 230,
    269-271, 277, 279
Oblates of the Blessed Virgin 175
oblation 33-35, 41, 54, 56, 148, 157,
    158, 160, 161, 178, 183, 205, 214,
    215, 220-222, 225, 227, 231, 232,
    234, 243, 280
Œuvres des Allemands 60
Œuvres des Italiens 60
ordination 10, 11, 22, 28, 40, 46, 50,
    59, 78, 81, 149, 154, 156, 157,
    182, 183, 187, 197, 198, 209, 210,
    220, 228, 231-233, 238, 241, 243,
    274, 281, 282, 284,
Oregon 61, 62, 66, 69, 166, 205, 206
Ottawa 6, 7, 21, 29, 30, 55, 58, 60, 61,
    69, 72, 85, 86, 95, 105, 118, 124,
    193, 201, 218, 244, 270, 277

Paris 1, 7, 9, 10, 12, 13, 18-20, 28, 32, 37-39, 71, 73, 84, 91, 124, 152, 153, 161, 168, 176, 178, 179, 197, 202, 270

Passionists 50, 80, 83, 127, 128, 174, 175

patrimony 51, 54, 116, 120, 121, 135, 137-139, 192, 239, 240, 242

Paul VI 1, 84, 107, 108, 110, 112, 130, 131, 135, 136, 138, 142-144, 163, 181, 188, 235, 272

pauvres 162, 168-170, 172

Pedicini, Cardinal 45-47, 221

Pelletier, Paul-Emile 99

père 33, 35, 70, 71, 168, 173

Perfectæ caritatis 103, 116, 121, 135, 138, 144, 191, 230, 234, 235, 239, 284, 285

Philip Neri, Saint 26

Pius V, Saint 125

Pius VII 9, 10, 13, 18, 19, 23, 39, 150, 194, 195

Pius VIII 46

Pius IX 72, 78, 79, 83, 91, 159, 195, 196, 220

Pius X 90, 93, 196

Pius XI 97, 196

Plattsburg 61

Preface 54, 55, 89, 100, 101, 112, 116, 117, 155, 163, 167, 169, 170, 185, 202, 230, 247, 269, 271, 274, 276

prefects apostolic 107, 191

procurator general 89, 113, 129, 181, 185, 191, 226, 243

Propaganda Fide, Congregaion de 62, 63, 70, 79, 80, 85, 92, 129, 134, 159, 160, 207

proportion of clerics 187

Provençal 2, 6, 15, 16, 20, 27, 37, 49, 151

Provence 1, 2, 14, 17, 18, 21-23, 25, 27-32, 34-40, 42, 49, 55, 148-151, 161, 162, 164, 167, 169, 175, 194, 195, 197, 222, 247

provinces 40, 65, 67-71, 83, 85, 97, 101, 104, 108, 117, 219, 224, 229, 277, 279, 280

provincials 67, 68, 70, 87, 88, 92, 98, 102, 107, 109, 110, 121, 181, 191, 208, 223, 225

Quaglia, Cardinal 82, 83

Quam multa 65, 195

Quanto fructuosius 125

Quebec 61, 69, 72, 172

Quum multa sit messis 65

Quum nullo unquam tempore 72, 196

Quum multa sit messis 195

Rauzan, Jean-Baptiste 19, 27, 150, 151, 171

Red River 61, 66, 69

Redemptorists 29, 37, 76, 79-83, 127-129, 174, 175

regular clergy 148, 202

Religious, Congregation of 93, 97, 103, 108, 109, 111, 112, 114, 137, 181, 182, 185, 199, 235, 236, 242, 243, 247

religious congregation 130, 147, 148, 241

religious garb 222, 224-226

religious institute 38, 40, 51, 102, 112, 124, 127, 131-133, 140, 141, 146, 147, 187, 192, 193, 198, 199, 226, 237, 238, 240-242, 281-283

Renovationis causam 114, 187, 218, 224, 233

Revolution 1-3, 6, 8, 11, 13, 15, 19, 22,

27, 29, 31, 50, 54-56, 128, 149, 150, 153

Rio Grande 77, 244

Roze-Joannis 5, 6, 37

Saint-Laurent-du-Verdon 2, 5, 29

Saint-Sulpice 6-9, 11, 12, 14, 15, 22, 270

Saint Paul University 95

San Antonio 86

Sardinia, kingdom of 3, 42, 45

Savior 7, 22, 30, 55, 101-103, 113, 117, 127, 164, 165, 170, 182, 210, 211, 247, 270, 273

Savoy 45

schools 17, 94-96, 126, 166, 177, 208, 221, 245, 285

secular priests 28, 30, 49, 55, 67, 94, 125, 127, 129, 131, 194, 198, 222, 245

Semeria, Jean-Étienne 63, 69, 158, 159, 176

seminaries 41, 42, 45, 48, 58, 59, 67, 96, 165, 171

simple vows 55, 67, 80, 82-84, 89, 92, 94, 123-130, 132, 133, 147-149, 198, 232

simples oblats 34, 35, 57, 205

Sion, Paul 110

Society for the Propagation of the Faith 160

Sodality of the Blessed Virgin Mary 8

Soullier, Louis 95, 178, 207

Spain 64, 74, 85, 197

special class of brothers 208, 219

spiritual prefect 203, 229, 230

St.-Pétersbourg, rue de 86

St. Charles Juniorate 189

Stockholm 197

Suzanne, Marius 32, 33

Sweden 197

Taché, A., archbishop 69, 167

Taché, Alexandre 110

Tamburini, Ambrose 78-80, 82

Tempier, Paul-Henry 22, 25-28, 32, 35, 38-40, 42-48, 50, 52-54, 58, 59, 64, 73, 74, 81, 148, 151, 158, 169, 171, 176, 202, 224, 248

Texas 61, 77, 86

Toronto 172

Trent, Council 125, 220, 224

Turin 3, 42, 43

United States 84, 85, 97, 106, 109, 172, 206, 237, 238

Vatican II 65, 98, 99, 103-105, 116, 123, 130, 134-136, 138, 140, 143, 145, 154, 162, 184, 185, 191, 192, 198, 211, 215, 234, 235, 239, 272

vicariates 67, 68, 71, 97

vicariates of mission 67

vicariates 190, 196, 197

vicars of missions 67, 68, 70, 71, 87, 98

vicars of missions 181, 190

vice-province 70, 102, 216, 237

Vincent de Paul, Saint 18, 27, 44, 126, 151, 152, 161

Vincentians 33, 43, 161, 174

vow of poverty 28, 31-33, 38, 50, 202

West Transval 118

Windhoek 189

Yukon 86

Zago, Marcello 118, 119, 182-184, 186, 192, 234, 280

Zinelli, Don Bartolo 3, 149

About the Author

William H. Woestman, O.M.I. was born on November 14, 1929 in Fort Smith, Arkansas. He made his first vows as a Missionary Oblate of Mary Immaculate in 1950 and was ordained to the priesthood in 1956.

He received licentiates in philosophy and theology from the Pontifical Gregorian University and a doctorate in canon law from the Pontifical University of St. Thomas Aquinas in Rome. He also obtained the Diploma of Advocate of the Roman Rota. His doctoral thesis is *The Missionary Oblates of Mary Immaculate, a Clerical Religious Congregation with Brothers.* In 1990 he published *Special Marriage Cases: Non-Consummation, Pauline Privilege, Favor of the Faith, Separation of Spouses, Validation, Sanation, Presumed Death.* A revised edition was printed in 1992 and a third edition in 1994. The French translation, *Les Procès spéciaux de mariage,* as well as *Papal Allocutions to the Roman Rota, 1939–1994* were published in 1994. In addition to this, he has published articles in *The Jurist, Monitor ecclesiasticus, Newsletter of the Canadian Canon Law Society Pastoral Sciences/Sciences pastorales, The Priest,* and *Studia canonica.*

From 1957 to 1965 he taught moral theology and canon law at the Oblate Scholasticate in Pass Christian, Mississippi. He was associate pastor and pastor of St. Patrick's Parish, McCook, Nebraska (1965–1969), director of the National Shrine of Our Lady of the Snows, Belleville, Illinois (1969–1975), provincial of the Oblate's Central United States Province (1975–1981), and director general of the Missionary Association of Mary Immaculate (1981–1986). Pope John Paul II appointed him consultor of the Congregation for the Evangelization of Peoples from 1985 to 1993. Since 1986 he has been teaching in the Faculty of Canon Law, Saint Paul University, Ottawa, where he is vice-dean and full professor.

The Faculty of Canon Law
Saint Paul University

The origin of Saint Paul University dates back to September 26, 1848, when "The College of Bytown" was founded by Bishop Joseph-Eugène Guigues, O.M.I., who in 1856 entrusted the College to the Missionary Oblates of Mary Immaculate. In 1861 the College of Bytown was renamed "College of Ottawa" and in August 1866 was granted university status by the Parliament of the United Canada. With the apostolic letter *Cum apostolica sedes* Leo XIII granted on February 5, 1989 the university its pontifical charter.

In the years following World War II, the University progressed rapidly and by 1965 had established nine faculties and four schools. On July 1 of that year, through an act of the Ontario Provincial Legislature, the institution heretofore designated as the University of Ottawa became Saint Paul University, nonetheless keeping its civil and canonical charters. At the same time the Provincial Government formed a new institution to be known as the University of Ottawa to which Saint Paul University conceded the majority of its holdings. The two Universities became a federated complex and according to mutual agreement were to share existing schools and faculties.

Under the terms of the present contract, Saint Paul University agrees to extend its teaching only to the Faculties of Theology and Canon Law and related Institutes. In addition to conferring its own degrees, Saint Paul University reserves the right to present its candidates to the Senate of the University of Ottawa for joint conferment (Saint Paul University–University of Ottawa) of its certificates, diplomas, and civil degrees.

At its inception in 1929, the Faculty of Canon Law was made up of Oblate professors and eleven students; the number of students has since fluctuated widely. The years before and during World War II were especially difficult ones; after the war, there was a brief surge of interest.

In 1968, the existence of the sole Faculty of Canon Law in Canada was in jeopardy. However, authorities decided to maintain the Faculty and hope for a better future; they were not disappointed. Spurred by conciliar renewal and the revision of the Code of Canon Law, bishops began to send more students. The international travels of Father Francis G. Morrisey, O.M.I., professor, then dean of the Faculty, contributed to the spread of the Faculty's reputation, making it one of the most respected in the world. Recently approximately one hundred students from more than fifteen different countries have registered each year.

In 1971, the languages of instruction became English and French, rather than Latin. Three years later, numbers were so high that the Faculty chose to offer two language streams; to this day, there exist within the same Faculty parallel programs in English and French. The program leading to the licentiate lasts two years; it consists of four modules and is cyclical, as in most faculties of canon law. All licentiate candidates are required to follow classes covering the entire Code of Canon Law.

Professors have more than once exhibited a timely awareness of the Church's needs. Many sessions have been organized for the benefit of religious, lay persons, members of ecclesiastical tribunals, or personnel from diocesan chanceries. After the Second Vatican Council, the Faculty hosted meetings for canonists from various countries preparing the new Code; then there were information sessions, in Ottawa or in other dioceses. Finally, the new Code having been promulgated, professors took part in translating it into French and English.

Since 1929, more than one hundred–twenty-five doctoral theses have been defended; the majority of these in recent years. Graduates of the Faculty can be found on every continent, working in every sphere of canonical activity.

In 1966, the Faculty was a prime instigator in the establishment of the Canadian Canon Law Society. The following year, the journal *Studia canonica* was begun; the publication, with a current circulation of 1,300 in twenty-six countries, is now a highly respected scholarly review.

With the beginning of the fall trimester in 1994, the Faculty was truly international with nine full time and six part time professors from four different countries, and an enrollment from the six continents and twenty-nine different countries. The number of students was about the same as in recent years with twenty-two doctoral candidates and seventy-five in the licentiate program.